THE
CASSELL

Atlas of the MEDIEVAL WORLD

AD 600–1492

John Haywood
with
Andrew Jotischky • Sean McGlynn

CASSELL

Project director Peter Furtado

Cartographic manager Richard Watts

Advisory editors

Jeremy Black
Professor of History, University of Exeter, UK

K.M. Chaudhuri
Vasco da Gama Professor of European Exploration, European University Institute, Florence, Italy

Barry Cunliffe
Professor of European Archaeology, University of Oxford, UK

Brian M. Fagan
Professor of Anthropology, University of California, Santa Barbara, USA

J.E. Spence
Associate Fellow, Royal Institute of International Affairs, UK

Academic advisors

J.I. Catto
Oriel College, University of Oxford, UK

Professor Robin Cohen
University of Warwick, UK

Professor J.H. Elliott
Regius Professor of Modern History, University of Oxford, UK

Professor Harold James
Princeton University, New Jersey, USA

Professor Maldwyn A. Jones
University of London, UK

Dr Stuart Kewley
University of Cambridge, UK

Dr Stewart Lone
Australian Defence Force Academy

Dr Oswyn Murray
Balliol College, University of Oxford, UK

Professor A.J.S. Reid
The Australian National University

Professor Francis Robinson
Royal Holloway, University of London, UK

Professor John K. Thornton
Millersville University, Pennsylvania, USA

This page:
Hieroglyph from a Mixtec codex, c.1000

Opposite above left:
Bronze statue of Charlemagne, c. 800

Opposite centre right:
French wall-painting of Black Death victims, c.1350

Opposite below left:
Image of Hindu deity Shiva, c.1000

Following page:
Portrait of Sultan Mehmet II c.1450

Art director Ayala Kingsley
Art editor Martin Anderson
Cartographic editor Tim Williams

Editors Susan Kennedy, Peter Lewis
(Encyclopedic dictionary) BCS Publishing
Cartographer Nathalie Johns
Picture research Claire Turner
Production Clive Sparling
Editorial assistance Marian Dreier
Typesetter Brian Blackmore
Illustrations Charles Raymond
Proof reader Lynne Elson
Index Ann Barrett

AN ANDROMEDA BOOK

Produced and prepared by
Andromeda Oxford Ltd
11–15 The Vineyard
Abingdon
Oxfordshire OX14 3PX

First published in the UK
by Cassell plc
Wellington House
125 Strand
London WC2R 0BB

ISBN 0-304-35042-7

10 9 8 7 6 5 4 3 2 1

Printed in Italy Petruzzi Città di Castello - PG

Contents

INTRODUCTION

Shortly after AD 600, the Islamic community was founded in Medina under the leadership of prophet Muhammad. For many centuries Islam and other civilizations farther east were the world's most dynamic cultures. The year 1492, however, saw Columbus reach the Antilles, the prelude to the conquest and settlement of the New World by Europeans; six years later Vasco da Gama sailed around Africa to India. The foundation of western hegemony was thus laid by the end of the fifteenth century.

Just as the "barbarian" invasions of the fifth century AD led to the eclipse of the classical civilization of Europe, so the Muslim Arab expansion ended the domination of old Persian empires in the Middle East and the surviving Roman empire in the eastern Mediterranean. The intensity of the success of Islam is still unexplained, but there is no doubt about its significance. The unification of large parts of the Mediterranean, the Middle East, and the Indian Ocean by the Umayyad and Abbasid caliphates was a cultural, technological, and economic as well as a political achievement. The use of the Arabic language played an important role: the Bedouins of the Arabian peninsula, the Berber converts of north Africa, Arab conquerors in Andalusia, the Copts of Egypt, the Nabateans of Mesopotamia, and the converted Iranians all shared the Koranic prayers recited in Arabic and a common body of family and civil law.

Islam revitalized old cities and founded new ones. Both Medina and Mecca attracted a huge number of pilgrims each year, while Damascus became the first Islamic capital under the Umayyads, greatly enlarged by successive caliphs. Under the Abbasids, the capital shifted to Baghdad, the first planned capital city to be built by Muslims. This in turn was followed by Samarra. The Islamic world's great cities included Basra, Alexandria, Fustat, Cairo, Tunis, and Córdoba.

The urban gravitation of Islamic expansion required an economic surplus and food resources. This was achieved by bringing new land under cultivation and reviving existing regions of agricultural production. Arab engineers and farmers proved skilful in constructing irrigation projects. New plants such as hard wheat, sugar cane, citrus fruits, vegetables, and legumes were imported from India and southeast Asia and disseminated throughout the oasis agriculture of north Africa and into the arid areas of southern Spain.

Similar developments took place in China and southeast Asia. The Chinese perfected ways of containing the rivers of northern China to develop the rice-growing areas of Szechuan and the Yangtze valley. Population expansion, combined with the instability of climate, created a problem of feeding the world's most advanced empire. The Song emperors knew this problem to be a product of previous agricultural success, which had created crowded cities and rural areas. Relief in times of scarcity was provided by the state, which encouraged the cultivation of a strain of rice that ripened in two months, as against the three to six taken by traditional varieties.

Chinese civilization and administration was a matter of wonder to the rest of the world. China developed a class of professional bureaucratic administrators who were given formal instructions in writing and who had to report to the imperial court through written memoranda. Science, mathematics, and engineering flourished, and papermaking, the moving-type printing press and gunpowder were invented.

China's capacity for industrial production was evident in the quality of its porcelain and silk textiles. The Indian subcontinent had a similar lead in the production of cotton textiles. These products sustained a trade from the South China Sea to the eastern Mediterranean. Luxury goods were not the only articles of international trade. A network of trading cities grew up in response to the needs of this trade. Chinese ports such as Hangzhou were linked to Malacca in the tip of Malay peninsula, in turn connected to the seaports of India, the Gulf and the Red Sea. The city-states in east Africa completed the commercial rectangle.

The Mongol conquests dealt a severe blow to the ancient civilizations of the Indian Ocean and prepared the way for a resurgent Europe, where Arab intellectual knowledge had slowly penetrated through the intermediary of Jewish scholars and scientists living and working in Spain.

Europe's main contribution to world history to this point was its fighting technique. The adoption of the stirrup made it possible to increase the armament of the mounted warrior using a heavy lance. Mounted knights on new breeds of more powerful horses were successful against the Turks during the Crusades. European success in the New World and the Indian Ocean later owed a great deal also to the invention of square-rigged ships armed with artillery capable of bombarding towns and cities. The reinforced hull made it possible to pierce gun-ports and add a gun-deck without reducing cargo capacity. The result was a floating fortress that was also a warehouse.

European expansion was embedded in a larger process of scientific and intellectual advance. The new navigational methods – the use of compass, marine charts, mapmaking and astronomical navigation – were linked to the development of fighting ships. As a result, in the 15th century, when Europeans sought routes to the east that would avoid the hostile Ottoman lands, the technology was at hand to enable them to dominate these new waters. The consequences of this were soon to become dramatically evident ■

USING THIS ATLAS

This atlas is part of a six-volume chronological set covering the Ancient (1), Classical (2), Medieval (3), Early Modern (4), 19th Century (5), and Modern (6) worlds. To help the user pinpoint straight away which era any particular map relates to, pages are numbered first by volume, and then by 2-page spread within that volume. Thus, map spread 14 in volume 3 is identified by the page number 3.14.

World map spreads outline global history on the date shown. Different typographical categories (see table opposite) denote different kinds of political or social entity. The text on these spreads includes many cross-references to other relevant spreads. The timelines here are organized by region.

Regional map spreads cover a part of the world over a specific period. Maps for a continent or major region are grouped in a section, named in the heading on the right-hand side of the spread. These sections also appear in the Contents page.

Maps are shown in true cartographic projections. North is generally at the top of the page. Some distortion is evident in those maps that cover huge areas of the world (e.g. Asia). Where necessary location maps have been included.

Each regional map has certain standard features: thick grey lines denote major borders, thin grey lines internal borders. Campaigns or journeys are shown by lines with arrowheads; thicker grey arrows are used for mass movements of people. Trade routes are thinner lines, with arrowheads when the trade is one-way. All map-key items are referred to in text. The main text explains and amplifies the information on the map.

The timelines on regional maps are arranged in geographical or thematic sections. Civilizations, cultures, and dynasties are shown with colored bands; broad historical phases (such as "Bronze Age") are indicated with grey bands. Every regional map also has several numbered "pointers", whose captions offer further historical detail on the places marked. Finally, the panel bottom right cross-refers to other spreads with related information, listing their numbers and themes.

A substantial encyclopedic section at the end of the book contains an A–Z guide to the people, places, and events of the period. It is cross-referenced both within the section and to the information that appears on the map spreads.

The index provides detailed references to the text, timelines, pointer captions and map keys. Space constraints have precluded indexing every location on the maps themselves.

TYPOGRAPHICAL CONVENTIONS

World maps	
FRANCE	state or empire
Belgian Congo	dependency or territory
Mongols	tribe, chiefdom or people
Anasazi culture	cultural group
Regional maps	
HUNGARY	state or empire
Bohemia	dependency or territory
Slavs	tribe, chiefdom or people
ANATOLIA	geographical region
⚔	battle
•	site or town

3.01 THE WORLD • AD 800 •

The years between AD 600 and 800 saw the final breakup of the world of classical antiquity and the dramatic rise of an Arab Islamic civilization. Islam has its origins in the teachings of Muhammad (c.570–632). Islam united the Arabs and created a theocratic state. Despite civil war after the prophet's death, the caliph or "successor" Umar turned Arab energies outward in campaigns of conquest and conversion (▷ *3.13*).

Circumstances were favorable to Arab expansion. From 602 to 627 the Persian Sasanian empire and the surviving eastern half of the Roman empire were locked in total war. The Romans emerged triumphant but the reforms introduced by the emperor Heraclius created an essentially new, Greek, state, known as the Byzantine empire. Neither Persia nor Byzantium was thus in a fit state to withstand the sudden invasions of Arab armies, which began with the capture of Damascus in 635. By 642 the Arabs had captured Syria, Palestine and Egypt from the Byzantines and completely destroyed the Sasanian empire. A second wave of conquests began after the Umayyad dynasty came to power in 661. In 698 Byzantine Carthage fell and in 711 the Arabs crossed the Straits of Gibraltar and conquered the Visigothic kingdom of Spain; in the east Arab armies reached the Indus and Samarkand. Failure to take Constantinople in 717 and defeat by the Franks at Poitiers in 732 marked the end of the Arab victories. The unity of the Arab world ended in 749–50 when the Umayyads were overthrown and slaughtered by the Abbasids, except for one who escaped to Spain and founded an independent state. By 800 the Abbasids had also lost control of Morocco and Tunisia (▷ *3.14*).

In 600 the Frankish kingdom was the leading state in western Europe but dynastic instability led to a decline in the late 7th century (▷ *3.06*). Frankish power recovered under the Carolingian dynasty, named for Charlemagne who controlled most of Christian western Europe and expanded into the pagan lands of eastern Europe. He was crowned Roman emperor by the pope in Rome on Christmas Day, 800. In the British Isles, the Anglo-Saxons confined the Celts to the hilly west. The Scandinavians were beginning state formation, a by-product of which was the onset of Viking raids on western Europe.

China, divided for almost four centuries, was reunited by the Sui dynasty in 589 (▷ *3.20*). The Sui's ambitions overstretched the empire's resources and they were overthrown by the Tang dynasty in 618. China flourished under the early Tang emperors and campaigns in central Asia extended

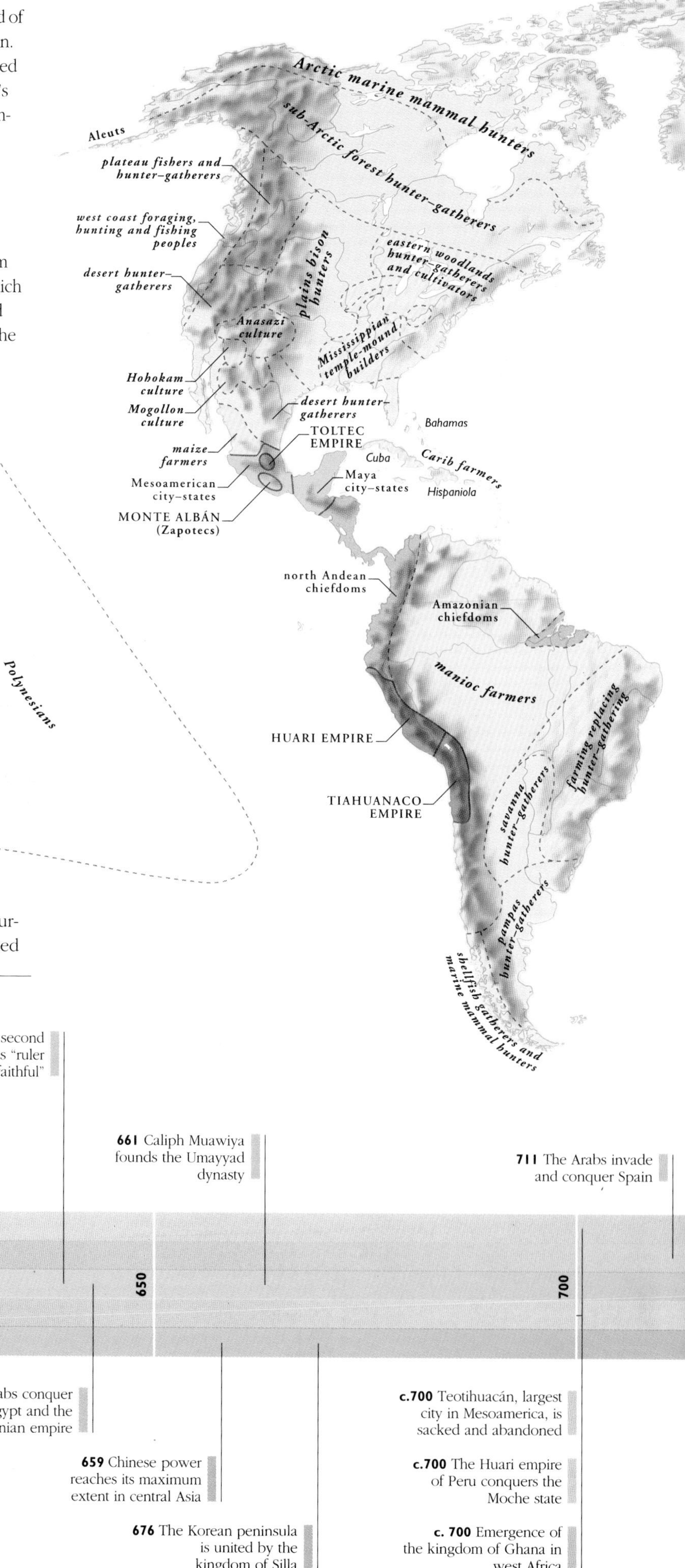

TIMELINE

The Americas · Europe · Middle East · Africa · East and South Asia — 600 · 650 · 700

589 The Sui dynasty reunifies China after 400 years of division

606 Harsha, king of Kanauj, conquers northern India

610 Accession of Heraclius; Eastern Roman empire is now known as the Byzantine empire

618 The Tang dynasty replaces the Sui in China

622 Muhammad flees from Mecca to Medina (*hijra*); beginning of the Islamic calendar

634 Umar, the second caliph, becomes "ruler of the faithful"

636–42 The Arabs conquer Palestine, Egypt and the Sasanian empire

659 Chinese power reaches its maximum extent in central Asia

661 Caliph Muawiya founds the Umayyad dynasty

676 The Korean peninsula is united by the kingdom of Silla

c.700 Teotihuacán, largest city in Mesoamerica, is sacked and abandoned

c.700 The Huari empire of Peru conquers the Moche state

c. 700 Emergence of the kingdom of Ghana in west Africa

711 The Arabs invade and conquer Spain

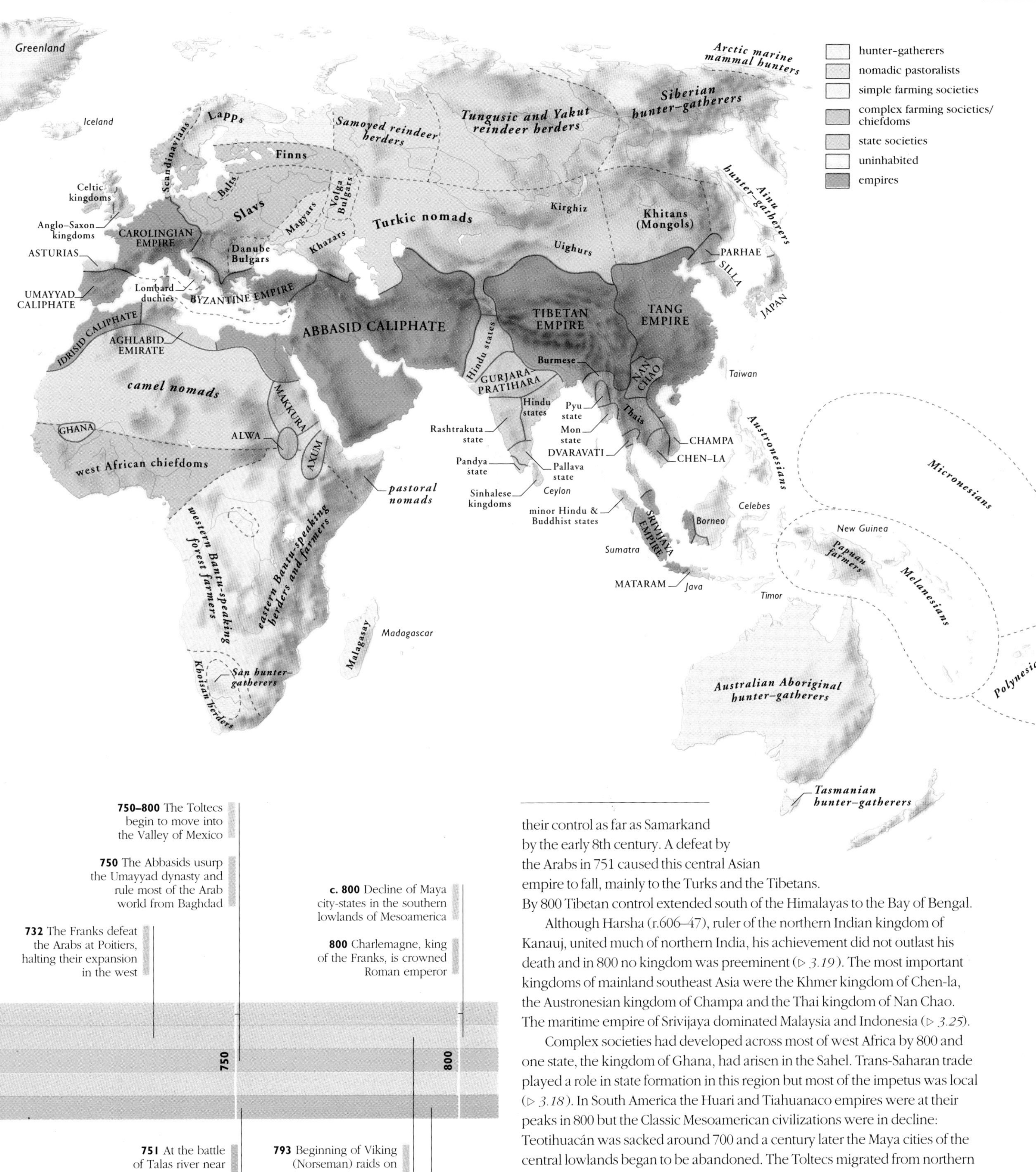

750–800 The Toltecs begin to move into the Valley of Mexico

750 The Abbasids usurp the Umayyad dynasty and rule most of the Arab world from Baghdad

732 The Franks defeat the Arabs at Poitiers, halting their expansion in the west

c. 800 Decline of Maya city-states in the southern lowlands of Mesoamerica

800 Charlemagne, king of the Franks, is crowned Roman emperor

751 At the battle of Talas river near Samarkand, Chinese expansion is halted by the Arab advance

793 Beginning of Viking (Norseman) raids on western Europe

794 The classical Heian period in Japan is established by emperor Kammu, who moves his capital to Kyoto

their control as far as Samarkand by the early 8th century. A defeat by the Arabs in 751 caused this central Asian empire to fall, mainly to the Turks and the Tibetans. By 800 Tibetan control extended south of the Himalayas to the Bay of Bengal.

Although Harsha (r.606–47), ruler of the northern Indian kingdom of Kanauj, united much of northern India, his achievement did not outlast his death and in 800 no kingdom was preeminent (▷ *3.19*). The most important kingdoms of mainland southeast Asia were the Khmer kingdom of Chen-la, the Austronesian kingdom of Champa and the Thai kingdom of Nan Chao. The maritime empire of Srivijaya dominated Malaysia and Indonesia (▷ *3.25*).

Complex societies had developed across most of west Africa by 800 and one state, the kingdom of Ghana, had arisen in the Sahel. Trans-Saharan trade played a role in state formation in this region but most of the impetus was local (▷ *3.18*). In South America the Huari and Tiahuanaco empires were at their peaks in 800 but the Classic Mesoamerican civilizations were in decline: Teotihuacán was sacked around 700 and a century later the Maya cities of the central lowlands began to be abandoned. The Toltecs migrated from northern Mexico into the power vacuum created by the fall of Teotihuacán (▷ *3.27*). The first North American societies to depend on farming developed in the southwestern deserts in the 7th–8th centuries. In the eastern woodlands maize was a widespread crop by 800. The Hopewell cultures were replaced by the more complex Mississippian temple-mound building cultures (▷ *3.26*) ■

3.02 THE WORLD • AD 1000 •

In the 9th century Christian Europe was under attack from Viking raiders from Scandinavia, Muslim pirates from Spain and north Africa, and steppe nomads, the Magyars and Bulgars (▷ *3.07*). The cultural and economic revival fostered by the Carolingian empire collapsed under the impact of the attacks and the empire itself broke up between 843 and 889. However, by 1000 European civilization was expanding and many of the states of medieval Europe had begun to emerge as stable political units: France was a decentralized, weak feudal kingdom but the German kings built a strong state based on their control of the church. In 962 the German king Otto I adopted the title Roman emperor, founding the Holy Roman empire. He ended the Magyar threat in 955, after which the Magyars founded the Christian kingdom of Hungary. Viking attacks on the British Isles were a catalyst in the formation of the kingdoms of England and Scotland and by 1000 stable kingdoms had developed in Scandinavia itself. Swedish Vikings founded the first Russian state about 862 but by 1000 this had lost its Scandinavian character and was a Slavic state under Byzantine influence.

The Arab world continued to fragment and by 1000 the Abbasid caliphs were no more than spiritual figureheads (▷ *3.14*). Persia passed under the control of native dynasties; Egypt, Syria and Palestine became independent under the Tulunid emirs in 868; most of Arabia was lost around 900; and the Christian Armenians recovered their independence in 886. Abbasid power revived in the early 10th century and control over Egypt and southern Iran was recovered, but it collapsed for good when the Persian Buwayhids seized Baghdad in 945: they ruled in the name of the caliph who was retained only for his spiritual authority. Between 967 and 973 the Tunisian Fatimid dynasty conquered Egypt, Palestine and Syria and were the most powerful Muslim rulers in 1000. Despite the disunity, the Muslim world continued to expand in the 9th and 10th centuries, the most important gain being the conversion of the Ghuzz Turks.

Despite the collapse of the Tibetan empire around 850, the Tang Chinese empire continued to decline in the 9th century (▷ *3.20*). The government's fiscal problems led to persecutions and expropriation of property belonging to Buddhists, Nestorian Christians and Manichaeans. Landlords began to reverse the earlier Tang land reforms, leading to a peasant uprising in 874–84 which broke the authority of the dynasty. Power devolved to provincial warlords and the empire split into several states. In 916 the far north was conquered by the nomad Khitans (a Mongol people), who founded the

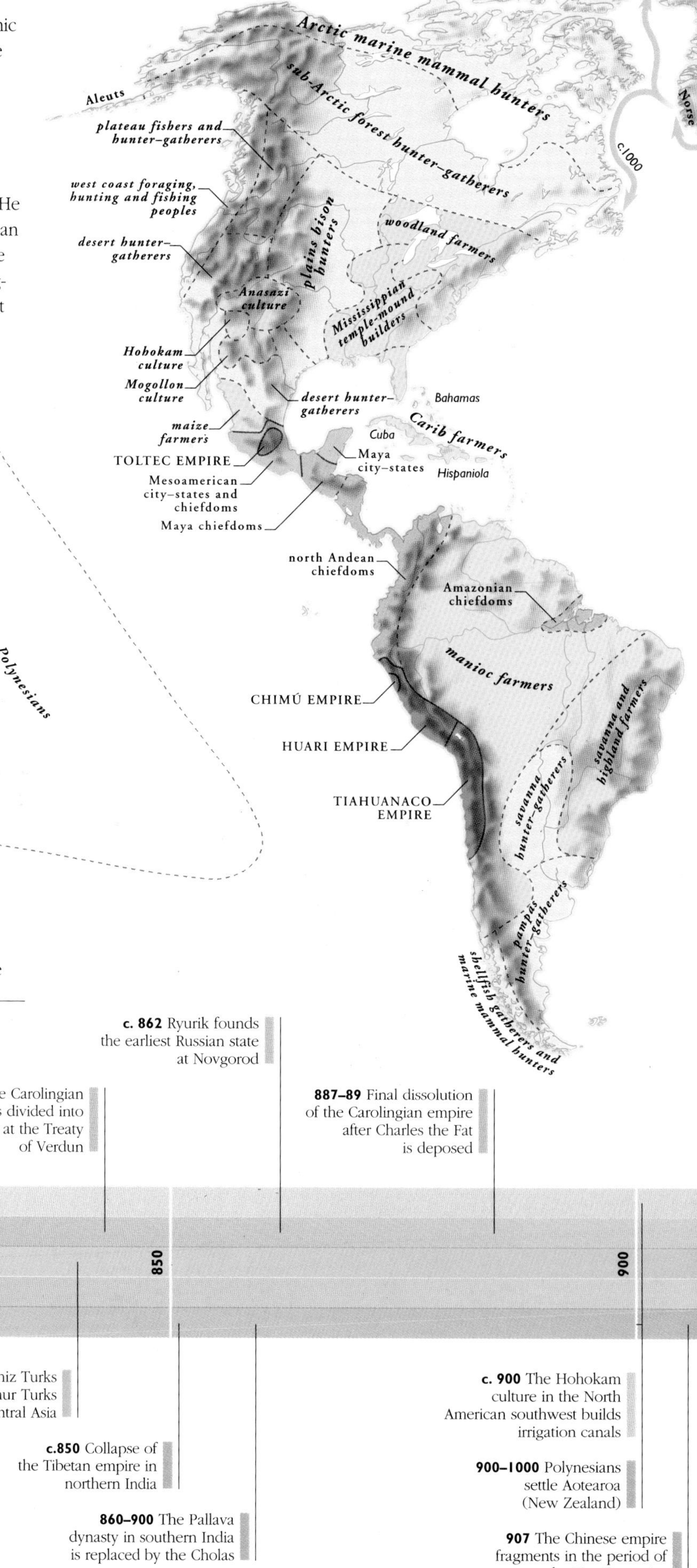

TIMELINE

	800	850	900
The Americas			
Europe			
Middle East			
Africa			
East and South Asia			

814 Death of the Frankish emperor, Charlemagne

800–900 Maize becomes an important source of food in the eastern woodlands of North America

c. 862 Ryurik founds the earliest Russian state at Novgorod

843 The Carolingian empire is divided into three parts at the Treaty of Verdun

887–89 Final dissolution of the Carolingian empire after Charles the Fat is deposed

c.800–20 Construction of the Buddhist temple at Borobudur, Java

840 The Kirghiz Turks conquer the Uighur Turks in central Asia

c.850 Collapse of the Tibetan empire in northern India

860–900 The Pallava dynasty in southern India is replaced by the Cholas

c. 900 The Hohokam culture in the North American southwest builds irrigation canals

900–1000 Polynesians settle Aotearoa (New Zealand)

907 The Chinese empire fragments in the period of the Five Dynasties

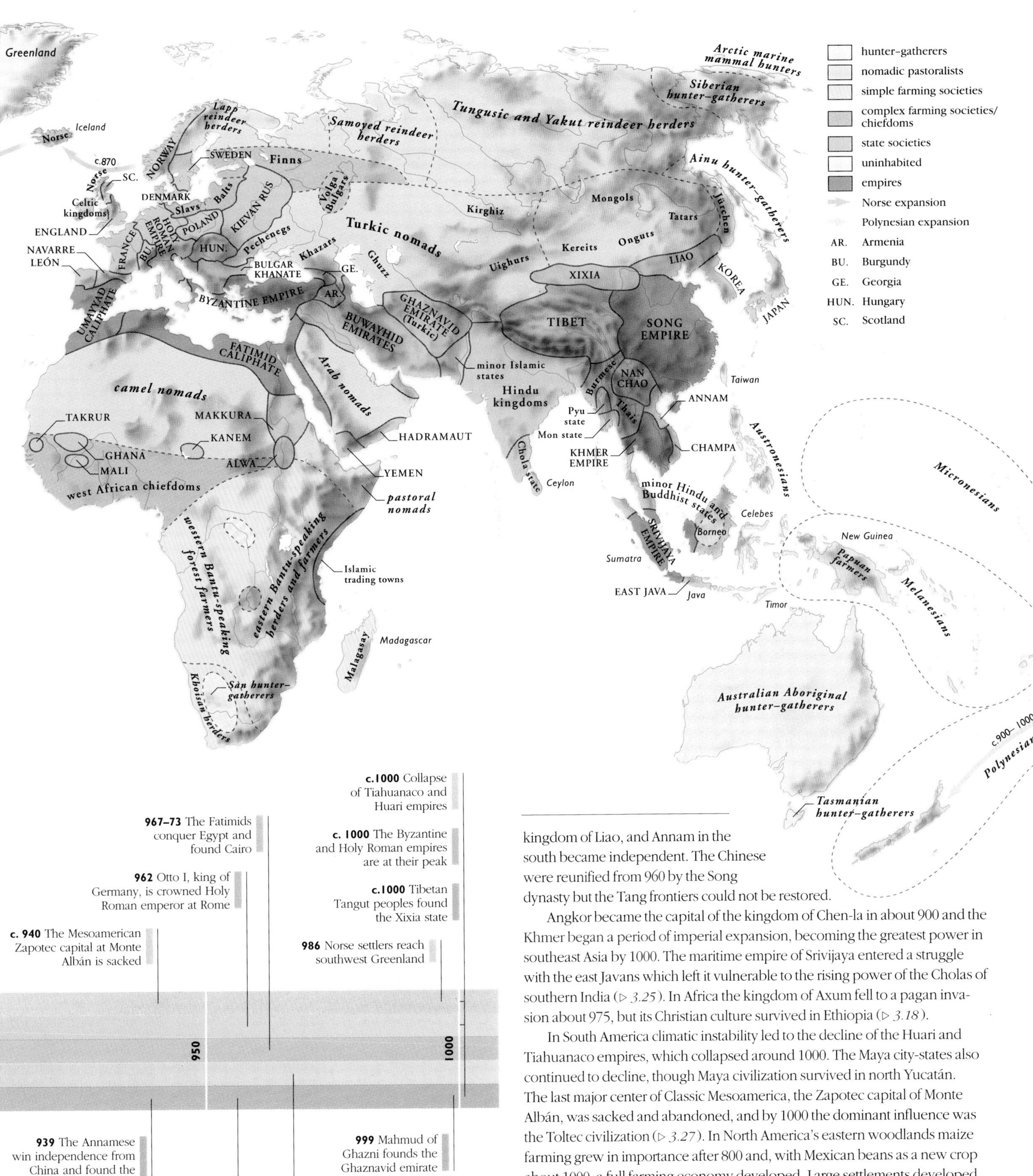

c.1000 Collapse of Tiahuanaco and Huari empires

967–73 The Fatimids conquer Egypt and found Cairo

c. 1000 The Byzantine and Holy Roman empires are at their peak

962 Otto I, king of Germany, is crowned Holy Roman emperor at Rome

c.1000 Tibetan Tangut peoples found the Xixia state

c. 940 The Mesoamerican Zapotec capital at Monte Albán is sacked

986 Norse settlers reach southwest Greenland

950

1000

939 The Annamese win independence from China and found the kingdom of Dai Viet

999 Mahmud of Ghazni founds the Ghaznavid emirate

960 The Chinese empire is restored by the Song dynasty

c.975 The Christian kingdom of Axum falls to pagan invaders

kingdom of Liao, and Annam in the south became independent. The Chinese were reunified from 960 by the Song dynasty but the Tang frontiers could not be restored.

Angkor became the capital of the kingdom of Chen-la in about 900 and the Khmer began a period of imperial expansion, becoming the greatest power in southeast Asia by 1000. The maritime empire of Srivijaya entered a struggle with the east Javans which left it vulnerable to the rising power of the Cholas of southern India (▷ *3.25*). In Africa the kingdom of Axum fell to a pagan invasion about 975, but its Christian culture survived in Ethiopia (▷ *3.18*).

In South America climatic instability led to the decline of the Huari and Tiahuanaco empires, which collapsed around 1000. The Maya city-states also continued to decline, though Maya civilization survived in north Yucatán. The last major center of Classic Mesoamerica, the Zapotec capital of Monte Albán, was sacked and abandoned, and by 1000 the dominant influence was the Toltec civilization (▷ *3.27*). In North America's eastern woodlands maize farming grew in importance after 800 and, with Mexican beans as a new crop about 1000, a full farming economy developed. Large settlements developed by 1000 in the southwestern deserts and the Mississippi area (▷ *3.26*).

Two large uninhabited landmasses were colonized at this time. Scandinavians, mainly from Norway, began to settle in Iceland about 870, and by 1000 had also settled southwest Greenland and reached the American mainland. At the same time Polynesians reached Aotearoa (New Zealand) ■

THE WORLD • AD 1279 •

Western Europe's confidence grew in the 11th and 12th centuries, as shown in its Gothic cathedrals and in crusades against the Muslims in the Holy Land and the pagan Slavs in eastern Europe (▷ 3.17). Spain's Christian kingdoms expanded until by 1279 the Muslims were confined to Granada. The Holy Roman empire looked impressive, but disputes with the papacy undermined its authority. By the mid-13th century the empire was becoming a confederation of semi-independent states. In contrast, England and France had become strong centralized kingdoms (▷ 3.08).

Although Islam lost ground in Europe it continued to expand elsewhere. The Ghaznavid emirate conquered northwest India and in 1206 a Muslim sultanate was founded at Delhi: by 1279 it was the largest state in India since the fall of the Gupta empire (▷ 3.19). Islam was spread by merchants to west Africa in the 11th century, and by the 13th century, Timbuktu, the capital of the kingdom of Mali, was a center of Muslim culture. Trade with the Muslim world was a factor in the emergence of the first powerful chiefdom of southern Africa at Great Zimbabwe around 1200 (▷ 3.18)

The dominant Muslim power in the 11th century was the Seljuks (▷ 3.16). Originally a clan of Ghuzz Turk mercenaries who rebelled against their employer, the Ghaznavid emir, in 1037, the Seljuks overran Persia, the Abbasid caliphate, Syria and the Holy Land, and in 1071 won control of Anatolia. Although the First Crusade, which captured Jerusalem in 1099, allowed the Byzantines to reclaim some lost territory, the empire never fully recovered. By this time Seljuk political unity had broken down, and hostility between them and the Fatimids of Egypt meant that Muslim counterattacks against the Crusaders were ineffective. The Crusaders were put on the defensive after the Seljuk Zangid sultanate of Aleppo overthrew the Fatimids 1169–71 and seized Egypt, but the Zangids were themselves overthrown five years later by Saladin, who retook Jerusalem in 1187. The Crusader states were finally destroyed in 1291 by the Mamlukes who had seized power in Egypt in 1250.

The nomadic Mongol peoples had been gradually expanding westward since the breakup of the Turkish steppe empire in the 8th century. Though superb cavalry fighters they did not threaten the settled civilizations of Eurasia until they were

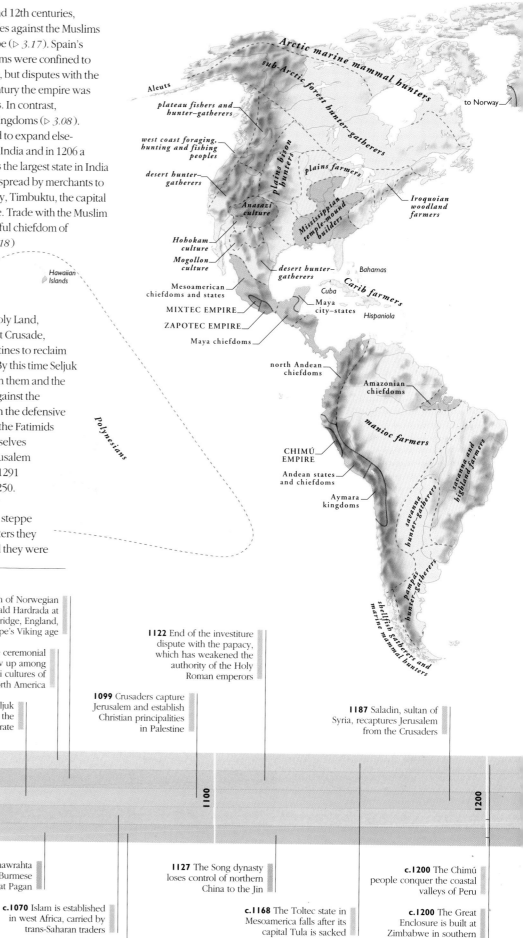

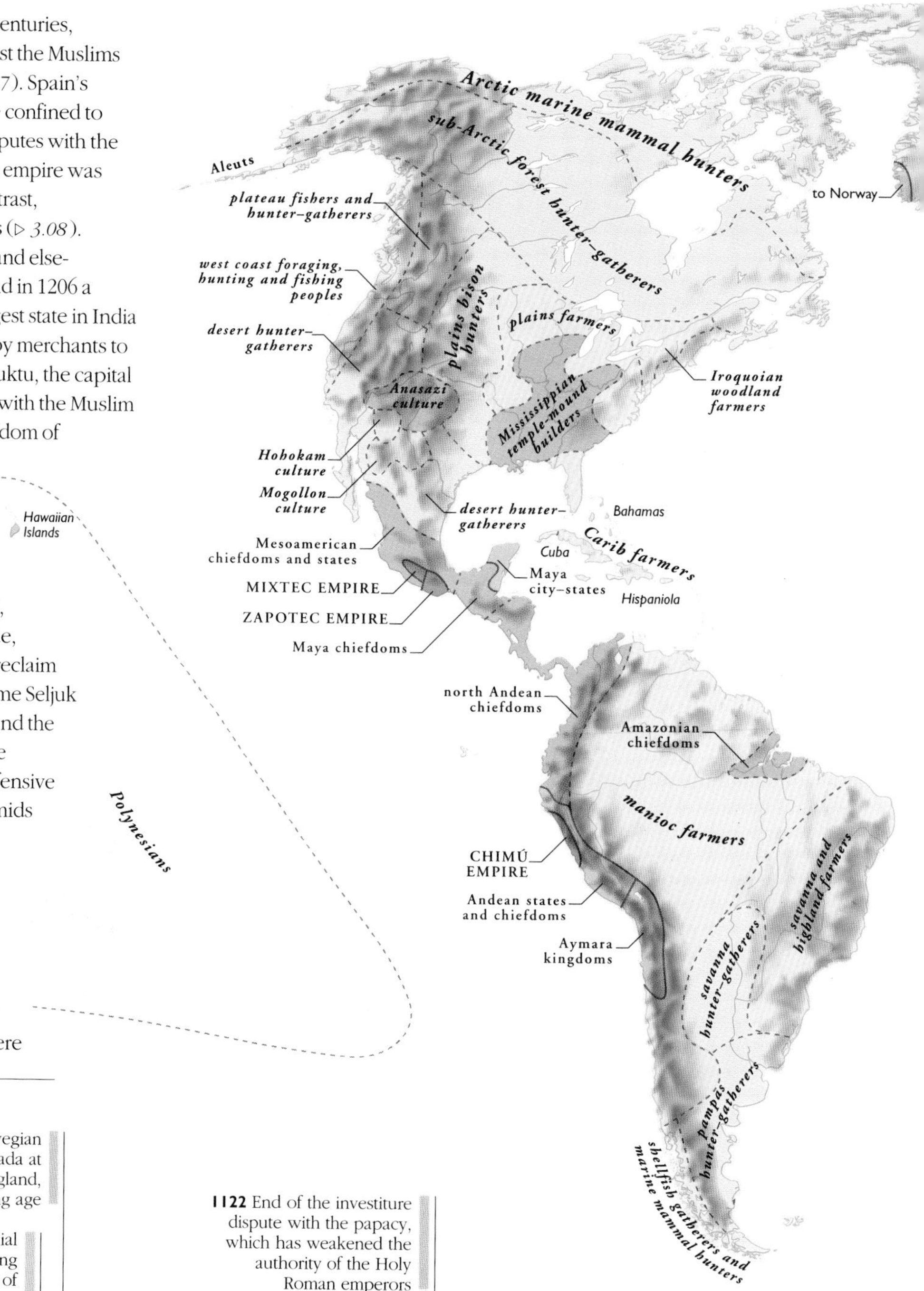

Arctic marine mammal hunters
sub-Arctic forest hunter-gatherers
Aleuts
to Norway
plateau fishers and hunter-gatherers
west coast foraging, hunting and fishing peoples
desert hunter-gatherers
plains bison hunters
plains farmers
Iroquoian woodland farmers
Anasazi culture
Mississippian temple-mound builders
Hohokam culture
Mogollon culture
desert hunter-gatherers
Bahamas
Hawaiian Islands
Mesoamerican chiefdoms and states
Carib farmers
Cuba
Maya city-states
Hispaniola
MIXTEC EMPIRE
ZAPOTEC EMPIRE
Maya chiefdoms
north Andean chiefdoms
Amazonian chiefdoms
Polynesians
manioc farmers
CHIMÚ EMPIRE
savanna and highland farmers
Andean states and chiefdoms
Aymara kingdoms
savanna hunter-gatherers
pampas hunter-gatherers
shellfish gatherers and marine mammal hunters

TIMELINE

The Americas · Europe · Middle East · Africa · East and South Asia

1000

1037 The Seljuk Turks rebel against the Ghaznavid emirate

1044–77 King Anawrahta creates a unified Burmese state based at Pagan

c.1050 Large ceremonial centers grow up among the Anasazi cultures of southwest North America

1066 Death of Norwegian king Harald Hardrada at Stamford Bridge, England, ends Europe's Viking age

c.1070 Islam is established in west Africa, carried by trans-Saharan traders

1071 The Byzantine empire is defeated by the Seljuk Turks at Manzikert

1099 Crusaders capture Jerusalem and establish Christian principalities in Palestine

1100

1122 End of the investiture dispute with the papacy, which has weakened the authority of the Holy Roman emperors

1127 The Song dynasty loses control of northern China to the Jin

c.1168 The Toltec state in Mesoamerica falls after its capital Tula is sacked

1187 Saladin, sultan of Syria, recaptures Jerusalem from the Crusaders

1200

c.1200 The Chimú people conquer the coastal valleys of Peru

c.1200 The Great Enclosure is built at Zimbabwe in southern Africa

c.1200 The first chiefdoms develop in Polynesia

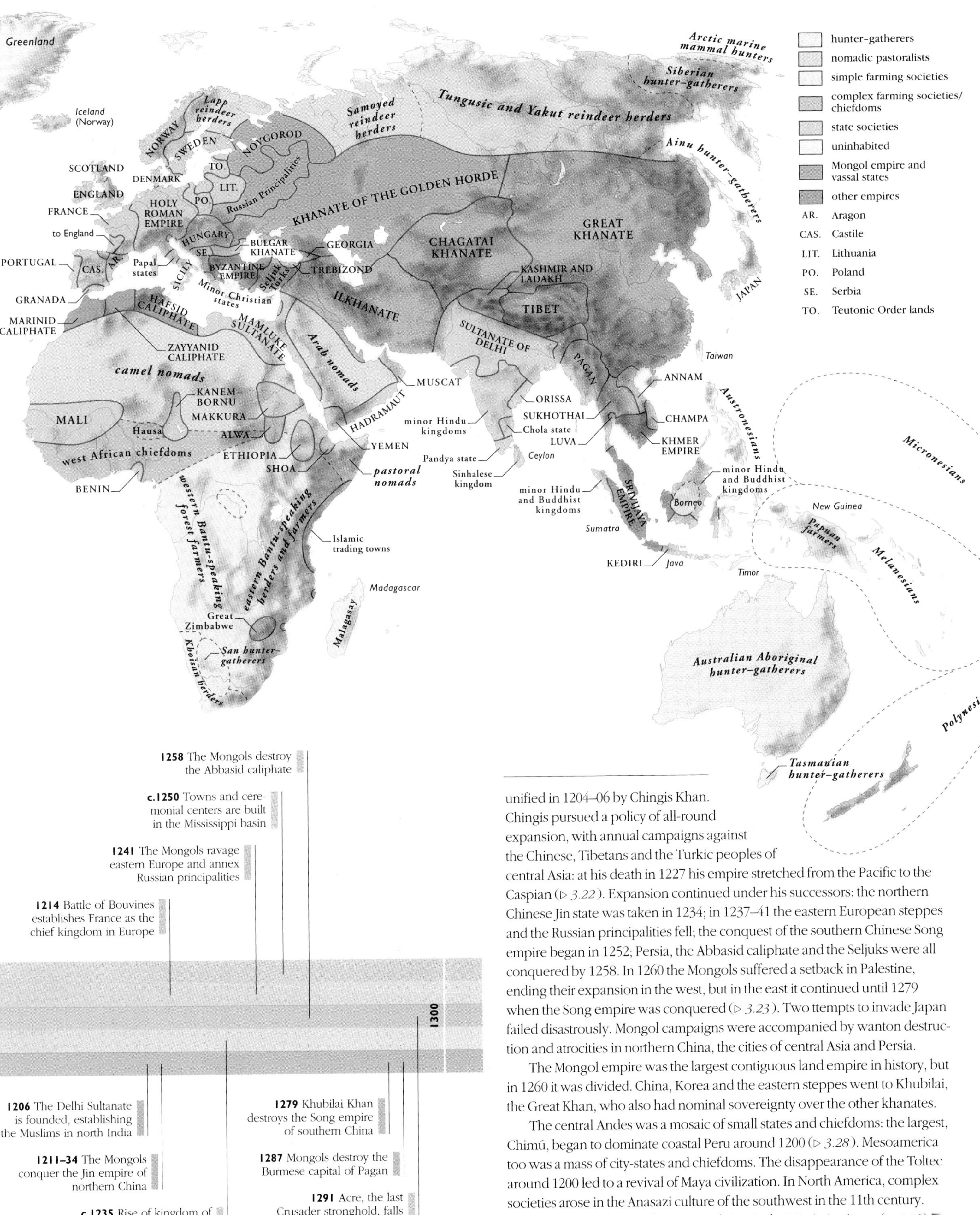

1258 The Mongols destroy the Abbasid caliphate

c.1250 Towns and ceremonial centers are built in the Mississippi basin

1241 The Mongols ravage eastern Europe and annex Russian principalities

1214 Battle of Bouvines establishes France as the chief kingdom in Europe

1206 The Delhi Sultanate is founded, establishing the Muslims in north India

1211–34 The Mongols conquer the Jin empire of northern China

c.1235 Rise of kingdom of Mali under Sun Diata Keita

1279 Khubilai Khan destroys the Song empire of southern China

1287 Mongols destroy the Burmese capital of Pagan

1291 Acre, the last Crusader stronghold, falls to the Mamlukes

unified in 1204–06 by Chingis Khan. Chingis pursued a policy of all-round expansion, with annual campaigns against the Chinese, Tibetans and the Turkic peoples of central Asia: at his death in 1227 his empire stretched from the Pacific to the Caspian (▷ *3.22*). Expansion continued under his successors: the northern Chinese Jin state was taken in 1234; in 1237–41 the eastern European steppes and the Russian principalities fell; the conquest of the southern Chinese Song empire began in 1252; Persia, the Abbasid caliphate and the Seljuks were all conquered by 1258. In 1260 the Mongols suffered a setback in Palestine, ending their expansion in the west, but in the east it continued until 1279 when the Song empire was conquered (▷ *3.23*). Two ttempts to invade Japan failed disastrously. Mongol campaigns were accompanied by wanton destruction and atrocities in northern China, the cities of central Asia and Persia.

The Mongol empire was the largest contiguous land empire in history, but in 1260 it was divided. China, Korea and the eastern steppes went to Khubilai, the Great Khan, who also had nominal sovereignty over the other khanates.

The central Andes was a mosaic of small states and chiefdoms: the largest, Chimú, began to dominate coastal Peru around 1200 (▷ *3.28*). Mesoamerica too was a mass of city-states and chiefdoms. The disappearance of the Toltec around 1200 led to a revival of Maya civilization. In North America, complex societies arose in the Anasazi culture of the southwest in the 11th century. Towns developed around ceremonial sites in the Mississippi area (▷ *3.26*) ■

3.04 THE WORLD • AD 1492 •

At the end of the 13th century Islam began to spread through Malaya and the islands of southeast Asia, gradually supplanting Hinduism and Buddhism. At the same time, the Mongols tried to expand into southeast Asia, but with little success. Their vast empire broke up in the 14th century. In China they were overthrown by the native Ming dynasty in 1368, following peasant rebellions and internal power struggles. The Ming ruled in the tradition of the Tang dynasty and reasserted Chinese power in southeast Asia. One of their first acts was to forbid Chinese from traveling abroad. This isolated China, ruined Chinese trade and led to a fateful neglect of maritime matters just as the Europeans were about to begin their own oceanic exploration. By the time the interdict was lifted in 1567, the initiative had passed irretrievably to the Europeans.

The Mongols remained a power on the eastern steppes and the khanates of the Chagatai and the Golden Horde survived at the end of the 15th century, but their mainly Turkic subjects had already reasserted their independence. In the Middle East the Mongols converted to Islam and were assimilated by their Persian and Turkic subjects. Fragmentation followed and by 1350 the Ilkhanate had dissolved into a number of Turkish, Persian and nominally Mongol states. One of these, the Ottoman Turk sultanate, had by 1400 conquered most of Anatolia and the Balkans and reduced the Byzantine empire to its capital Constantinople (▷ *3.16*). Attempts to build a united Christian front to counter this new Muslim threat to Europe foundered amid international rivalries. The Ottomans, however, were defeated in 1402 by Timur the Lame (r.1361–1405), ruler of Samarkand, who claimed Chingis Khan as his ancestor and saw himself as restorer of the Mongol empire, though he was culturally more Turk than Mongol. In a devastating reign of terror, Timur rebuilt the Ilkhanate, broke the power of the Delhi sultanate and was only prevented from invading China by his death. The empire he had built broke up shortly after.

Ottoman power revived after Timur's death and the advance into Europe began again. In 1453 Constantinople fell after an epic siege and the Byzantine empire finally died. In 1475 the Ottomans crossed the Danube and pushed west. Although Byzantium had fallen, much of its heritage survived in the

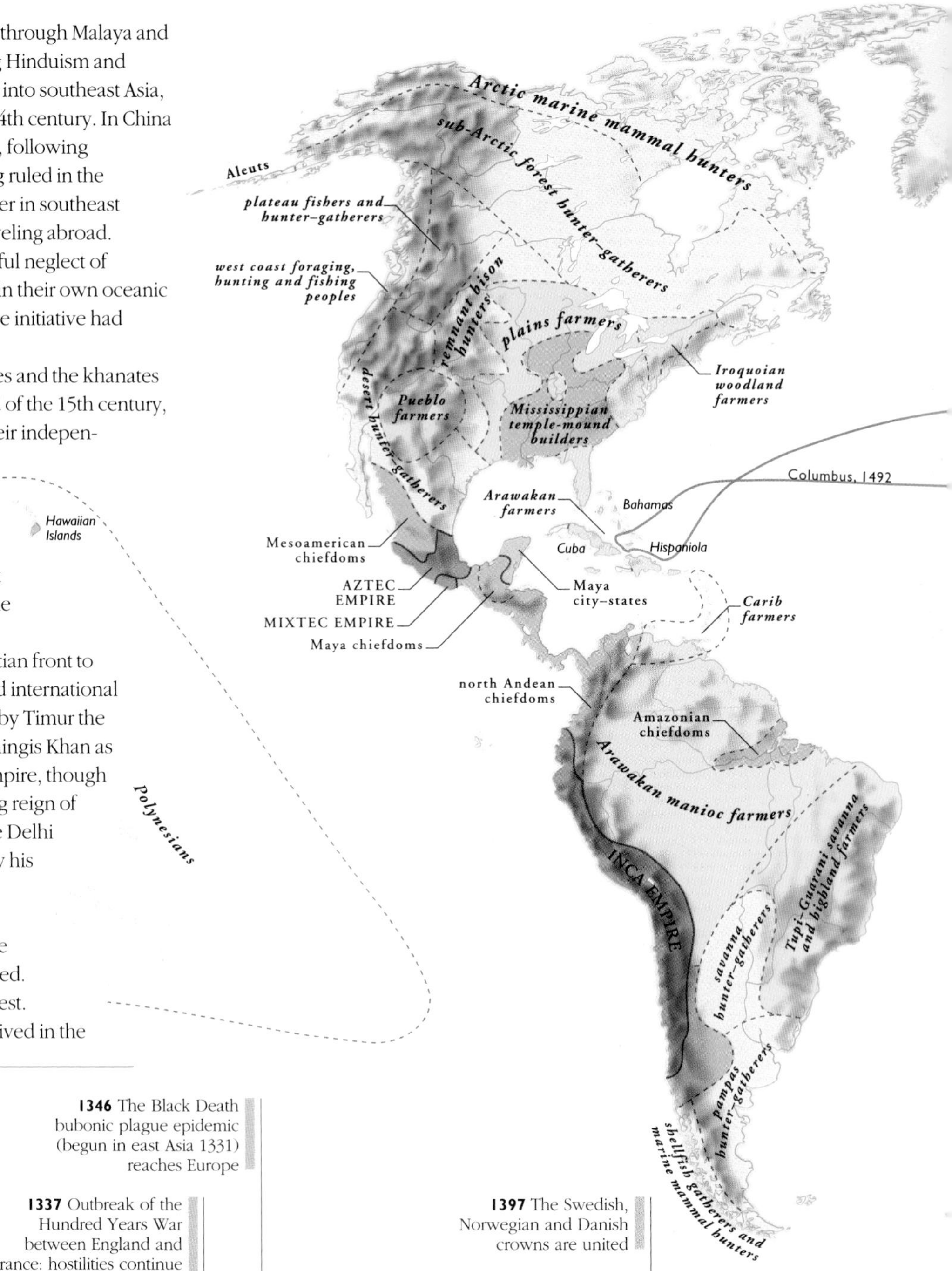

TIMELINE

The Americas · Europe · Middle East · Africa · East and South Asia

1290 Merchants introduce Islam into Indonesia and Malaysia

1293 Osman I, a Turkish chief in Anatolia, founds the Ottoman dynasty

c.1300 Decline of the Anasazi and other farmers of southwestern deserts

c.1300 The Renaissance begins in Italy as Classical forms in art, architecture and literature are revived

1300

1317 Christian Makkura is overthrown by Muslim Arab nomads

c.1325 Arrival of the Aztecs in Mexico

c.1330 The sultanate of Delhi reaches its maximum extent under Muhammad ibn Tughluk

1337 Outbreak of the Hundred Years War between England and France: hostilities continue sporadically until 1453

1346 The Black Death bubonic plague epidemic (begun in east Asia 1331) reaches Europe

1361–1405 From his capital at Samarkand Timur the Lame leads a resurgence of Mongol power in the Middle East

1368 The establishment of the Ming dynasty ends Mongol rule in China

1370 The kingdom of Vijayanagara dominates southern India

1378 The "Great Schism" in the Catholic church begins, with popes in both Rome and Avignon

1397 The Swedish, Norwegian and Danish crowns are united

1400

1415 The Portuguese take Ceuta in Morocco, their first African possession

1428 The Aztec empire is founded by Itzcóatl (r.1428–40)

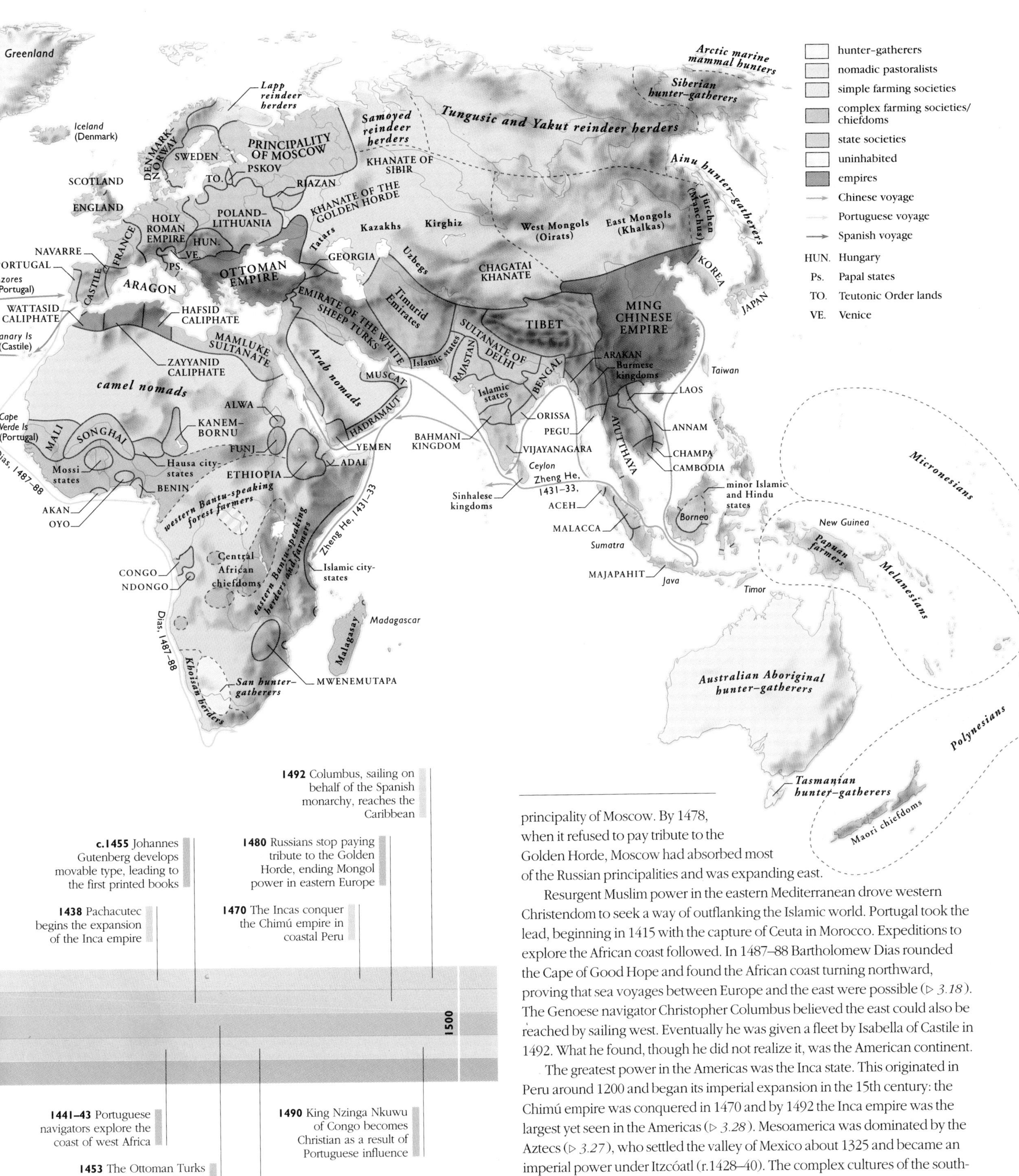

1492 Columbus, sailing on behalf of the Spanish monarchy, reaches the Caribbean

c.1455 Johannes Gutenberg develops movable type, leading to the first printed books

1480 Russians stop paying tribute to the Golden Horde, ending Mongol power in eastern Europe

1438 Pachacutec begins the expansion of the Inca empire

1470 The Incas conquer the Chimú empire in coastal Peru

1441–43 Portuguese navigators explore the coast of west Africa

1490 King Nzinga Nkuwu of Congo becomes Christian as a result of Portuguese influence

1453 The Ottoman Turks take Constantinople and end the Byzantine empire

1464 Songhai eclipses Mali as the chief power in west Africa

principality of Moscow. By 1478, when it refused to pay tribute to the Golden Horde, Moscow had absorbed most of the Russian principalities and was expanding east.

Resurgent Muslim power in the eastern Mediterranean drove western Christendom to seek a way of outflanking the Islamic world. Portugal took the lead, beginning in 1415 with the capture of Ceuta in Morocco. Expeditions to explore the African coast followed. In 1487–88 Bartholomew Dias rounded the Cape of Good Hope and found the African coast turning northward, proving that sea voyages between Europe and the east were possible (▷ *3.18*). The Genoese navigator Christopher Columbus believed the east could also be reached by sailing west. Eventually he was given a fleet by Isabella of Castile in 1492. What he found, though he did not realize it, was the American continent.

The greatest power in the Americas was the Inca state. This originated in Peru around 1200 and began its imperial expansion in the 15th century: the Chimú empire was conquered in 1470 and by 1492 the Inca empire was the largest yet seen in the Americas (▷ *3.28*). Mesoamerica was dominated by the Aztecs (▷ *3.27*), who settled the valley of Mexico about 1325 and became an imperial power under Itzcóatl (r.1428–40). The complex cultures of the south-western deserts of North America collapsed at the end of the 13th century after prolonged droughts. The towns of the Mississippian cultures were in decline by 1492 and the region's center had lost its population. Buffalo-hunting on the Great Plains was dying out as farming spread along river valleys (▷ *3.26*) ■

3.05 The spread of the world religions • AD 600 – 1500 •

The birth of Islam, the most recent of the world religions, dominated the era known to Europeans as the Middle Ages, and it deeply affected all the established world religions.

Islam originated in the teachings of the prophet Muhammad. From 610 Muhammad received a series of revelations which are recorded in the sacred book of Islam, the *Koran*. Islam drew much from Judaism and, to a lesser extent, Christianity; the *Koran* asserts that Muhammad is the last of a line of prophets that included Adam, Abraham, Noah, Moses and Jesus.

By the time of Muhammad's death in 632 Arabs had generally acknowledged him as their religious and political leader and had accepted Islam. Muhammad had no male heir and the decades following his deathwere marked by prolonged disputes over the succession, which erupted into civil war during the caliphate of Muhammad's son-in-law Ali (r.656–61). When Ali was murdered in 661, his supporters recognized his son Husain as successor (caliph) in preference to Muawiya, founder of the Umayyad dynasty. Husain's death in battle at Karbala in 680 led to his martyrdom, and the development among his supporters of the Shiite tradition of Islam.

Shiism has continued to be distinguished from the majority Sunni tradition by its stress on martyrdom and its radically different theories of religious leadership. In the 9th century doctrinal disputes resulted in the secession from Shiism of the Ismaili sect. Until the 13th century, the Ismailis (who are also known as the Assassins) habitually murdered their enemies. Moreover, the spread of both the Sunni and Shiite Islamic traditions was promoted by the growth, from the 8th century onward, of the mystical movement known as Sufism, which laid a heavy emphasis on piety and zeal.

The rise of Islam halved the area under Christian domination between 600 and 750. Islam tolerated Christians but the social and financial advantages of conversion were great and Christianity soon declined in the areas conquered by the Arabs. However, freedom from Orthodox persecution enabled some minority Christian sects, such as the Nestorians, to spread widely in Asia. Although it regained some ground through missionary work and military conquest – most notably the Crusades that temporarily restored Christian

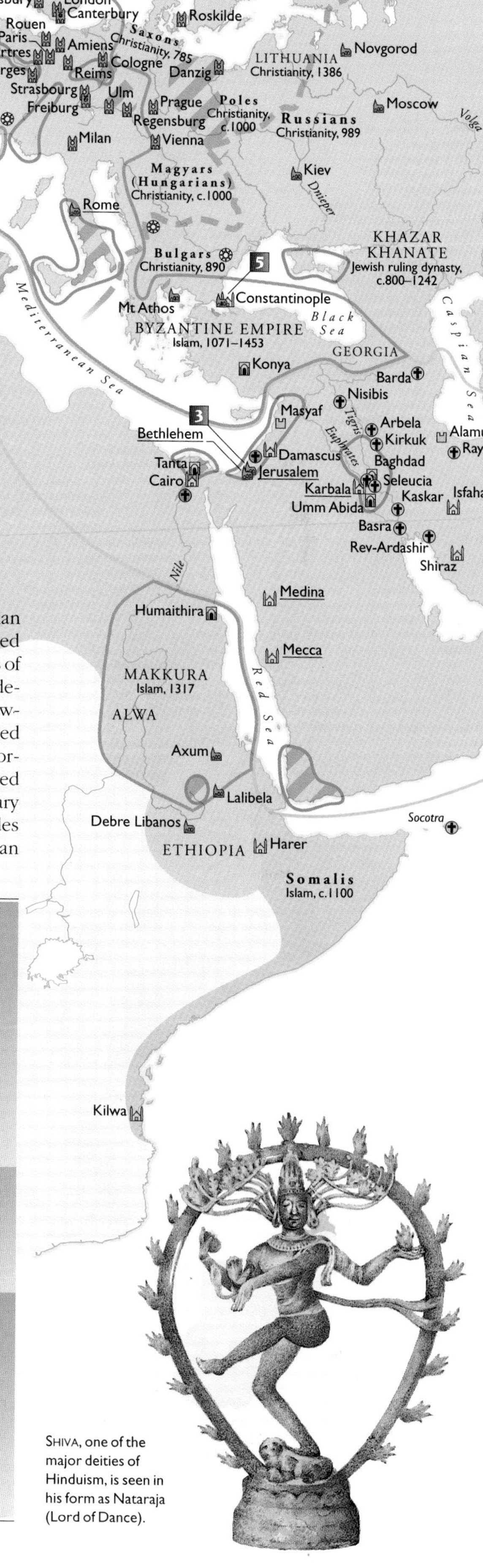

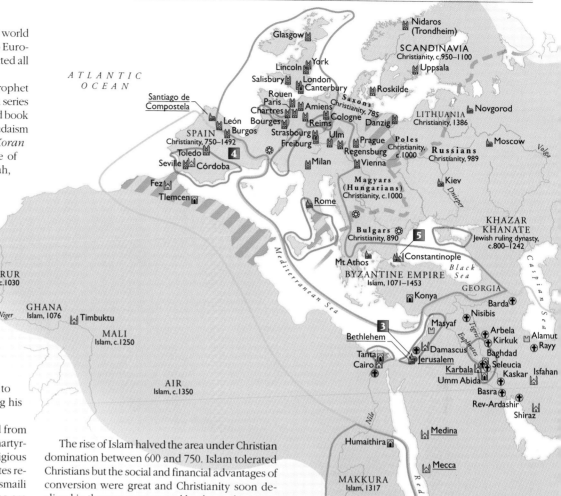

SHIVA, one of the major deities of Hinduism, is seen in his form as Nataraja (Lord of Dance).

TIMELINE

	700	1000	1300
South and east Asia	**600–700** Beginning of the Bakhti revival of Hinduism in India **600–800** Spread of Chan and Pure Land Buddhism in China **c.700** Persian Zoroastrians settle in India: origin of Parsis **762** Uighur nomads adopt Manichaeanism as religion **791** Buddhism becomes the state religion in Tibet **843** Manichaeanism in China is destroyed by persecution **845** Buddhists face persecution in China **900–1000** Pilgrimages are established as an important expression of Hindu devotion	**1191** Zen (Chan) Buddhism is introduced to Japan **1200–1300** Buddhism dies out in northern India	
Middle East	**622** Muhammad's flight (*hijra*) from Mecca to Medina **700–800** Growth of the Sufi mystical movement in Islam	**c.970** Turks convert to Islam **c.1070** Islam spreads to sub-Saharan Africa **1258** Mongols destroy the Abbasid caliphate of Baghdad	
Europe	**726–843** Iconoclast controversy: destruction of religious images in Byzantine empire	**965** Harald Bluetooth of Denmark is baptized: the first Christian king of Scandinavia **1054** Roman–Orthodox schism becomes permanent **1095–99** The First Crusade is called; Jerusalem is taken **1209–29** Crusades are launched against Cathar (Manichaean) heretics **1232** The Church sets up the Inquisition to fight heresy	**1378–1417** Great Schism damages papal authority
	700	1000	1300

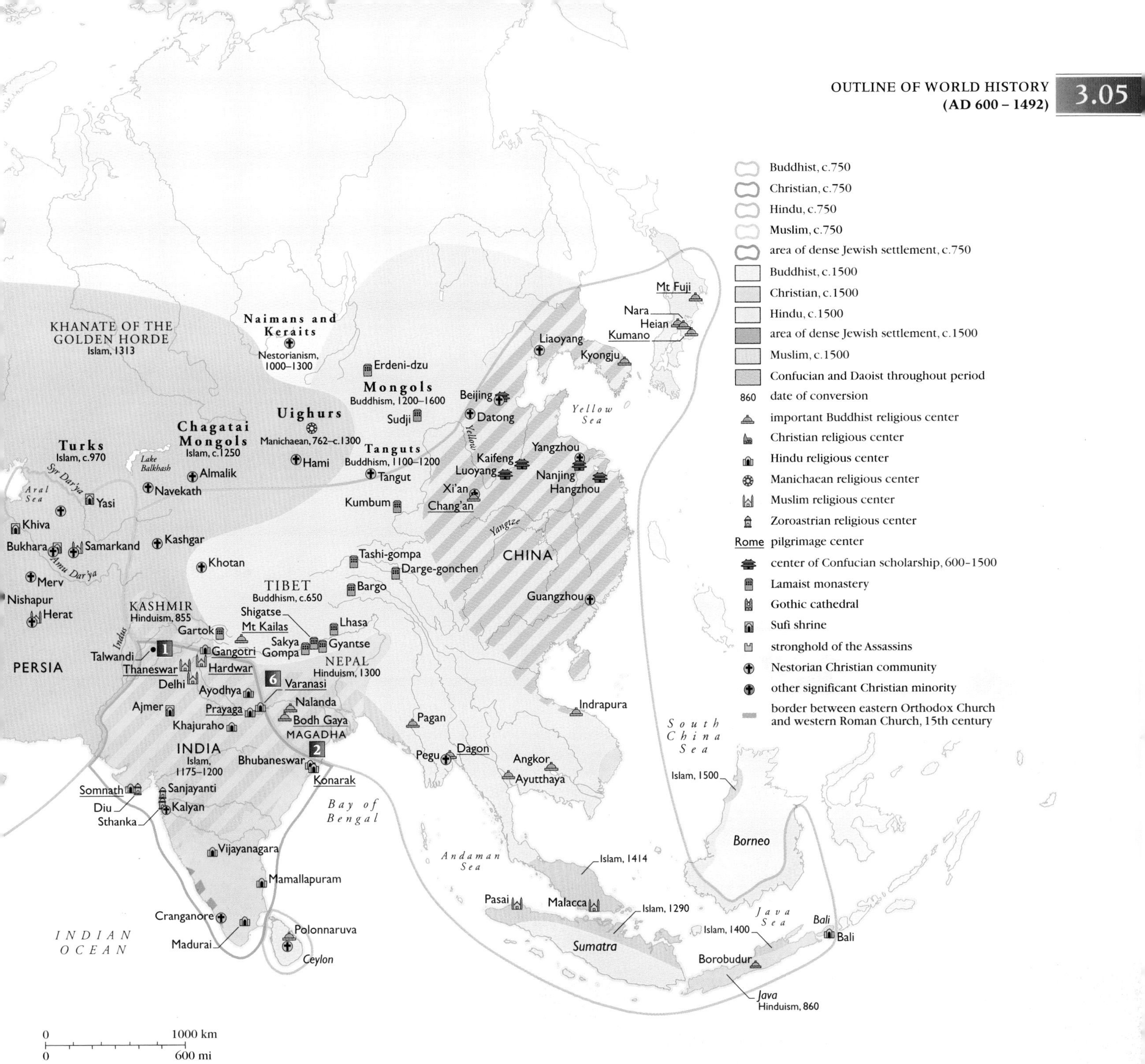

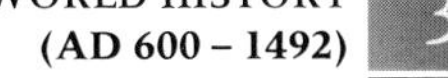

- Buddhist, c.750
- Christian, c.750
- Hindu, c.750
- Muslim, c.750
- area of dense Jewish settlement, c.750
- Buddhist, c.1500
- Christian, c.1500
- Hindu, c.1500
- area of dense Jewish settlement, c.1500
- Muslim, c.1500
- Confucian and Daoist throughout period
- 860 date of conversion
- important Buddhist religious center
- Christian religious center
- Hindu religious center
- Manichaean religious center
- Muslim religious center
- Zoroastrian religious center
- Rome pilgrimage center
- center of Confucian scholarship, 600–1500
- Lamaist monastery
- Gothic cathedral
- Sufi shrine
- stronghold of the Assassins
- Nestorian Christian community
- other significant Christian minority
- border between eastern Orthodox Church and western Roman Church, 15th century

0 1000 km
0 600 mi

control to the Holy Land – Christianity was again in retreat by the 15th century, as the Muslim Ottoman Turks overran the Byzantine empire and moved into the Balkans.

The Arab conquests destroyed Zoroastrianism in its Persian homeland but small communities of emigrants established themselves on India's west coast where the religion still survives among the Parsis.

The Bakhti (devotional) revival movement in the 7th century caused Hinduism to reassert itself against Buddhism, which had been dominant in the preceding centuries. The 8th-century philosopher Shankara gave impetus to the recovery by assimilating popular aspects of Buddhist devotion into Hinduism. An important aspect of the Bakhti revival was the great increase in the popularity of pilgrimages to sacred sites such as Varanasi on the River Ganges. A number of Hindus, especially from the lower castes, converted to Islam following the Muslim conquest around 1200, yet Hinduism remained India's principal religion.

Indian Buddhism, however, was destroyed by the Muslim conquest, continuing to flourish only in Ceylon. Buddhism also declined in southeast Asia following the introduction there of Islam in the 13th century. Chinese Buddhism reached the peak of its influence in the 7th and 8th centuries as a result of patronage by the Tang court. The period saw the spread of the meditative school of Chan (known in Japan as Zen) Buddhism and the populist Pure Land school which promised its adherents rebirth in paradise. Some 40,000 Buddhist temples and monasteries, all with tax-exempt estates, sprang up; they proved a severe drain on state income by 800. A brief imperial persecution in 845 closed many of these monasteries and forced 250,000 monks back into secular life. Buddhism recovered but never regained its former prestige.

The most important new converts to Buddhism in this period were the Tibetans. Here elements of Tibetan shamanism were assimilated to Buddhism to form a distinctive tradition known as Lamaism.

1 Talwandi was the birthplace in 1469 of Guru Nanak, founder of the Sikh religion.

2 Buddhism declined in its original heartland of Magadha after 600 and had been supplanted by Hinduism and Islam by the 13th century.

3 Jerusalem, site of Jesus' crucifixion, was believed by medieval Christians to be the center of the world.

4 Jews were tolerated in Muslim Spain but faced expulsion or forcible conversion after the Christian reconquest.

5 Constantinople, the greatest Christian city of the East, became a leading center of Islamic culture after its conquest by the Ottoman Turks in 1453.

6 Varanasi is Hinduism's most holy site: pilgrimages to bathe in the Ganges had become popular by 1050.

See also 3.09 (religion in medieval Europe); 3.17 (the Crusades); 3.19 (medieval India)

Of the Germanic kingdoms set up within the territory of the western Roman empire in the 5th century, only the Frankish and the Visigothic still survived in 600. The Visigothic kings preserved the late Roman administrative structure but, in contrast to the Franks who were able to win the cooperation and loyalty of their subjects, they remained distant from their Hispano-Roman subjects. This was a fatal weakness. Faced with an invasion of Muslim Arabs and Berbers from North Africa in 711, the Visigoths received no support and the kingdom abruptly collapsed. The invaders took only two years to overrun most of the Iberian peninsula, bringing it within the Umayyad caliphate. Only in the mountains of the far north was there substantial resistance. Here the small Christian kingdom of Asturias developed, based at Oviedo. By 800 it had won back a sizable part of the northwest peninsula from the Arabs.

Since the mid 5th century the Merovingian dynasty had ruled the Frankish kingdom. They followed the Germanic custom of dividing the kingdom between all male heirs, leading to a complex sequence of subdivisions as generation succeeded generation. The succession was rarely a simple matter, and civil wars and assassinations were frequent. In the mid 7th century real authority passed into the hands of court officials known as the mayors of the palace. Frankish power declined and some peripheral areas of the kingdom were lost: most were recovered early in the 8th century but Aquitaine, which broke away in 670, was not taken back until 768. The most successful of the mayors was Pepin II of Herstal (mayor 679–714), who was effective ruler of the entire kingdom by 687. Founder of the Carolingian dynasty, he began an expansion of Frankish power which continued under his son Charles Martel (mayor 714–41). In 732 he turned back an Arab invasion at Poitiers, ending Muslim expansion in the west.

Charles' successor Pepin III (r.741–68) formed an alliance with the papacy in 751. The year before, the Lombards (rulers of most of Italy since 568) had conquered the Byzantine exarchate of Ravenna and were threatening Rome itself. In return for military aid, the pope authorized Pepin to depose the last Merovingian king and assume the kingship of the Franks himself. Pepin died in 768, and the kingdom was divided between his two sons, Charlemagne and Carloman. On the latter's death in 771 Charlemagne was sole ruler; he doubled the size of the Frankish realm in thirty years of campaigning. He was also an energetic legislator and administrator and was devoutly religious, even intervening in matters of doctrine. He promoted missionary activity among the pagan Saxons in the northeast and, anxious to improve the quality of the clergy, encouraged the revival of classical learning known as the Carolingian renaissance. Charlemagne made considerable donations of land to the papacy and, influenced by Byzantine ideas of rulership, had himself crowned emperor by the pope on Christmas Day 800, an act he probably saw as restoring the Roman empire in the west. In line with Frankish custom, Charlemagne made provisions for his empire to be divided between his three sons after his death but was survived by only one, Louis the Pious.

In the British Isles, the Anglo-Saxons had overrun most of the fertile lowland zone by 600 and were

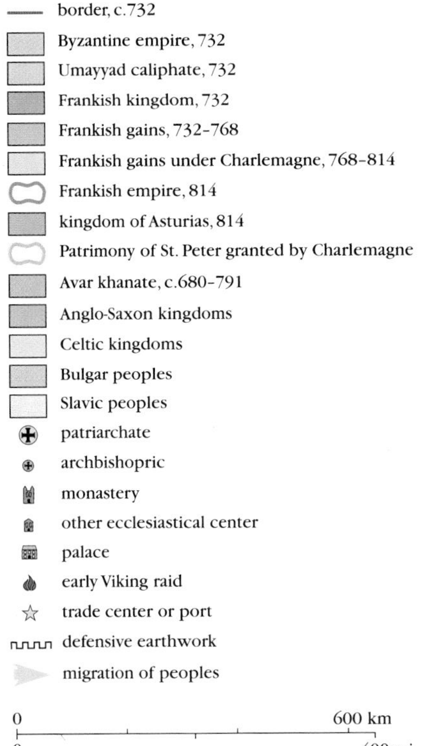

TIMELINE

The Franks

- **639** With the death of King Dagobert, a succession of short-lived kings sees power pass from the Merovingians to the mayors of the palace
- **689** Mayor Pepin II begins the conquest of the Frisians
- **732** Charles Martel defeats Arab invasion at Poitiers
- **751** Pope Zacharias authorizes the deposition of the last Merovingian king by Pepin III (d. 768)
- **771** Charlemagne becomes sole ruler of the Frankish kingdom
- **774** Charlemagne conquers Lombard kingdom of Italy
- **800** Charlemagne is crowned Roman emperor by Pope Leo III in Rome
- **814** Death of Charlemagne, succession of Louis the Pious

Western Christendom

- **c.600–635** Life of Isidore of Seville, theologian, historian and encyclopedist
- **616** The Visigoths expel the Byzantines from southern Spain
- **664** British churches adopt Roman Christianity at the Synod of Whitby: decline of Celtic Christianity
- **c.672–735** Life of Bede: monk, scholar, theologian and historian of early England
- **711–13** Arabs and Berbers conquer the Visigothic kingdom of Spain
- **718** The Danes fortify their southern border against Saxon attack
- **726** Iconoclast controversy causes a breach between the Byzantine and Roman churches
- **750** Lombards capture Ravenna, ending Byzantine power in central Italy
- **790** A dispute between King Offa of Mercia and Charlemagne disrupts cross-channel trade
- **793** The monastery of Lindisfarne is sacked by Viking raiders

700 800

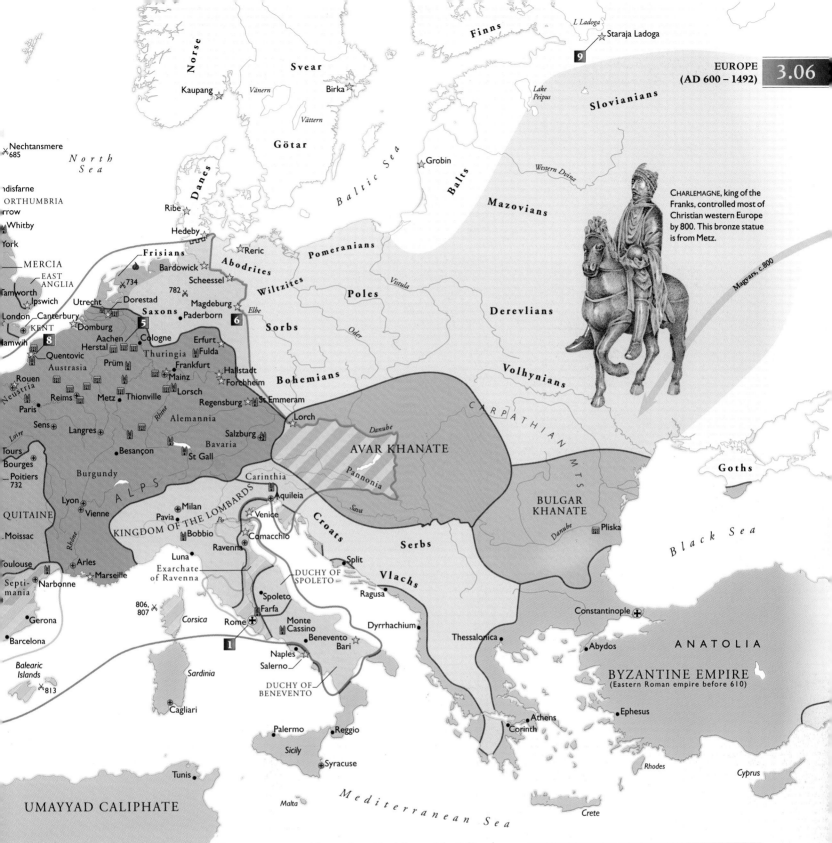

CHARLEMAGNE, king of the Franks, controlled most of Christian western Europe by 800. This bronze statue is from Metz.

UMAYYAD CALIPHATE

beginning to form regional kingdoms, the most powerful being Northumbria. The Anglo-Saxon migrations into southern Britain had cut off British Christianity from contact with the Roman church. The Celtic church developed a distinctive identity and in Ireland fostered the creation of a monastic civilization that was to have significant influence on cultural and religious life in Europe. Irish and Roman missionaries both won converts among the Anglo-Saxons in the 7th century, and it was only with difficulty that the Celtic church was persuaded to rejoin the Roman church in 664. Northumbrian power declined after defeat by the Picts in 685, and in the 8th century the Mercian kingdom rose to dominance under Aethelbald (r.716–57) and Offa (r.757–96).

Frankish overrule brought a modest revival of trade and towns to western Europe, most marked around the southern North Sea and the Baltic where ports and seasonal trading places developed by 800. Though threatened by the Viking raids that broke out in the 790s, it was the start of the process that shifted the focus of economic life from the Mediterranean to the North Sea and Atlantic coasts.

1 Rome found a new role as the seat of the papacy and the spiritual capital of western Christendom.

2 The Asturian victory at Covadonga is regarded as the beginning of the Christian reconquest of Spain.

3 King Offa of Mercia built a 240km (185 mile) earth and timber rampart on his frontier with the Welsh.

4 The Bretons fiercely resisted Frankish expansion: subdued by Charlemagne in 799, they revolted in 812.

5 Charlemagne built an impressive palace, administrative and ecclesiastical complex at Aachen in the 790s.

6 Charlemagne set up a chain of customs posts to regulate trade with the Slavs in 806.

7 Córdoba, the capital of Muslim Spain, was the largest city in western Europe by the 9th century.

8 Trading centers such as Hamwih and Quentovic were evidence of the growing commercial importance of northern Europe.

9 Scandinavian merchants were established at the Finnic settlement of Staraja Ladoga by 750.

See also 3.07 (Viking age), 3.13 (Arab conquests); 3.15 (Byzantine empire)

3.07 Viking Age Europe • 793 – 1050 •

The Vikings – pagan raiders from Denmark and Norway – burst upon western Europe at the end of the 8th century as a bolt from the blue. The targets for their attacks were defenseless coastal monasteries which offered rich plunder. Their first known raid was against the monastery at Lindisfarne, the center of Northumbrian Christianity, in 793. Six years later they raided the Frankish coast, prompting Charlemagne to set up coastal defenses. But the full weight of Viking raids came in the 830s, when they arrived each year in ever greater numbers and began to sail up navigable rivers like the Rhine to sack inland ports such as Dorestad. Viking activity entered a new phase in 865 when the Danish "Great Army" invaded England with permanent settlement rather than plunder in mind. Much of eastern and northern England was overrun and settled (the area known as the Danelaw, with its capital at York) but the Wessex king Alfred (r.871–99) resisted the Danish advance. By 954 Alfred's successors had conquered the Scandinavian settlements and in the process created a united English kingdom. Traders and farmers as well as pirates, the Vikings also established colonies in Normandy, the Shetland and Orkney Islands, Ireland, the Faroe Islands and Iceland. A final migration across the Atlantic about 1000 led to the colonization of Greenland and the first European exploration in the Americas. In eastern Europe, Swedish venturers known as Rus pioneered trade routes along the rivers of Russia to the Black and Caspian Seas, giving their name to the Russian state which developed at Novgorod around 862.

The Viking raids and settlements were prompted by developments within Scandinavia itself. By the late 8th century power was becoming centralized, creating an intensely competitive society. For many, pirate raids overseas became a means to acquire wealth, a reputation and an armed following to support their ambitions at home. Others, denied the chance to rule at home, sought to conquer lands for themselves and their followers abroad. Trade and land hunger, caused by a rising population, were other important factors in the Viking phenomenon.

During the 10th century Denmark and Norway emerged as stable territorial states, a process completed in Sweden by the 12th century. The same period saw the start of the Scandinavians' conversion to Christianity. Denmark's hegemony briefly included England and Norway under Cnut (r.1016–35). In the east the Slavs assimilated the Rus ruling class and by 1000 Kievan Rus was a powerful Slavic state, strongly influenced by the Byzantines who introduced Orthodox Christianity. In Normandy the Vikings adopted French culture and language by 1000, but remained effectively independent of the French monarchy, which had passed from the Carolingian line with the accession of Hugh Capet in 987.

The Viking invasions occurred at a time when the Carolingian empire was weakened by internal squabbles. The emperor Louis the Pious (r.814–40) was not willing, as Charlemagne had been, to contemplate the equal division of the empire between his sons. Louis' younger sons and many of the Franks regarded the settlement as unjust and in 827 civil war broke out. The succession was not resolved until the Treaty of Verdun (843) which saw the empire divided into three parts. By this time royal authority was weakened and defenses against the Vikings had collapsed. Charles the Fat briefly reunited the Carolingian empire from 885–87, but it broke

borders, c.888
Danish Viking settlement, 800–1000
Norwegian Viking settlement, 800–1000
Swedish Viking settlement, 800–1000
Byzantine empire, 888
Carolingian kingdoms, 888
Muslim states, 888
Bulgar peoples
Slavic peoples
Magyar settlement, c.900
temporary gain by Germany, 929–82
kingdom of Hungary, 1000
empire of Cnut, 1019–35
Kievan Rus, c.1050
Holy Roman empire, 1050
Duchy of Normandy, 1051
Viking raids, trade and colonization routes, 793–1000
Magyar raids, 899–955
Muslim raids, 800–1000
Viking controlled trade center
Viking ship find
migration of peoples

0 600 km
0 400 mi

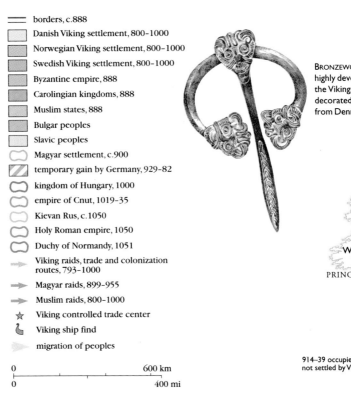

BRONZEWORKING was highly developed among the Vikings, as in this decorated brooch from Denmark.

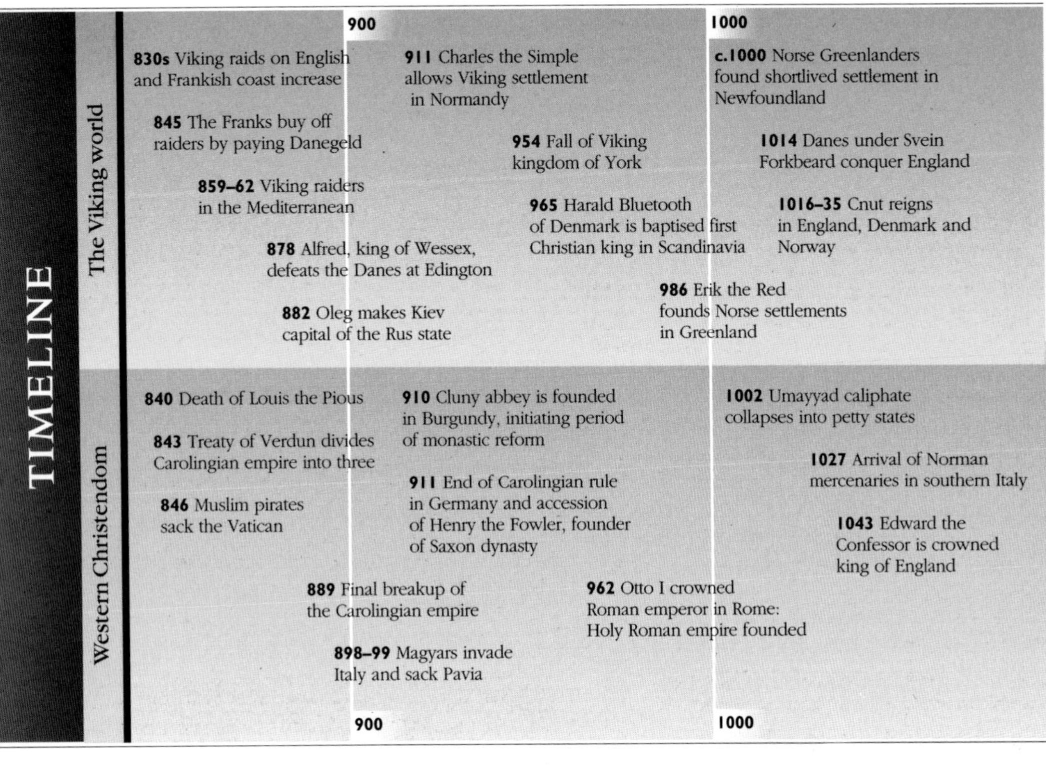

up finally in 889 into five kingdoms: West Francia (France), East Francia (Germany), Italy, Burgundy and Provence.

The Vikings were not the only threat facing western Christendom. Muslim pirates from Spain and Tunisia raided the Mediterranean coast and preyed on travelers over the Alpine passes. In the east a nomadic people, the Magyars, crossed the Carpathians around 900 to settle in the Danube plain in the old Roman province of Pannonia, from where they raided Italy, Germany and France. By 1000, however, the Muslim and Magyar threats had ended and Viking activity was limited mainly to the British Isles. Leading the recovery was Germany. With the ending of Carolingian rule there in 911, power passed into the hands of the Saxon kings. Under Otto I (r.936–73) the Magyars were defeated at the battle of Lechfeld (955) and were converted to Christianity. Expansion against the Slavs continued, and Otto annexed the kingdom of Italy in 951–61. Crowned Roman emperor in 962, he founded what became known as the Holy Roman empire. By the 11th century the German emperors had emerged as the clear leaders of western Christendom.

1 The monastery of Luxeuil was sacked successively by Viking raiders, Muslim pirates and Magyars between 886 and 924.

2 The Viking raids damaged Ireland's monastic culture, but also founded its first towns at Dublin, Wexford, Waterford and Limerick in the 9th century.

3 Paris first rose to prominence as a result of its determined resistance to a Viking siege in 885–86.

4 Conversion of the Poles to Christianity began in 966: the first Polish archbishopric, at Gniezno, was founded in 1000.

5 German protectorates from 935, Burgundy and Provence were united in a single kingdom in 948 and absorbed into the Holy Roman empire in 1033.

6 Rus traders traveled down the river Volga to Bulgar to trade slaves and furs with Arab merchants.

7 Strategically placed, Gotland was an important center of Baltic trade: over 40,000 Arab, 38,000 Frankish and 28,000 Anglo-Saxon silver coins have been found there.

See also 3.05 (world religions);
3.06 (Carolingians); 3.26 (North America)

Feudalism was a contractual system by which a lord granted a fief (or estate) to a vassal, usually a knight or nobleman, in return for sworn homage and military service. The Carolingian kings used the system to bind the nobility in loyalty to the crown, but under a weak ruler it could undermine royal authority and decentralize power. By the late 11th century feudalism had been introduced to England and Sicily by the Normans and was highly developed in Spain. It was present, though less dominant, in Scotland, Scandinavia, northern Italy and eastern Europe. By 1200 the military importance of feudalism was in decline, as kings could raise money to hire professional soldiers, and vassals could make a cash payment in lieu of military service. Fiefs had become heritable and were treated by vassals as family estates.

Decentralization was most extreme in France, where the royal lands (the demesne) were confined in the 11th century to the area around Paris and Orléans, while powerful vassals like the dukes of Normandy and the counts of Anjou and Aquitaine were semi-independent rulers of vast fiefs. When William of Normandy became king of England by conquest in 1066, he became more powerful than his feudal lord, the French king. In the 1150s Henry Plantagenet of Anjou accumulated, through inheritance and marriage, fiefs covering half of France, dwarfing the royal demesne. In 1154 he inherited the English throne to become, as Henry II, the most powerful ruler in Europe. Yet he tried to avoid open warfare with the French king, feeling he should not set a bad example to his own vassals. Philip Augustus (r.1180–1223) revived the French monarchy and recovered all the Angevin fiefs except Gascony. In 1214 he repulsed a German invasion at Bouvines, making France the strongest power in Europe.

The German kings and emperors avoided the problems of the French monarchy by granting land as fiefs to the church. Literate priests and abbots were well equipped to administer its fiefs, and celibate churchmen could not found dynasties, so the lands returned into the gift of the king. As long as the king retained control over ecclesiastical appointments, this system offered a counterweight to the territorial nobility. But when emperor Henry III died in 1056, leaving his son Henry IV (r.1056–1106) in the control of a weak regency, the papacy asserted itself. The ensuing Investiture Contest (1075–1122), a dispute over who had the right to nominate to vacant sees, gave the popes greatly enhanced authority. A sign of their new prestige was the summoning of the First Crusade in 1095, which led to the capture of Jerusalem in 1099.

The Hohenstaufen emperor Frederick Barbarossa (r. 1152–90) found his authority challenged in Germany by powerful territorial princes, such as Henry the Lion of the Welf family. He tried to compensate by tightening imperial control in Italy but was defeated by the Lombard league of cities in 1176. His successors did little better. Though the Hohenstaufens won control of the Norman kingdom of Sicily in 1194, they failed to assert their authority over the German princes, and the Holy Roman empire disintegrated into a loose federation of states. The emperor Frederick II (r.1210–50) attempted to consolidate his

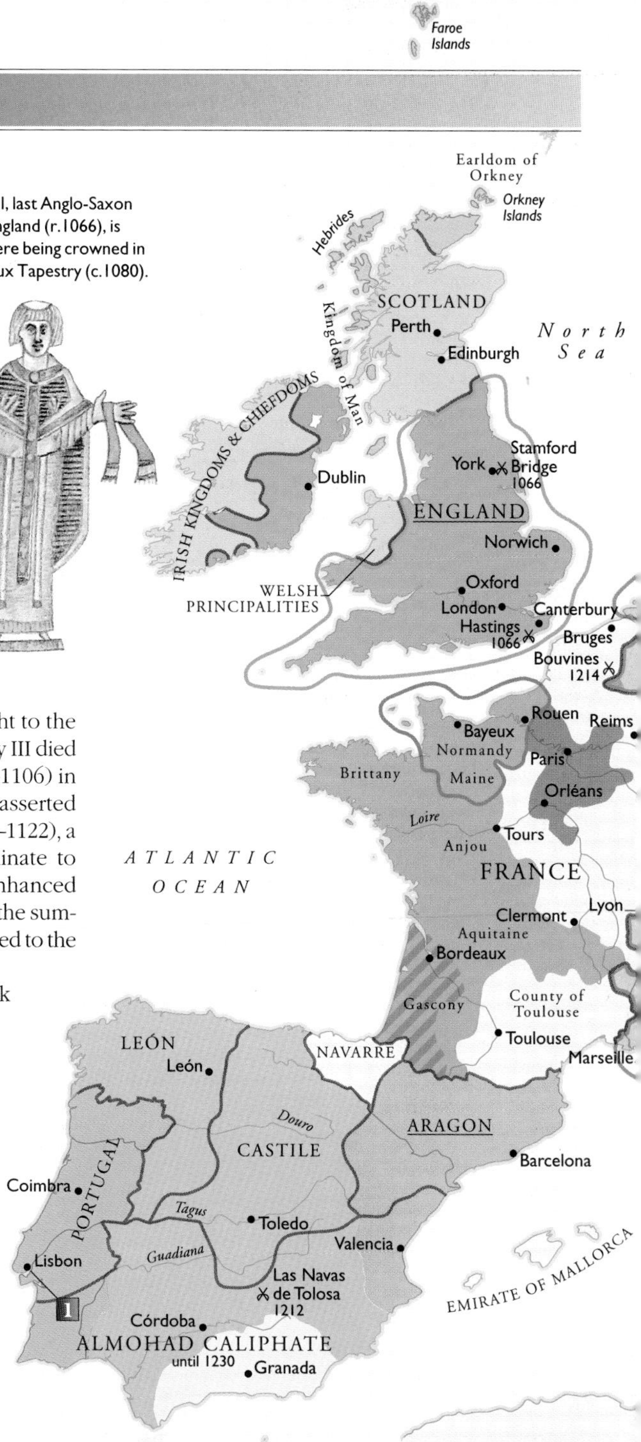

HAROLD II, last Anglo-Saxon king of England (r.1066), is shown here being crowned in the Bayeux Tapestry (c.1080).

TIMELINE

Political change

- **1047–90** Normans conquer southern Italy and Sicily
- **1066** William the Conquerer, Duke of Normandy, invades and conquers England
- **1075–1122** Investiture Contest with popes damages authority of the Holy Roman emperors
- **1095** Pope Urban II calls the First Crusade at Clermont
- **1099** Crusaders take Jerusalem
- **1128** Portugal becomes independent of León
- **1154** Henry II becomes the first Angevin king of England
- **1170** Murder of Thomas Becket, archbishop of Canterbury
- **1187** Defeat of crusading army by Saladin at the Horns of Hattin leads to fall of Jerusalem to the Muslims
- **1194** Henry VI conquers Norman kingdom of Sicily
- **1212** Christian victory at Las Navas de Tolosa breaks Muslim power in Spain
- **1215** King John of England signs the Magna Carta
- **1230** Union of the kingdoms of Castile and León
- **1237–41** Mongols invade Russia and eastern Europe
- **1253–99** Commercial rivalry leads to war between Genoa and Venice
- **1254–73** Interregnum in Germany inaugurates period of political chaos

Cultural change

- **1079–1142** Peter Abelard: theologian and philosopher
- **c.1095** "Song of Roland", *chanson de geste*, celebrates chivalric ideals
- **c.1136** Geoffrey of Monmouth's *History of the Kings of Britain* popularizes Arthurian romances
- **c.1140** Abbey church of St Denis near Paris, regarded as first building in Gothic style
- **c.1200–75** Sagas (fictionalized family histories of early settlers) written in Iceland
- **c.1220–92** Roger Bacon: philosopher and early advocate of scientific experiment
- **c.1270–1300** Invention of the mechanical clock
- **1298** Marco Polo's account of his travels in Asia between 1271 and 1295 becomes an instant success

1100 1200 1300

position in Italy but, faced with the hostility of the papacy and the Lombard cities, his reign ended in failure and the dynasty was overthrown in 1266. Despite the political fragmentation of the empire, the 13th century saw German influence expand to the east through the establishment of peasant settlements and new towns, and the activities of traders and the crusading order of the Teutonic Knights in the Baltic.

The Slavic state of Kievan Rus broke up into several principalities in 1132, most of which were overrun by the Mongols in 1237–41. Alexander Nevsky (r.1236–63), ruler of Novgorod, submitted voluntarily to the Mongol invasion, and was therefore able to concentrate his resources on resisting incursions by Swedish forces and the Teutonic Knights. In 1252, he added the principality of Vladimir to his possessions.

1 Lisbon was captured from the Muslims by a fleet from northern Europe *en route* to the Second Crusade in the Holy Land in 1147.

2 Alexander Nevsky's victory at the river Neva in 1240 halted further Swedish expansion eastward.

3 Austria was founded as a duchy by Frederick Barbarossa in 1156 to counter Welf power in Bavaria.

4 The wealthy cities of Lombardy formed defensive leagues in 1167 and 1226 to resist imperial attempts to restrict their freedoms.

5 A major concern of the Papacy was to prevent a political union between the Holy Roman empire and the kingdom of Sicily.

6 Sicily passed to the Normans (1091); to emperor Henry IV (1194); to the Angevin dynasty (1266); to the Aragonese (1282); to independence (1295).

See also 3.09 (religion in medieval Europe); 3.17 (Crusades); 3.22 (Mongol empire)

3.09 Religion in medieval Europe • 800 – 1300 •

The church's split into the opposing camps of eastern Orthodoxy and western Catholicism dated from late Roman times. Five sees – Jerusalem, Alexandria, Antioch, Constantinople and Rome – were recognized as having patriarchal status. As the direct heirs of St Peter, the popes (the name given to the Roman patriarchs) claimed, but failed to establish, primacy over the rest. In the 7th century Antioch, Jerusalem and Alexandria came under Muslim rule and declined in importance, but the popes continued to press their claims against the patriarch of Constantinople. Animosity hardened as the two churches competed for influence among the Magyars and Slavs: the conversion of Hungary and Poland was brought about by Catholic missionaries; Serbia, Bulgaria and Russia by Orthodox. Schisms between the two branches of the church were frequent, and in 1054 the breach became permanent when the pope excommunicated the patriarch for refusing to accept his authority. Although the Byzantine emperor appealed to the west for help in expelling the Turks from Asia Minor after the battle of Manzikert, relations between the Greeks and the Latin Crusaders were always strained, even before the sack of Constantinople in 1204.

Standards in the western church had declined in the 9th century: the papacy itself was corrupt and under the control of the Roman nobility, and clerical morals were lax. A reform movement spreading out from monastic centers such as Gorze in Germany and Cluny in Burgundy during the 10th century gradually widened the demand for church reform. In 1046 emperor Henry III (r.1039–56) deposed three rival popes at the synod of Sutri and appointed his own reformist candidate. But a strengthened and reformed papacy soon determined to assert its independence of imperial control. Reform in Rome was led by the German churchman Hildebrand who, as Pope Gregory VII (r.1073–85), banned laymen from investing bishops and claimed papal primacy in secular affairs. Papal authority increased through the 12th century, reaching its zenith under Innocent III (r.1198–1216), an able lawyer and administrator.

In the hands of such men the church became a wealthy and worldly institution. By the 12th century abbeys such as Cluny had moved away from their ideals of poverty, prompting a new call for monastic reform. The Cistercian order, with an austere rule of labor, prayer and study, spread throughout Europe under the charismatic leadership of St Bernard of Clairvaux. The dissatisfaction of many lay people with the laxity of the church fed the growth of anticlerical movements, such as the Waldensians. Others embraced the antimaterialistic Cathar heresy, which held that the universe is ruled by two powers, one good, one evil. To combat such heresies the papacy authorized new preaching orders of friars and launched the Albigensian Crusade against the Cathars of southwest France.

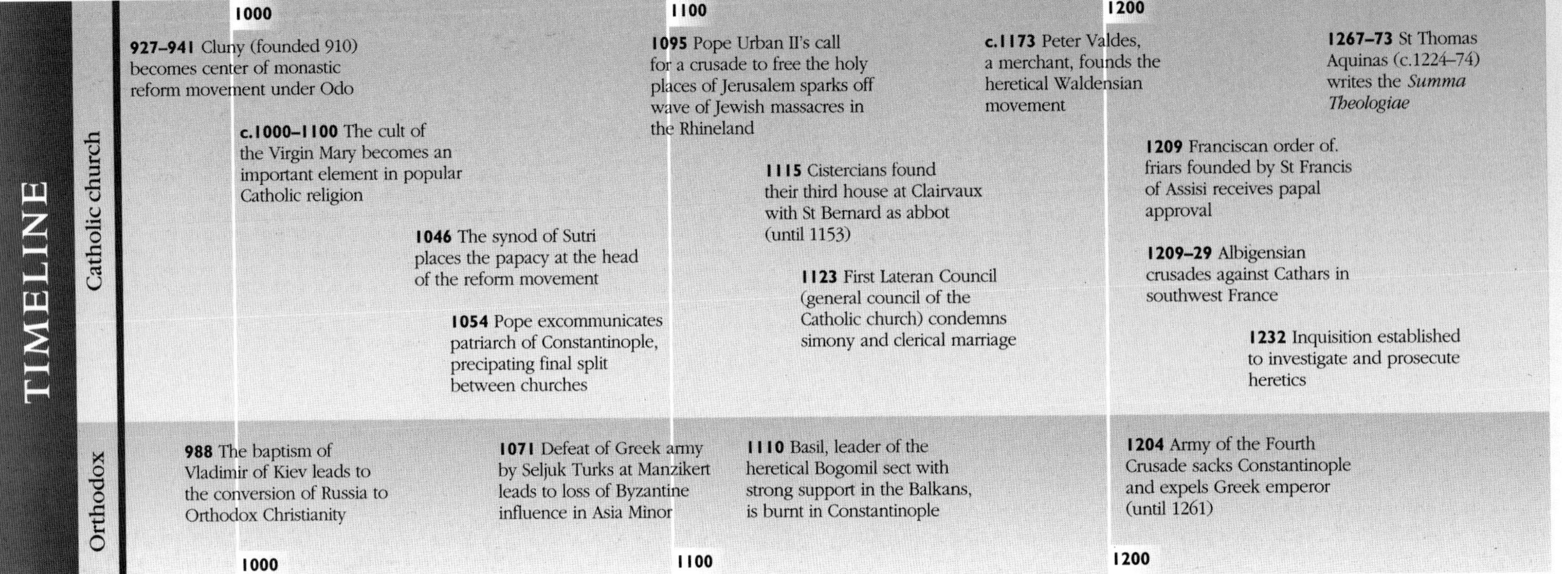

1 Under Muslim rule Spanish towns such as Toledo were important centers of Islamic scholarship. They enabled knowledge of classical learning, preserved in Arabic translations and commentaries, to enter the cathedral schools of western Europe.

2 It was the discovery in 812 of what were claimed to be the bones of St James the Apostle that gave Santiago de Compostela its eminent position as a pilgrimage center, second only to Rome.

3 The austerity-seeking Cistercians chose remote sites for their new religious houses, such as inaccessible upland areas of Yorkshire.

4 The university of Bologna, the earliest in Europe, was largely responsible for the revival of Roman law in the 12th century.

5 The peninsula of Mount Athos was the most important center of Orthodox monasticism with over 20 monasteries, some dating back to the 10th century.

6 Crusaders had both political and military motivation. The Sicilian Norman Bohemond I led the Crusaders in the siege of Antioch in 1098 and then acquired it as his own principality.

DEVOTION to the figure of Christ crucified was a new theme in the religion of the 12th century, as shown in this crucifix from the Rhineland.

Pilgrimages – penitential journeys to holy places or shrines containing relics of saints to which were ascribed miraculous cures – were an important part of medieval religion. Particular merit was acquired by those who made the difficult journey to Rome, Santiago or Jerusalem. Hundreds of charitable hostels along the main routes provided safe lodgings for pilgrims. The church was also the main repository of literacy in early medieval Europe. In the 11th century cathedral schools grew in importance as centers of education, and universities developed from them for the formal study of theology and law.

Western Europe's Jewish communities were most densely concentrated in the towns of Germany, France and Sicily. Jews faced restrictions on what occupations they could follow and where they could live. They often served as moneylenders, which Christians were forbidden to do by canon law. This added to popular dislike of Jews, though cash-hungry kings often called upon their services. At times of religious enthusiasm, such as accompanied Crusades, Jews faced pogroms and expulsions.

Unlike the pope, the patriarch of Constantinople had no monarchical authority but was respected as "the first among equals". Major doctrinal controversies were resolved by church councils. Monasticism was strongly established in Greek-speaking areas from late Roman times, but its expansion among the Slavs occurred only in the late Middle Ages.

0 600 km
0 400 mi

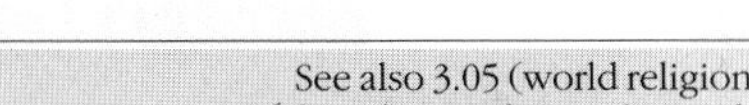
See also 3.05 (world religions); 3.06 (Carolingians); 3.17 (Crusades)

3.10 War, revolt and plague in 14th-century Europe • 1300–1400 •

The authority of the papacy – already in decline in the face of royal attempts to build centralized nation-states – faced a further setback in 1303 when it fell under the domination of the French monarchy. In 1309 it took up residence at Avignon. It returned to Rome in 1377, but a disputed papal election led to the Great Schism in 1378, with rival popes sitting at Rome and Avignon. The schism stayed unresolved until 1417 as neither pope would submit to the judgment of a church council. It divided Europe and exacerbated existing political differences. France supported the Avignon papacy, for example, so England – then involved in the Hundred Years War (1337–1453) with France – gave its allegiance to the Roman papacy while Scotland, antagonistic to England, joined the French party.

The Hundred Years War had been sparked off by French attempts to recover English lands in France. After English victories at Crécy (1346) and Poitiers (1356), the French ceded Aquitaine and Gascony at the treaty of Bretigny (1360). But fighting broke out again and when a 28-year truce was agreed in 1396 the English held less land in France than they had in 1337. In 1363, the French monarchy stored up future trouble by granting the duchy of Burgundy out of the royal desmesne to Philip the Bold, the younger son of John II. Through marriage to the heiress of the Count of Flanders (1369), Philip later added the imperial county of Burgundy (the Franche-Comté) and the wool towns of Flanders to his possessions.

War was endemic throughout the Holy Roman empire.The powerful city-states of northern Italy, where imperial control was now purely nominal, engaged armies of mercenaries to fight one another. The German princes were occupied in dynastic struggles to gain primacy and thus win control of imperial elections. The Wittelsbachs gained the upper hand from the Habsburgs in 1325, only to lose it to the Luxembourgs (1346–1438). From 1377–89 the princes formed a united front to reduce the independence of the cities of south Germany and the Rhineland. In 1388, after a century of rebellion, the Swiss confederation of eight cantons secured their independence from the dukes of Habsburg. In eastern Europe in 1354, the Ottoman Turks took

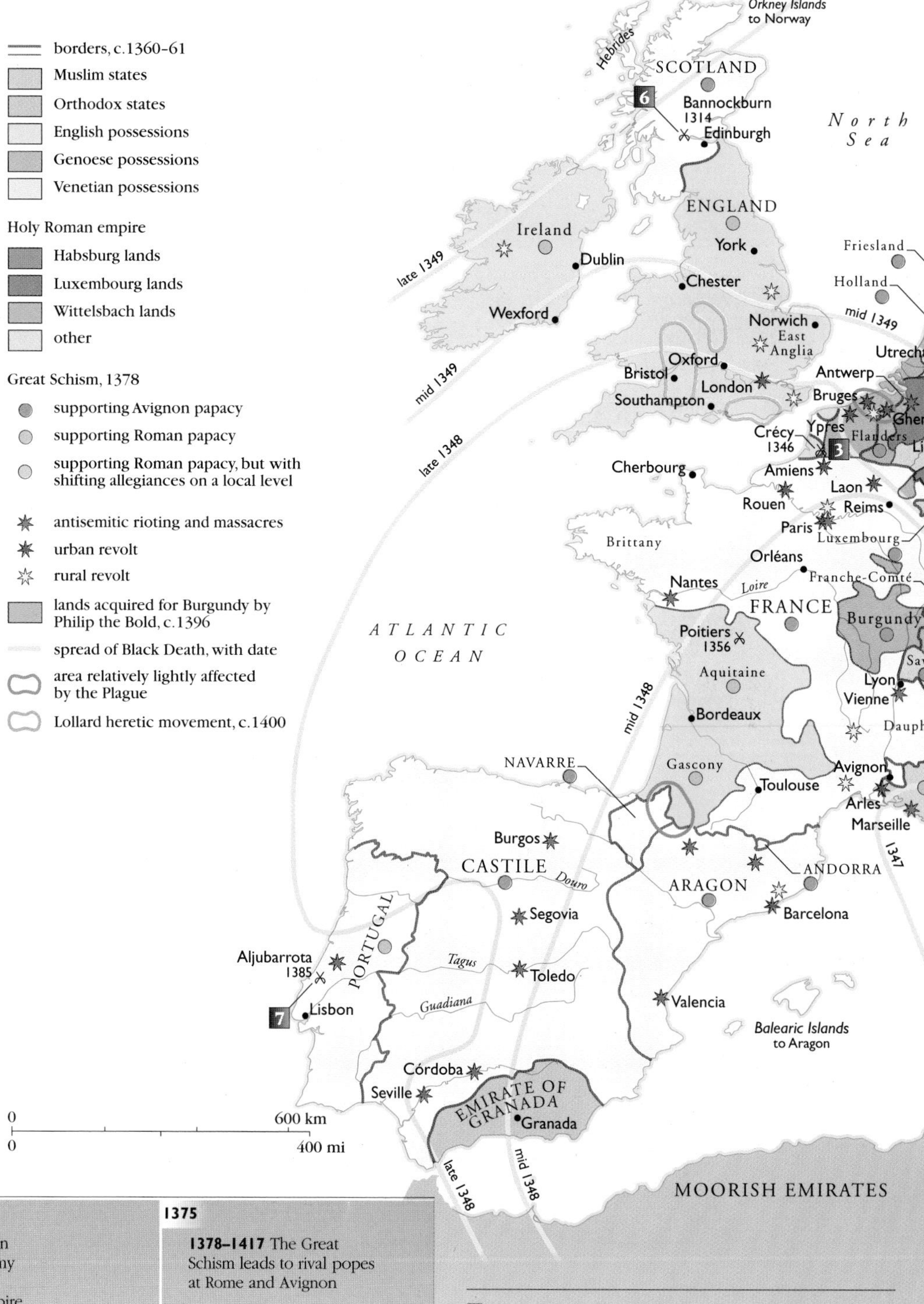

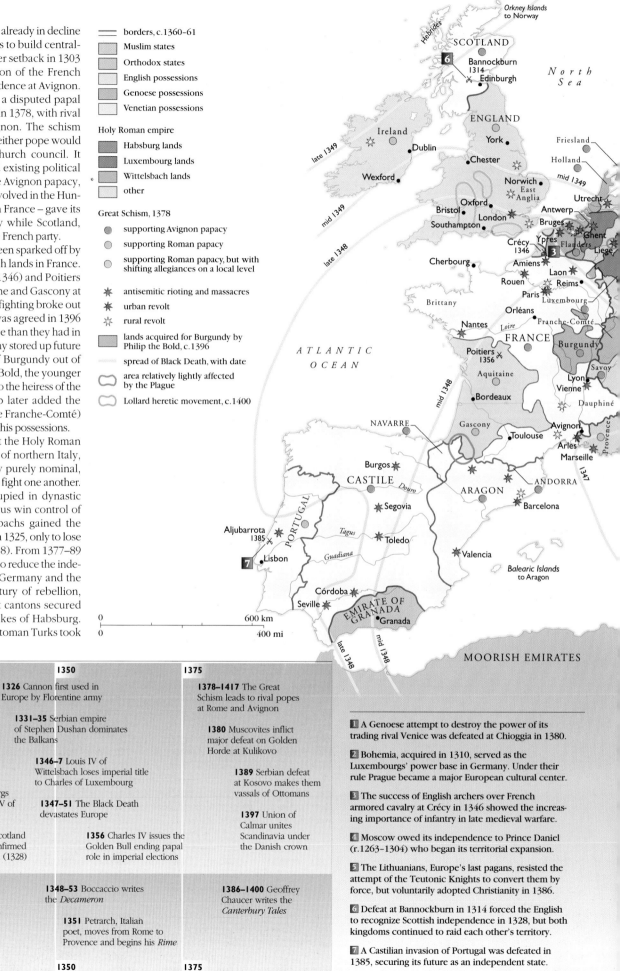

TIMELINE

Political change

- **1302** Territorial expansion of Muscovy begins
- **1309–77** The papacy is resident at Avignon
- **1310** John of Luxembourg becomes king of Bohemia
- **1314–25** War between Wittelsbachs and Habsburgs ends in victory for Louis IV of Wittelsbach
- **1323** Wars between Scotland and England ends; confirmed by treaty of Edinburgh (1328)
- **1326** Cannon first used in Europe by Florentine army
- **1331–35** Serbian empire of Stephen Dushan dominates the Balkans
- **1346–7** Louis IV of Wittelsbach loses imperial title to Charles of Luxembourg
- **1347–51** The Black Death devastates Europe
- **1356** Charles IV issues the Golden Bull ending papal role in imperial elections
- **1378–1417** The Great Schism leads to rival popes at Rome and Avignon
- **1380** Muscovites inflict major defeat on Golden Horde at Kulikovo
- **1389** Serbian defeat at Kosovo makes them vassals of Ottomans
- **1397** Union of Calmar unites Scandinavia under the Danish crown

Cultural change

- **1305** Frescoes of the Arena Chapel, Padua painted by Giotto
- **c.1314–21** Dante writes the *Divine Comedy*
- **1348–53** Boccaccio writes the *Decameron*
- **1351** Petrarch, Italian poet, moves from Rome to Provence and begins his *Rime*
- **1386–1400** Geoffrey Chaucer writes the *Canterbury Tales*

1325 | 1350 | 1375

1 A Genoese attempt to destroy the power of its trading rival Venice was defeated at Chioggia in 1380.

2 Bohemia, acquired in 1310, served as the Luxembourgs' power base in Germany. Under their rule Prague became a major European cultural center.

3 The success of English archers over French armored cavalry at Crécy in 1346 showed the increasing importance of infantry in late medieval warfare.

4 Moscow owed its independence to Prince Daniel (r.1263–1304) who began its territorial expansion.

5 The Lithuanians, Europe's last pagans, resisted the attempt of the Teutonic Knights to convert them by force, but voluntarily adopted Christianity in 1386.

6 Defeat at Bannockburn in 1314 forced the English to recognize Scottish independence in 1328, but both kingdoms continued to raid each other's territory.

7 A Castilian invasion of Portugal was defeated in 1385, securing its future as an independent state.

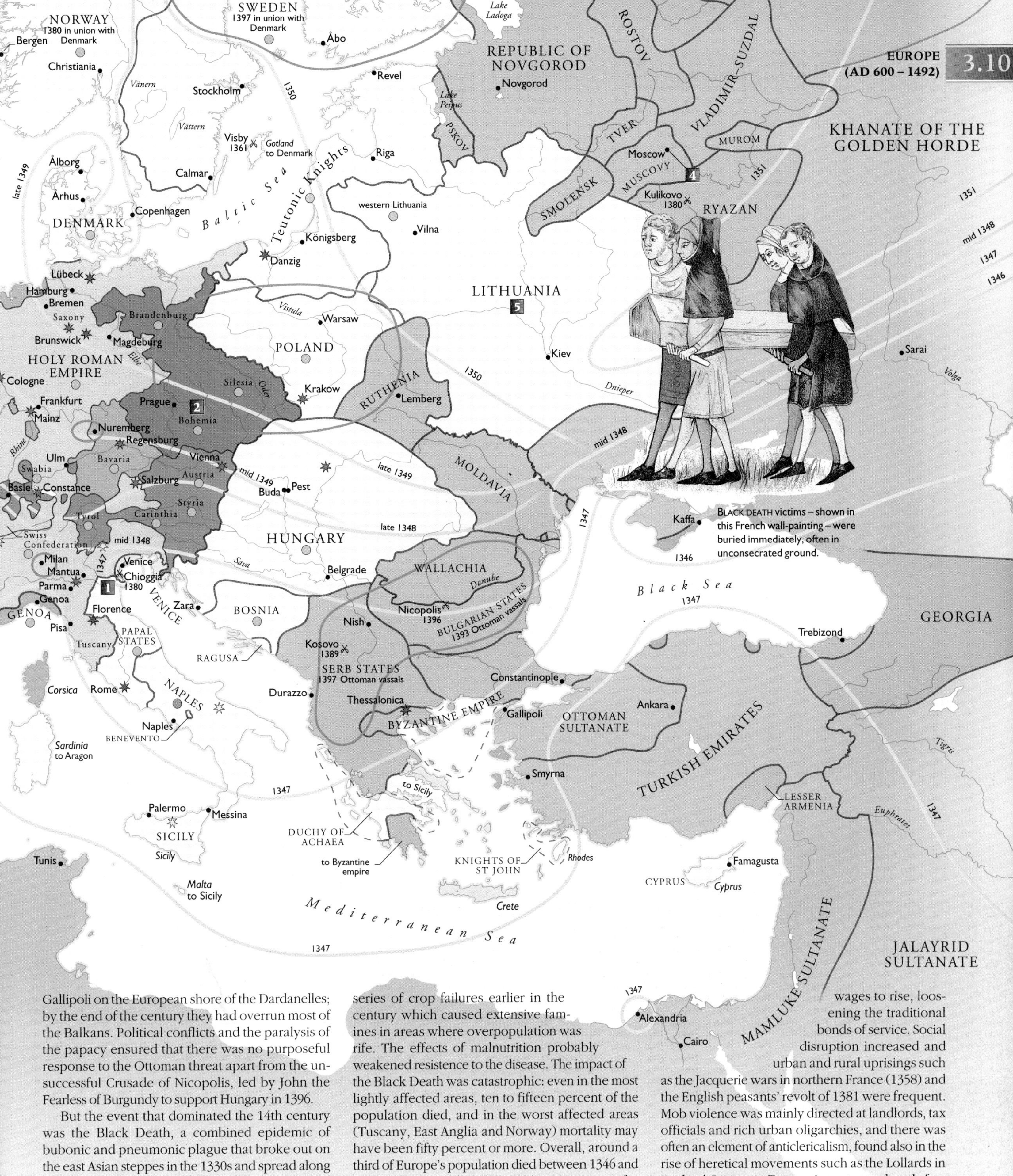

BLACK DEATH victims – shown in this French wall-painting – were buried immediately, often in unconsecrated ground.

Gallipoli on the European shore of the Dardanelles; by the end of the century they had overrun most of the Balkans. Political conflicts and the paralysis of the papacy ensured that there was no purposeful response to the Ottoman threat apart from the unsuccessful Crusade of Nicopolis, led by John the Fearless of Burgundy to support Hungary in 1396.

But the event that dominated the 14th century was the Black Death, a combined epidemic of bubonic and pneumonic plague that broke out on the east Asian steppes in the 1330s and spread along the Silk Road to reach the Genoese port of Kaffa in the Crimea in late 1346. From here it was carried (by the parasitic fleas that infested ships' rats) to Venice, Genoa and Marseille, all ports with strong links to the east, and then spread amazingly quickly along the main trade routes of Europe. One factor explaining the Black Death's rapid inroads may lie in the series of crop failures earlier in the century which caused extensive famines in areas where overpopulation was rife. The effects of malnutrition probably weakened resistence to the disease. The impact of the Black Death was catastrophic: even in the most lightly affected areas, ten to fifteen percent of the population died, and in the worst affected areas (Tuscany, East Anglia and Norway) mortality may have been fifty percent or more. Overall, around a third of Europe's population died between 1346 and 1351. The plague remained endemic in Europe for 250 years and many cities had still not regained their pre-plague population levels by the 16th century.

Outbreaks of the plague were often accompanied by religious hysteria, and blame fell on Jews and foreigners who were subjected to attacks. Depopulation caused prices and rents to fall and wages to rise, loosening the traditional bonds of service. Social disruption increased and urban and rural uprisings such as the Jacquerie wars in northern France (1358) and the English peasants' revolt of 1381 were frequent. Mob violence was mainly directed at landlords, tax officials and rich urban oligarchies, and there was often an element of anticlericalism, found also in the rise of heretical movements such as the Lollards in England. In eastern Europe, in contrast, a largely free peasantry had serfdom imposed upon them by lords who were anxious not to lose tenants.

See also 3.09 (religion in medieval Europe); 3.23 (break-up of the Mongol empire)

.11 The economy of medieval Europe • 1000 – 1500 •

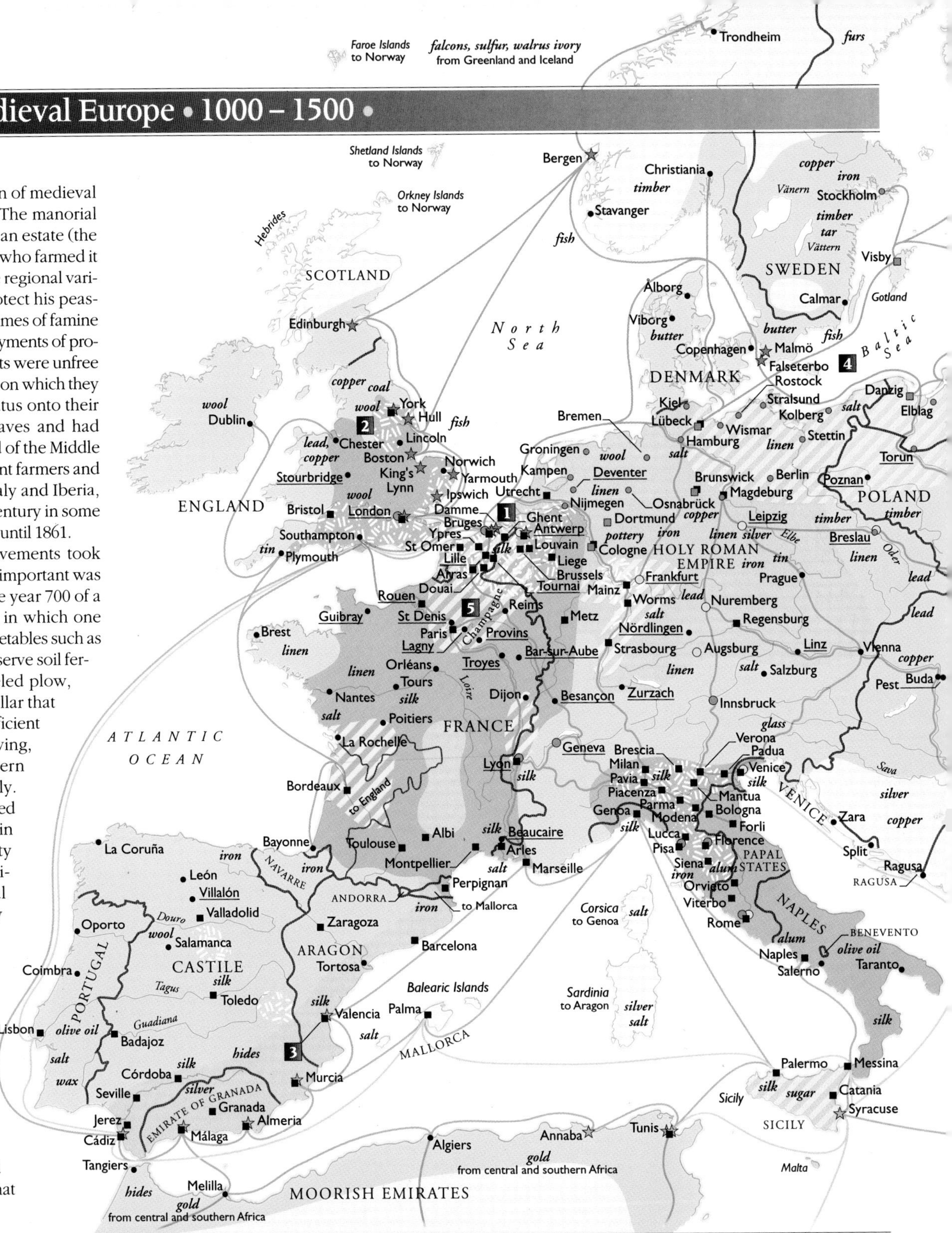

Over 90 percent of the population of medieval Europe were peasant farmers. The manorial system – by which a lord divided up an estate (the manor) between individual peasants who farmed it – was widespread, though there were regional variations. The lord was expected to protect his peasants in times of war, provide relief in times of famine and administer justice, in return for payments of produce, labor and money. Many peasants were unfree serfs or villeins, tied for life to the land on which they worked and passing their servile status onto their descendants, but they were not slaves and had certain established rights. By the end of the Middle Ages serfs had been replaced by tenant farmers and wage laborers in the British Isles, Italy and Iberia, but serfdom survived into the 18th century in some parts of western Europe and in Russia until 1861.

A number of agricultural improvements took place in the early Middle Ages. Most important was the widespread adoption around the year 700 of a three-field system of crop rotation, in which one field was used for cereals, one for vegetables such as beans and the third left fallow, to preserve soil fertility. The introduction of the wheeled plow, and later of the padded shoulder collar that enabled horses – 50 percent more efficient than oxen – to be used for plowing, allowed the heavy soils of northern Europe to be worked more efficiently. In these ways productivity was boosted far beyond the levels achieved in Roman times and peasant prosperity increased steadily. Most surplus agricultural produce was sold at local markets but wool, hides, wine, dairy products, salt, fish and grain were traded in large quantities over long distances. Moving goods by land was slow and expensive, so most bulk trade went by sea or river boat. Various industrial activities such as mining, ore smelting, logging, charcoal burning, quarrying and salt extraction were also important in the countryside. Both agriculture and rural industry benefited from technological improvements that

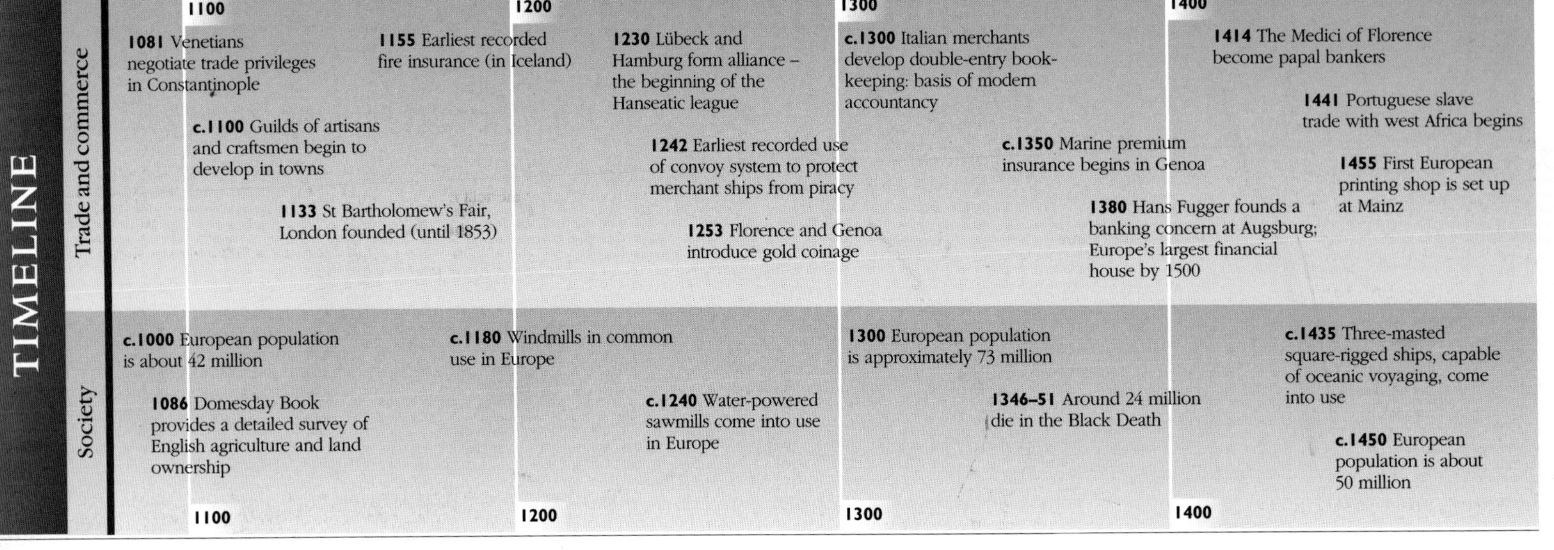
TIMELINE
Trade and commerce
1100
1200
1300
1400
1081 Venetians negotiate trade privileges in Constantinople
c.1100 Guilds of artisans and craftsmen begin to develop in towns
1133 St Bartholomew's Fair, London founded (until 1853)
1155 Earliest recorded fire insurance (in Iceland)
1230 Lübeck and Hamburg form alliance – the beginning of the Hanseatic league
1242 Earliest recorded use of convoy system to protect merchant ships from piracy
1253 Florence and Genoa introduce gold coinage
c.1300 Italian merchants develop double-entry book-keeping: basis of modern accountancy
c.1350 Marine premium insurance begins in Genoa
1380 Hans Fugger founds a banking concern at Augsburg; Europe's largest financial house by 1500
1414 The Medici of Florence become papal bankers
1441 Portuguese slave trade with west Africa begins
1455 First European printing shop is set up at Mainz
Society
c.1000 European population is about 42 million
1086 Domesday Book provides a detailed survey of English agriculture and land ownership
c.1180 Windmills in common use in Europe
c.1240 Water-powered sawmills come into use in Europe
1300 European population is approximately 73 million
1346–51 Around 24 million die in the Black Death
c.1435 Three-masted square-rigged ships, capable of oceanic voyaging, come into use
c.1450 European population is about 50 million
1100
1200
1300
1400

LÜBECK was a center of the Hanseatic trade in the Baltic, using sturdy ships called cogs, as shown on this seal of 1258.

made possible greater use of water and wind power to mill grain and work pumps, bellows and sawmills.

Except in Italy, urban life declined dramatically in western Europe during the late Roman empire and did not fully recover until the 11th century. Italy remained the most urbanized region of Europe throughout the Middle Ages. Compared with contemporary towns in the Arab world and China, medieval European towns were small and, outside northern Italy and Flanders, rarely had populations above 10,000. They were unhygienic places and, as deaths exceeded births, they relied on immigration from the countryside to maintain their populations. Townspeople were free of servile obligations but citizenship, and with it a right to participate in local government, was normally restricted to property owners. The trade and craft activities of towns were regulated by associations of merchants or craftsmen known as guilds. These prescribed standards of quality and training and provided members with welfare benefits, but their principal function was protectionist, to exclude outside competition. Manufactured goods produced in towns were generally intended for the local market but production of high-quality goods for export was important in some areas, such as Flanders where there was a flourishing woolen textile industry. Seasonal trade fairs were important commercial events, attracting merchants from a far wider area than the weekly town markets; some, for example the Champagne fairs, developed into major centers of international business.

One of the most powerful trade associations of the Middle Ages was the Hanseatic league, membership of which extended to 37 north German and Baltic towns at its peak in the 14th century. The league negotiated trading privileges for its members, prepared navigational charts, suppressed piracy and even waged war. It maintained offices called *kontors* in London, Bergen, Bruges and Novgorod where its merchants lived and traded permanently, as well as subsidiary depots in many other cities. The league's power declined at the end of the Middle Ages, when it was faced with greater competition from England and the Netherlands. In the Mediterranean, maritime trade was dominated by Venice and Genoa. Both took advantage of the Crusades to build up trade links with Asia, the source of luxury products such as silks, spices and gems, and maintained a bitter rivalry between themselves.

By the 13th century merchants were assuming the role of capitalists to finance craft production, so that productivity increased but craftsmen lost their independence. International banking houses such as the Medici and the Fuggers emerged, and the principles of modern insurance and accountancy were established.

1 Flanders was a leading center of Europe's growing textile industry; its prosperity was enshrined in grand town halls, as at Ghent.

2 England's prosperity resulted from it being Europe's main source of wool for cloth-making.

3 The Arabs introduced papermaking to Europe at Valencia in the 12th century.

4 The church's prohibition on eating meat on fast days maintained demand for salted fish from the Baltic and North Seas.

5 The fairs of Champagne flourished as centers of north–south trade in the 12th and 13th centuries.

6 The importance of the Black Sea as a trading area increased after the 13th-century Mongol invasions improved access to the east for European traders.

population density per sq km, early 14th century
- over 30
- 21-30
- 11-20
- 10 or under
- city with population over 10,000, c.1300
- branch of Fugger bank
- branch of Medici bank
- Kiev — city with important trade fair
- major Hanseatic league member
- other Hanseatic league member
- Hanseatic *kontor* (foreign depot)
- Genoese trading center
- Venetian trading center
- grain exporting area
- wine exporting area
- woollen cloth producing area
- *furs* — main trade commodity
- borders, c.1325
- Hanseatic trade route
- Genoese trade route
- Venetian trade route
- Gascon wine trade route
- other trade route

0 600 km
0 400 mi

See also 3.10 (war, revolt and plague)

3.12 Renaissance Europe • 1400 – 1492 •

The Renaissance, the great cultural movement of 15th-century Europe, had its origins in the revival of interest in classical philosophy, science and literature that first emerged during the 12th century, but its immediate roots lay in 14th-century Italy in the work of artists such as Giotto and humanist scholars such as Petrarch. By the early 15th century, men like Masaccio and Donatello in Florence were evolving new styles of painting and sculpture, while Brunelleschi was leading the revival of classical forms of architecture. In the course of the century Italy's city-states came to be ruled by dynastic princes. Italian Renaissance rulers – whether the powerful Medici family in Florence or the heads of ducal courts such as Mantua or Urbino – dispensed patronage as an arm of government, to secure prestige and influence. In Venice, a large urban aristocracy was keen to publicize its wealth and status. The technology of printing, developed in Germany in the mid-1450s, aided the spread of the new arts and learning outside Italy. By the early 16th century they were beginning to find their place in the courts of Europe's "new monarchs", who were emerging from periods of dynastic rivalry and civil war with strong centralized governments.

In the early 15th century France was divided by the rivalry between the Burgundian and Armagnac families, who disputed control of mad king Charles VI (r.1380–1422). Henry V of England (r.1413–22), anxious to secure the legitimacy of the Lancastrian dynasty established by his father Henry IV in 1399, seized the opportunity to reopen the Hundred Years War. His major victory at Agincourt (1415) and conquest of northern France led to his recognition as Charles VI's heir in 1420. After Henry's death and the revival of French morale under the leadership of Joan of Arc, English fortunes declined. By 1453 they had lost all their French possessions except Calais. Defeat provoked dynastic wars in England (the Wars of the Roses) until Henry VII (r.1485–1509), founder of the Tudor dynasty, restored stable government.

The dukes of Burgundy profited from France's troubles to enhance their own position by forming an alliance with the English which lasted until 1435. Under Philip the Good (r.1419–67) they acquired further territory in the Netherlands. His successor Charles the Bold wanted to establish an independent kingdom and tried to build a corridor of lands to link his southern and northern possessions, but died in battle against the Swiss at Nancy in 1477. When his heiress Mary married Maximilian of Habsburg, the Burgundian lands descended to the Habsburgs, who had ruled the Holy Roman empire since 1438, having already united their lands with those of Luxembourg. Louis XI (r.1461– 83) seized and retained the lands of the duchy of Burgundy in France. Franche-Comté was ceded to France on the betrothal of the *dauphin* (later Charles VIII) to Mary's daughter in 1482, but reverted to the Habsburgs when the engagement was revoked.

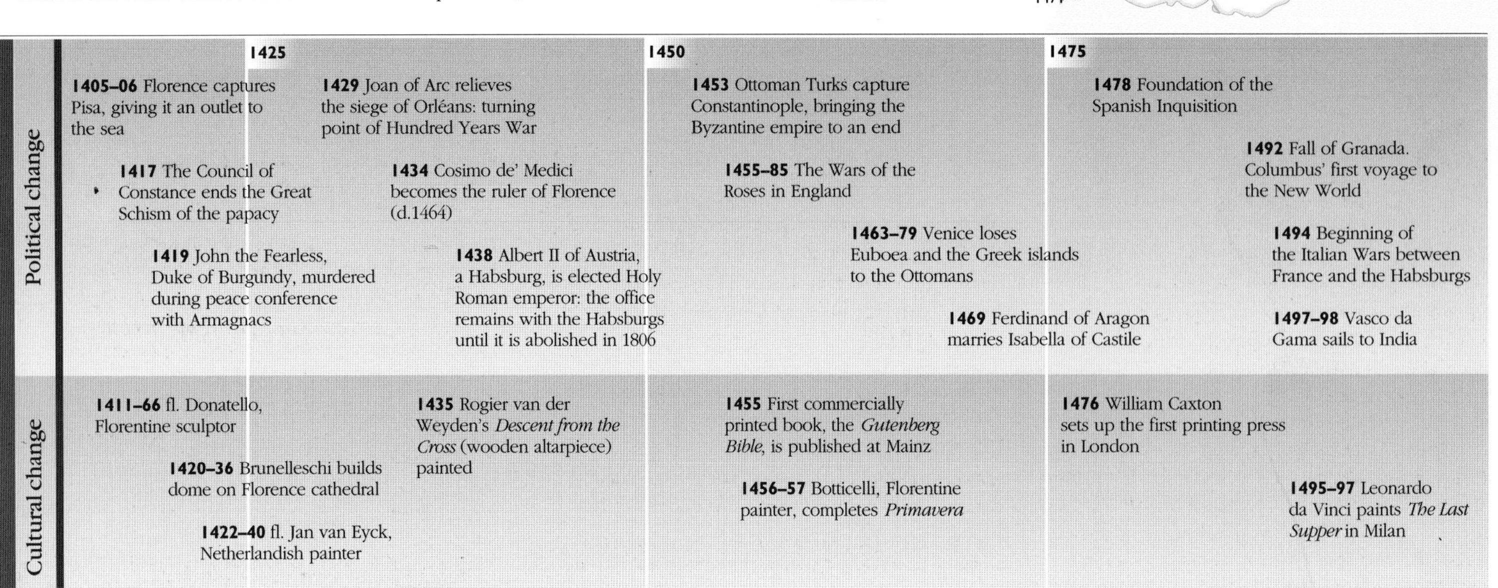

TIMELINE

1425 | 1450 | 1475

Political change

1405–06 Florence captures Pisa, giving it an outlet to the sea

1417 The Council of Constance ends the Great Schism of the papacy

1419 John the Fearless, Duke of Burgundy, murdered during peace conference with Armagnacs

1429 Joan of Arc relieves the siege of Orléans: turning point of Hundred Years War

1434 Cosimo de' Medici becomes the ruler of Florence (d.1464)

1438 Albert II of Austria, a Habsburg, is elected Holy Roman emperor: the office remains with the Habsburgs until it is abolished in 1806

1453 Ottoman Turks capture Constantinople, bringing the Byzantine empire to an end

1455–85 The Wars of the Roses in England

1463–79 Venice loses Euboea and the Greek islands to the Ottomans

1469 Ferdinand of Aragon marries Isabella of Castile

1478 Foundation of the Spanish Inquisition

1492 Fall of Granada. Columbus' first voyage to the New World

1494 Beginning of the Italian Wars between France and the Habsburgs

1497–98 Vasco da Gama sails to India

Cultural change

1411–66 fl. Donatello, Florentine sculptor

1420–36 Brunelleschi builds dome on Florence cathedral

1422–40 fl. Jan van Eyck, Netherlandish painter

1435 Rogier van der Weyden's *Descent from the Cross* (wooden altarpiece) painted

1455 First commercially printed book, the *Gutenberg Bible*, is published at Mainz

1456–57 Botticelli, Florentine painter, completes *Primavera*

1476 William Caxton sets up the first printing press in London

1495–97 Leonardo da Vinci paints *The Last Supper* in Milan

1425 | 1450 | 1475

GERMAN and Italian armorers brought plate armor to its highest development in the 15th century. This finely-crafted plumed helmet was made for Ferdinand of Aragon.

In the Iberian peninsula a century or more of rivalry between Castile and Aragon (which added the kingdom of Naples to its extensive Mediterranean empire in 1442), came to an end in 1469 with the marriage of Ferdinand of Aragon to Isabella of Castile. Under their joint leadership Granada, the last Muslim state in Spain, was conquered in 1485–92. Portugal, prevented from expanding in the peninsula by Castile, turned its attention to North Africa, beginning with the capture of Ceuta in 1415. In the 1430s Portuguese navigators began to explore the African coast and in 1487 entered the Indian Ocean. Even more significant was the voyage of Columbus, commissioned by Isabella of Castile, which led to the discovery of the New World in 1492.

Eastern Europe saw the creation of a strong but short-lived kingdom: Poland–Lithuania, under Casimir IV (r.1447–92) the largest state in Europe. Hungary, which resisted Ottoman expansion in the Balkans, dominated central Europe under Matthias Corvinus (r.1477–90). By the end of the century Muscovy had absorbed most of the other Russian principalities. With the fall of the Byzantine empire in 1453, it was left as the only significant Orthodox state: Ivan III married a Byzantine princess in 1472, adopting the title of *czar* (caesar).

1 The Union of Calmar, proclaimed in 1397, was unpopular in Sweden, where it led to several revolts before its final collapse in 1523.

2 The defeat by Poland–Lithuania of the Teutonic Knights at Tannenberg saw the start of their decline.

3 The burning for heresy of the Bohemian religious reformer Jan Hus at Constance in 1415 sparked a 20-year revolutionary uprising by his followers.

4 In 1480 Ivan III of Muscovy ceased paying tribute to buy off the Golden Horde, by now a shadow of its former strength.

5 In 1492, after their victory over the Muslims, Ferdinand and Isabella expelled from Spain around 150,000 Jews who refused to convert to Christianity.

6 England's preoccupation with war in France in the 15th century allowed much of Ireland to achieve effective independence.

7 The patronage of the wealthy Medici family made Florence the leading cultural center of the age, as well as a center for banking and trade, and the dominant political entity of central Italy.

See also 3.11 (economy of medieval Europe); 3.23 (decline of the Mongol empire)

3.13 The great Arab conquests • 632 – 750 •

The great empires of the Mediterranean and the Middle East had for centuries been accustomed to raids by Arab border tribes. Though troublesome, these raids were prevented from becoming a serious threat by the political disunity of the Arabs. However, this situation changed dramatically in the early 7th century as a result of the rise of Islam.

The faith of Islam (meaning "submission to the will of God") was founded by Muhammad (c.570–632), a member of the Meccan Quraysh tribe. From about 610, Muhammad began to experience the revelations that formed the basis of the *Koran*. Muhammad's espousal of monotheism met with opposition from the Quraysh, so to escape persecution the prophet and his followers fled in 622 to Medina, a commercial rival of Mecca. This event, the *hijra* (flight), marks the beginning of the Muslim era and is the first year of the Islamic calendar. Muhammad used Medina as a base to fight the Quraysh and in 630 he returned to Mecca in triumph. However, Muhammad continued to live at Medina, which became the capital of a theocratic Islamic state. In the last two years of his life, Muhammad used diplomacy and force to spread Islam to other Arab tribes.

Muhammad was succeeded by his father-in-law Abu Bakr, the first *caliph* (successor). After putting down an anti-Islamic rebellion, Abu Bakr completed the political and religious unification of the Arabs. Under the next two caliphs, Umar and Uthman, the Arabs began an explosive expansion which saw the Byzantine empire lose the rich and populous provinces of Syria, Palestine, Egypt and Libya, and the complete destruction of the Persian Sasanian empire. On Uthman's death civil war broke out between supporters of the caliph Ali, Muhammad's son-in-law, and Muawiya, a member of Uthman's Umayyad family. After Ali's murder in 661, Muawiya became caliph, founding the Umayyad dynasty. Ali's son Husain tried to win the caliphate on Muawiya's death but was killed in battle with the Umayyads at Karbala in 680. Consequently, Islam split into its two main branches: the Sunnites (from *sunna*, "tradition of Muhammad"), who formed a majority, and the Shiites (from *shi'atu Ali*, "party of Ali").

Arab expansion continued under the early Umayyads and by 715 the Islamic caliphate, extending from the Indus and central Asia to the Pyrenees, was the largest state the world had yet seen. Yet their attempts to complete the conquest of the Byzantine empire and the west failed, with two unsuccessful sieges of Constantinople in 677 and 717 and defeat by the Franks at Poitiers in 732.

The caliphs were both religious and political leaders. Whereas the early caliphs had been elected, the Umayyads introduced hereditary succession, claiming divine appointment and demanding total obedience. By adapting Byzantine bureaucracy, they created an administrative system capable of ruling a world empire. As this empire could not be ruled effectively from the remote Arabian city of Medina, Muawiya moved the capital to Damascus in 661. The Umayyad period saw the beginning of the successful Arabization of the conquered populations through conversion to Islam, the adoption of Arabic as a common language, and by intermarriage. The Arabs in turn were influenced by the Persian and Byzantine civilizations that they had conquered. One of the most important cultural developments of

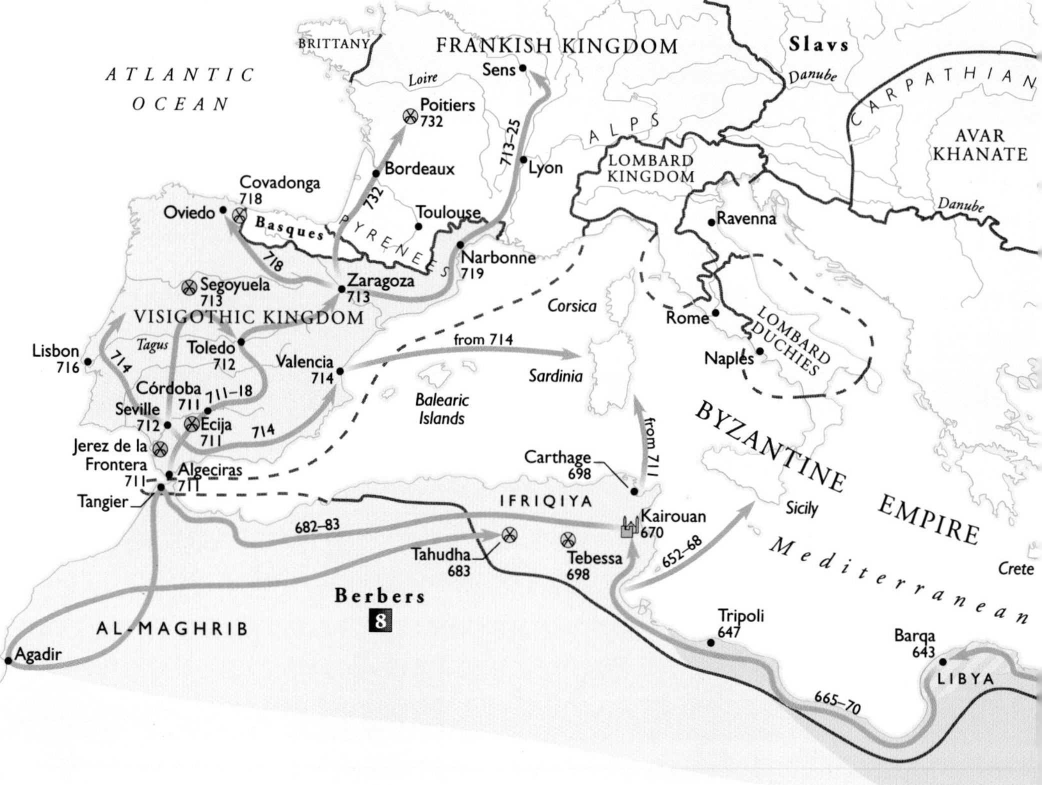

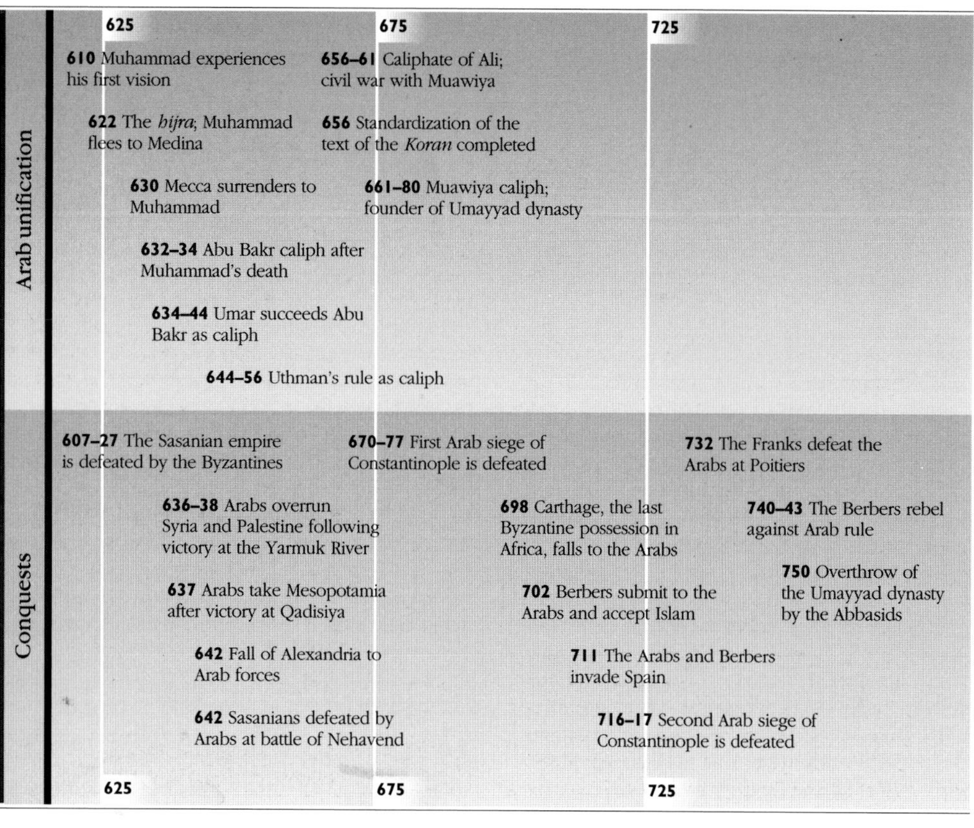

TIMELINE
Arab unification
625
675
725
610 Muhammad experiences his first vision
622 The *hijra*; Muhammad flees to Medina
630 Mecca surrenders to Muhammad
632–34 Abu Bakr caliph after Muhammad's death
634–44 Umar succeeds Abu Bakr as caliph
644–56 Uthman's rule as caliph
656–61 Caliphate of Ali; civil war with Muawiya
656 Standardization of the text of the *Koran* completed
661–80 Muawiya caliph; founder of Umayyad dynasty
Conquests
607–27 The Sasanian empire is defeated by the Byzantines
636–38 Arabs overrun Syria and Palestine following victory at the Yarmuk River
637 Arabs take Mesopotamia after victory at Qadisiya
642 Fall of Alexandria to Arab forces
642 Sasanians defeated by Arabs at battle of Nehavend
670–77 First Arab siege of Constantinople is defeated
698 Carthage, the last Byzantine possession in Africa, falls to the Arabs
702 Berbers submit to the Arabs and accept Islam
711 The Arabs and Berbers invade Spain
716–17 Second Arab siege of Constantinople is defeated
732 The Franks defeat the Arabs at Poitiers
740–43 The Berbers rebel against Arab rule
750 Overthrow of the Umayyad dynasty by the Abbasids
625
675
725

1 Mecca was an important trading city and the main cult center for the pre-Islamic Arabs' pagan religion.

2 Arab military settlements, such as Al-Fustat (Cairo), were sited close to the edge of the desert, where the Arabs could take refuge in the event of rebellions.

3 The Taurus mountains proved an effective barrier against further Arab conquests in Anatolia.

4 The last Sasanian king, Yezdegird III, was murdered near Merv in 652, so ending Persian resistance.

5 Karbala became a major pilgrimage site for Shiite Muslims after Husain, Muhammad's grandson, was killed there by the Umayyads.

6 With the transfer of the Arab capital to Damascus in 661, Arabia gradually declined in significance.

7 The two attempts by the Arabs to take the heavily fortified city of Constantinople were costly failures.

8 Berber resistance to the Arabs was fierce; they were only subdued and converted to Islam in 702.

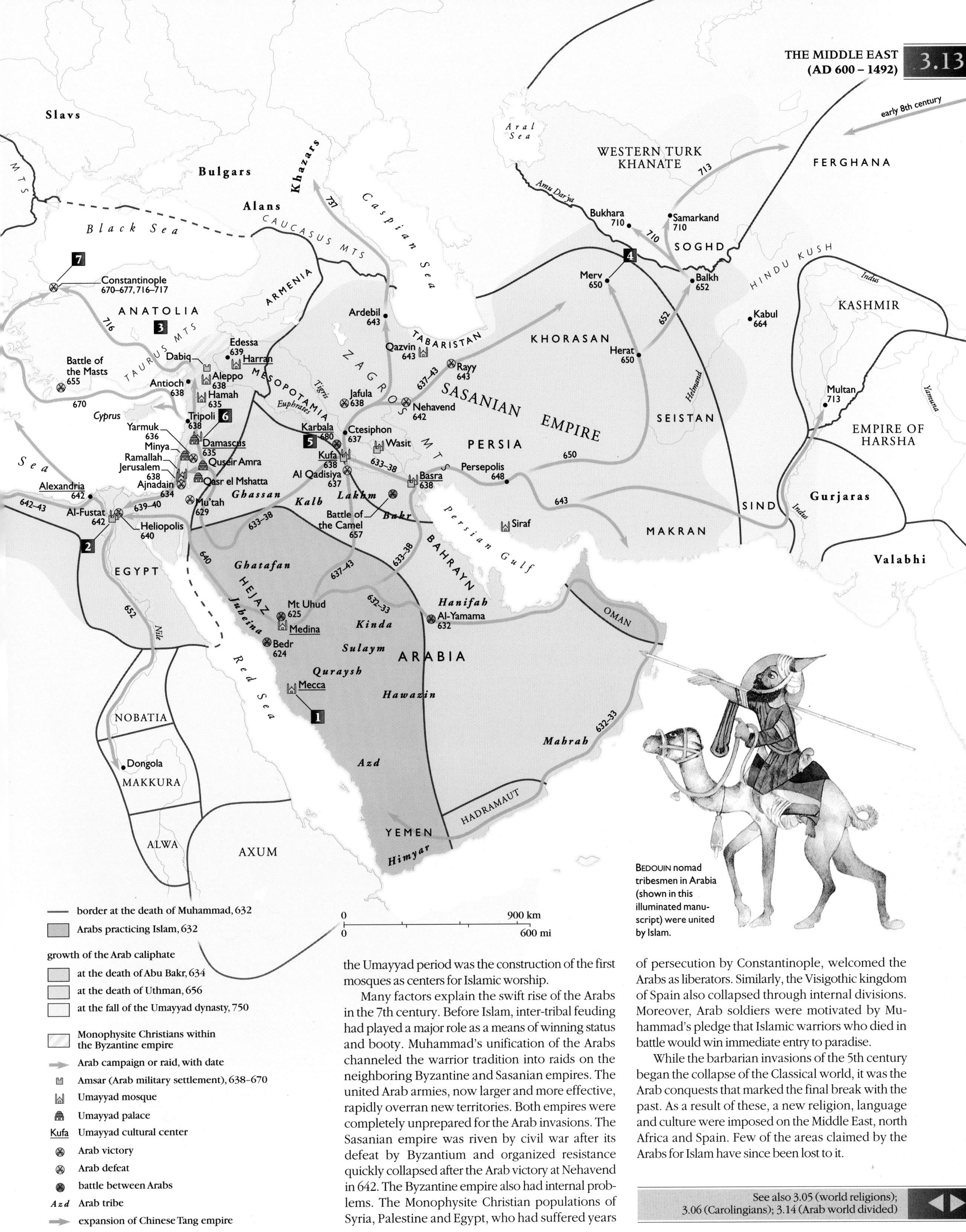

BEDOUIN nomad tribesmen in Arabia (shown in this illuminated manuscript) were united by Islam.

the Umayyad period was the construction of the first mosques as centers for Islamic worship.

Many factors explain the swift rise of the Arabs in the 7th century. Before Islam, inter-tribal feuding had played a major role as a means of winning status and booty. Muhammad's unification of the Arabs channeled the warrior tradition into raids on the neighboring Byzantine and Sasanian empires. The united Arab armies, now larger and more effective, rapidly overran new territories. Both empires were completely unprepared for the Arab invasions. The Sasanian empire was riven by civil war after its defeat by Byzantium and organized resistance quickly collapsed after the Arab victory at Nehavend in 642. The Byzantine empire also had internal problems. The Monophysite Christian populations of Syria, Palestine and Egypt, who had suffered years of persecution by Constantinople, welcomed the Arabs as liberators. Similarly, the Visigothic kingdom of Spain also collapsed through internal divisions. Moreover, Arab soldiers were motivated by Muhammad's pledge that Islamic warriors who died in battle would win immediate entry to paradise.

While the barbarian invasions of the 5th century began the collapse of the Classical world, it was the Arab conquests that marked the final break with the past. As a result of these, a new religion, language and culture were imposed on the Middle East, north Africa and Spain. Few of the areas claimed by the Arabs for Islam have since been lost to it.

See also 3.05 (world religions); 3.06 (Carolingians); 3.14 (Arab world divided)

3.14 The Arab world divided • 750 – 1037 •

The authority of the Umayyad caliphs was gradually undermined in the 8th century by the Shiite-Sunnite conflict, the re-emergence of tribal feuding among the Arabs and by discontent among new converts to Islam in the conquered lands who were resentful of the tax and political privileges enjoyed by the Arabs. Rebellion broke out in the province of Khorasan in 747 and in 749 Abu al-Abbas of the Sunni Abbasid family was proclaimed caliph by the rebels. Following the Abbasid victory at the Battle of the Zab in 750, there was a general massacre of the Umayyad family. One of the few to survive, Abd al-Rahman (r.756–88), escaped to Spain and seized power in Córdoba in 756. His founding of an independent emirate began the political fragmentation of the Arab world. Abd al-Rahman faced internal opposition to his rule for several years, which allowed the Christians of Asturias to regain Galicia and give their kingdom a firm territorial base: the Franks were also able to recapture Narbonne. The Abbasid caliphate suffered further losses in 789 when the Idrisid emirs of the Maghrib rejected its political and spiritual authority and founded a Shiite caliphate. In 800 the Aghlabid emirs of Ifriqiya (Tunisia) also became independent.

Despite these losses the accession of the Abbasids ushered in a "golden age" of Islamic civilization. The caliphate's vast wealth, acquired partly from the exploitation of rich silver mines in the Hindu Kush Mountains, funded lavish building projects and patronage of the arts and sciences. Baghdad, founded as a new capital to replace Damascus in 763, had within forty years become probably the world's largest city and its greatest cultural center. The assimilation of Persian literary forms and Greek science and philosophy to Islamic and Arab tradition initiated a period of great achievements in many intellectual fields. Medieval Europe would owe most of its knowledge of astronomy, geography, medicine, mathematics and even Greek philosophy to Arab scholars. Religious and racial pluralism also characterized Abbasid rule: strict observance of Islam did not preclude tolerance of the faith of people of other religions, while Arabs were no longer accorded a privileged status.

The Abbasids reached their zenith under Harun al-Rashid but civil war broke out between his sons soon after his death. The caliph's authority began to decline in favour of the provincial emirs. In 868 Egypt and Palestine became independent under the Tulunids, while the eastern provinces seceded under the native Persian Saffarid and Samanid dynasties. The Abbasids lost Arabia after the rebellion of the Shiite Qarmatian sect in 899. The Christians of Armenia had also regained their independence in 886. The Abbasids recovered briefly around 900, retaking Palestine and Egypt in 905, and aided by the Sunnite Samanid emirate's annexation of the troublesome Shiite Ṣaffarid emirate. However, in 914 the Fatimids, who had come to power in Ifriqiya in 909, began the conquest of Egypt; by 1000 they were the dominant Islamic power. In about 913 the Buwayhids, a tribal confederation from Daylam, conquered Persia. Their capture of Baghdad in 945 ended Abbasid territorial power. Though the caliphate was kept as a spiritual office, the Sunnite caliph was merely a figurehead, behind whom the Shiite Buwayhids held real power.

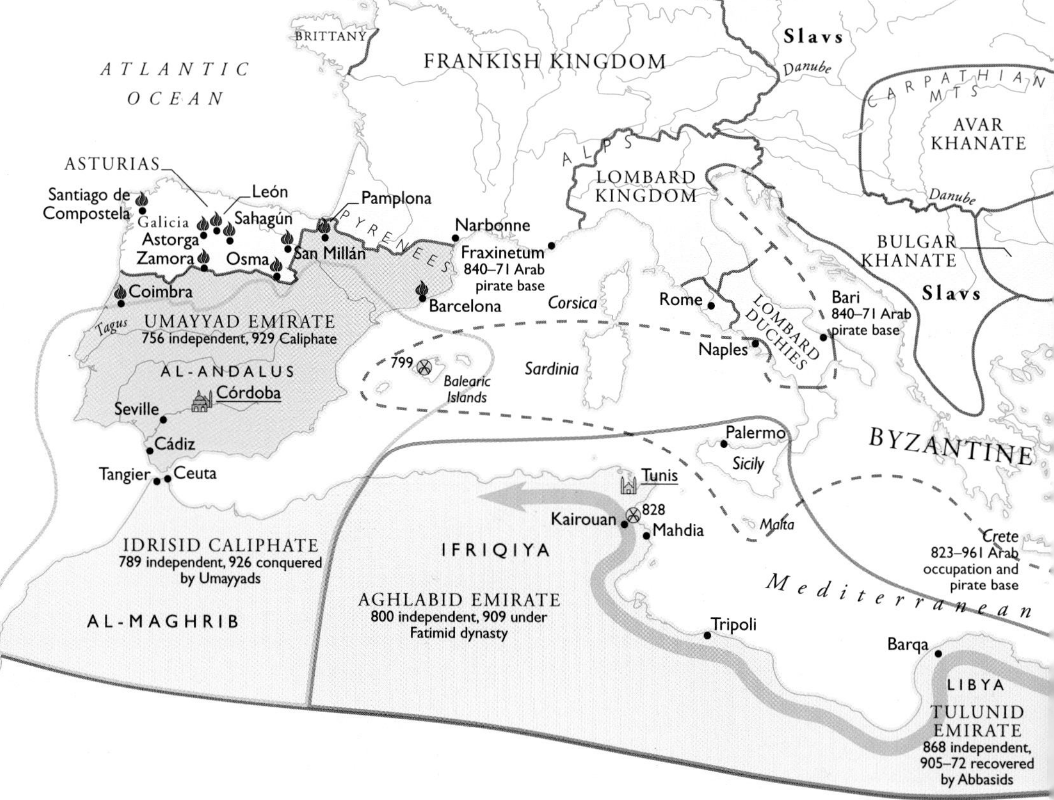

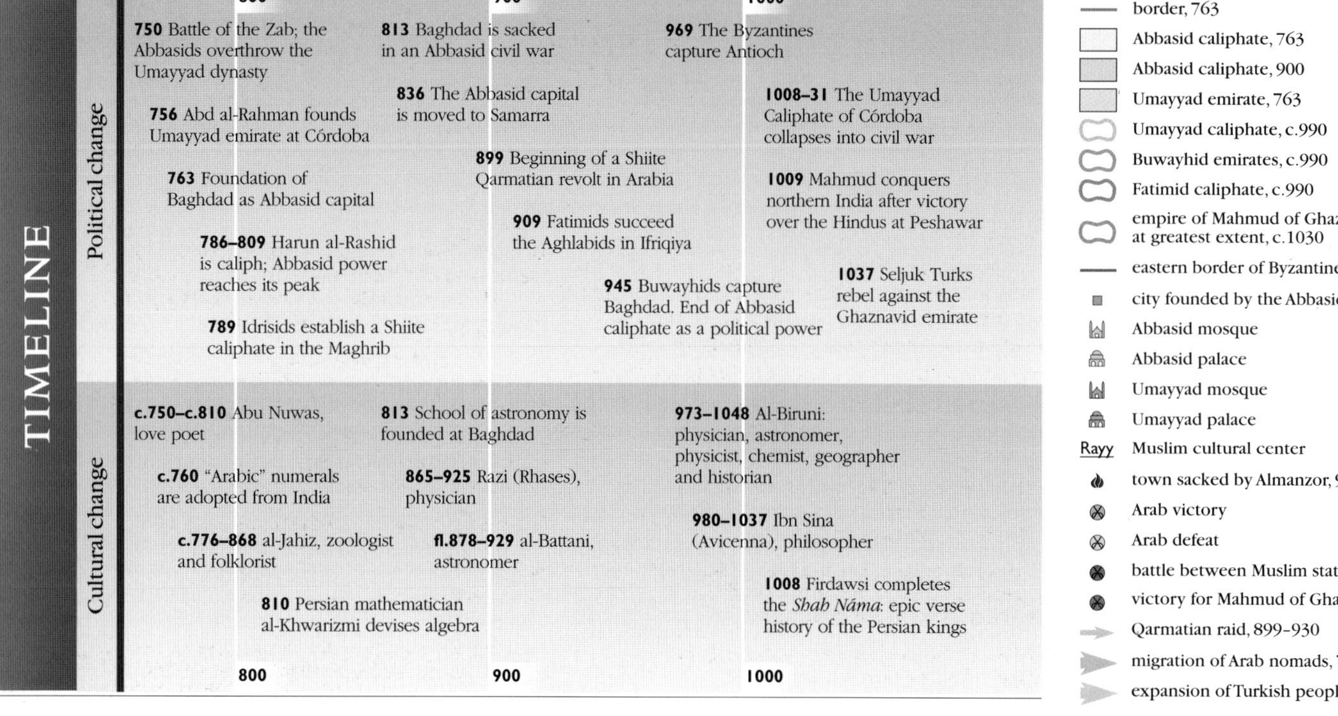

TIMELINE

Political change

750 Battle of the Zab; the Abbasids overthrow the Umayyad dynasty

756 Abd al-Rahman founds Umayyad emirate at Córdoba

763 Foundation of Baghdad as Abbasid capital

786–809 Harun al-Rashid is caliph; Abbasid power reaches its peak

789 Idrisids establish a Shiite caliphate in the Maghrib

813 Baghdad is sacked in an Abbasid civil war

836 The Abbasid capital is moved to Samarra

899 Beginning of a Shiite Qarmatian revolt in Arabia

909 Fatimids succeed the Aghlabids in Ifriqiya

945 Buwayhids capture Baghdad. End of Abbasid caliphate as a political power

969 The Byzantines capture Antioch

1008–31 The Umayyad Caliphate of Córdoba collapses into civil war

1009 Mahmud conquers northern India after victory over the Hindus at Peshawar

1037 Seljuk Turks rebel against the Ghaznavid emirate

Cultural change

c.750–c.810 Abu Nuwas, love poet

c.760 "Arabic" numerals are adopted from India

c.776–868 al-Jahiz, zoologist and folklorist

810 Persian mathematician al-Khwarizmi devises algebra

813 School of astronomy is founded at Baghdad

865–925 Razi (Rhases), physician

fl.878–929 al-Battani, astronomer

973–1048 Al-Biruni: physician, astronomer, physicist, chemist, geographer and historian

980–1037 Ibn Sina (Avicenna), philosopher

1008 Firdawsi completes the *Shah Náma*: epic verse history of the Persian kings

800 900 1000

- border, 763
- Abbasid caliphate, 763
- Abbasid caliphate, 900
- Umayyad emirate, 763
- Umayyad caliphate, c.990
- Buwayhid emirates, c.990
- Fatimid caliphate, c.990
- empire of Mahmud of Ghazni at greatest extent, c.1030
- eastern border of Byzantine empire, 1022–71
- city founded by the Abbasids
- Abbasid mosque
- Abbasid palace
- Umayyad mosque
- Umayyad palace
- Rayy Muslim cultural center
- town sacked by Almanzor, 985–1002
- Arab victory
- Arab defeat
- battle between Muslim states
- victory for Mahmud of Ghazni
- Qarmatian raid, 899–930
- migration of Arab nomads, 7th to 11th centuries
- expansion of Turkish peoples

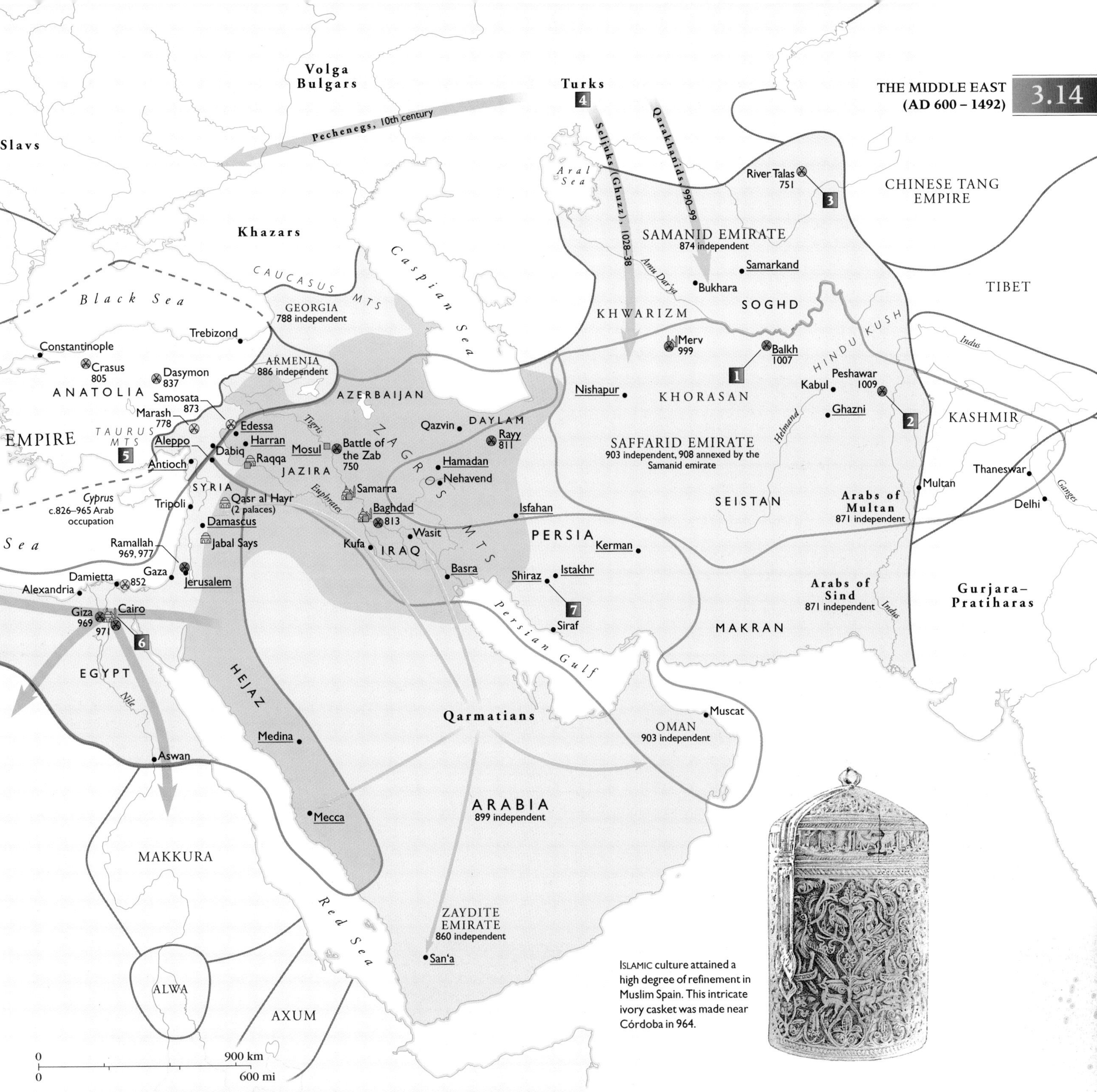

ISLAMIC culture attained a high degree of refinement in Muslim Spain. This intricate ivory casket was made near Córdoba in 964.

The rise of the Buwayhids was accompanied by the decline of the Samanid emirate. Its northern provinces were lost to the Qarakhanid Turks in the 990s while the rest was seized by a rebel Turkish mercenary, Mahmud of Ghazni, who defeated the Samanids near Merv. Thereafter, Mahmud expanded into the Buwayhid emirates and northern India. A militant Muslim, Mahmud conducted holy wars against the Hindu kingdoms, deliberately destroying Hindu temples. The Ghaznavid emirate was the first of the Turkish empires of the Middle East, yet it declined rapidly following an invasion by the Ghuzz Turks led by members of the Seljuk clan in 1037.

After its initial setbacks, the Umayyad emirate in Spain consolidated its position, and in 929 Abd al-Rahman III (r.912–61) declared himself caliph. Conquest of the Maghrib in 973 and the great successes of his general Almanzor (al-Mansur) against the Christians of the north seemed to justify his confidence. However, in 1008 civil war broke out: the caliphate collapsed and Muslim power in Spain never fully recovered. Despite mainly hostile relations, Muslim Spain was, with Sicily, the most important route for the transmission of Arab culture to Christian Europe.

1 The Qarakhanid Turks overran Soghd in 990–95, but further expansion was halted by their defeat by Mahmud of Ghazni at Balkh in 1007.

2 Mahmud of Ghazni's victory over a coalition of Hindu princes at Peshawar in 1009 made him the dominant power in northwest India.

3 The Arab victory at the River Talas led to the collapse of China's central Asian empire.

4 The Turks, who converted to Islam c.970, were an important source of mercenaries for the armies of the Abbasid caliphate and its successor states: many Turks achieved positions of power and influence.

5 The long Arab-Byzantine struggle for control of the Taurus Mountains was won by the Byzantines in the 960s, after which they occupied northern Syria.

6 Cairo (Al-Qahirah) was founded in 969 as the capital of the Fatimid dynasty, and began to supplant Alexandria as Egypt's most important city.

7 The Shiite Buwayhids established their capital at Shiraz c.913 after conquering Persia. They captured Baghdad in 945.

See also 3.06 (Carolingians); 3.13 (the rise of Islam); 3.19 (medieval India)

3.15 The Byzantine empire • 610 – 1204 •

The Byzantine empire is the term modern historians use to describe the continuation of the eastern Roman empire after the accession of Heraclius (r.610–41). When Heraclius came to the throne, the empire was facing defeat by the neighboring Persian Sasanian empire. To save it Heraclius reformed the army and administration to create what was effectively a new state. Greek, which had always been the majority language of the eastern Roman empire, replaced Latin as the official language of government. Because of this, medieval western Europeans saw the Byzantine empire as a Hellenistic state; however, the Byzantines continued to think of themselves as Romans, until the final fall of their empire to the Ottoman Turks in 1453.

Heraclius' reforms saw Byzantium emerge victorious from its war with Persia in 627. However, the exhausted empire was unprepared for the attacks by the Arabs, newly united by Islam, that began in 633. Syria, Palestine, Egypt and North Africa were lost by 698 but Arab attempts to take Constantinople in 670–77 and 716–17 failed. Other powers also benefited from Byzantine weakness: the Lombards captured Genoa in 640 and the Bulgars overran much of the Balkans in 679. The empire continued to lose ground in the 8th and early 9th centuries: the Lombards conquered the exarchate of Ravenna in 751 and the Arabs began the conquest of Sicily in 827.

The shrinkage of the empire was eventually reversed by the emperors of the Macedonian dynasty (867–1059), who restored the frontiers in the north and the east close to where they had been in late Roman times. Though the Macedonians were fine soldiers, they were also helped by the political fragmentation of the Arab world in the 9th century and the weakening of the Bulgars by Magyar and Rus attacks in the 10th. Under Basil II (r.976–1025; the "Bulgar-slayer"), the Byzantine empire reigned supreme in Europe and the Middle East, yet within 20 years of his death it was again losing ground. By 1071 the Normans had largely driven the Byzantines out of Italy. In the same year a crushing defeat by the Seljuk Turks at Manzikert was followed by the loss of Anatolia, the empire's main source of army recruits.

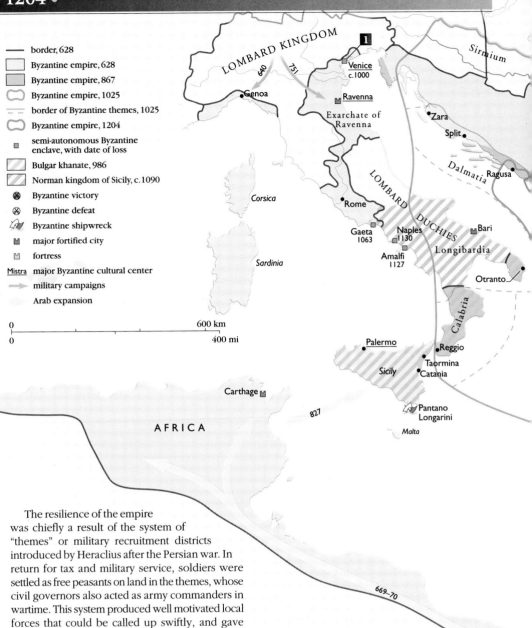

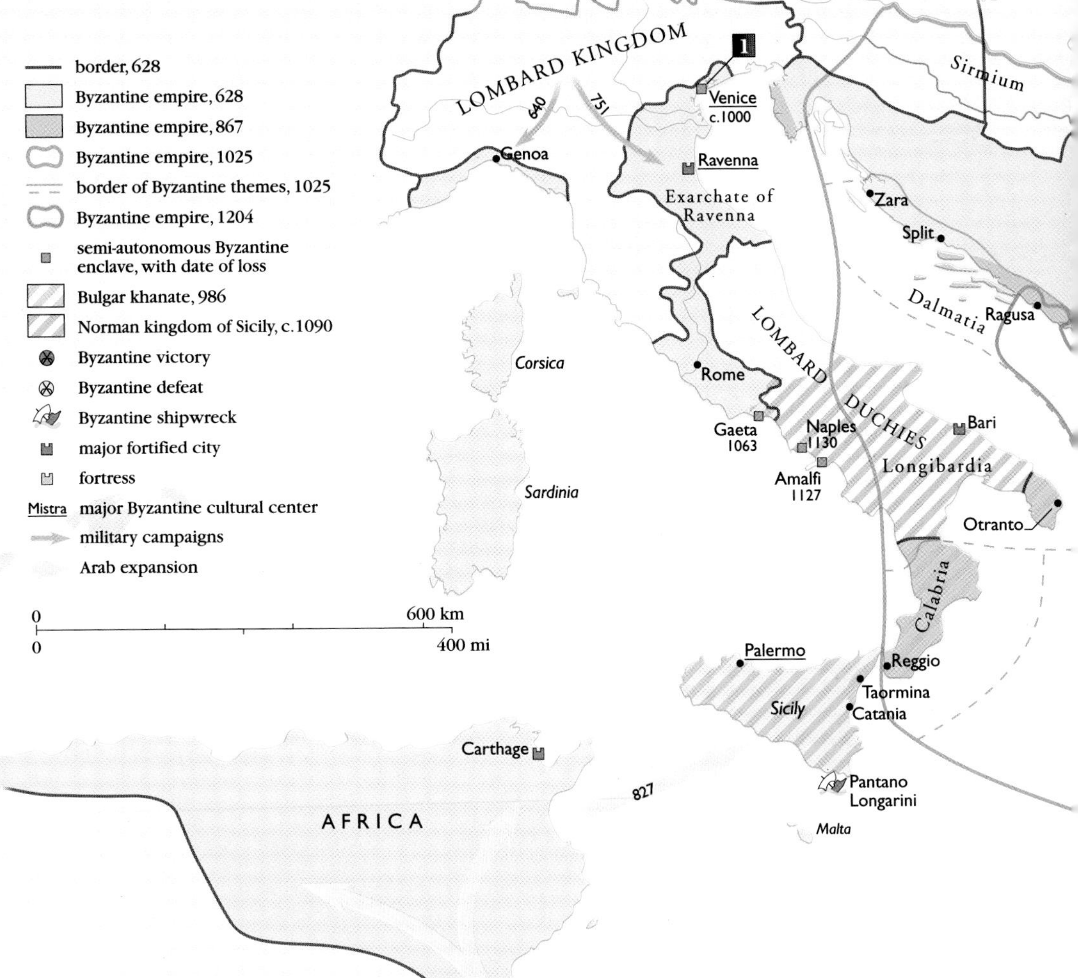

border, 628
Byzantine empire, 628
Byzantine empire, 867
Byzantine empire, 1025
border of Byzantine themes, 1025
Byzantine empire, 1204
semi-autonomous Byzantine enclave, with date of loss
Bulgar khanate, 986
Norman kingdom of Sicily, c.1090
Byzantine victory
Byzantine defeat
Byzantine shipwreck
major fortified city
fortress
Mistra major Byzantine cultural center
military campaigns
Arab expansion

0 600 km
0 400 mi

The resilience of the empire was chiefly a result of the system of "themes" or military recruitment districts introduced by Heraclius after the Persian war. In return for tax and military service, soldiers were settled as free peasants on land in the themes, whose civil governors also acted as army commanders in wartime. This system produced well motivated local forces that could be called up swiftly, and gave the state a reliable source of revenue. Originally

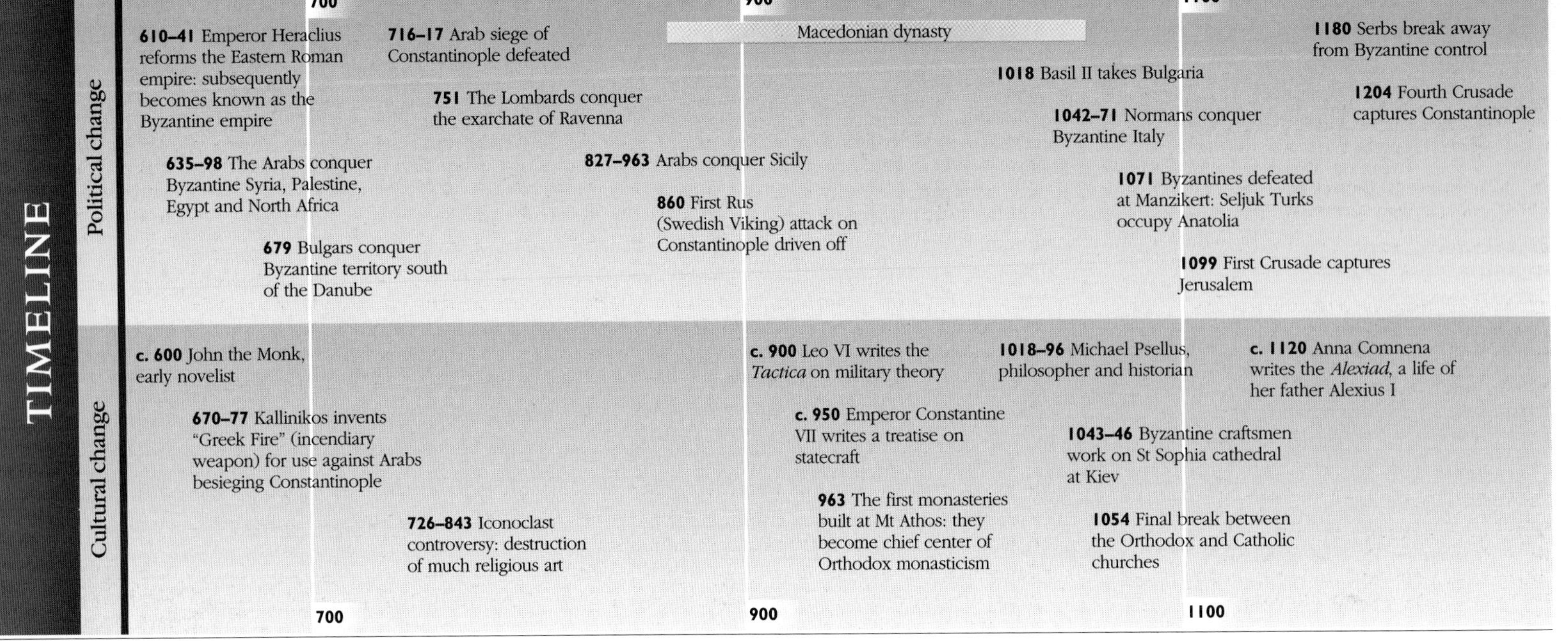

TIMELINE
Political change
700
900
1100
610–41 Emperor Heraclius reforms the Eastern Roman empire: subsequently becomes known as the Byzantine empire
716–17 Arab siege of Constantinople defeated
Macedonian dynasty
1180 Serbs break away from Byzantine control
1018 Basil II takes Bulgaria
751 The Lombards conquer the exarchate of Ravenna
1204 Fourth Crusade captures Constantinople
1042–71 Normans conquer Byzantine Italy
635–98 The Arabs conquer Byzantine Syria, Palestine, Egypt and North Africa
827–963 Arabs conquer Sicily
1071 Byzantines defeated at Manzikert: Seljuk Turks occupy Anatolia
860 First Rus (Swedish Viking) attack on Constantinople driven off
679 Bulgars conquer Byzantine territory south of the Danube
1099 First Crusade captures Jerusalem
Cultural change
c. 600 John the Monk, early novelist
c. 900 Leo VI writes the Tactica on military theory
1018–96 Michael Psellus, philosopher and historian
c. 1120 Anna Comnena writes the Alexiad, a life of her father Alexius I
670–77 Kallinikos invents "Greek Fire" (incendiary weapon) for use against Arabs besieging Constantinople
c. 950 Emperor Constantine VII writes a treatise on statecraft
1043–46 Byzantine craftsmen work on St Sophia cathedral at Kiev
963 The first monasteries built at Mt Athos: they become chief center of Orthodox monasticism
726–843 Iconoclast controversy: destruction of much religious art
1054 Final break between the Orthodox and Catholic churches
700
900
1100

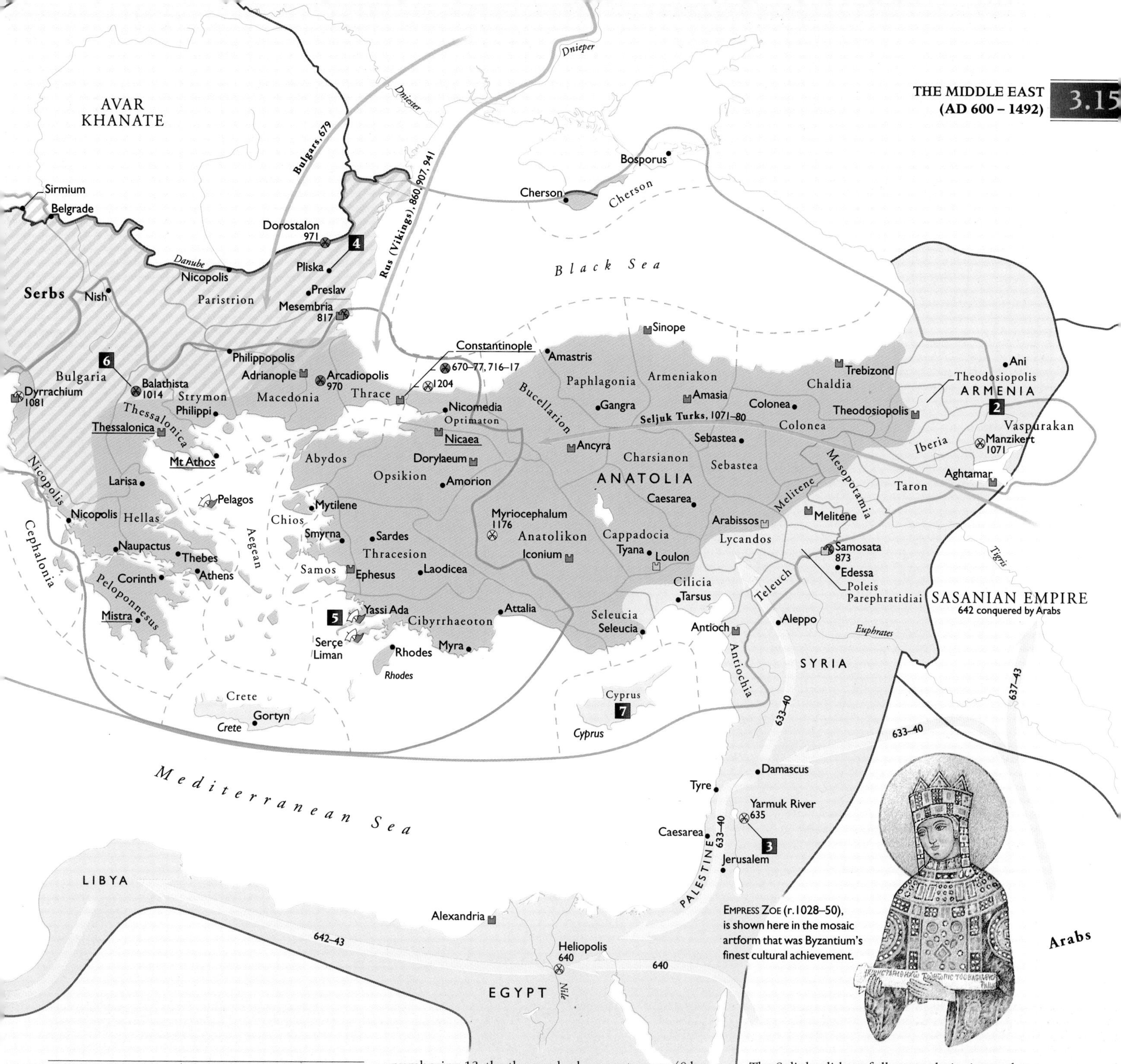

EMPRESS ZOE (r.1028–50), is shown here in the mosaic artform that was Byzantium's finest cultural achievement.

1 Byzantine influence endured in Venice long after the city's independence. St Mark's Cathedral (begun 1063) is a fine example of Byzantine architecture.

2 Christian Armenia joined the empire voluntarily in 1020, seeking protection from its Muslim neighbors.

3 The Byzantine defeat on the Yarmuk River led to the Arab occupation of Palestine and Syria.

4 The Bulgarian capital at Pliska was built around a fortified palace; at its height (c.800) the city covered a larger area than Constantinople.

5 Wreck of a 7th-century Byzantine merchant ship carrying wine; long-distance trade flourished in the Byzantine empire in the early Middle Ages.

6 After their defeat of the Bulgars at Balathista (1014), the Byzantines pushed their frontier to the Danube.

7 Cyprus changed hands several times: Arab 649–746, Byzantine 746–c.826, Arab c.826–965, Byzantine 965–1191 when it was captured by Richard I of England during the Third Crusade.

numbering 13, the themes had grown to over 40 by the 11th century. After Basil II's death, the system was deliberately neglected by weak rulers who feared the army's strength, and the empire was unprepared to face the Seljuk invasions.

The loss of Anatolia was a fatal blow for the empire. Though the western districts were regained by Alexius I Comnenus (r.1081–1118) following the success of the First Crusade, the themes had been obliterated and the area depopulated. The landed aristocracy reduced the surviving free peasantry to servile status, leading to the total collapse of the theme system. Thus the empire was left dependent on expensive mercenaries at a time when its income base was being undermined. The state was further impoverished in the 12th century as Venice and Genoa gradually took control of Byzantine trade. Byzantium's residual prestige and its proverbially devious diplomacy maintained the semblance of a great power until the Seljuks inflicted another crushing defeat, at Myriocephalum, in 1176.

The Seljuks did not follow up their victory, however, and it was the Fourth Crusade's capture and plunder of Constantinople that delivered the fatal blow in 1204. Although the Byzantines retook their capital in 1261, the restored empire was a shadow of its former self: prone to civil war, its survival depended on its enemies' weaknesses and misfortunes.

For most of the Middle Ages Byzantium was Christendom's most sophisticated state, producing outstanding sacred art, literature and architecture. Yet its frequent schisms with the western (Roman) church engendered mutual suspicion and hostility. As a result, Byzantium's cultural influence was strongest in areas where Orthodox Christianity prevailed: the Balkans, Georgia and, especially, Russia, which came to see itself as the legitimate successor to the Byzantine state after 1453.

See also 3.16 (the rise of the Turks; 3.17 (the Crusades)

3.16 The medieval Turkish empires • 1038 – 1492 •

Turkish power in the Middle East grew rapidly after the Seljuk invasion of the Ghaznavid emirate in 1037. Three years later, under Toghril Beg (r.1038–63), they had occupied the emirate's western provinces. In 1054–55 the Seljuks, heeding an appeal for help by the Abbasid caliph of Baghdad, drove the Buwayhids from the city. As Sunni Muslims, the Seljuks accorded the caliph greater respect than had the Shiite Buwayhids, but they were no less firm in ruling the city. Under Toghril Beg's successor, Alp Arslan (r.1063–72), the Seljuks overran Syria and routed the Byzantines at Manzikert. Alp Arslan was killed in 1072 repelling a Qarakhanid Turk invasion at Berzem but in the reign of his successor Malik Shah (r.1072–92), Byzantine Anatolia was occupied and the Fatimids expelled from Palestine.

Malik Shah's death sparked civil war and the Seljuk sultanate began to fragment. By 1095 the sultanate of Rum and the Danishmend emirate in Anatolia had seceded and by 1100 there were dozens of independent Seljuk states. The main beneficiaries were the Byzantine empire and the First Crusade, which between them deprived the Seljuks of western Anatolia and northern Syria, and the Fatimids, who retook Palestine in 1098, only to lose it again almost at once to the Crusaders.

Turkish power in the west began to recover under Zangi, the *atabeg* (governor) of Mosul (r.1127–46), who united northern Syria and recaptured Edessa from the Crusaders in 1144. Zangi's son Nur al-Din (r.1146–74) conquered the rest of Muslim Syria and destroyed the Shiite Fatimid caliphate of Egypt. After his death, Saladin, Kurdish governor of Egypt, rebelled against the Zangids and by 1177 controlled the emirate. The Ayyubid dynasty founded by Saladin held power until 1250 when the Mamlukes, a caste of mainly Turkish slave soldiers, seized power. This military elite continued to rule Egypt and Syria until 1517, surviving as a class until 1811. The Seljuks of Rum also recovered their power and defeated the Byzantines at Myriocephalum in 1176.

In the east Turkish power continued to wane in the 12th century and in 1156 the Abbasid caliphate enjoyed a revival. Although its political authority extended only to Iraq, its spiritual authority enabled it to arbitrate in disputes between the Seljuk states. Then in the early 13th century the eastern Seljuk states were absorbed by a new Turkish power, the shahdom of Khwarizm. However, its growth was abruptly halted by the Mongol invasion of 1219. At a stroke, Chingis Khan broke the shahdom's power.

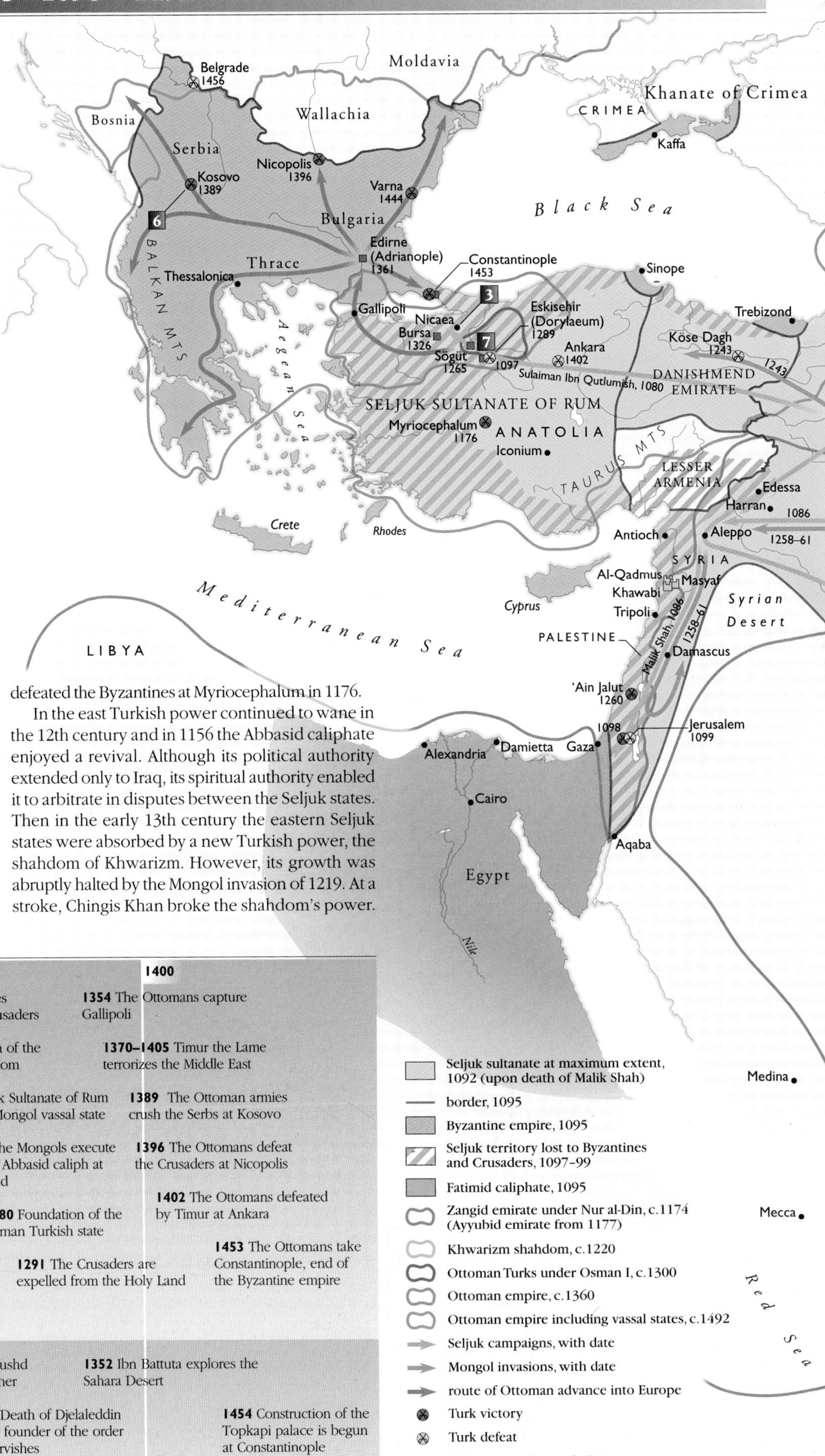

TIMELINE

1100 | 1250 | 1400

Political change

- **1038–40** The Seljuks conquer Khorasan
- **1055** Seljiks capture Baghdad
- **1071** The Seljuks defeat Byzantines at Manzikert
- **1092** Death of Malik Shah; Seljuk sultanate disintegrates
- **1099** The First Crusade captures Jerusalem
- **1127–46** Zangi, emir of Mosul, unites Turkish emirates of Syria
- **1169–71** Saladin conquers Egypt for the Zangid emirate
- **1187** Saladin recaptures Jerusalem from the Crusaders
- **1210** Foundation of the Khwarizm shahdom
- **1243** Seljuk Sultanate of Rum becomes Mongol vassal state
- **1258** The Mongols execute the last Abbasid caliph at Baghdad
- **c.1280** Foundation of the Ottoman Turkish state
- **1291** The Crusaders are expelled from the Holy Land
- **1354** The Ottomans capture Gallipoli
- **1370–1405** Timur the Lame terrorizes the Middle East
- **1389** The Ottoman armies crush the Serbs at Kosovo
- **1396** The Ottomans defeat the Crusaders at Nicopolis
- **1402** The Ottomans defeated by Timur at Ankara
- **1453** The Ottomans take Constantinople, end of the Byzantine empire

Cultural change

- **1027–1123** Omar Khayyam: Persian scientist and poet
- **1065–67** Nizamayeh academy (Baghdad) is founded
- **c. 1080** Construction of the Friday Mosque in Isfahan
- **1198** Death of Ibn Rushd (Averröes): philosopher
- **1273** Death of Djelaleddin Rumi, founder of the order of Dervishes
- **1352** Ibn Battuta explores the Sahara Desert
- **1347** The Black Death reaches Baghdad
- **1454** Construction of the Topkapi palace is begun at Constantinople

1100 | 1250 | 1400

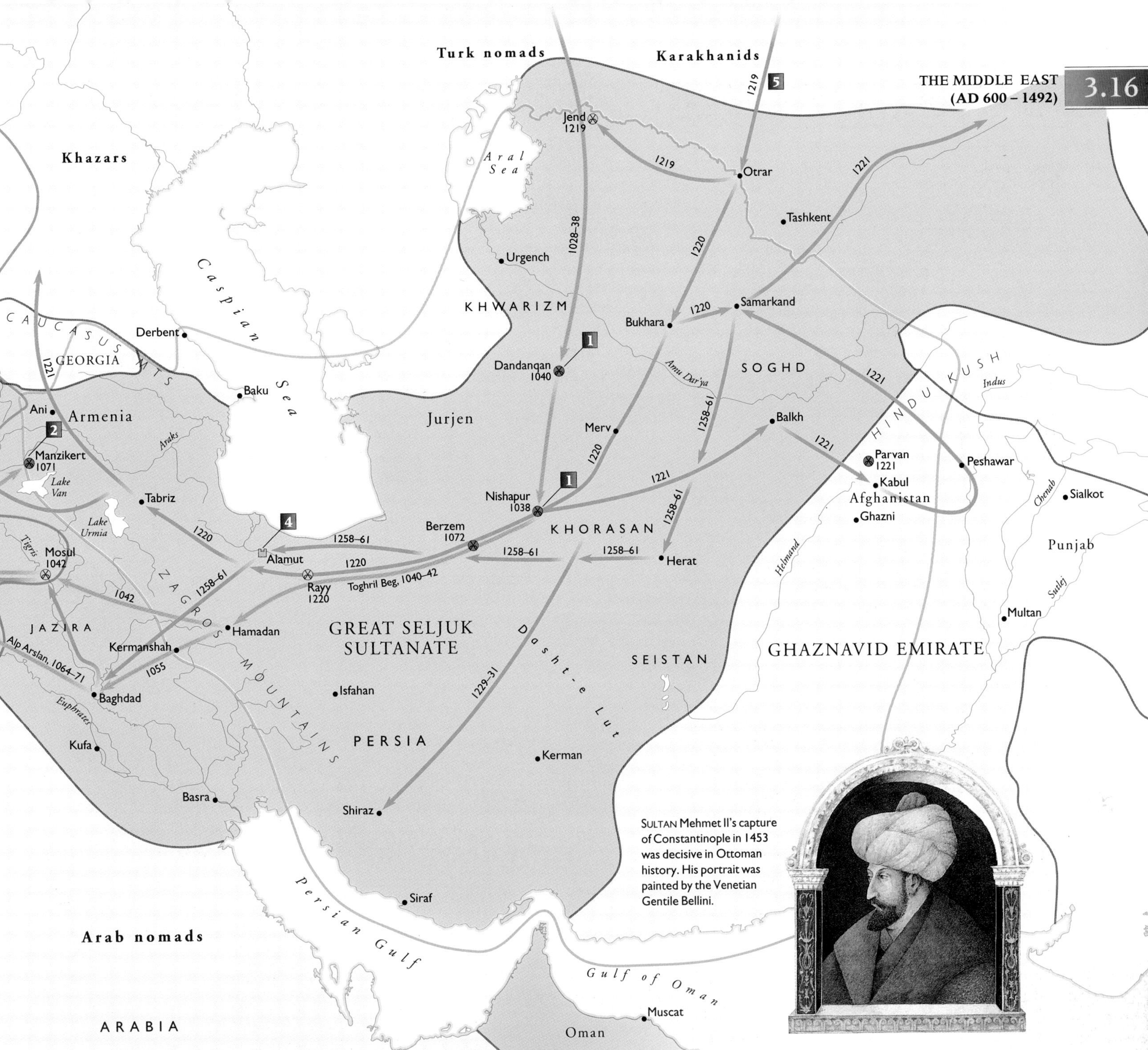

SULTAN Mehmet II's capture of Constantinople in 1453 was decisive in Ottoman history. His portrait was painted by the Venetian Gentile Bellini.

1 The Ghaznavids lost their western territories to the Seljuks after defeats at Nishapur and Dandanqan.

2 Sultan Alp Arslan's victory over the Byzantines at Manzikert began the Seljuk conquest of Anatolia.

3 Nicaea became the capital of the Seljuk sultanate of Rum ("Rome", from *Romaivi*, as the Byzantine Greeks called themselves) in 1080; when it fell to the Crusaders in 1097, the capital was moved to Iconium.

4 Alamut was the main stronghold of the Shiite Ismaili Nizari sect (the Assassins).

5 The Mongol invaders of the 13th century occupied or imposed vassalage on all the Middle East except Palestine, Egypt, Syria and Arabia.

6 Their defeat by the Ottomans at Kosovo is deeply ingrained on the Serbian national consciousness; for many, it justified the "ethnic cleansing" of Muslims in the Bosnian civil war of 1992–95.

7 The Ottoman state is named after Osman I (r.1280–1324), a Turkish chieftain who ruled Sögüt.

The Seljuks of Rum were reduced to vassals in 1243, the Abbasid caliphate was destroyed, this time for good, in 1258 and in 1260 the Mongols drove the Mamlukes out of Syria. Though the Mamlukes recovered much of this territory after their victory over the Mongols at 'Ain Jalut later that year, the Mongols remained the dominant power in the Middle East until Timur the Lame's death in 1405.

Following the Mongol conquests, the Seljuk sultanate of Rum broke up. The Byzantine empire was now too weak to benefit, while the Serbs, Bulgars and the Latins were busy arguing over the remains of the dying empire. The Ottoman state began its growth under the minor Anatolian chief Osman I, and by the death of Orhan (r.1324–60) the Ottomans occupied most of northwest Anatolia and had begun to expand into Europe, capturing Gallipoli in 1354. In 1361 Murad I (r.1360–89) captured Adrianople and, renaming it Edirne, transferred the capital there. Timur the Lame's invasion in 1402, and his victory at Ankara, led to the temporary collapse of the sultanate but the Ottomans rallied quickly, expanding again by 1430. Constantinople, and with it the Byzantine empire, fell in 1453. Although further expansion into central Europe was checked by the Hungarians at Belgrade in 1456, the Ottoman sultanate was still a rising power in 1492.

A major factor in Ottoman success was the weakness of the neighboring Christian and Turkish states. The divisions in Europe caused by the Hundred Years' War and the Great Schism precluded a concerted Christian resistance, while the Seljuks were weakened by the Mongols, who subsequently withdrew from Anatolia. Religious zeal was another vital element. Osman I had been a *ghazi*, an Islamic warrior, and commitment to spreading the faith through holy war motivated the Ottoman armies. This was especially true of its elite Janissary corps which was composed of the children of Christians, who were raised as devout Muslims.

See also 3.14 (the rise of the Turks); 3.17 (the Crusades)

3.17 The Crusades • 1096 – 1291 •

The Crusades were holy wars fought to defend the Catholic church and the Christian people against those who were regarded as external and internal enemies of Christendom. Although the main crusading effort was directed against the Muslims in the Holy Land, Crusades were also conducted against the pagan Slavs of the Baltic, Muslim Spain, the Ottoman Turks in the Balkans and heretics, such as the Cathars, within western Christendom itself. Though considered peripheral at the time, it was these campaigns, particularly those in Spain and the Baltic, that were ultimately the most successful. The movement did not die out completely until the 18th century; however, the main period of crusading activity lasted from 1096 to 1291, which saw eight major campaigns and dozens of smaller expeditions.

The Crusaders saw their role as part of the pilgrimage tradition. Pilgrimages to holy places were undertaken as penance and to acquire spiritual merit. The ultimate pilgrimage was to Jerusalem, and when the Turks began to harass pilgrims in the 11th century an armed pilgrimage to restore Christian control was thought fully justified. This appealed both to the piety and the adventurous spirit of the feudal knightly class, who saw themselves as protectors of Christendom. As an inducement the papacy offered Crusaders spiritual and legal privileges, most important of which was remission of the penances due for sin. This was popularly interpreted as a guarantee of immediate entry to heaven if the Crusader were to die on the expedition.

The First Crusade was called by Pope Urban II at the Council of Clermont in 1095 in response to an appeal from the Byzantine emperor Alexius I Comnenus for military help against the Seljuk Turks. The first army to set out, a motley band of poorly armed pilgrims, was wiped out near Nicomedia. However, the main army, mostly French and Norman knights, fought its way across Anatolia to Antioch and on to Jerusalem, which was taken in 1099. The First Crusade was the most successful, thanks in part to divisions in the Muslim world. Four Crusader states were set up in Syria and Palestine: the Kingdom of Jerusalem, the County of Tripoli, the Principality of Antioch and the County of Edessa.

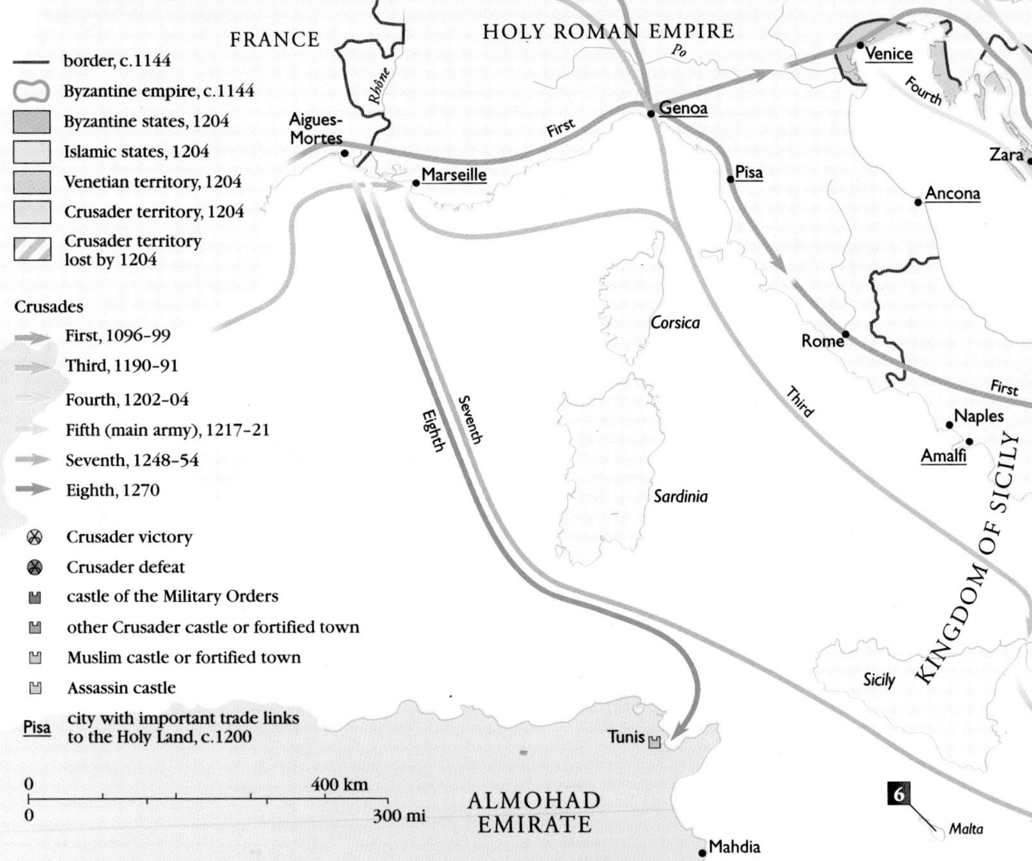

Muslim unity began to be restored by Zangi, governor of Mosul, who retook Edessa in 1144; this loss prompted the Second Crusade (1147–49), which was badly mauled crossing Anatolia and achieved nothing. The loss of Jerusalem after Saladin's victory at Hattin in 1187 led to the calling of the Third Crusade under Richard I (Lionheart) of England and Philip II Augustus of France. Although this failed to recover Jerusalem, by retaking the coast of Palestine it ensured the survival of the Crusader states.

In the 13th century, Crusaders showed an increasingly sophisticated strategic approach to defense of the Holy Land. It was realized that Christian control of the region could never be secure so long as Egypt remained the center of Muslim power. The Fourth Crusade (1202–04) was the first called with the intention of attacking Egypt but it never reached its destination. Assembled in Venice, the Crusaders were unable to pay for their transit to Egypt, and so agreed to help the Venetians capture the Hungarian city of Zara. Thereafter, the Crusade was diverted to Constantinople in support of a claimant for the Byzantine throne who promised support for the expedition. When this was not forthcoming, the Crusaders sacked Constantinople and made it the center of a Latin Empire. The Fifth Crusade (1217–21) took Damietta at the mouth of the Nile but was defeated by river flooding as it

TIMELINE

Eastern Mediterranean

1095 Pope Urban II calls the First Crusade at Clermont

1098 Crusaders take Edessa and Antioch

1099 Crusaders capture Jerusalem. Defeat of Egyptian relief army at Ascalon

1113 Founding of Order of the Hospital of St John in Jerusalem (Hospitallers)

1118 Founding of the Order of the Knights Templar

1144 Zangi, governor of Mosul takes Edessa

1149 The Second Crusade ends in failure

1187 Saladin defeats Christians at Hattin and recaptures Jerusalem

1190–92 Third Crusade under Richard I: Cyprus captured

1200

1204 The Fourth Crusade takes Constantinople; founding of the Latin Empire

1217–21 The Fifth Crusade attacks Egypt

1228–29 The Sixth Crusade secures Jerusalem

1248–54 Louis IX leads the Seventh Crusade in Egypt

1261 Byzantines recapture Constantinople: fall of the Latin Empire

1270 Louis IX (St Louis) dies besieging Tunis on the Eighth Crusade

1291 Mamlukes capture Acre: fall of Kingdom of Jerusalem

1300

1302 Fall of Ruad. Crusaders are expelled from Holy Land

1310 The Hospitallers are established on Rhodes

1312 The Order of the Knights Templar is dissolved

1400

1396 The Ottomans defeat Burgundian–Hungarian Crusade at Nicopolis

1456 Crusaders defend Belgrade against the Ottomans

Other Crusades

1096 Urban II offers privileges to Crusaders fighting the Spanish Muslims

1147 Crusades against the pagan Wends (Slavs) in the Baltic. Crusaders take Lisbon

1200

1208 Pope Innocent III calls a Crusade against the Cathar heretics in southern France

1227 The Teutonic Knights begin crusading against the pagan Prussians

1300

1309 The Teutonic Knights launch a permanent Crusade against the pagan Lithuanians

1400

1420 A Crusade is proclaimed against the Hussite heretics in Bohemia

1492 The fall of Granada completes the Christian reconquest of Spain

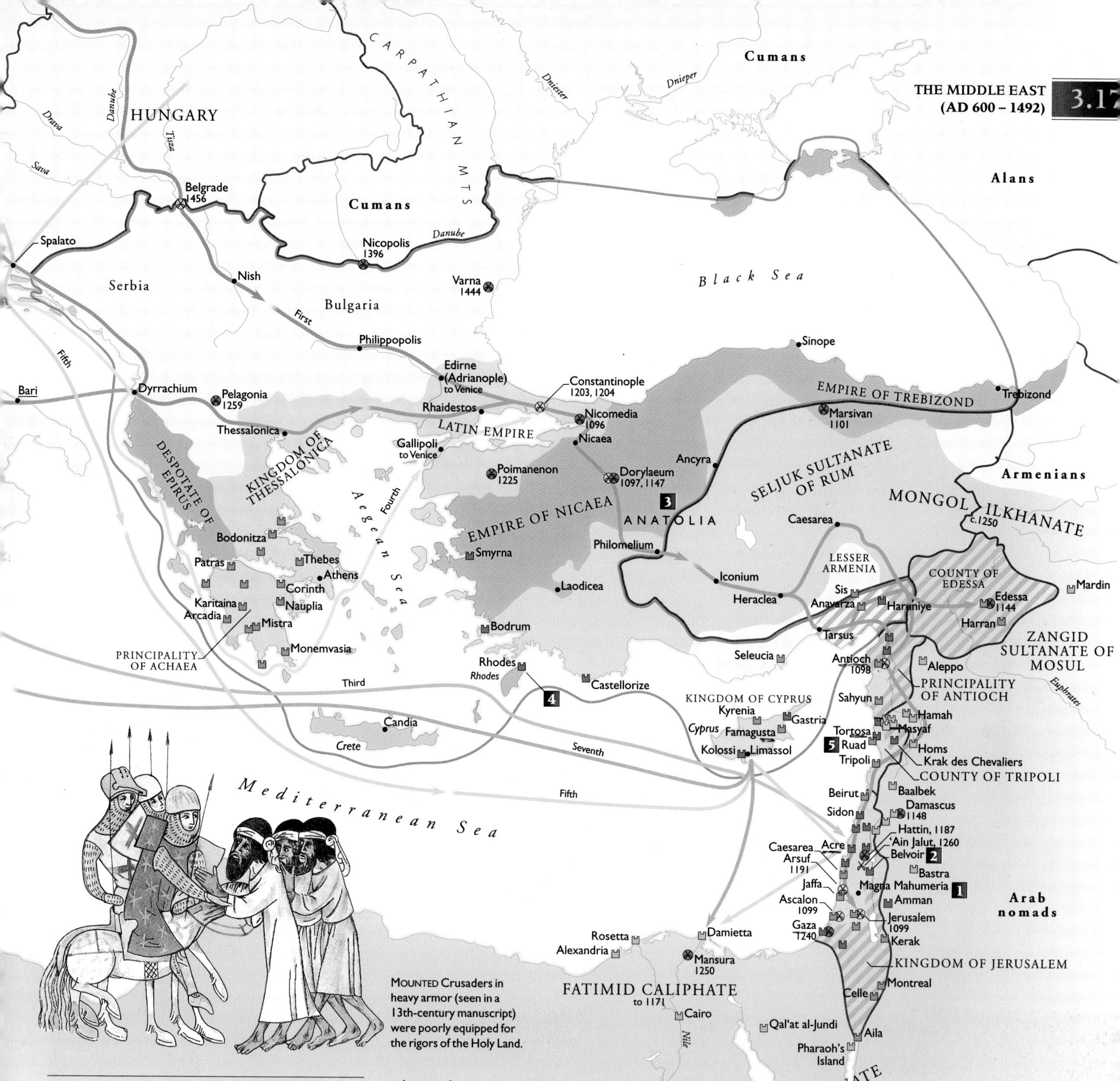

MOUNTED Crusaders in heavy armor (seen in a 13th-century manuscript) were poorly equipped for the rigors of the Holy Land.

1 Magna Mahumeria was a farming settlement of volunteers from France, Spain and Italy, occupied 1120–87 with a population of c.700. Settlers received land on easy terms in return for military service.

2 The concentric castle was the most important innovation of Crusader military architecture. The earliest, begun in 1168, is at Belvoir.

3 Food and water shortages and Turkish attacks made Anatolia highly dangerous for Crusaders. After the Second Crusade failed, most went to Palestine by sea.

4 Occupied by the Hospitallers in 1310, Rhodes became an major Crusader base for campaigns against the Turks until its capture by the Ottomans in 1522.

5 The fortress island of Ruad was the last Christian stronghold in the Holy Land to fall to the Muslims, being taken by the Mamlukes in 1302.

6 Malta, the last bastion of the Crusading movement, was home to the Hospitallers from 1530 to 1798, when they were expelled by Napoleon.

advanced on Cairo. The Holy Roman emperor Frederick II gained Jerusalem through diplomacy on the Sixth Crusade (1228–29) but did not win enough territory to ensure its defense once the truce broke down, and the city was lost again in 1244. The Seventh Crusade (1248–54) under Louis IX of France was an exact repeat of the Fifth. The Eighth Crusade (1270), also led by Louis IX and directed against Tunis with the intention of using it as a base for further attacks on Egypt, was also a costly failure. Far more significant than the Crusades in ensuring the survival of the Crusader states in the 13th century were the Mongol attacks on the Muslim world. After decisively defeating the Mongols at 'Ain Jalut in 1260 the Mamlukes turned their full attention to the Crusader states, which finally fell in 1291.

Throughout their existence the Crusader states suffered from a critical shortage of manpower. Attempts to attract settlers foundered on the extreme inhospitability of the region. Instead, castle building became highly sophisticated; these castles were often garrisoned by military monastic orders, such as the Knights Templars and the Knights Hospitallers, founded to help defend the Holy Land.

The Crusades had considerable effects on the Islamic world, where they briefly revived the concept of the *jihad* (holy war). Nevertheless, Arab historians of the time gave them only scanty attention, and saw the Mongols as a far more potent threat to Islamic civilization.

See also 3.05 (the world religions); 3.09 (medieval Christianity); 3.16 (the medieval Turkish empires)

3.18 Africa • 600 – 1500 •

In sub-Saharan Africa, the period 600–1500 witnessed the rise of chiefdoms, cities, states and empires so that by 1500 most Africans lived in complex societies of some sort. While the causes of state formation were primarily internal, Islam, introduced by Arab merchants, also exerted a strong influence on west and east Africa from the 10th century onward. From the mid-15th century Catholicism was introduced to west and central Africa by the Portuguese. Except possibly in the far southwest, iron was in everyday use in sub-Saharan Africa by the 11th century and in west Africa metalworkers made artifacts of high technical and artistic quality.

Too little is known at present to determine the exact causes of state formation in sub-Saharan Africa. In the west African part of the Sahel (the southern fringe of the Sahara), state formation had begun by 600 and the earliest known state, the kingdom of Ghana, had emerged by 700. Population growth and the development of regional trade routes in the early first millennium AD led to the growth of many large settlements along rivers and at waterholes even before AD 600. It is unclear whether state formation was a response to urbanization or a cause of it, but the west African states grew out of amalgamations of smaller units – chiefdoms with populations of between two and ten thousand people, which dominated areas no more that 30–50 kilometers (20–30 miles) across and were often centered on a single large settlement. These units did not lose their identities in the early states but remained the focus for local loyalties.

The first west African state about which any substantial information exists is the empire of Mali. Arising in the 13th century, Mali centered on fertile farmlands on the inland delta of the upper Niger and controlled access to rich goldfields. Its government and army, which included a strong cavalry element, were strongly influenced by the Muslim states of north Africa. Trans-Saharan trade by camel caravan played an important part in the economy of Mali. Cities such as Koumbi Saleh and Timbuktu at the southern termini of the caravan routes grew rapidly to be centers where African slaves, ivory and gold were exchanged for salt, cloth, glass, ceramics, horses and other luxuries from the north. By 1500 Songhai, another cavalry state, had supplanted Mali as the chief west African power. By 1300 small states such as Benin were developing in the west African forest. State formation here is presumed to have had internal causes: contact with the Sahelian states and, later, the Portuguese was too fleeting to be decisive.

Trade was vital to the growth of city-states on the east African coast. These cities were founded before the arrival of Islam by local Bantu-speaking peoples, perhaps to exploit trade links with the Mediterranean, Middle East and India that had existed since Classical times. Islam was brought by Arab merchants in about AD 1000, yet despite strong cultural influence (such as literacy and stone architecture), no large scale immigration occurred.

States had also begun to emerge in southern Africa by 1500. From about AD 1000, many small chiefdoms had developed between the Zambezi and Limpopo rivers. As cattle formed the basis of the region's wealth, competition over grazing rights possibly led to state formation, and by the 13th century Great Zimbabwe was predominant. Its imposing stone architecture was unequalled in sub-Saharan Africa at the time. Yet as power shifted north to the emerging state of Mwenemutapa in about 1450, Great Zimbabwe declined.

The oldest states in sub-Saharan Africa in 600 were the Christian states in Nubia and Ethiopia. Makkura, the strongest Nubian state, conquered its neighbor Nobatia in the 8th century but finally succumbed to Arab pressure in the 14th century. Another, Alwa, survived until 1505 when it was conquered by an alliance of Arabs and the southern Funj people. By 600 the Ethiopian kingdom of Axum was in decline and the city of Axum itself was abandoned. The last traces of the state survived until 975 when they were destroyed by pagan invaders from the southeast, and through them Christianity survived in the highlands. By the 12th century a successor state, the kingdom of Ethiopia, had emerged around Lalibela. Under the Solomonid dynasty (1270–1777), Ethiopia expanded, bringing most of the Ethiopian highlands under its control by the 15th century and often exacting tribute from its Muslim neighbors.

1 Cruciform churches of solid rock, such as that at Lalibela (c.1300), are the most important monuments of the medieval Ethiopian kingdom.

2 In c.1400, Great Zimbabwe had a population of between 5,000 and 18,000: its Great Enclosure was the largest stone building in sub-Saharan Africa.

3 Cemetery of Mecca-oriented burials with rich grave goods from Persia, Egypt and China indicates settlement by Muslim traders by the 10th–13th centuries.

4 Under the Songhais in the 15th century, Timbuktu became the main center of Islamic culture in west Africa and of trade in salt, gold, ivory and slaves.

5 A fortress was built in 1482 by the Portuguese to protect their trade in gold from Spanish interference: the coast became known as Elmina, "the mine".

6 To mark where they had been, Portuguese explorers built stone columns ("mariners' milestones") with their country's arms and the date of arrival.

SCULPTURES of chieftains and kings were made in bronze and terracotta at Ife, west Africa, from the 12th century.

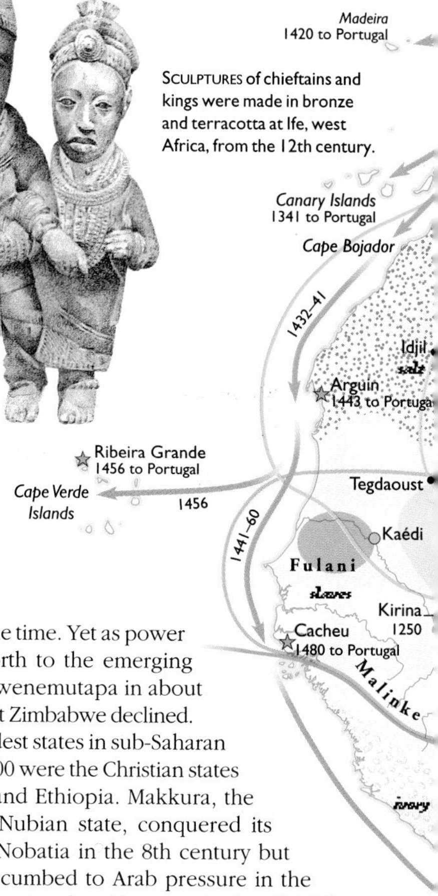

TIMELINE

	600–900	900–1200	1200–1500
West	**c.700** Foundation of the kingdom of Ghana **738** The Arabs raid west Africa for slaves **c.750** Trans-Saharan trade begins to increase	**c.1000** Islam becomes established in west Africa **1056–94** Yahya ibn Masa creates the Sanhaja Berber Almoravid emirate **c.1076** Ghana is invaded by the Almoravids	**c.1250** The empire of Malinke becomes the predominant state of west Africa **c.1250** Founding of kingdom of Benin **c.1260–77** Mansa Uli, king of Mali, makes the pilgrimage to Mecca (*hajj*) **c.1400** The lost-wax bronze casting technique introduced to west Africa **1432** Portuguese navigators begin the exploration of the west African coast **1464** Sanni Ali makes Songhai the leading power in west Africa
East and south	**c.800** Trading towns are founded on the east African coast, including Kilwa Kisiwani	**c.1000** Islamic influence begins at Kilwa	**c.1200** Construction of the Great Enclosure at Zimbabwe **c.1200** The first coinage in east Africa is issued at Kilwa **c.1450** Great Zimbabwe is superseded by Mwenemutapa **1490** Portuguese convert King Nzinga Nkuwu of Congo to Christianity
Northeast	**652** The first Islamic Arab invasion of Makkura	**c.975** Pagan invaders destroy kingdom of Axum	**1270** Solomonid dynasty comes to power in Ethiopia **1317** Muslim Arab nomads destroy kingdom of Makkura **1415** Ethiopians kill the Muslim ruler of Saylac

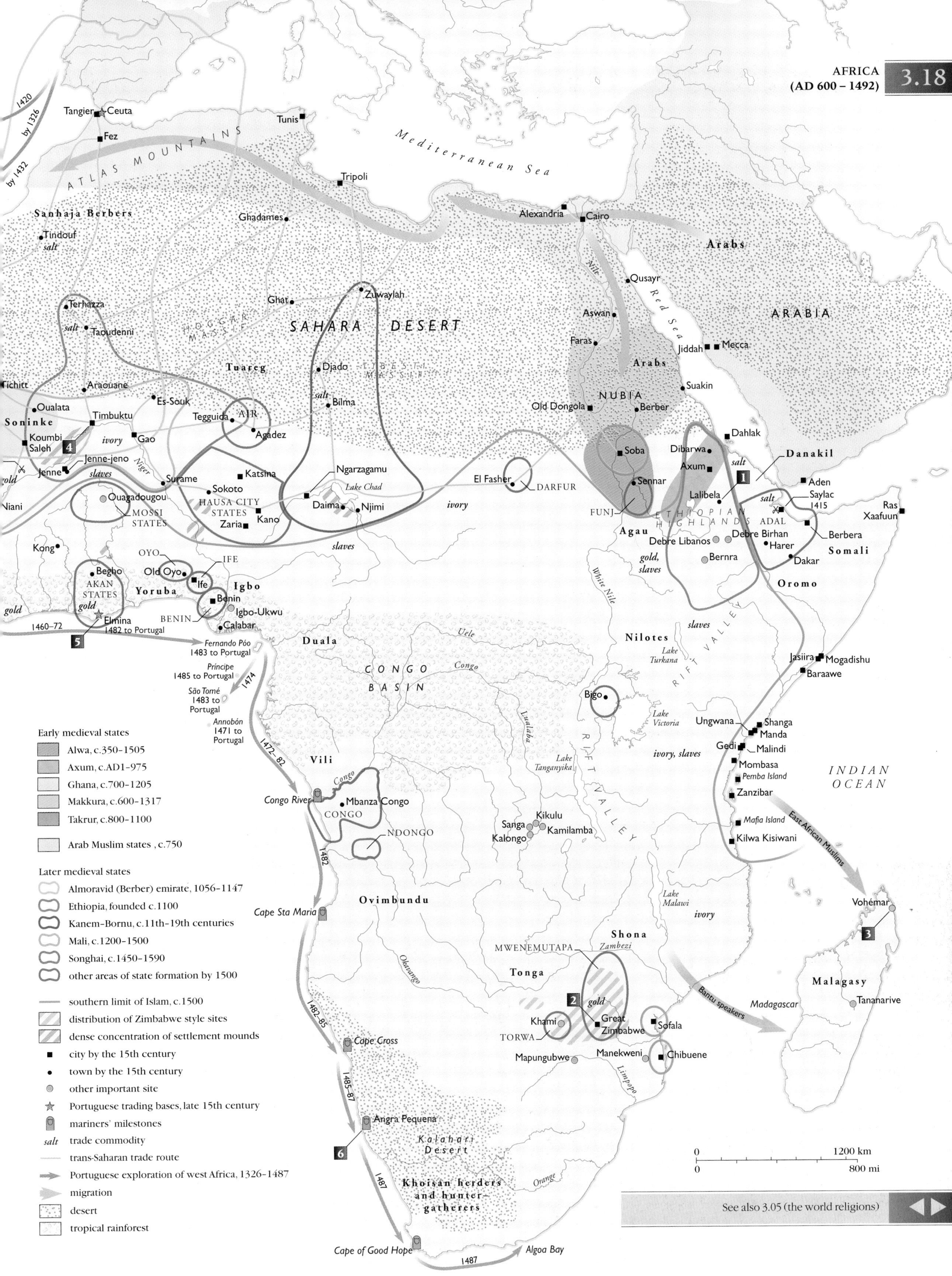

by 1326
by 1432
1420

Tangier Ceuta
Fez
Tunis

Mediterranean Sea

ATLAS MOUNTAINS

Tripoli

Alexandria Cairo

Arabs

Sanhaja Berbers

Tindouf
salt

Ghadames

Ghat

Zuwaylah

SAHARA DESERT

Qusayr

Nile

ARABIA

Terhazza
salt Taoudenni
Tichitt
Araouane

HOGGAR MASSIF

Aswan

Red Sea

Jiddah Mecca

Soninke
Oualata
Koumbi
Saleh **4**
Timbuktu
ivory Gao
Jenne-jeno

gold

Jenne

Niani

Kong

Tuareg

Es-Souk
Teggida AÏR
Agadez

Djado

salt Bilma

TIBESTI MASSIF

Faras

Old Dongola Berber

NUBIA

Suakin

Dahlak

Dibarwa
Soba Axum
salt

Danakil

Aden
Saylac
1415

Ras
Xaafuun

Niger
slaves
Surame
Katsina
Sokoto
Zaria Kano

Ngarzagamu

El Fasher DARFUR

Lake Chad
Daima Njimi

HAUSA CITY
STATES

Ougadougou
MOSSI
STATES

OYO
Old Oyo
Ife IFE
Begho
AKAN
STATES **Yoruba**
gold Elmina
1460–72 1482 to Portugal

5

Igbo
Benin
Igbo-Ukwu
BENIN Calabar

ivory

slaves

Sennar Lalibela
FUNJ
Agau ETHIOPIAN
HIGHLANDS ADAL
Debre Libanos
Debre Birhan
Bernra
Harer
Dakar

Somali

Oromo

*gold,
slaves*

slaves

Berbera

RIFT VALLEY

Duala

Fernando Póo
1483 to Portugal

Príncipe
1485 to Portugal
São Tomé
1483 to
Portugal
Annobón
1471 to
Portugal

1474

CONGO
BASIN

Uele
Congo

Nilotes

Lake
Turkana

Jasiira Mogadishu
Baraawe

INDIAN
OCEAN

White Nile

Bigo

Lake
Victoria

Ungwana Shanga
Gedi Manda
Malindi
Mombasa
Pemba Island
Zanzibar

ivory, slaves

East African Muslims

1472–82

Vili

CONGO

Congo

Mbanza Congo

Congo River

NDONGO

Lualaba

Lake
Tanganyika

Kikulu
Sanga Kamilamba
Kalongo
Kikulu

Mafia Island
Kilwa Kisiwani

Cape Sta Maria

1482

Ovimbundu

Okavango

Lake
Malawi

ivory

Vohémar

3

Malagasy

Tananarive

1485–87

Cape Cross

Angra Pequena

6

Kalahari
Desert

*Kalahari
Desert*

Khoisan herders
and hunter-
gatherers

Cape of Good Hope

1487

Algoa Bay

1487

Shona

MWENEMUTAPA Zambezi

Tonga

2 *gold*

Khami
TORWA
Mapungubwe

Great
Zimbabwe Sofala

Manekweni Chibuene

Limpopo

Orange

Bantu speakers

Madagascar

Early medieval states

▨	Alwa, c.350–1505
▨	Axum, c.AD1–975
▨	Ghana, c.700–1205
▨	Makkura, c.600–1317
▨	Takrur, c.800–1100
▢	Arab Muslim states , c.750

Later medieval states

- Almoravid (Berber) emirate, 1056–1147
- Ethiopia, founded c.1100
- Kanem–Bornu, c.11th–19th centuries
- Mali, c.1200–1500
- Songhai, c.1450–1590
- other areas of state formation by 1500

— southern limit of Islam, c.1500

▨ distribution of Zimbabwe style sites

▨ dense concentration of settlement mounds

■ city by the 15th century

● town by the 15th century

◉ other important site

★ Portuguese trading bases, late 15th century

⬗ mariners' milestones

salt trade commodity

— trans-Saharan trade route

➤ Portuguese exploration of west Africa, 1326–1487

➤ migration

⣿ desert

⣿ tropical rainforest

0 1200 km
0 800 mi

See also 3.05 (the world religions)

3.19 Medieval India • 600 – 1500 •

At the beginning of the 7th century the most powerful Indian kingdom was Kanauj, which dominated the Gangetic plain. Shortly after his ascending the throne of the minor kingdom of Thaneswar, Harsha also became king of Kanauj and began a career of conquest that united most of northern India under his rule. However, Harsha's attempt to conquer the Deccan was defeated in 633 by the Chalukyas, the dominant power of central India. Harsha's empire fell apart after he was murdered in 647; no other northern ruler would again attempt to conquer the south until the 13th century.

For the 600 years after the fall of Harsha's empire, the history of India is dominated by the rise and fall of regional kingdoms and short-lived dynasties. Regional wars were frequent; however, because the main kingdoms were roughly comparable in wealth, population, military strength and tactics, a balance of power existed that precluded the formation of supraregional states. The period saw a strong revival of Hinduism and a commensurate decline of Buddhism throughout India with the exception of Ceylon. Hinduism also began to replace Buddhism in much of southeast Asia, largely through the influence of the Tamil kingdom of the Cholas, a major mercantile and naval power.

The entire period from 700 to 1500 was dominated by the spread of Islam as a cultural and political force. Introduced into India by the Arabs, who conquered Sind and Multan in the early 8th century, Islam's advance under the Arabs was halted by the Gurjara-Pratiharas, a military Rajput dynasty that had become the main power in the north after the fall of Harsha's empire. However, in 1000 the militant Muslim ruler Mahmud of Ghazni (r.999–1030) launched the first of his 17 invasions of India. Mahmud broke the power of the Gurjara-Pratiharas and the Chandellas but only incorporated the Punjab into his empire, as his main concern was with plunder, and with despoiling Hindu temples. After Mahmud's death the Ghaznavid emirate declined and for 150 years there was no further Islamic advance in India. In 1151 the Ghaznavids were overthrown by the governor of Ghur. From 1175 onwards, Muhammad of Ghur (r.1173–1206) made a concerted effort to conquer northern India. Following his victory over a confederation of Rajput rulers at the second battle of Tarain in 1192, Hindu resistance began to crumble. By 1200 he was master of the Indus and Gangetic plains and had laid the foundations for 600 years of Muslim dominance in India. Muhammad's victory was the result of both Muslim strength and Hindu weakness. The Muslim army was a professional force of disciplined and highly mobile horse archers. Many Muslim soldiers were slaves, trained for battle from childhood, but a military career was open to all – unlike in the Hindu states – and rapid advancement was possible for anyone who showed ability, enslaved or free. Also, the Muslims were invading a country rich in plunder, and were further motivated by religious fervor.

On the death of Muhammad in 1206 the Turkish slave-general Qutb-ud-Din broke away from the Ghurid empire, founding an independent sultanate at Delhi. Qutb-ud-Din faced widespread Hindu rebellions and his successor Iltutmish (r.1211–36) consolidated the Muslim conquest of northern India. Qutb-ud-Din's dynasty was overthrown in 1290 by the Khalji dynasty (1290–1320). Under the second Khalji ruler Ala-ud-Din, the sultanate's control was extended south of the Narmada river in the Deccan. The sultanate reached its greatest territorial extent under Muhammad ibn Tughluk (d.1351). Determined to make the whole of the Deccan an integral part of the Delhi sultanate, he transferred his center of government to the massive hilltop fortress of Daulatabad in central India but by moving away from Delhi he lost control of the north while failing to consolidate his hold on the south. Muhammad was forced to return to Delhi to restore order, leaving the Deccan in the charge of a governor, Hasan Gungu, who revolted in 1347 to establish the independent Bahmani sultanate. At the same time the Hindu kingdom of Vijayanagara started to establish

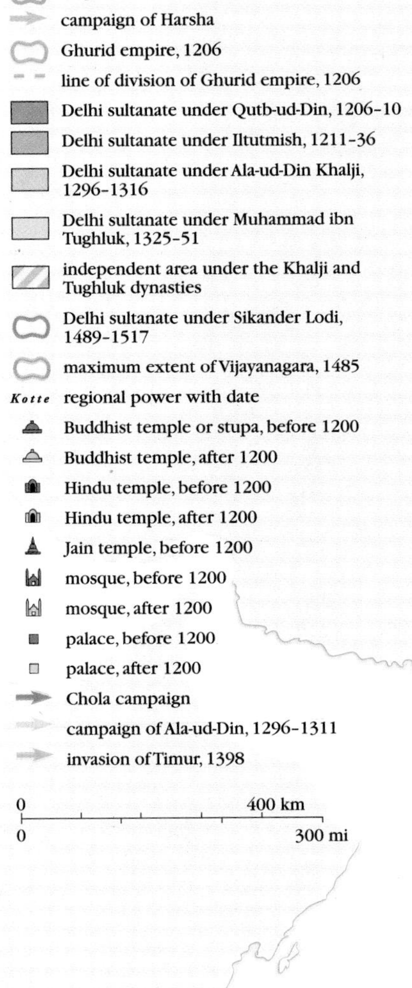

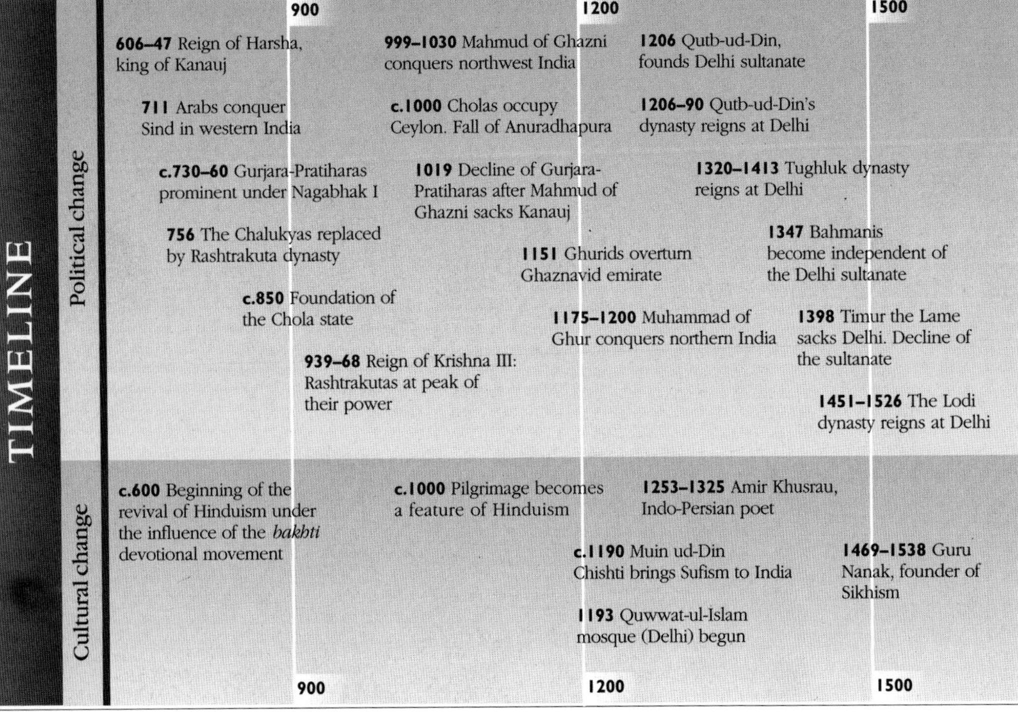

TIMELINE
Political change
900
1200
1500
606–47 Reign of Harsha, king of Kanauj
711 Arabs conquer Sind in western India
c.730–60 Gurjara-Pratiharas prominent under Nagabhak I
756 The Chalukyas replaced by Rashtrakuta dynasty
c.850 Foundation of the Chola state
939–68 Reign of Krishna III: Rashtrakutas at peak of their power
999–1030 Mahmud of Ghazni conquers northwest India
c.1000 Cholas occupy Ceylon. Fall of Anuradhapura
1019 Decline of Gurjara-Pratiharas after Mahmud of Ghazni sacks Kanauj
1151 Ghurids overturn Ghaznavid emirate
1175–1200 Muhammad of Ghur conquers northern India
1206 Qutb-ud-Din, founds Delhi sultanate
1206–90 Qutb-ud-Din's dynasty reigns at Delhi
1320–1413 Tughluk dynasty reigns at Delhi
1347 Bahmanis become independent of the Delhi sultanate
1398 Timur the Lame sacks Delhi. Decline of the sultanate
1451–1526 The Lodi dynasty reigns at Delhi
Cultural change
c.600 Beginning of the revival of Hinduism under the influence of the *bakhti* devotional movement
c.1000 Pilgrimage becomes a feature of Hinduism
c.1190 Muin ud-Din Chishti brings Sufism to India
1193 Quwwat-ul-Islam mosque (Delhi) begun
1253–1325 Amir Khusrau, Indo-Persian poet
1469–1538 Guru Nanak, founder of Sikhism
900
1200
1500

1 Harsha's attempt to capture the Deccan in 633 was decisively repulsed by the Chalukyas.

2 The complex of over 20 Hindu and Jain temples of the 9th–11th centuries at Khajuraho is virtually the sole relic of the powerful Chandella kingdom.

3 Delhi was a minor fortress town until Qutb-ud-Din, its first sultan, adopted it as his capital.

4 The Cholas were the dominant south Indian power in the 10th and 11th centuries, with a major naval and trading empire. The kingdom survived until 1279.

5 Two battles fought at Tarain 1191 and 1192 between the Rajputs and Muhammad of Ghur were followed by the Muslim conquest of northern India.

6 Buddhism, long in decline in India, was finally extinguished when the Ghurids destroyed the university at Nalanda in 1199.

7 The ruins of Vijayanagara ("city of victory"), capital of the largest Hindu state from the 14th century onward, cover some 25 sq km (9 sq miles).

8 Daulatabad, a massive hilltop fortress and walled city, was chosen by Muhammad Tughluk as a new capital in the Deccan in 1339.

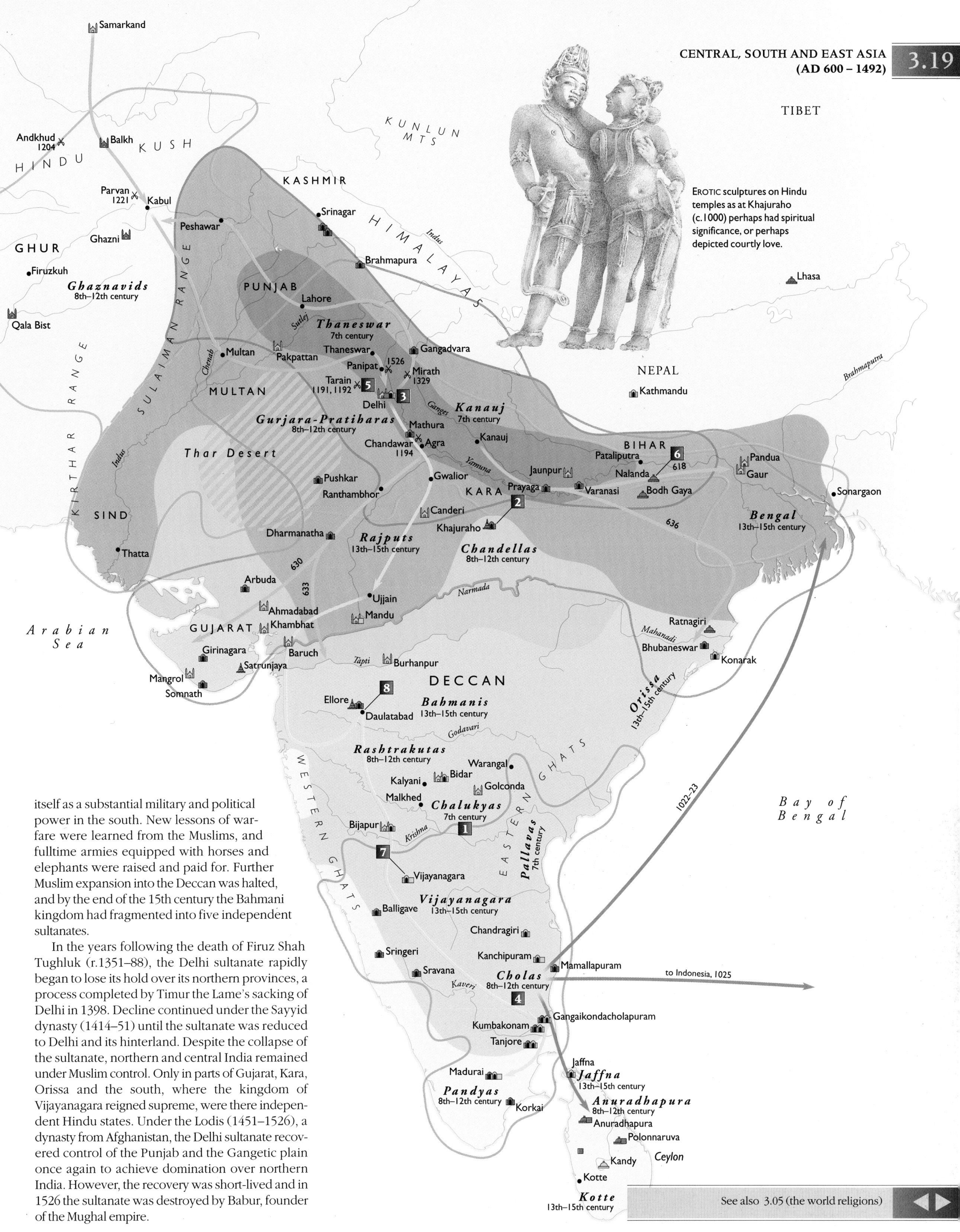

EROTIC sculptures on Hindu temples as at Khajuraho (c.1000) perhaps had spiritual significance, or perhaps depicted courtly love.

itself as a substantial military and political power in the south. New lessons of warfare were learned from the Muslims, and fulltime armies equipped with horses and elephants were raised and paid for. Further Muslim expansion into the Deccan was halted, and by the end of the 15th century the Bahmani kingdom had fragmented into five independent sultanates.

In the years following the death of Firuz Shah Tughluk (r.1351–88), the Delhi sultanate rapidly began to lose its hold over its northern provinces, a process completed by Timur the Lame's sacking of Delhi in 1398. Decline continued under the Sayyid dynasty (1414–51) until the sultanate was reduced to Delhi and its hinterland. Despite the collapse of the sultanate, northern and central India remained under Muslim control. Only in parts of Gujarat, Kara, Orissa and the south, where the kingdom of Vijayanagara reigned supreme, were there independent Hindu states. Under the Lodis (1451–1526), a dynasty from Afghanistan, the Delhi sultanate recovered control of the Punjab and the Gangetic plain once again to achieve domination over northern India. However, the recovery was short-lived and in 1526 the sultanate was destroyed by Babur, founder of the Mughal empire.

See also 3.05 (the world religions)

3.20 Sui and Tang China • 589 – 907 •

The centralized Chinese empire created by Shi Huangdi survived until AD 220, when it split into three rival states. Unity was restored in 589 by Yang Jian, who as emperor Wen (r.589–604) became the founder of the Sui dynasty. Wen, a tyrannical but able ruler, re-established a strong centralized bureaucracy and increased the prosperity of the peasantry through a land redistribution scheme. Granaries were built and the canal system expanded. As a result of Wen's reforms, the economy grew rapidly and the state amassed large reserves of cash and commodities. These were squandered by Wen's successor Yang (r.604–17) on building projects and opulent court life. Moreover, a disastrous war against the Korean kingdom of Koguryo caused the peasants of the northeast to rebel. The empire was saved only by the coup of Li Yuan, military governor of Taiyuan, who captured the Sui capital at Luoyang in 617 and became, after Yang's murder in 618, the first emperor of the Tang dynasty (as Gaozu, r.618– 26). Gaozong was then deposed by his son Taizong (r.626–49), one of Chinese history's ablest rulers.

Taizong based his government loosely on the Han model but without the feudal elements. At its head was the emperor, whose authority (in theory if not always in practice) was absolute. The central administration consisted of three bodies, the Imperial Chancellery, the Imperial Secretariat and the Department for State Affairs. This latter department supervised the six ministries – officials, finances, religious rites, the army, justice and public works – while a Board of Censors oversaw the actions of officials. The empire was divided into 15 administrative regions or "circuits", under an inspecting commissioner. The examination system became more important for selecting bureaucratic staff, yet the cost of education precluded all but the rich landowning classes from pursuing a career in administration.

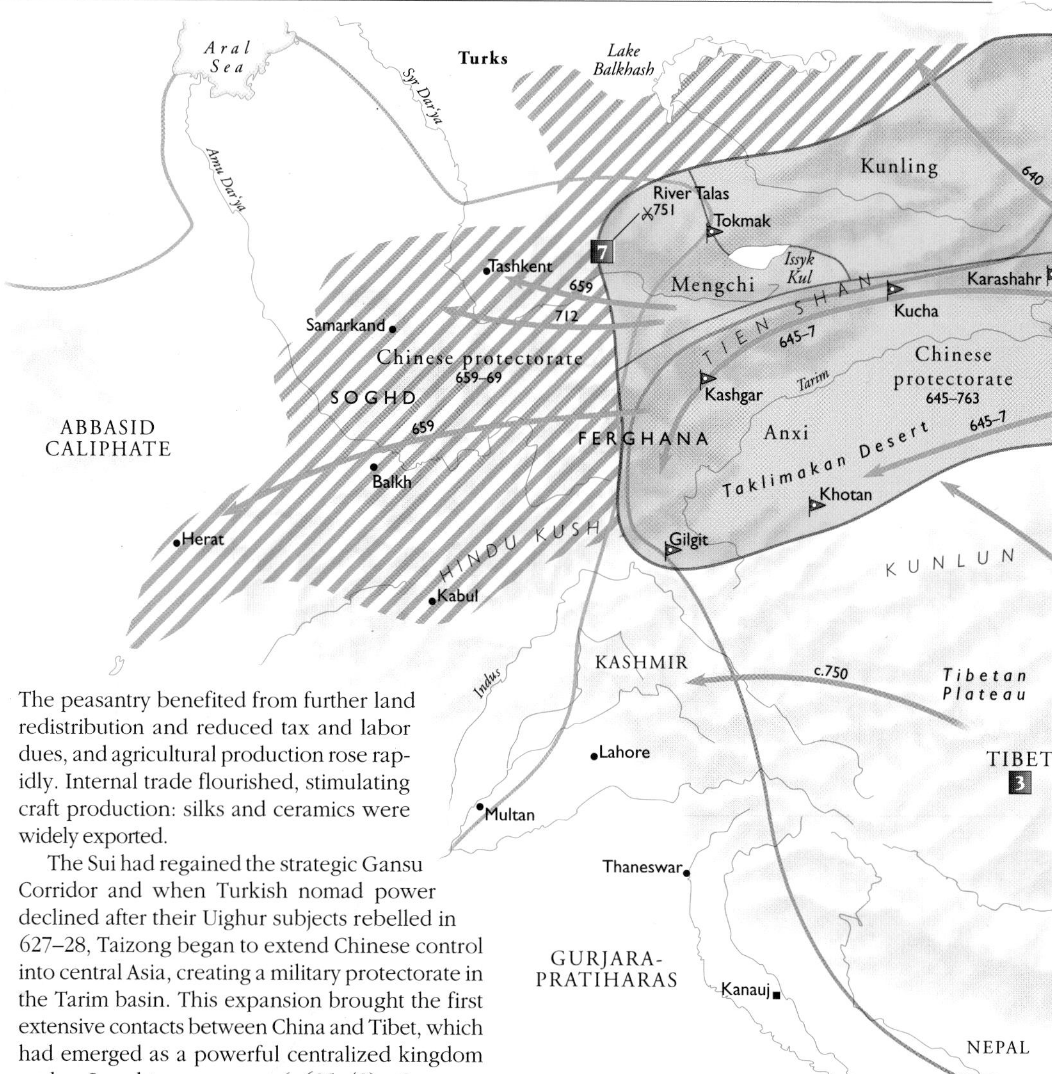

The peasantry benefited from further land redistribution and reduced tax and labor dues, and agricultural production rose rapidly. Internal trade flourished, stimulating craft production: silks and ceramics were widely exported.

The Sui had regained the strategic Gansu Corridor and when Turkish nomad power declined after their Uighur subjects rebelled in 627–28, Taizong began to extend Chinese control into central Asia, creating a military protectorate in the Tarim basin. This expansion brought the first extensive contacts between China and Tibet, which had emerged as a powerful centralized kingdom under Sron-btsan-sgampo (r.605–49). Gaozong

TIMELINE

700 800 900

Political change

589 Yang Jian unites China and founds Sui dynasty

c. 600 Emergence of Tibet and Nan Chao states

611–14 A Sui attempt to conquer Koguryo defeated with heavy loss

618 Li Yuan becomes the first emperor of the Tang dynasty

640–59 The Chinese expand into central Asia

676 Silla becomes the leading Korean kingdom

751 Arab victory over the Tang at the River Talas

755–63 Rebellion of An Lushan leads to breakdown of central administration

780 Collapse of the kingdom of Silla

791 Chinese lose control of Gansu corridor after defeat of Chinese–Uighur army by Tibetans at Tingzhou

874–84 Major peasant rebellions: decline of the Tang dynasty

907–60 The Five Dynasties and Ten Kingdoms

907 Final collapse of the Tang dynasty

936 Foundation of the kingdom of Koryo (Korea)

939 Annam becomes independent of China

960–79 Song Taizu and Song taizong reunite China

Cultural change

606–09 The Grand Canal from Beijing to Yue is built

635 Nestorian Christian missionaries reach China

c. 700–800 Earliest text produced by block printing

c. 701–761 Life of the poet Li Po

713–68 Life of the poet Du Fu

780 Lu Yu's *The Classic of Tea* describes tea use

c.825 Chamber lock in use on Chinese canals

845 Persecution of non-Chinese religions including Buddhism and Christianity

c.850 Possible earliest use of gunpowder

700 800 900

border, 750
"circuits" of Tang empire, 742
civil administration
military government
temporary expansion, 7th century
Abbasid caliphate, c.751
maximum extent of Tibetan kingdom, c.800
capital
seat of circuit-inspecting commissioner, 742
seat of government-general, 800
Chinese garrison
non-Chinese capital
outbreak of An Lushan's rebellion, 755
other rebellion against the Tang
concentration of pottery kilns
Sui campaign
Tang campaign
Tibetan expansion
frontier wall
major migration
major canal
modern coastline and drainage where altered

0 800 km
0 500 mi

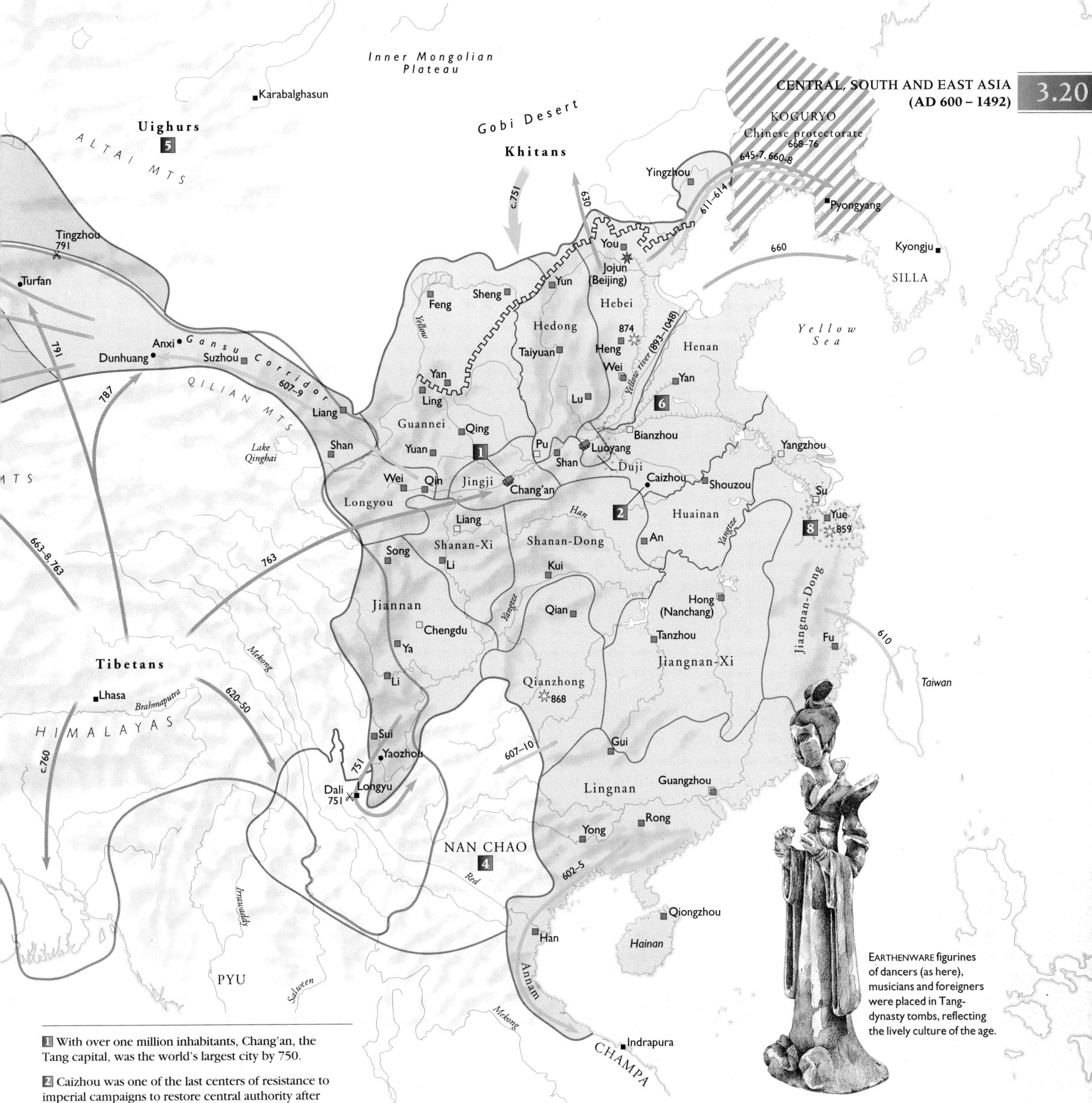

EARTHENWARE figurines of dancers (as here), musicians and foreigners were placed in Tang-dynasty tombs, reflecting the lively culture of the age.

1 With over one million inhabitants, Chang'an, the Tang capital, was the world's largest city by 750.

2 Caizhou was one of the last centers of resistance to imperial campaigns to restore central authority after An Lushan's rebellion. It fell in 817.

3 Tibet emerged as a united kingdom c.600 and reached its greatest extent c.800.

4 Nan Chao, a Thai kingdom in modern Yunnan province, emerged c.600.

5 The Uighurs were a Turkic nomad tribe allied with the Chinese against the Turks and Tibetans.

6 The canal system linked the grain-producing Yangtze valley with the political center of the empire and the northern frontier zone.

7 The decisive battle at the River Talas, which led to the fall of China's central Asian empire, followed an appeal to the Arabs from the ruler of Tashkent for protection against the Chinese.

8 The first true porcelain was made in eastern China during the Tang period.

(r.649–83) brought Ferghana and Soghd under Chinese control in 659. However, these conquests overextended the empire and they were lost by 665. In the east, the Chinese subdued Koguryo in 668 but the Korean kingdom of Silla expelled them in 676.

The Chinese position in central Asia was dealt further blows in 751, with defeats by the Arabs at the River Talas and by the Thai kingdom of Nan Chao at Dali. The Mongol Khitan nomads emerged as a threat in the north in the 8th century. At home, landlord–peasant conflict increased, and the emperors from Gaozong onward proved ineffectual. A rebellion of the general An Lushan in 755 threatened the Tang; it was suppressed in 763 but central authority did not recover and power devolved to around forty semi-independent military governments-general. In 791 the empire lost control of the Gansu Corridor to the Tibetans following their victory over a Chinese and Uighur army at Tingzhou. In 859, 868 and 874–84 peasant rebellions broke out. The emperor's authority was damaged beyond repair and power was again seized by provincial warlords. The Tang struggled on until 907, finally collapsing in a period of disunity known as the Five Dynasties and Ten Kingdoms (907–960).

The Tang period is regarded as the golden age of Chinese poetry. The dynasty also presided over major achievements in historiography and painting, and restored Confucianism as the state ideology after it had declined during the Period of Disunion.

See also 3.05 (the world religions); 3.21 (the Song dynasty)

.21 Song China • 907 – 1279 •

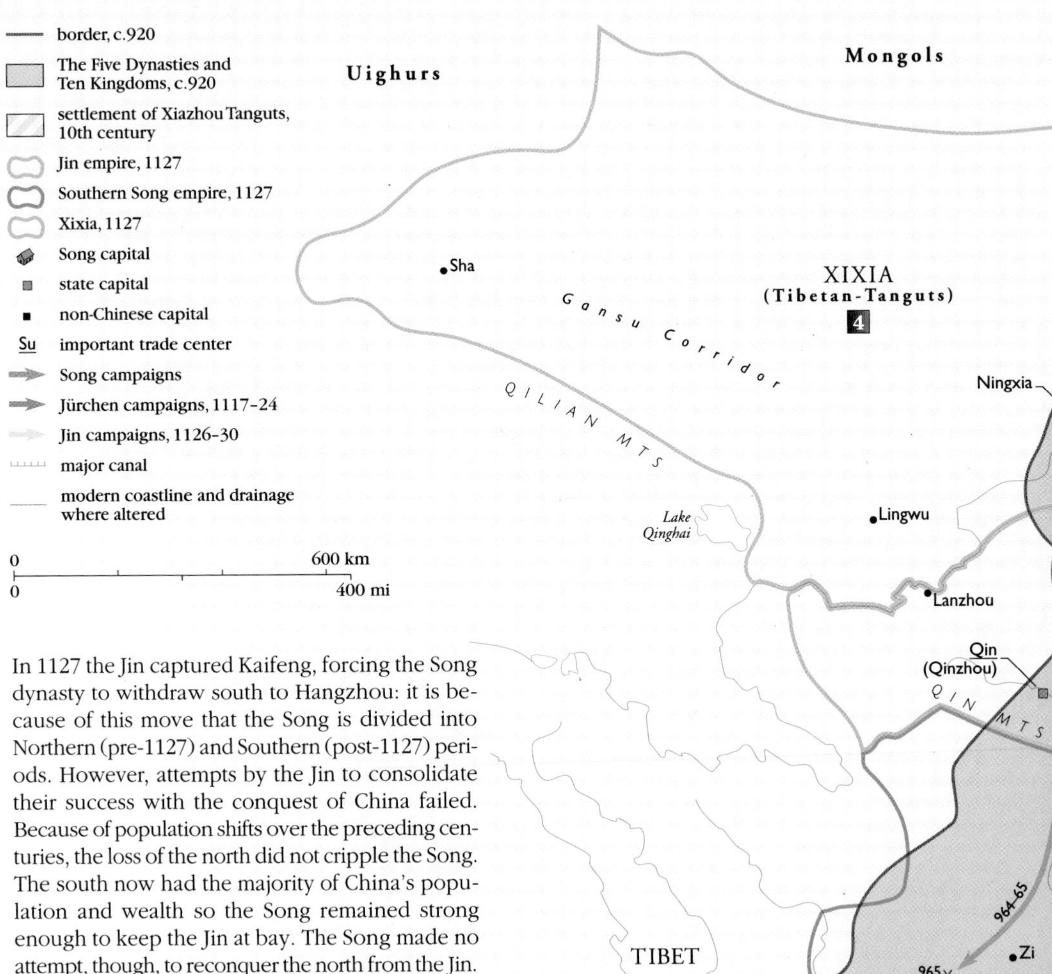

The disunity of the Five Dynasties and Ten Kingdoms period began to come to an end when Song Taizu (r.960–76) overthrew the last of the Five Dynasties, which had ruled the Yellow River valley since 907, in a military coup. Taizu skillfully consolidated his hold on power by bringing the military under effective civilian political control and in 963 he began a series of diplomatic and military campaigns to reunify China. This process was completed by his equally able brother Song Taizong (r.976–97), so creating the third Chinese empire. In accomplishing this, the Song benefited from the idea of China as an indivisible state, which had become established under the Tang. Only in Taiyuan, which had the support of the nomadic Khitans, and Houshu did the Song meet determined resistance, while Wuyue was secured through diplomacy alone. However, the Song were not able to restore the borders of the Tang empire and its authority was confined to areas of ethnic Chinese settlement. Unlike the Tang, the Song empire was surrounded by well-organized states that effectively blocked Chinese expansion.

The most powerful of these states was the Khitan Liao kingdom. The Khitans were a Turko-Mongol nomadic people, who had won control of the northern Chinese plains in 916 and went on to dominate the eastern steppes. Taizong attempted to drive the Khitans back to the steppes in 979 but was badly defeated near Beijing. A Khitan attack on the Song capital Kaifeng in 1004 was bought off for a heavy annual tribute of silver, silk and tea and thereafter relations between Song and Liao were peaceful. The Khitans adopted Chinese administrative practices to govern their kingdom and by the end of the 11th century they had become thoroughly assimilated. In 1114 the Jürchen people of Manchuria broke off payments of tribute to the Khitans and three years later launched an invasion of Liao, which collapsed in 1124. The Song initially supported the Jürchen attack on Liao but when the Jürchen created their own state under the Jin dynasty they found themselves faced with an even more formidable enemy.

In 1127 the Jin captured Kaifeng, forcing the Song dynasty to withdraw south to Hangzhou: it is because of this move that the Song is divided into Northern (pre-1127) and Southern (post-1127) periods. However, attempts by the Jin to consolidate their success with the conquest of China failed. Because of population shifts over the preceding centuries, the loss of the north did not cripple the Song. The south now had the majority of China's population and wealth so the Song remained strong enough to keep the Jin at bay. The Song made no attempt, though, to reconquer the north from the Jin.

Less powerful than Liao but a more serious obstacle to Chinese expansion was the kingdom of Xixia, which dominated the Gansu corridor, shutting the Song out of central Asia. Xixia was founded in the late 10th century by the Xiazhou clan of the nomadic Tangut people. With a mixed Tangut, Tibetan and Chinese population, it never became as sinicized as Liao. In the south the Thai kingdom of Nan Chao and the Viet kingdom of Annam blocked expansion.

Unlike the previous Chinese imperial dynasties, the Song fell not as a result of internal rebellion but from outside aggression. The Mongol steppe nomads were unified at the beginning of the 13th century by Chingis Khan, who then turned on Xixia and Jin. The Song refused appeals by Jin for help and, repeating their earlier disastrous policy towards the Jürchen, even supplied the Mongols with much-needed troops who were skilled in siege warfare. When the Song tried to profit from the fall of Jin in 1234 by seizing Kaifeng and Luoyang, they simply caused the Mongols to turn on them. Song resistance to the Mongols was determined but swiftly collapsed after the capture of Hangzhou in 1276. The last Song emperor was drowned three years later following a naval battle off the island of Yaishan.

Although theirs was the smallest of the Chinese empires, the Song are regarded as one of the most capable and humane dynasties in Chinese history. The Song period was one of remarkable economic prosperity, technological innovation and rapid population growth, especially in the south, which experienced an influx of refugees from the Jin in the 12th century. Agricultural productivity was greatly increased by the introduction of Vietnamese strains

TIMELINE

1000 | 1100 | 1200

Northern Song period | Southern Song period

Political change

960 Song Taizu is declared emperor in the Five Dynasties state

963 Song Taizu begins the reunification of China

979 Song Taizong completes the reunification of China

1068–86 Minister Wang Anshi introduces unsuccessful land reform program

1117–24 Jürchen destroy Liao state and establish Jin empire

1127 Jin take Kaifeng. Song capital is moved to Hangzhou

1226 Xixia is destroyed by the Mongols

1234 Jin empire conquered by the Mongols. First Mongol attack on Southern Song

1279 Mongols conquer Southern Song empire

Cultural change

969 Gunpowder rockets are first used in warfare

c.1000 Rise of Song school of landscape painting

c.1000 Movable type printing is invented

c.1086 Scientist Shen Gua writes the *Dreampool Jottings*

1090 Water-driven mechanical clock built for Song court

1130–1200 Zhu Xi, neo-Confucian philosopher

1130 Paddle-wheel-driven ships are in use

1150 Chinese navigators use the magnetic compass

1259 Song forces use bamboo-tube firearms

c.1200 Chinese ships built with watertight bulkheads

c.1200 Waterpowered textile machinery is in use

1000 | 1100 | 1200

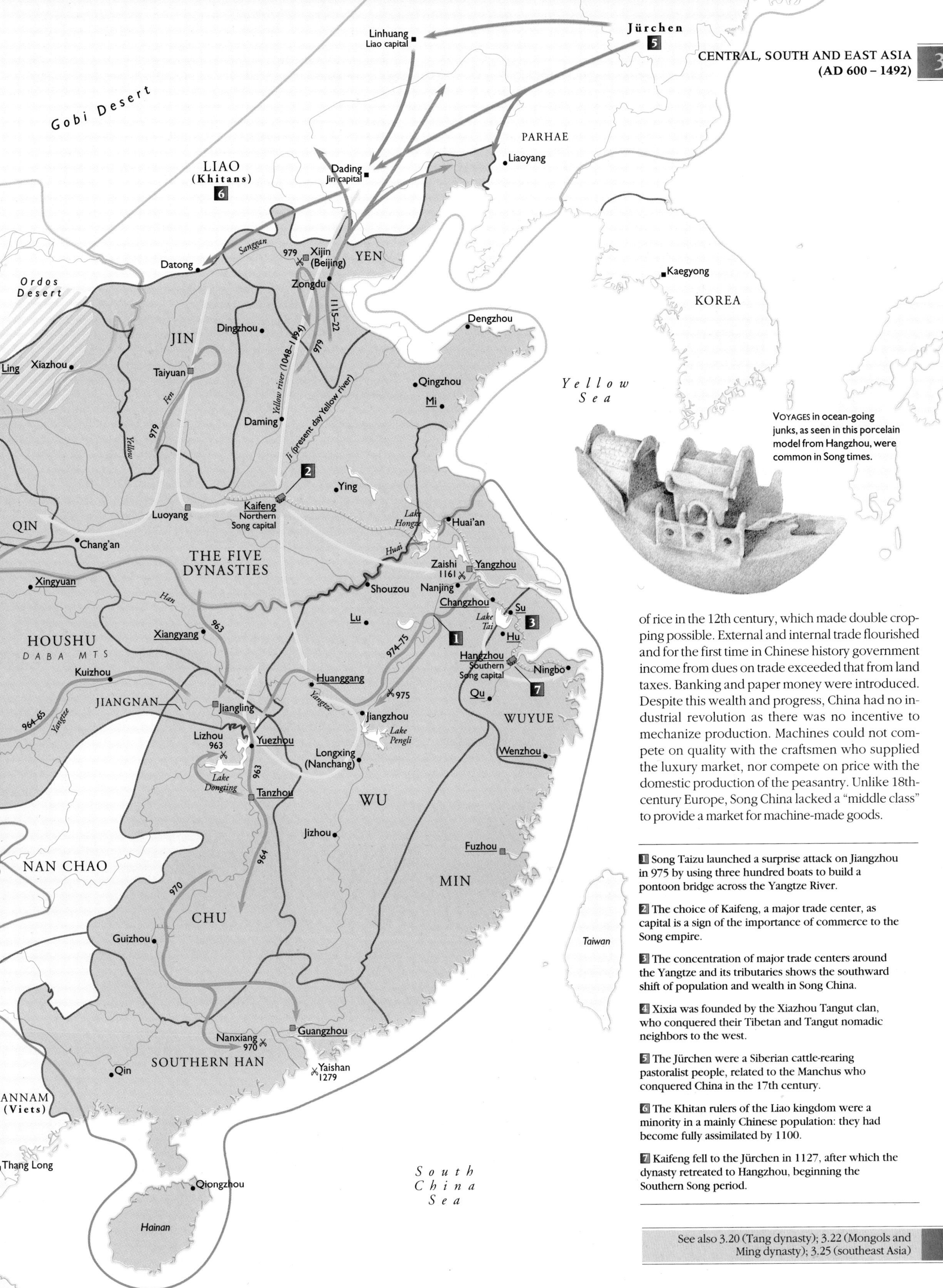

VOYAGES in ocean-going junks, as seen in this porcelain model from Hangzhou, were common in Song times.

of rice in the 12th century, which made double cropping possible. External and internal trade flourished and for the first time in Chinese history government income from dues on trade exceeded that from land taxes. Banking and paper money were introduced. Despite this wealth and progress, China had no industrial revolution as there was no incentive to mechanize production. Machines could not compete on quality with the craftsmen who supplied the luxury market, nor compete on price with the domestic production of the peasantry. Unlike 18th-century Europe, Song China lacked a "middle class" to provide a market for machine-made goods.

1 Song Taizu launched a surprise attack on Jiangzhou in 975 by using three hundred boats to build a pontoon bridge across the Yangtze River.

2 The choice of Kaifeng, a major trade center, as capital is a sign of the importance of commerce to the Song empire.

3 The concentration of major trade centers around the Yangtze and its tributaries shows the southward shift of population and wealth in Song China.

4 Xixia was founded by the Xiazhou Tangut clan, who conquered their Tibetan and Tangut nomadic neighbors to the west.

5 The Jürchen were a Siberian cattle-rearing pastoralist people, related to the Manchus who conquered China in the 17th century.

6 The Khitan rulers of the Liao kingdom were a minority in a mainly Chinese population: they had become fully assimilated by 1100.

7 Kaifeng fell to the Jürchen in 1127, after which the dynasty retreated to Hangzhou, beginning the Southern Song period.

See also 3.20 (Tang dynasty); 3.22 (Mongols and Ming dynasty); 3.25 (southeast Asia)

3.22 The creation of the Mongol empire • 1204 – 1260 •

The dramatic expansion of the Mongols that began under Temujin was the most important event in world history in the 13th century. The son of a minor Mongol chief, Temujin's brilliant leadership in inter-tribal warfare enabled him to unify the Mongol peoples in a ruthless two-year campaign.

To mark his success he was proclaimed Chingis ("universal") Khan in 1206. During his unification campaign, he created what has often been called the finest cavalry army that the world has ever seen. If the army was not to break up, and his khandom with it, he had to find work for it to do and wealth with which to reward it. He therefore adopted a policy of all-round aggression and by his death in 1227 he had conquered an empire that included most of central Asia and northern China.

His successors, his son Ogedai and grandsons Küyük and Möngke, continued his expansionist policy and by 1259 they had carried the Mongol conquests into Europe and the Middle East. In China only the southern Song empire stood out against the Mongols, though it too would fall within 20 years. However, Mongol unity was fragile and already the achievement of Chingis Khan had started to unravel.

The Mongol conquests formed the largest land empire in history. The achievement is all the more remarkable in that the Mongols had few governmental institutions and did not even possess basic metal-working skills. They were fortunate in being able to exploit existing disunity among their enemies: China was divided into three hostile kingdoms; the powerful Turkish empires of Kara-Khitai and Khwarizm were mutually hostile and had dynastic problems; and Russia, like most of Europe, was a mosaic of quarrelsome states which cooperated only reluctantly and ineffectually against the common enemy.

The key factor in the Mongol success, however, was the magnificent army that Chingis created. Unlike the armies of their opponents, where birth usually determined rank, promotion in the Mongol army was by merit only. The discipline and mobility of the Mongol army enabled it to execute complex battlefield maneuvers, giving it decisive advantages over any opponent. A frequent tactic was the feigned retreat, used to lure rash pursuers into ambushes on unfavorable ground where they could be destroyed. The Mongols had an excellent long-range weapon in the composite bow, which enabled them to inflict casualties while keeping out of danger themselves. The Mongols also committed horrific atrocities, systematically creating terror to sap their enemies' will to resist. This persuaded many Turks, Uighurs, Kipchaks and Chinese to defect to the Mongols rather than risk defeat.

The Mongol military machine had its limitations. Except in China, the boundaries of the Mongol empire were very close to those of the Eurasian

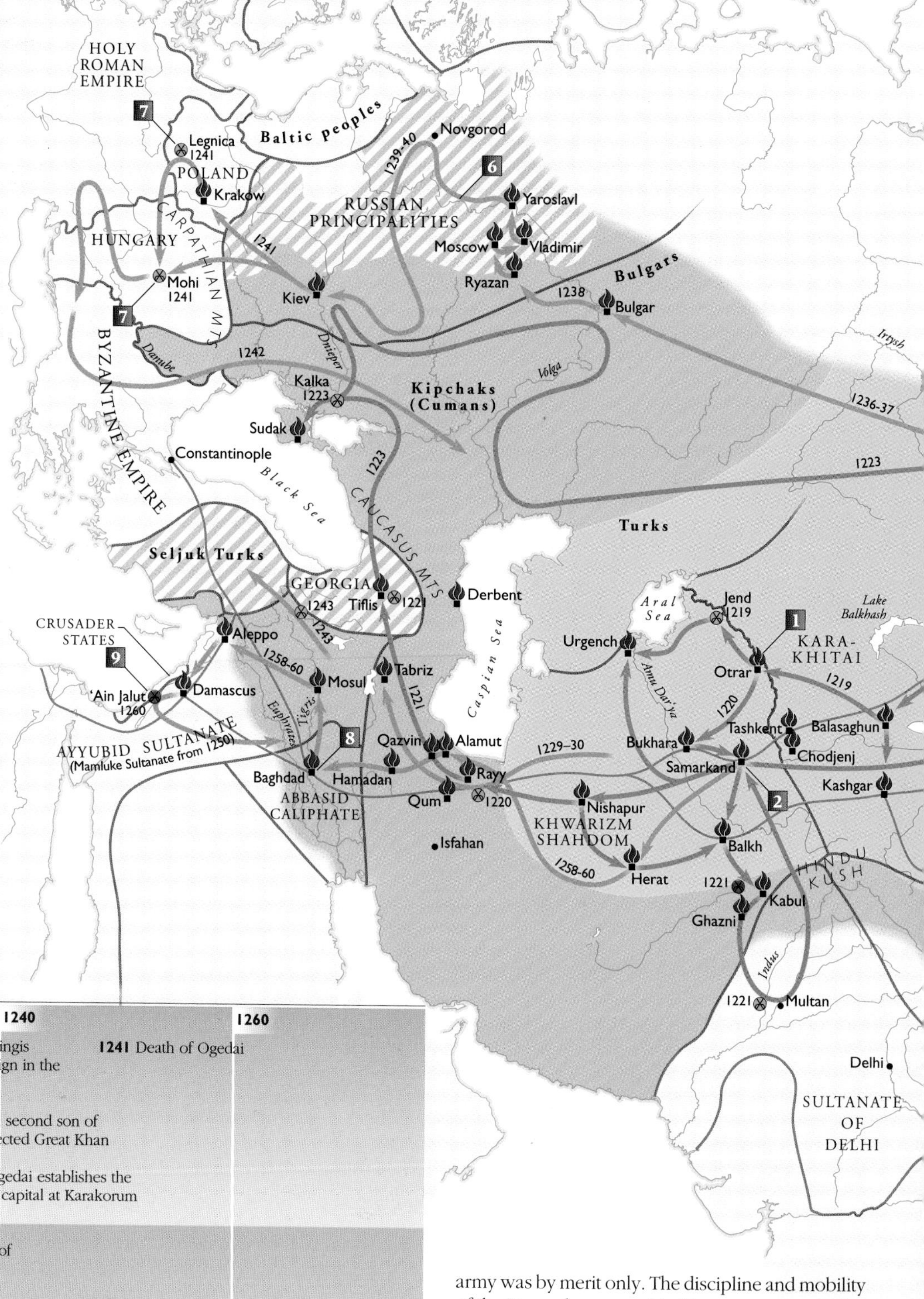

TIMELINE

The Mongol world

- **c1167** Birth of Temujin (Chingis Khan)
- **1204–06** Temujin unites the Mongol tribes and is proclaimed Chingis Khan
- **1227** Death of Chingis Khan on a campaign in the Jin empire
- **1229** Ogedai, second son of Chingis, is elected Great Khan
- **1235** Ogedai establishes the Mongol capital at Karakorum
- **1241** Death of Ogedai

Eastern conquests

- **1209** The Mongols attack Xixia and Uighurs
- **1211** The first Mongol attacks on China (Jin empire)
- **1215** The Mongols capture Dadu (Beijing)
- **1218** Kara-Khitai empire is conquered by the Mongols
- **1226** The conquest of Xixia is complete
- **1234** The Jin capital Kaifeng falls to the Mongols
- **1252** The conquest of the Song empire (southern China) begins

The West

- **1219–21** Chingis Khan invades Khwarizm shahdom
- **1220–23** Chingis Khan sends a force to Russia
- **1237–41** The Mongols invade Russia and eastern Europe
- **1258** Baghdad falls to the Mongols, and the last Abbasid caliph is executed
- **1260** The Mongols are defeated by the Mamlukes at 'Ain Jalut

1220 1240 1260

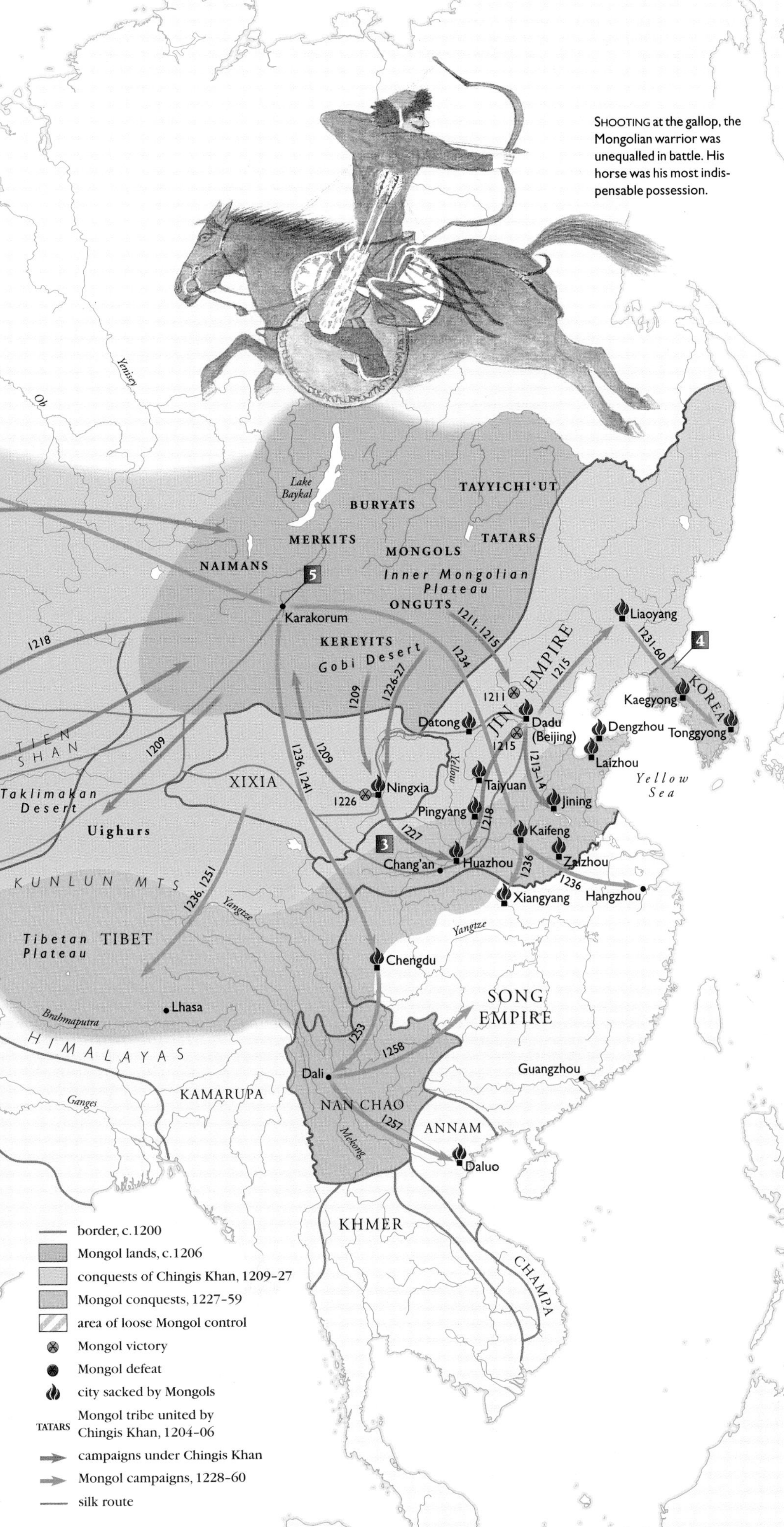

SHOOTING at the gallop, the Mongolian warrior was unequalled in battle. His horse was his most indispensable possession.

steppes and grasslands which alone could provide the necessary grazing for the vast herds of horses that accompanied every Mongol army. The defeat suffered by the Mongols at the hands of the Mamlukes at 'Ain Jalut in 1260 was to some extent the result of poor grazing in the Syrian desert. This, rather than the strength of local resistance, was probably also the reason why the Mongols never returned to Europe after their invasion of 1241–42. The army also needed plenty of room for maneuver, so it was less effective in forested, mountainous or intensively farmed areas than in open country. This helps to explain, for example, the relative slowness of the conquest of China.

The period of the Mongols' expansion had few beneficial results: they destroyed far more than they built. The most sophisticated civilizations of the time – the Muslim and the Chinese – suffered the worst. The Abbasid caliphate of Baghdad, spiritual, cultural and (for much of the time) political leader of the Muslim world since the 8th century, was overthrown. The ancient cities of central Asia were devastated and never recovered their former prosperity. Depopulation and the neglect of irrigation channels meant that most of Iraq and west Persia was reduced to desert for centuries. Northern China suffered depopulation and the Mongol conquest isolated Russia from the mainstream of European development for almost two centuries. The impact of the Mongols on the rest of Christendom was fleeting, and by disrupting the Muslim world they granted a brief stay of execution to the Crusader states and allowed a shortlived revival of the crumbling Byzantine empire. Eventually, Christendom benefited from the Mongol conquests in Asia, as Muslim control of the silk route ended and the way was opened for westerners such as Marco Polo to travel to east Asia for the first time.

1 The governor of Otrar provoked Chingis Khan's invasion of the Khwarizm shahdom by executing merchants and envoys from the Mongols in 1218.

2 Chingis Khan divided his army at Samarkand, despatching a smaller force to pursue the Khwarizm Shah and then cross the Caucasus to gather intelligence in Europe.

3 Chingis Khan died here in 1227 on campaign against the Jin empire.

4 Fighting in unfavorable mountainous terrain, it took the Mongols 30 years to force the Koreans to submit. Thereafter the Koreans became close allies.

5 Karakorum, favorite campsite of Chingis, became the capital of the Mongol empire in 1235.

6 Using frozen rivers as highways, the Mongols launched the only successful winter invasion in Russian history in 1238–39. The Russians paid tribute to the Mongols for two centuries.

7 The combined armies of eastern Europe were routed at Legnica and Mohi in 1241. The Mongols withdrew on news of Ogedai Khan's death.

8 The fall of Baghdad was followed by the massacre of 200,000 captives (20 percent of the population).

9 The first major defeat of the Mongols was at the hands of the Mamlukes at 'Ain Jalut in 1260.

See also 3.08 (Europe); 3.16 (Muslim world); 3.23 (later Mongols)

3.23 The break-up of the Mongol empire • 1260 – 1502 •

The empire created by Chingis Khan was too vast to be ruled by one man and in the reigns of his successors as Great Khan, Ogedai (r.1229–41) and Möngke (r.1251–59), subordinate khanates were created to govern the western conquests. After Möngke's death the western khanates became in effect fully independent states and Khubilai (r.1260–94), his successor as Great Khan, had a purely nominal sovereignty over them. Khubilai's conquest of the Song empire in 1268–79 brought the period of the Mongol conquests to an end. Khubilai's attempts at expansion in southeast Asia and Japan were costly failures and the Chagatai khanate's campaigns in India were stoutly resisted by the Delhi sultanate.

Khubilai Khan was the last great Mongol ruler: his successors as Great Khan were all mediocrities who failed to give their empire a stable centralized administration. Peasant rebellions became common in the 14th century and by 1355 the Great Khanate had broken up into separate states. A Chinese rebel leader of peasant stock, Zhu Yuanzhang, seized control of Nanjing in 1356 and by 1367 had won control of southern China. The following year Zhu recaptured Beijing and declared himself the first emperor of the Ming dynasty (1368–1644). Zhu's success in unifying China from the south – the reverse of the Qin, Sui and Song unifications – was possible because the Mongol invasions had left the north much poorer and less densely populated than the south. The early Ming emperors refortified the northern frontier and launched frequent punitive campaigns into Mongolia but the two main tribal confederacies, the Oirats (or Kalmyks) and Kalkhas, were only finally subjugated in the mid-18th century.

Trade and cultural contacts between China and the rest of the world increased greatly under Mongol rule. Many European missionaries and merchants – most famously the Venetian Marco Polo – found their way to China, taking home with them the first

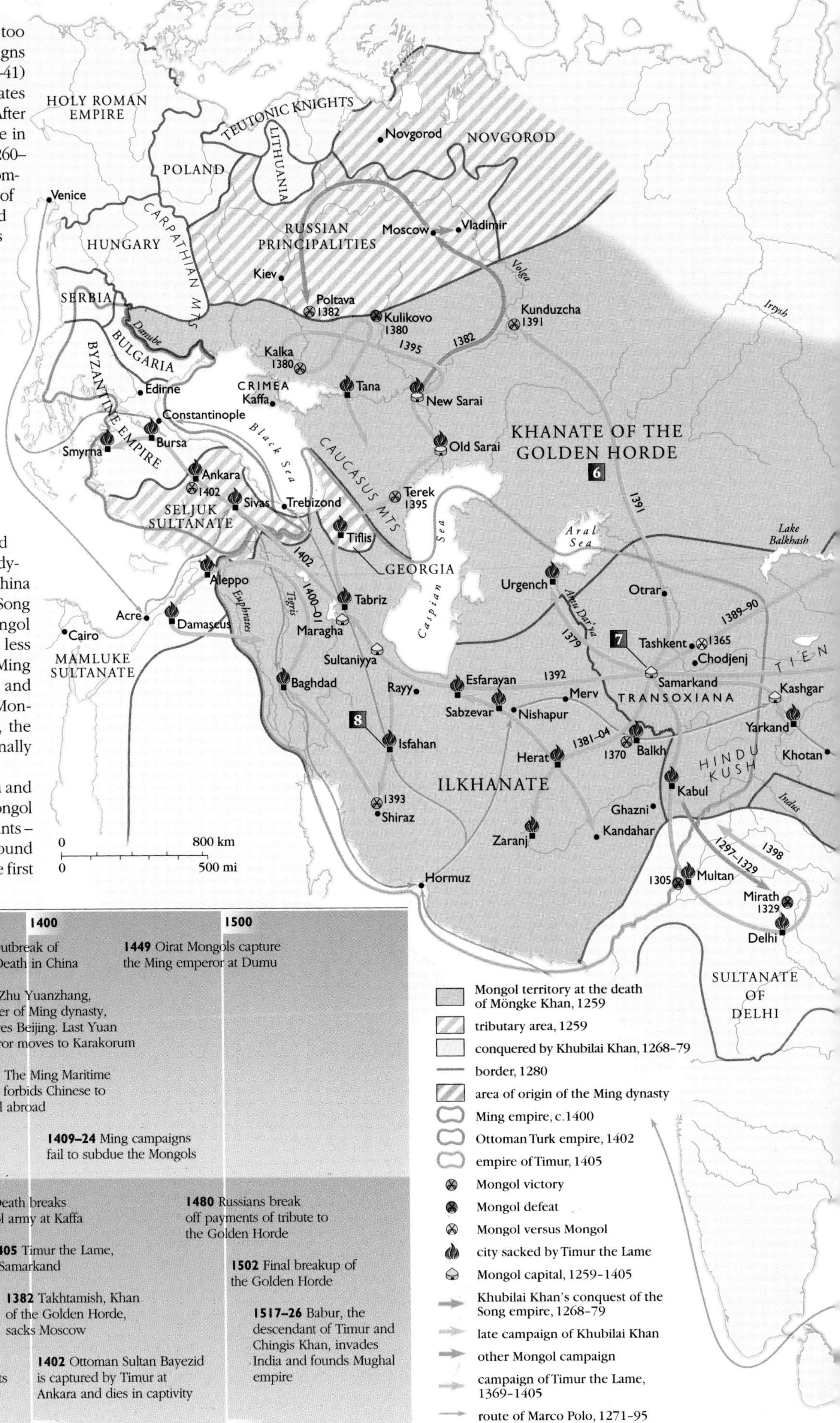

TIMELINE

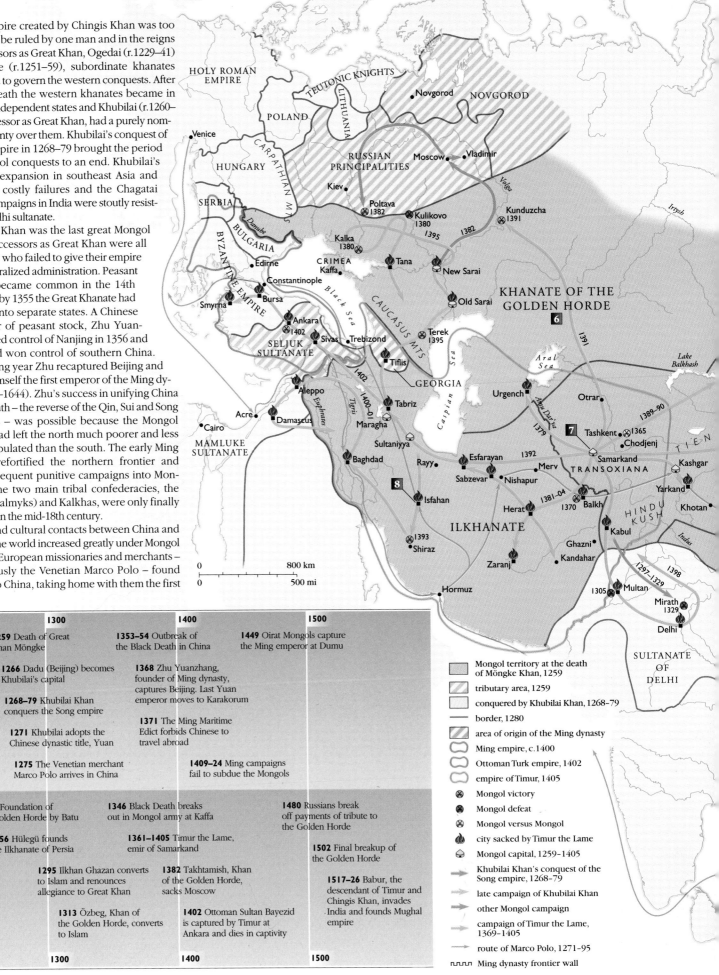

East Asia

1300 — 1400 — 1500

1259 Death of Great Khan Möngke

1266 Dadu (Beijing) becomes Khubilai's capital

1268–79 Khubilai Khan conquers the Song empire

1271 Khubilai adopts the Chinese dynastic title, Yuan

1275 The Venetian merchant Marco Polo arrives in China

1353–54 Outbreak of the Black Death in China

1368 Zhu Yuanzhang, founder of Ming dynasty, captures Beijing. Last Yuan emperor moves to Karakorum

1371 The Ming Maritime Edict forbids Chinese to travel abroad

1409–24 Ming campaigns fail to subdue the Mongols

1449 Oirat Mongols capture the Ming emperor at Dumu

Europe and west Asia

1241 Foundation of the Golden Horde by Batu

1256 Hülegü founds the Ilkhanate of Persia

1295 Ilkhan Ghazan converts to Islam and renounces allegiance to Great Khan

1313 Özbeg, Khan of the Golden Horde, converts to Islam

1346 Black Death breaks out in Mongol army at Kaffa

1361–1405 Timur the Lame, emir of Samarkand

1382 Takhtamish, Khan of the Golden Horde, sacks Moscow

1402 Ottoman Sultan Bayezid is captured by Timur at Ankara and dies in captivity

1480 Russians break off payments of tribute to the Golden Horde

1502 Final breakup of the Golden Horde

1517–26 Babur, the descendant of Timur and Chingis Khan, invades India and founds Mughal empire

1300 — 1400 — 1500

detailed accounts of Chinese civilization. Although the Christian and Islamic worlds benefited from these cultural contacts, China itself did not. Most trade was controlled by foreigners and currency drained out of China. The painful experience of Mongol rule seemed to the Chinese to vindicate their ancient xenophobia and sense of cultural superiority. Thus, when Mongol rule ended, they unwisely renounced all foreign influences just as China was losing its economic and technological lead.

The Ilkhanate of Persia, founded in 1256, was the shortest-lived of the Mongol khanates, lasting only until 1335 despite a series of able rulers. By 1300 most Mongols had converted to Islam, while their lavish patronage of scholarship and the arts had helped repair the damage inflicted by their conquests. On the death of the last khan, the Ilkhanate split into several Mongol, Turkish and Persian states.

The steppe khanates of the Golden Horde and the Chagatai, where the Mongols could pursue their traditional way of life, survived the longest. The population of the Golden Horde was mainly Turkish: their adoption of Turkish as the official language in about 1280 and of Islam in the early 14th century alienated them from their Christian Russian tributaries. The Chagatai khanate was divided into an eastern area, characterized by paganism and nomadism, and a western, dominated by the great Muslim cities of the Silk Route. Antagonism between them was exploited by the last Mongol conqueror, Timur the Lame (r.1361–1405). Though a nomad who claimed descent from Chingis Khan, Timur was a Muslim and culturally and linguistically Turkish. Timur was appointed emir of Samarkand in 1361, and established a power base in Transoxiana by organizing defenses against nomad raiders from Mughulistan. In 1370 he captured Balkh, murdered its ruler and massacred its populace. Timur spent the rest of his life in almost constant campaigning, yet the empire he built died with him. His campaigns were marked by appalling savagery and widespread plundering, and he made no attempt to impose institutional unity on the lands he gained. Samarkand thrived on war booty, but Timur's legacy was otherwise entirely negative. A militant Muslim, he left the Islamic world in ruins; moreover, though claiming to restore Chingis Khan's empire, he weakened the Golden Horde and the Chagatai khanate. These states did, however, survive Timur's attacks. The Chagatai khanate was reduced to the lands around Kashgar; it was ultimately annexed by the Manchus in the late 17th century. The Golden Horde split up in 1438, finally disappearing from history in 1502. The khanate of the Crimean Tatars, virtually the last vestige of the Mongol empire, was annexed by Russia in 1783.

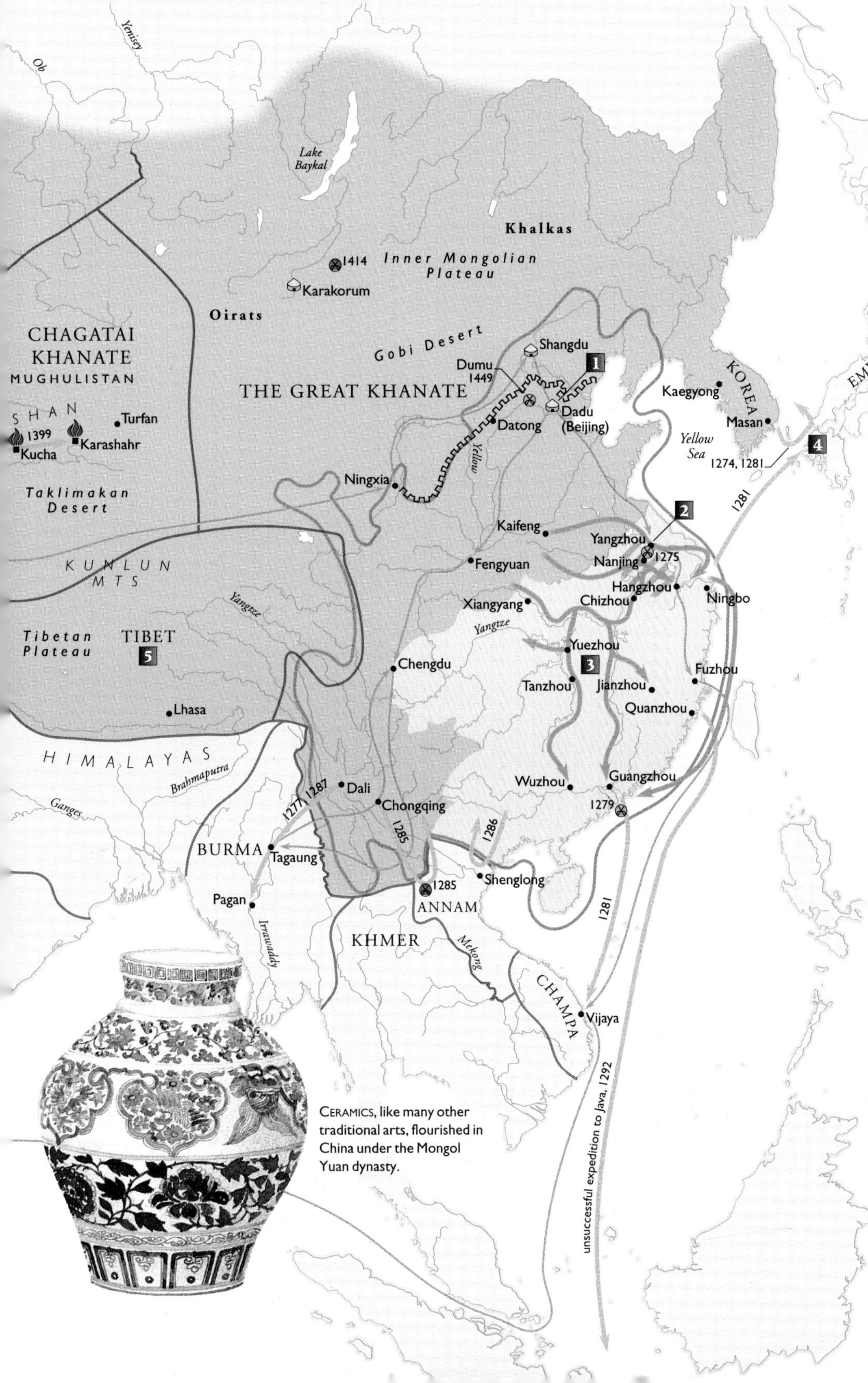

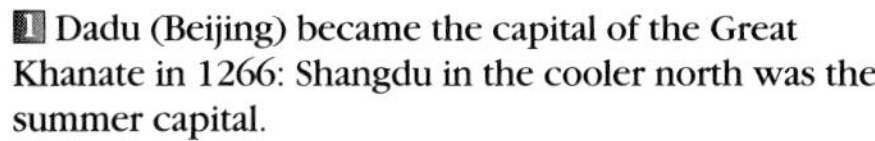

1 Dadu (Beijing) became the capital of the Great Khanate in 1266: Shangdu in the cooler north was the summer capital.

2 Marco Polo claimed to have been appointed governor of Yangzhou for three years by Khubilai, though he was probably only a minor trade official.

3 Khubilai Khan wanted to capture the Song empire intact, and so avoided the pillaging and massacres that had characterized earlier Mongol campaigns.

4 The myth of Mongol invincibility was shattered by the failure of Khubilai Khan's attempted invasions of Japan in 1274 and 1281. The invasion fleets were scattered by a typhoon, from which the Japanese term *kamikaze* ("divine wind") is derived.

5 After Khubilai Khan's death in 1294, Tibet regained its independence: the Mongols retained nominal superiority until 1368.

6 The Golden Horde is thought to be named for the color of the first Khan's tent.

7 Enslaved craftsmen from throughout the Middle East labored to build some of the Islamic world's finest surviving mosques, mausoleums and public buildings at Timur's capital Samarkand.

8 Isfahan was the scene of one of Timur the Lame's worst atrocities: 70,000 people were slaughtered so that he could build towers with their skulls.

CERAMICS, like many other traditional arts, flourished in China under the Mongol Yuan dynasty.

See also 3.22 (rise of the Mongols); 3.24 (medieval Japan)

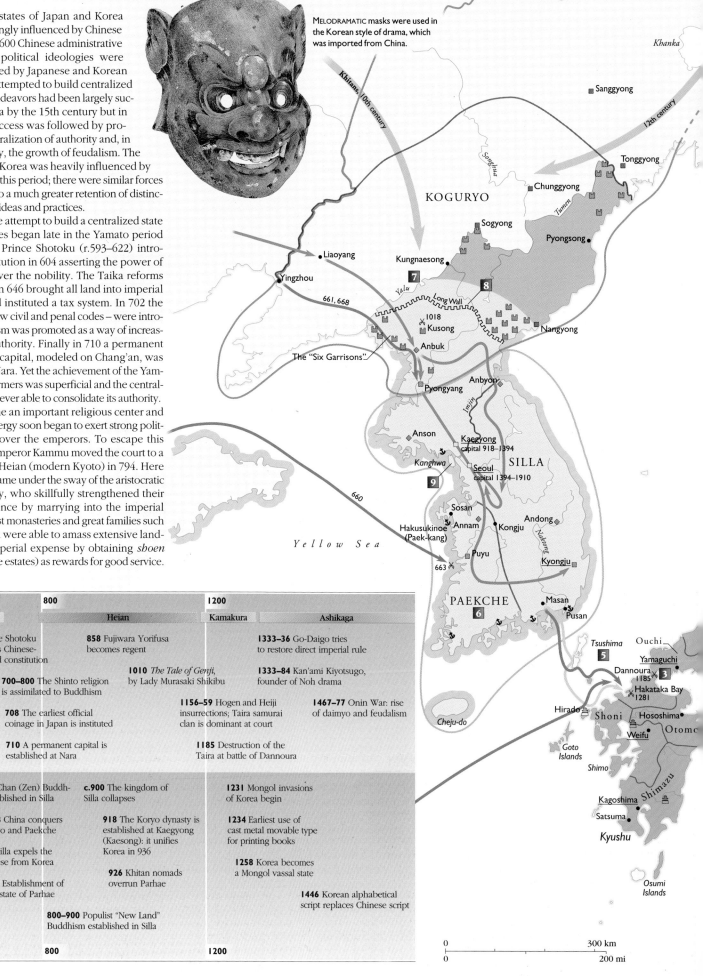

3.24 Medieval Japan and Korea • 600 – 1500 •

The early states of Japan and Korea were strongly influenced by Chinese civilization. By 600 Chinese administrative practices and political ideologies were being introduced by Japanese and Korean rulers as they attempted to build centralized states. These endeavors had been largely successful in Korea by the 15th century but in Japan initial success was followed by progressive decentralization of authority and, in the 15th century, the growth of feudalism. The elite culture of Korea was heavily influenced by that of China in this period; there were similar forces in Japan but also a much greater retention of distinctively Japanese ideas and practices.

In Japan, the attempt to build a centralized state on Chinese lines began late in the Yamato period (AD 300–710). Prince Shotoku (r.593–622) introduced a constitution in 604 asserting the power of the emperor over the nobility. The Taika reforms that followed in 646 brought all land into imperial ownership and instituted a tax system. In 702 the Taiho laws – new civil and penal codes – were introduced. Buddhism was promoted as a way of increasing imperial authority. Finally in 710 a permanent administrative capital, modeled on Chang'an, was established at Nara. Yet the achievement of the Yamato period reformers was superficial and the centralized state was never able to consolidate its authority.

Nara became an important religious center and the Buddhist clergy soon began to exert strong political influence over the emperors. To escape this interference, emperor Kammu moved the court to a new capital at Heian (modern Kyoto) in 794. Here the emperors came under the sway of the aristocratic Fujiwara family, who skillfully strengthened their political influence by marrying into the imperial family. Buddhist monasteries and great families such as the Fujiwara were able to amass extensive landholdings at imperial expense by obtaining *shoen* (private tax-free estates) as rewards for good service.

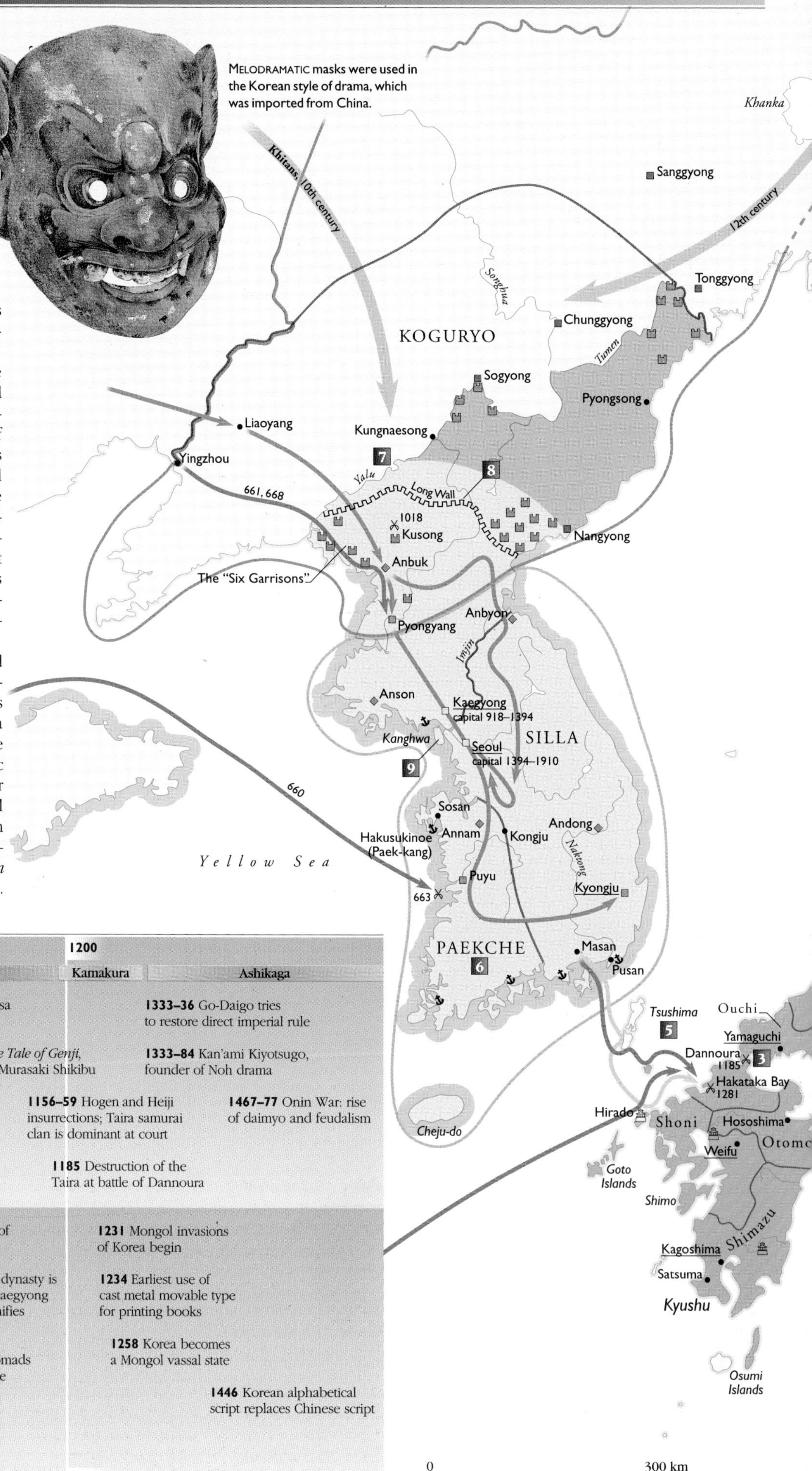

MELODRAMATIC masks were used in the Korean style of drama, which was imported from China.

TIMELINE

800 | 1200

Japan — Yamato | Heian | Kamakura | Ashikaga

- **604** Prince Shotoku introduces Chinese-influenced constitution
- **700–800** The Shinto religion is assimilated to Buddhism
- **708** The earliest official coinage in Japan is instituted
- **710** A permanent capital is established at Nara
- **858** Fujiwara Yorifusa becomes regent
- **1010** *The Tale of Genji*, by Lady Murasaki Shikibu
- **1156–59** Hogen and Heiji insurrections; Taira samurai clan is dominant at court
- **1185** Destruction of the Taira at battle of Dannoura
- **1333–36** Go-Daigo tries to restore direct imperial rule
- **1333–84** Kan'ami Kiyotsugo, founder of Noh drama
- **1467–77** Onin War: rise of daimyo and feudalism

Korea

- **600–700** Chan (Zen) Buddhism is established in Silla
- **660–68** China conquers Koguryo and Paekche
- **676** Silla expels the Chinese from Korea
- **694** Establishment of the state of Parhae
- **800–900** Populist "New Land" Buddhism established in Silla
- **c.900** The kingdom of Silla collapses
- **918** The Koryo dynasty is established at Kaegyong (Kaesong): it unifies Korea in 936
- **926** Khitan nomads overrun Parhae
- **1231** Mongol invasions of Korea begin
- **1234** Earliest use of cast metal movable type for printing books
- **1258** Korea becomes a Mongol vassal state
- **1446** Korean alphabetical script replaces Chinese script

800 | 1200

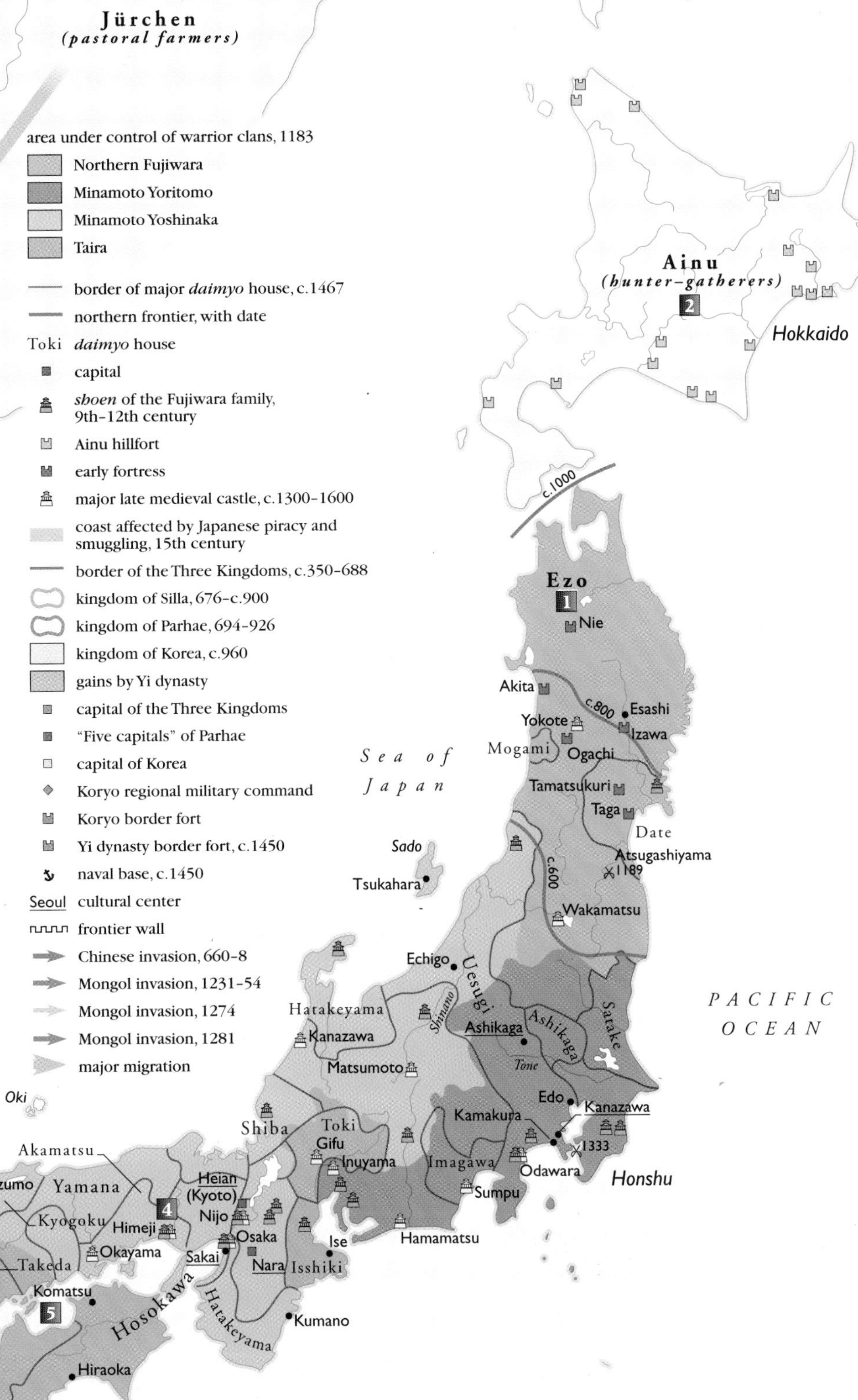

1 The Ezo people of Honshu, related to the Ainu, fiercely resisted Japanese expansion but were conquered by the 12th century.

2 The Ainu were an aboriginal hunter-gatherer people, linguistically and physically unrelated to any other east Asian peoples, who were only brought under Japanese rule in the 17th century.

3 The destruction of the Taira at the battle of Dannoura was made the subject of the *Tale of the Heike*, the major literary work of 13th-century Japan.

4 One of the best preserved Japanese medieval castles is White Heron Castle at Himeji (14th century).

5 Fishing villages in the Inland Sea and on Tsushima became bases for smugglers and pirates, breaking tight Korean and Chinese restrictions on trade.

6 The kingdom of Paekche fell after its Japanese allies were defeated by Silla in a naval battle in 663.

7 The Koryo dynasty extended its control to the Yalu River c.960, since when it has remained Korea's northwestern border.

8 The Long Wall was built in 1033–44 to defend Korea against Khitan and Jürchen invasions.

9 During the Mongol invasions, the Korean royal court moved to the greater safety of Kanghwa Island.

The exquisitely refined culture of Heian court life contrasted with growing disorder in the provinces. In the absence of a centralized military system, monasteries and aristocratic houses formed private armies and a class of rural warriors – the *samurai* – developed. Sporadic warfare increased, and with it arose the culture of the warrior.

In the 12th century samurai clans became involved in court politics and Fujiwara influence declined. Following the Gempei war (1180–85) between the Taira and Minamoto clans, Minamoto Yoritomo founded the Kamakura shogunate, beginning a period of military government that would last until 1868. The Kamakura shogunate was overthrown in 1333 and replaced five years later by the Ashikaga shogunate. The shoguns ruled in alliance with the *shugo* (military constables), who gradually became powerful regional rulers, undermining the authority of the shoguns. When a dispute over the shogunal succession escalated into a fullscale civil war between 1467–77, the shugo lost control of their regional power bases. Control of the provinces fell to new feudal warlords, or *daimyo*. The daimyo feuded almost constantly among themselves, deploying armies of samurai vassals who held small estates in return for military service. The castles of the daimyo became the main centers of government and of warrior culture. Castles attracted craftsmen and merchants and many became a focus for urban development. Though the Ashikaga shogunate survived until 1573, the civil war destroyed its remaining authority and by 1500 Japan had fragmented into almost 400 effectively independent states. The emperors continued to reign in Heian (Kyoto) but they were powerless and impoverished figureheads.

In Korea three kingdoms – Koguryo, Silla and Paekche – had emerged by 600. In 660 the expansionist Chinese Tang dynasty invaded the peninsula and in alliance with Silla conquered Paekche and Koguryo. On finding that it was not to share in the spoils, Silla drove the Chinese from the peninsula in 676. Silla occupied Paekche and southern Koguryo: northern Koguryo remained in chaos until a successor state, Parhae, emerged in 694. Both Korean states developed as centralized kingdoms on the Tang model. In 780 a struggle between the monarchy and the aristocracy broke out in Silla and in the 9th century the kingdom broke up. A new kingdom was created in 918–36 by Wang Kon (r.918–45), founder of the Koryo dynasty from which Korea gets its name. Parhae was extinguished about the same time by the Khitan nomads. Despite Khitan opposition, Korea had established a heavily fortified frontier on the Yalu River by the early 11th century.

A coup in 1170 deprived the monarchy of real power, leaving Korea leaderless until the military Choe family seized power in 1196. The Choe led resistance to the Mongols but unrest grew more widespread as the wars dragged on: the dynasty was overthrown in 1258 and Korea became a Mongol vassal state. The end of Mongol rule in 1356 brought a return to political instability and the Koryo dynasty was eventually overthrown with Chinese help by the general Yi Songgye (r.1392–98), founder of the Yi dynasty (1392–1910). Under the Yi, Confucianism replaced Buddhism as Korea's main ethical code and was made the basis of the bureaucratic and educational systems. The Yi resumed expansion to the northeast and by the 15th century the country's modern borders had been established.

See also 3.05 (the world religions); 3.23 (Mongol invasion)

3.25 The kingdoms of southeast Asia • 600 – 1500 •

Several small and unstable states arose in mainland and island southeast Asia during the first half of the first millennium AD. Yet by 1000 many stable kingdoms and large empires had emerged. Local rulers, influenced by India, consolidated their power by adopting Buddhist and Hindu concepts of sacred kingship: most southeast Asian states before 1500 were royal theocracies. Indeed, Indian cultural influences remained strong throughout the period; China, however, despite close trade and diplomatic links with some southeast Asian states, only exerted influence on states directly bordering on it.

The most powerful mainland state for much of this period was the Khmer empire of Cambodia. The Khmers had been united in the state of Chen-la around AD 400: this peaked under Jayavarman I in about 700 but soon declined. In 802 Jayavarman II (r.802–50), a minor king in the Angkor district, proclaimed himself *devaraja* ("god-king"), reuniting the Khmer peoples. By the reign of Indravarman I (r.877–89) the Khmer ruled the Mon and Thai peoples to the north and west. Yasovarman I (r.889–910) founded a new capital at Angkor, the Khmer empire's most impressive monument. The empire was at its height under Suryavarman I (r.1010–50) and Suryavarman II (r.1113–50). Under pressure from the expanding Thai peoples and the pull of maritime commerce, the Khmer capital moved to the safer location of Caturmukha (near Phnom Penh) in 1431 and abandoned Angkor in 1440. By 1500 the Khmer had become a minor regional power.

The earliest Thai state, the warlike Nan Chao, emerged in about 600; it was finally conquered by the Mongols in 1253. From about 1000 Thai peoples began moving south into Mon and Khmer territories. Around 1250, a Thai dynasty established a powerful kingdom at Sukhothai and a century later another Thai kingdom was founded at Ayutthaya. Ayutthaya conquered Sukhothai in about 1378 and became the dominant power of the Gulf of Thailand by the 15th century after driving the Khmers from Angkor.

About 600, Buddhist states began to form among the Mon and Pyu peoples of the Irrawaddy valley.

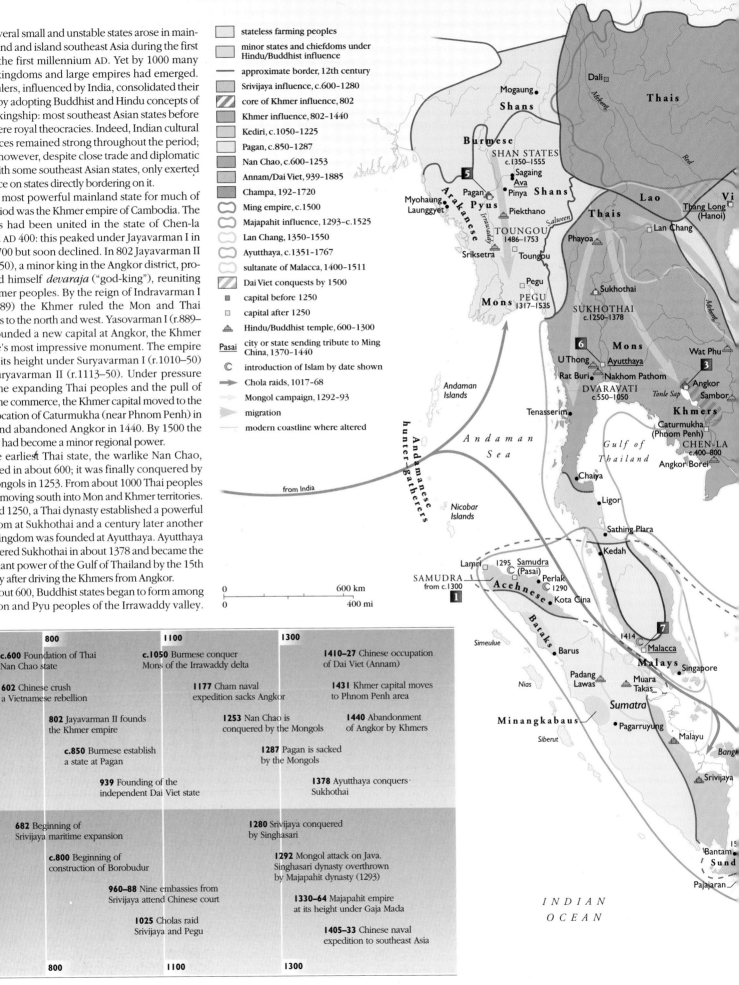

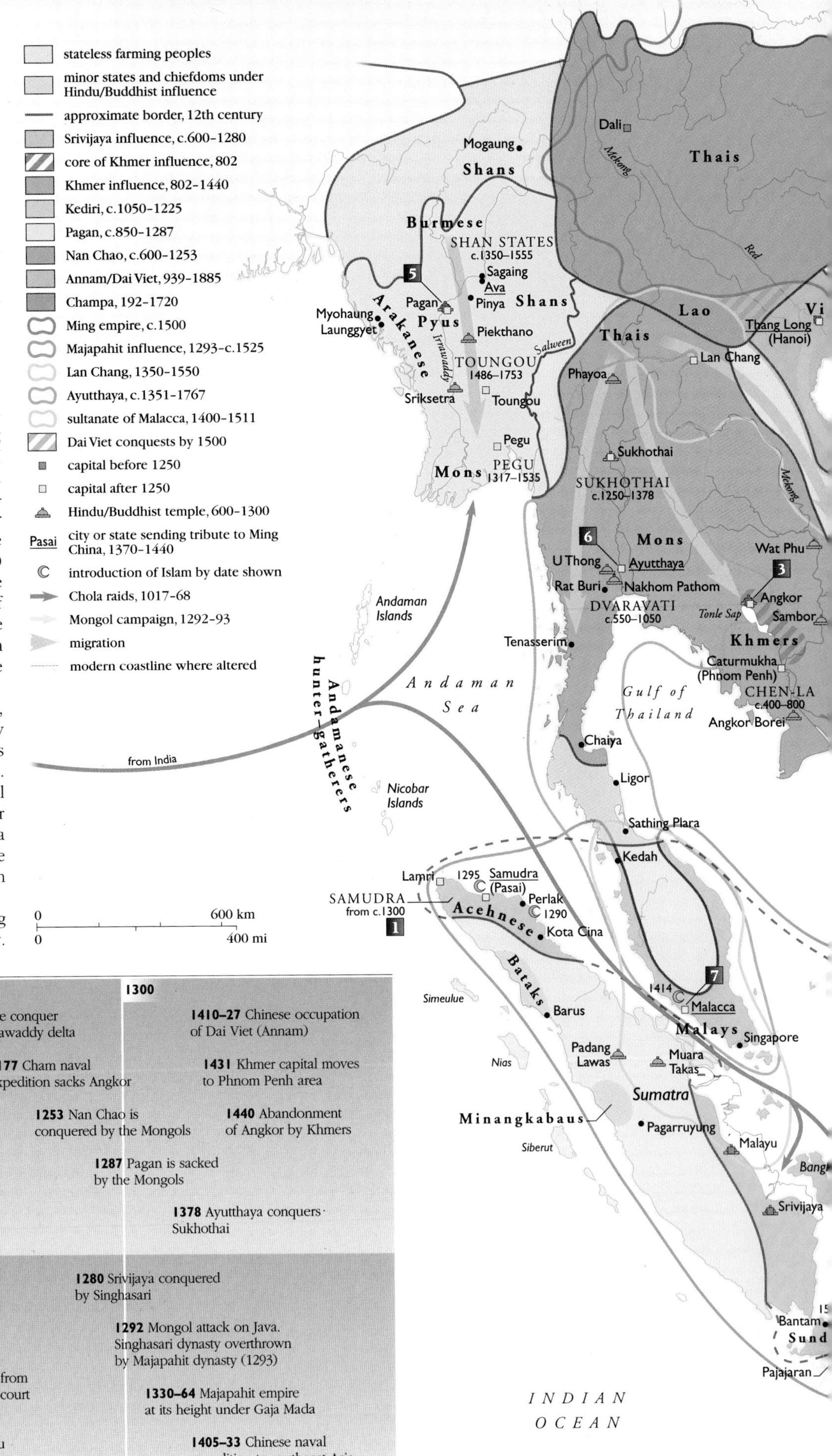

TIMELINE

Mainland southeast Asia

- **c.600** Foundation of Thai Nan Chao state
- **602** Chinese crush a Vietnamese rebellion
- **802** Jayavarman II founds the Khmer empire
- **c.850** Burmese establish a state at Pagan
- **939** Founding of the independent Dai Viet state
- **c.1050** Burmese conquer Mons of the Irrawaddy delta
- **1177** Cham naval expedition sacks Angkor
- **1253** Nan Chao is conquered by the Mongols
- **1287** Pagan is sacked by the Mongols
- **1378** Ayutthaya conquers Sukhothai
- **1410–27** Chinese occupation of Dai Viet (Annam)
- **1431** Khmer capital moves to Phnom Penh area
- **1440** Abandonment of Angkor by Khmers

Island Southeast Asia

- **682** Beginning of Srivijaya maritime expansion
- **c.800** Beginning of construction of Borobudur
- **960–88** Nine embassies from Srivijaya attend Chinese court
- **1025** Cholas raid Srivijaya and Pegu
- **1280** Srivijaya conquered by Singhasari
- **1292** Mongol attack on Java. Singhasari dynasty overthrown by Majapahit dynasty (1293)
- **1330–64** Majapahit empire at its height under Gaja Mada
- **1405–33** Chinese naval expedition to southeast Asia

800 1100 1300

The Pyu states were destroyed by Nan Chao about 835; shortly after the Burmese moved into the valley and built a state around Pagan. By the mid-11th century Pagan subdued the Mons, the coastal Arakanese and the Thai-speaking Shan hill peoples, building the first unified state in the Irrawaddy basin. Pagan was eventually destroyed by the Mongols. The Shan, Mon and Arakanese were reconquered by the Burmese Toungou dynasty (16th century).

Vietnam had been the site of complex societies from early times and occupied by the Chinese since the 3rd century BC. Only in 939, after centuries of rebellion, did the Vietnamese found an independent state, known to them as Dai Viet and to the Chinese as Annam. This was the sole state of southeast Asia in which Chinese cultural influences predominated. Once China had abandoned hopes of reconquest in 1427, relations between the two states improved.

The first large state to dominate the sea passages was Srivijaya, in Sumatra. Srivijaya began its imperial expansion in 682 and reached its peak in 800. Raids by the Cholas of south India in the 11th century eroded its power but its demise was hastened in the first quarter of the 13th century by the imperial expansion of the east Javan Singhasari dynasty. This was in turn succeeded by a new dynasty at Majapahit in 1293. For the next century Majapahit dominated maritime Indonesia but was in decline by 1400. Like the earlier maritime empires, Majapahit was not centralized: only central and east Java was under its direct control, while provincial rulers retained power locally. Payment of tribute was enforced by the threat of punitive naval action.

Islam, which was brought to island southeast Asia by Indian Muslim merchants at the end of the 13th century, undermined theocratic kingship, founded coastal states and defeated the remnants of Hindu–Buddhist Majapahit by 1527. When the Europeans arrived in the 16th century, they found island southeast Asia divided into dozens of petty states.

STONE GUARDIAN for a temple in Pagan, Burma, where Indian and Chinese influences merged to form a distinctive Burmese identity.

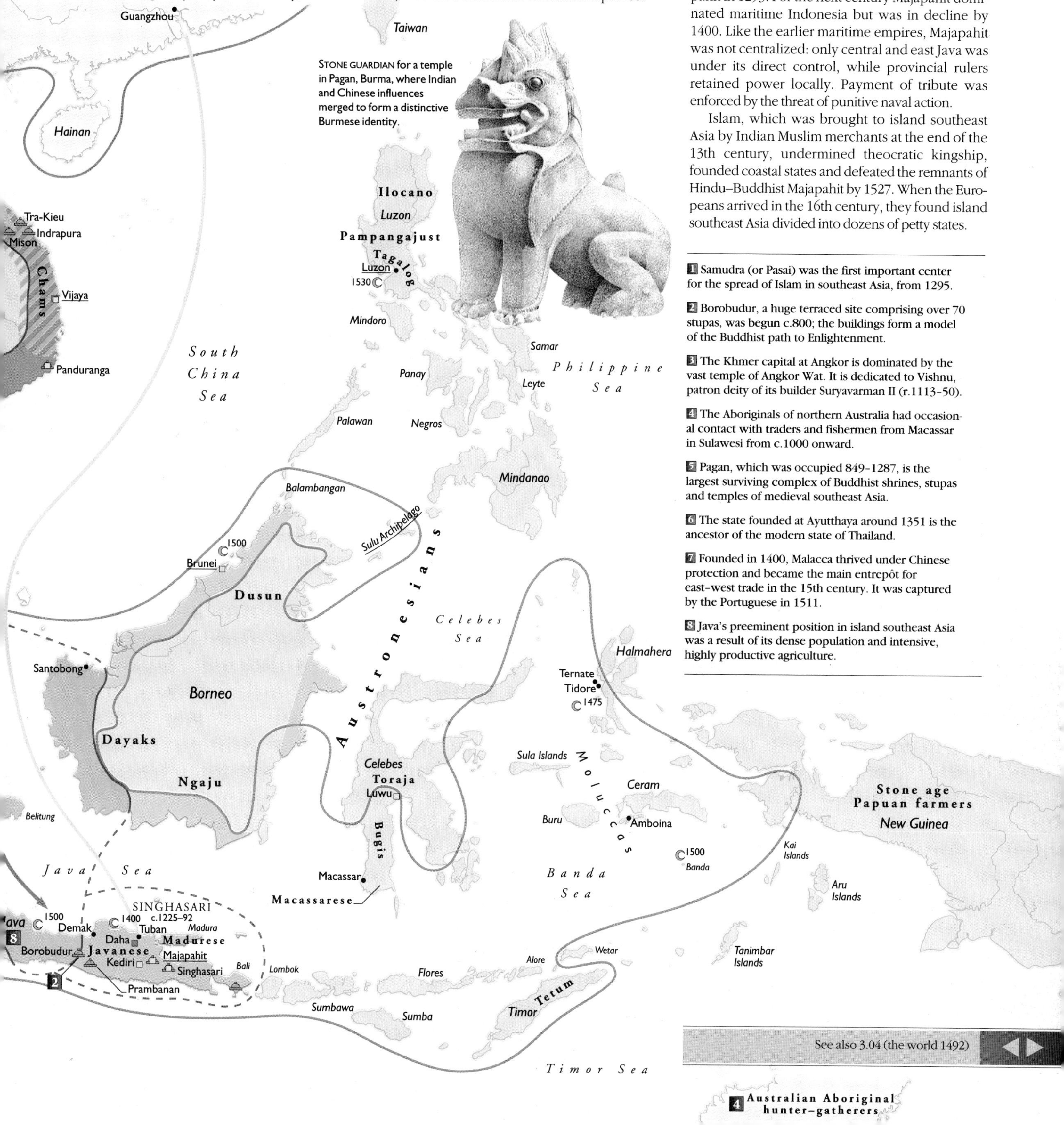

1 Samudra (or Pasai) was the first important center for the spread of Islam in southeast Asia, from 1295.

2 Borobudur, a huge terraced site comprising over 70 stupas, was begun c.800; the buildings form a model of the Buddhist path to Enlightenment.

3 The Khmer capital at Angkor is dominated by the vast temple of Angkor Wat. It is dedicated to Vishnu, patron deity of its builder Suryavarman II (r.1113–50).

4 The Aboriginals of northern Australia had occasional contact with traders and fishermen from Macassar in Sulawesi from c.1000 onward.

5 Pagan, which was occupied 849–1287, is the largest surviving complex of Buddhist shrines, stupas and temples of medieval southeast Asia.

6 The state founded at Ayutthaya around 1351 is the ancestor of the modern state of Thailand.

7 Founded in 1400, Malacca thrived under Chinese protection and became the main entrepôt for east–west trade in the 15th century. It was captured by the Portuguese in 1511.

8 Java's preeminent position in island southeast Asia was a result of its dense population and intensive, highly productive agriculture.

See also 3.04 (the world 1492)

3.26 Native cultures of North America • 600 – 1500 •

The initial settlement of North America began around 12,000 years ago as bands of Paleoindians, the ancestors of modern Native Americans, spread south from Alaska. At first, Paleoindian culture was relatively homogeneous but adaptation to particular environments led to the emergence of well defined regional cultures by the end of the first millennium BC. From early times hunter–gatherers in many areas of North America had cultivated favored food plants on a small scale. Some native plant species, such as sunflowers, had been domesticated by the end of the first millennium BC and maize and beans had been introduced from Mexico. As wild food sources remained abundant, true farming communities were slow to develop.

The first mainly agricultural North American societies developed in the southwest deserts in about AD 300. Maize, beans, squash and cotton were first cultivated close to permanent water sources but by about 900 elaborate irrigation systems were in use. By the 9th century three main cultural traditions had developed – the Hohokam, Mogollon and Anasazi – together with two subsidiary cultures, the Patayan and the Fremont. In some areas (such as Chaco Canyon) these cultures developed considerable social complexity. Their most distinctive remains are the multi-roomed dwellings known as pueblos, and their fine pottery. Droughts caused their decline from around 1300.

True farming began to emerge in the eastern woodlands once hardier strains of maize and beans appeared after 700. The resulting growth in food production stimulated the rise of North America's first towns, in the Mississippi basin, by the 12th century. These centered around large earthwork temple mounds. The Mississippian cultures shared a common religion known as the Southern Cult, and were hierarchical; their rulers were buried in mound-top mortuaries with rich grave goods and even human sacrifices. Large Mississippian towns, such as Cahokia, were the centers of powerful chiefdoms. By the 15th century, Mississippian culture was declining and its heartland was depopulated (the so-called "vacant quarter"). By about 1000 permanent farming villages were established throughout the eastern woodlands. Warfare spread and by the time of European contact defensive tribal confederacies, such as the Iroquois league, were forming.

Elsewhere in North America hunting, fishing and gathering remained the dominant way of life. On the Pacific coast, ocean resources were so abundant that relatively dense populations and permanent village settlements emerged, with a level of social and cultural complexity far beyond that normally achieved by hunter–gatherer peoples. The Great Plains and the sub-Arctic forests were sparsely populated, though the advent of the bow and arrow in the first millennium AD made big-game hunting more efficient. At the time of European contact buffalo hunting was gradually giving way to farming, but the introduction of the horse (native American horses died out around 10,000 years ago), led many settled Plains peoples to abandon farming for nomadism.

The Paleoindians did not for the most part settle in Arctic North America. The region was uninhabited until about 2500–1900 BC when the ancestors of the modern Inuit peoples arrived in Alaska from Siberia. Early Inuit cultures became increasingly well adapted to the Arctic environment, culminating in the Thule tradition which survived to the modern age. This originated during the Old Bering Sea Stage (200 BC–AD 800) among specialized marine mammal hunters on St Lawrence and other Bering Sea islands, from where it spread along Alaska's west coast and north to Point Barrow. From there Thule Inuit migrated east, displacing or assimilating the earlier Dorset Inuit until they reached Greenland in the 13th century. Here they made contact with Norse settlers, with whom they traded and fought. The Norse were not well adapted to life in the Arctic and by about 1500 their settlements had died out and been occupied by the Thule.

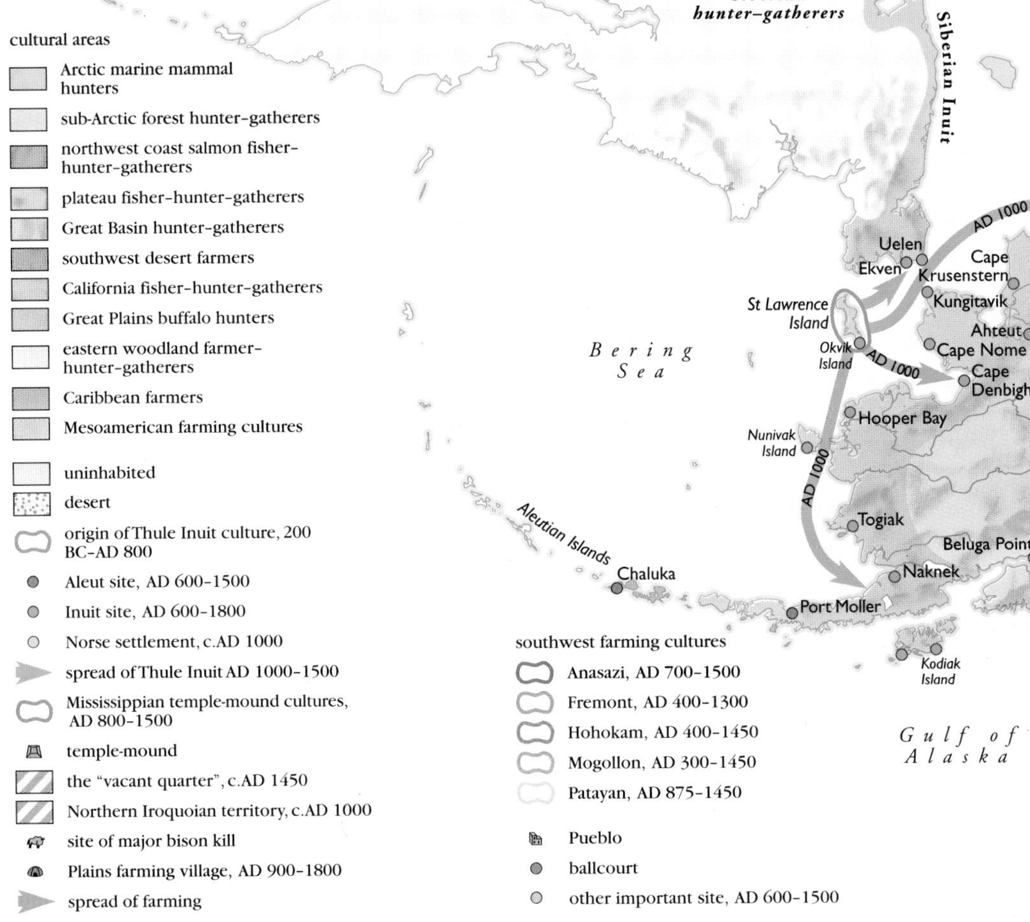

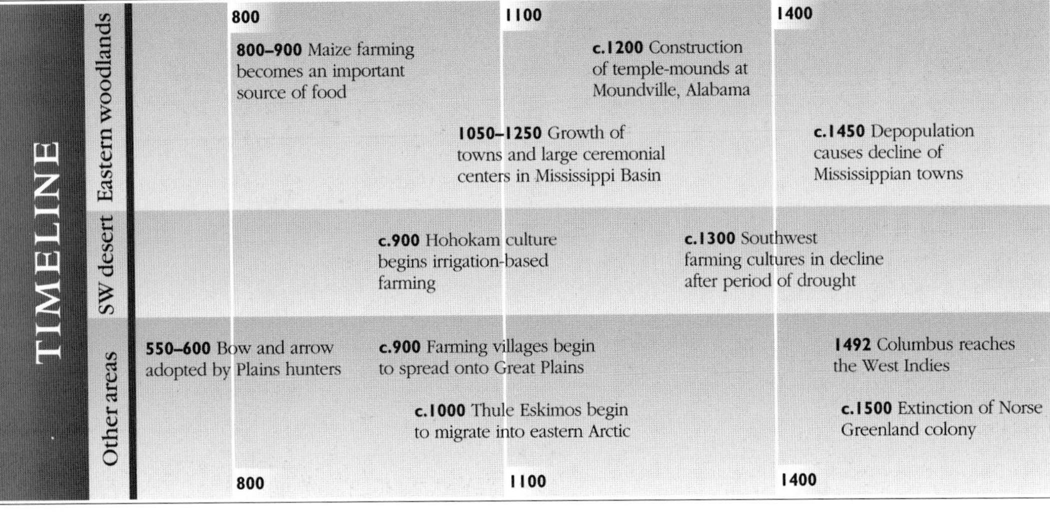

TIMELINE
Eastern woodlands
SW desert
Other areas
800
1100
1400
800–900 Maize farming becomes an important source of food
c.1200 Construction of temple-mounds at Moundville, Alabama
1050–1250 Growth of towns and large ceremonial centers in Mississippi Basin
c.1450 Depopulation causes decline of Mississippian towns
c.900 Hohokam culture begins irrigation-based farming
c.1300 Southwest farming cultures in decline after period of drought
550–600 Bow and arrow adopted by Plains hunters
c.900 Farming villages begin to spread onto Great Plains
1492 Columbus reaches the West Indies
c.1000 Thule Eskimos begin to migrate into eastern Arctic
c.1500 Extinction of Norse Greenland colony
800
1100
1400

1 Here a cliff was used as a "jump" over which buffalo were stampeded to their deaths, from c.5400 BC to European contact.

2 A small Norse settlement occupied for about twenty years c.AD 1000 is the only sure evidence that Europeans reached the Americas before Columbus.

3 Ritual ball courts at Snaketown and Casa Grande indicate that the Hohokam culture was influenced by Mesoamerican civilizations.

4 From 900–1300, Chaco Canyon was the hub of a network of 125 planned villages linked by 400 kilometers (250 miles) of roads.

5 Iron ship rivets, textiles and chain mail found at sites at Flagler Bay show contact between the Thule Inuit and the Norse Greenlanders.

6 Sub-Arctic hunters typically sited their camps at river crossings used by herds of caribou (reindeer).

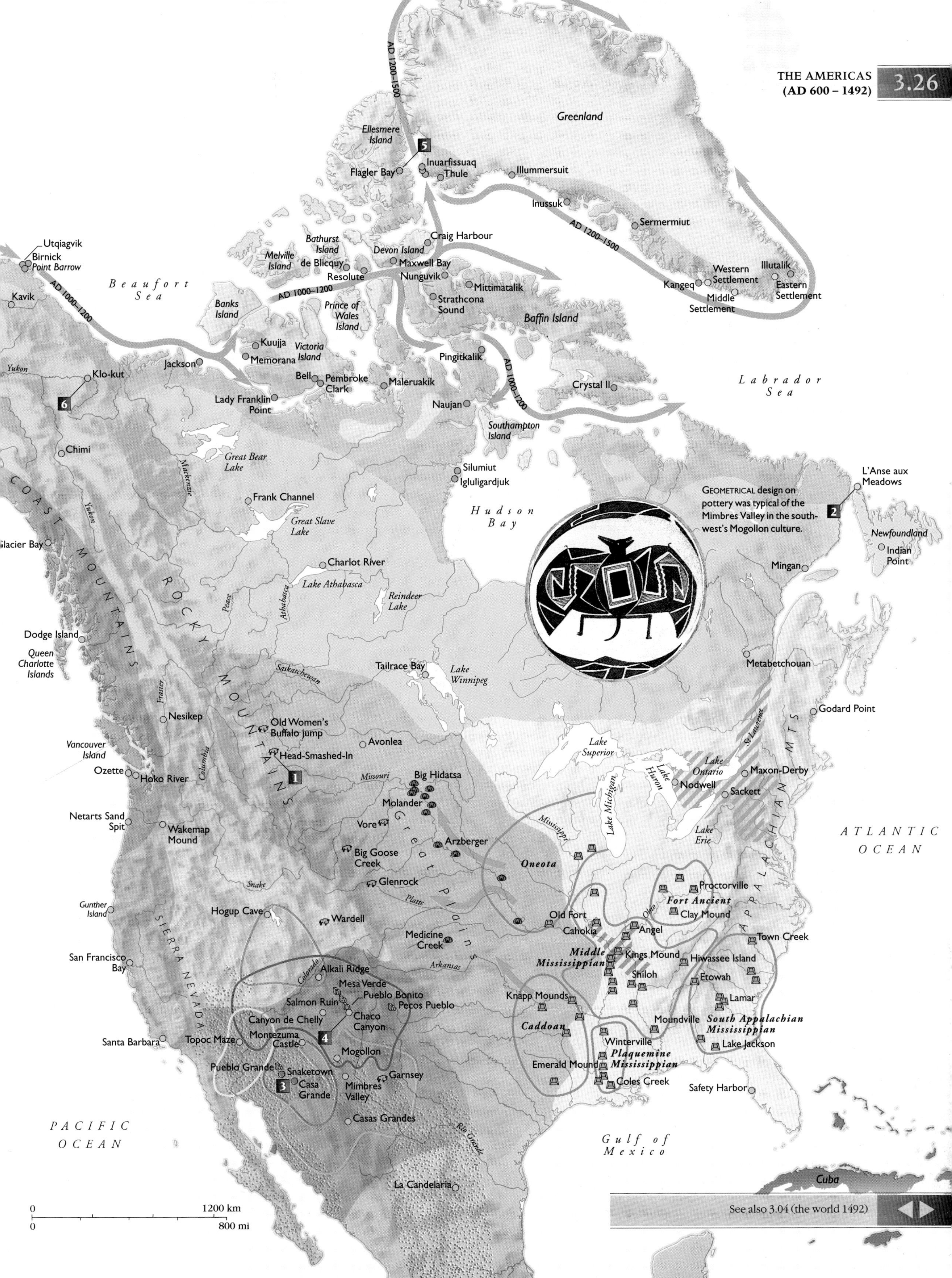

GEOMETRICAL design on pottery was typical of the Mimbres Valley in the south-west's Mogollon culture.

See also 3.04 (the world 1492)

3.27 Toltecs and Aztecs • 800 – 1520 •

The destruction of Teotihuacán in the 8th century left a power vacuum in central Mexico, which allowed new peoples to migrate to the region. The Chichimeca and the Nonoalca settled to the north of the Valley of Mexico, where they merged to form the Toltec nation. By around 900 a Toltec state was established around Tula, from where they expanded over the Valley of Mexico. Little is known of the history of the Toltecs, but their legends feature prominently in the traditions of the Aztecs, who claimed descent from them. The most important legend concerns the Toltec ruler Topiltzin-Quetzalcóatl, a real person born in 935 or 947, who soon came to be identified with the god Quetzalcóatl ("feathered serpent"). His opposition to human sacrifice offended the god Tezcatlipoca, who overthrew him: Topiltzin-Quetzalcóatl fled east overseas, vowing to return one day to reclaim his kingdom. Intriguingly, Mayan records show that in 987 a man called Kukulcán ("feathered serpent" in Mayan) conquered Yucatán. Whether or not this was the Toltec Quetzalcóatl, archeological evidence confirms that in about 1000 the main Mayan city of Chichén Itzá was occupied by Toltecs.

Tula was sacked in about 1168 and the Toltec empire was supplanted by many rival city-states. Around 1200 the Aztecs, a farming people from the west, moved into the Valley of Mexico, eventually founding a permanent settlement at Tenochtitlán in 1325. First serving as mercenaries for Tezozomoc, ruler of Azcapotzalco, the Aztecs allied with Texcoco to destroy Azcapotzalco after Tezozomoc's death in 1426. Two years later Itzcóatl established a strong Aztec monarchy. In 1434 Tenochtitlán, Texcoco and Tlacopan formed the Triple Alliance, imposing tributary status on the other states of the Valley of Mexico. Expansion continued under Itzcóatl's successors; by 1500 the alliance ruled over some 10 million people. The empire peaked under Moctezuma II (r.1502–20) but was abruptly ended by Hernán Cortés' invasion of 1519–21. Though Cortés had great advantages in weaponry and armor, these were not decisive against overwhelming Aztec superiority of numbers. Moctezuma vacillated, believing Cortés to be the returning Quetzalcóatl, whom the legends described as fair-skinned and bearded. The Mesoamerican custom of taking prisoners for sacrifice also hampered the Aztecs against the conquistadors, who fought to kill. Moreover, Cortés found willing allies in the Tlaxcallans, the Aztecs' main source of sacrificial victims. Finally, diseases brought by the Spanish, such as smallpox, decimated the Aztecs.

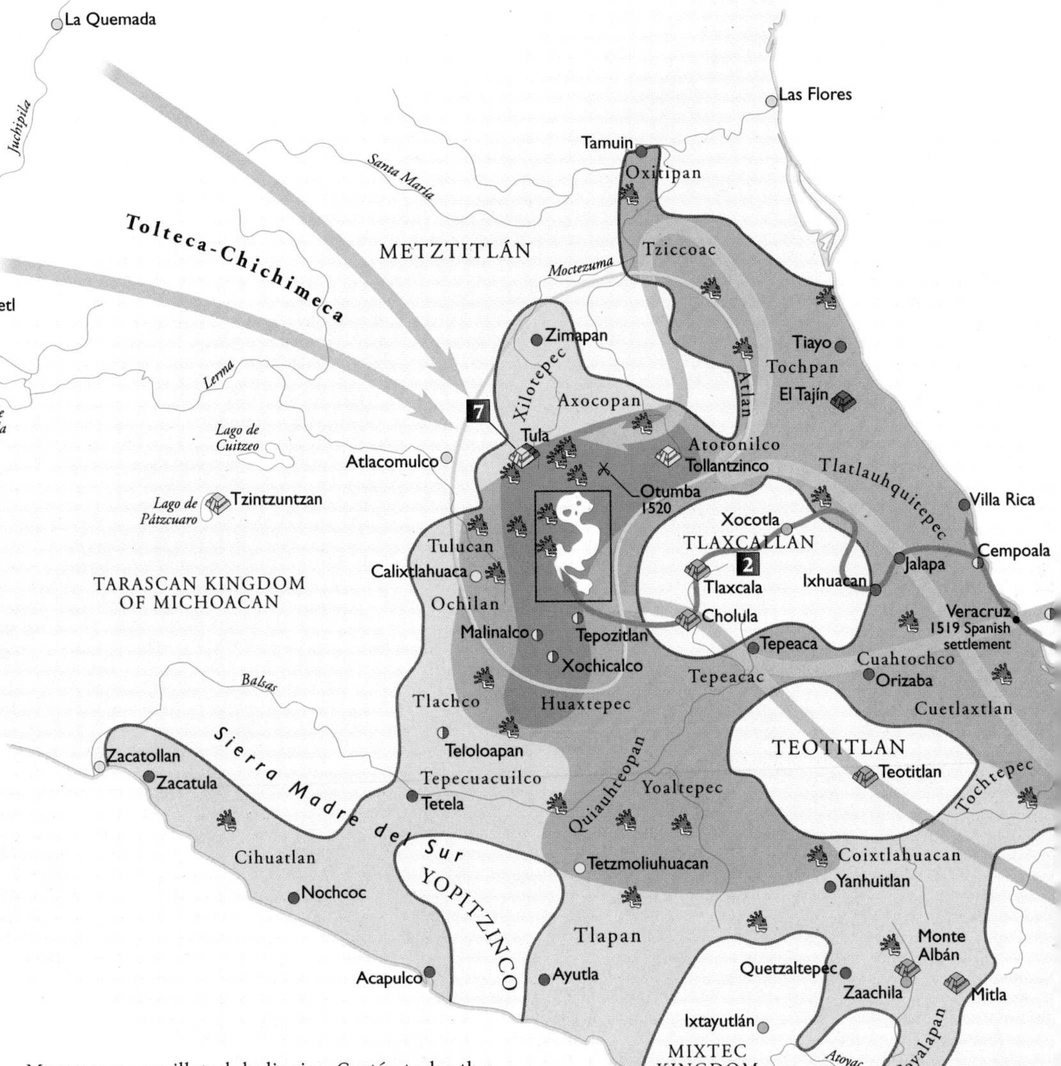

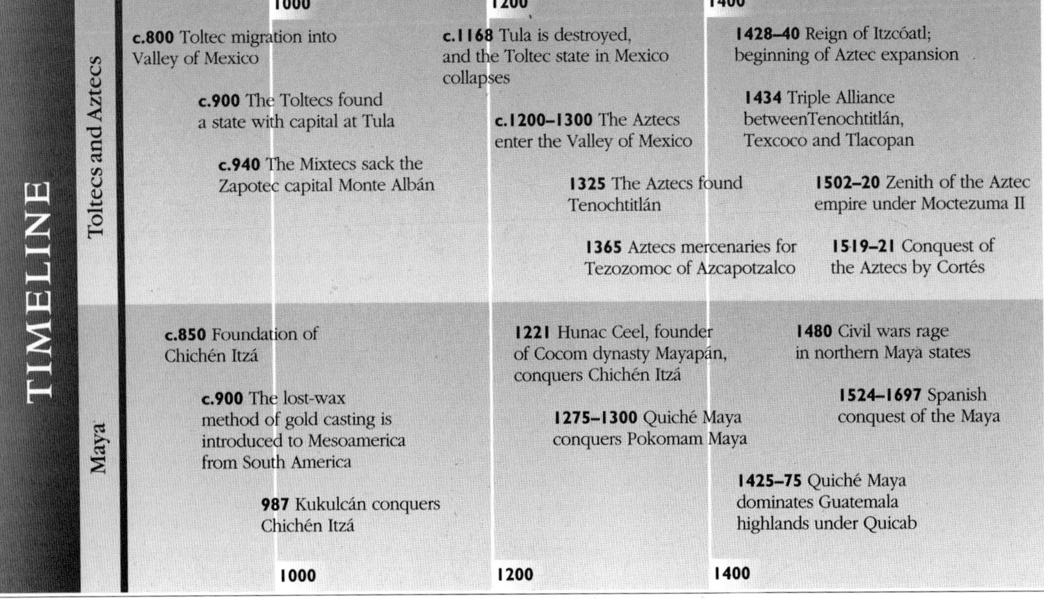

TIMELINE
Toltecs and Aztecs
1000
1200
1400
c.800 Toltec migration into Valley of Mexico
c.900 The Toltecs found a state with capital at Tula
c.940 The Mixtecs sack the Zapotec capital Monte Albán
c.1168 Tula is destroyed, and the Toltec state in Mexico collapses
c.1200–1300 The Aztecs enter the Valley of Mexico
1325 The Aztecs found Tenochtitlán
1365 Aztecs mercenaries for Tezozomoc of Azcapotzalco
1428–40 Reign of Itzcóatl; beginning of Aztec expansion
1434 Triple Alliance betweenTenochtitlán, Texcoco and Tlacopan
1502–20 Zenith of the Aztec empire under Moctezuma II
1519–21 Conquest of the Aztecs by Cortés
Maya
c.850 Foundation of Chichén Itzá
c.900 The lost-wax method of gold casting is introduced to Mesoamerica from South America
987 Kukulcán conquers Chichén Itzá
1221 Hunac Ceel, founder of Cocom dynasty Mayapán, conquers Chichén Itzá
1275–1300 Quiché Maya conquers Pokomam Maya
1425–75 Quiché Maya dominates Guatemala highlands under Quicab
1480 Civil wars rage in northern Maya states
1524–1697 Spanish conquest of the Maya
1000
1200
1400

At the time of the conquest, Aztec society was a class-based hierarchy. Relatives of the king formed the aristocracy, while the commoners (the largest class) comprised members of 20 clans. Each clan had its own quarter of the city with its own schools, temples and communal farms. The lowest class were conquered peoples, who served the aristocracy as farmers and laborers. There were also slaves, usually war captives, and a merchant class, the *pochteca*.

After the Classic Maya cities of the Petén lowlands were abandoned in about 800, Mayan civilization continued in northern Yucatán. Around 850–900 the Putún or Itza Maya settled at Chichén Itzá, which quickly became the dominant Maya center. Around 1000 Yucatán was conquered by the Toltecs, whose rule ended in 1221 with the fall of Chichén Itzá to Hunac Ceel, ruler of Mayapán. The Cocom dynasty he founded dominated Yucatán for over 200 years. When the Spanish landed on Yucatán in 1517 the northern Maya were divided into 16 rival states. This made them harder to subdue than the Aztecs, as there were no key institutions. Thus, Tayasal, the last independent Maya state, did not fall until 1697.

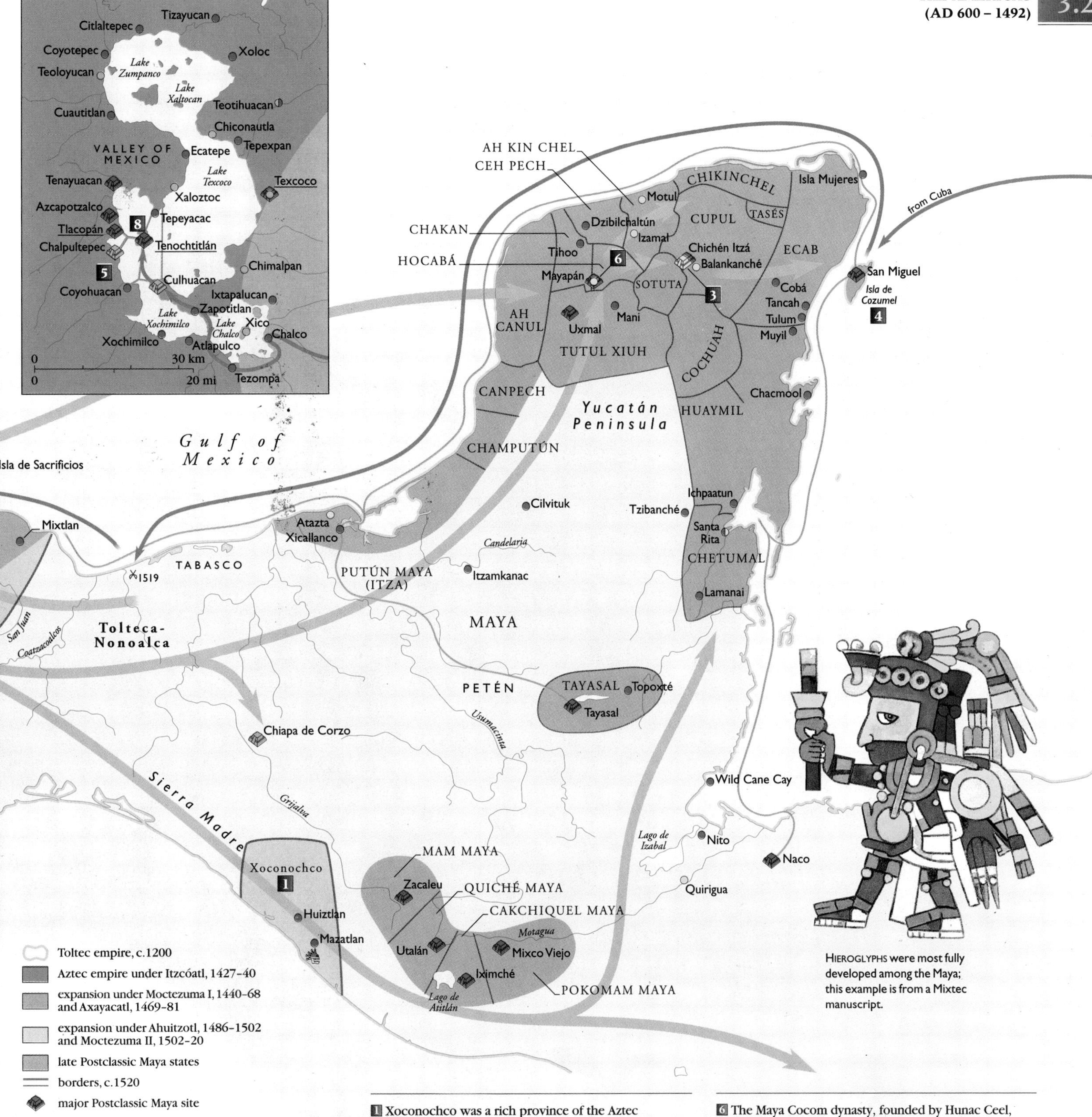

HIEROGLYPHS were most fully developed among the Maya; this example is from a Mixtec manuscript.

- Toltec empire, c.1200
- Aztec empire under Itzcóatl, 1427–40
- expansion under Moctezuma I, 1440–68 and Axayacatl, 1469–81
- expansion under Ahuitzotl, 1486–1502 and Moctezuma II, 1502–20
- late Postclassic Maya states
- borders, c.1520
- major Postclassic Maya site
- other Postclassic Maya site
- major Toltec site
- other Toltec site
- major Aztec site
- other Aztec site
- other major Postclassic site
- other site
- Aztec garrison
- Tlacopán city of the Triple Alliance
- Putún Maya trade route
- migration, c.900
- Toltec migration, c.980–1200
- route of Cortés, April to November 1519

1 Xoconochco was a rich province of the Aztec empire, conquered for its cocoa.

2 The Aztecs allowed Tlaxcallan to remain independent so that they could raid it for sacrificial victims.

3 Chichén Itzá: founded by the Putún Maya c.850, it was the Toltec capital of Yucatán c.987–1221. Many of its buildings were modeled on the old Toltec capital of Tula.

4 Isla de Cozumel was settled by the Putún Maya, who used the island as a storage depot for their coastal trade routes.

5 The key to Aztec power was intensive agriculture on fertile reclaimed swampland, or *chinampas*, on the southern shores of Lake Texcoco.

6 The Maya Cocom dynasty, founded by Hunac Ceel, ruled Yucatán from Mayapán from 1283 until their empire broke up in 1441.

7 The Toltec state, founded at Tula c.900, became the model for the later Mesoamerican states of the Aztecs and northern Maya.

8 With a population of 500,000 at the time of the Spanish conquest, Tenochtitlán ("place of the high priest Tenoch") was far larger than most contemporary European cities. Its site is now buried under Mexico City.

See also 3.04 (the world 1492)

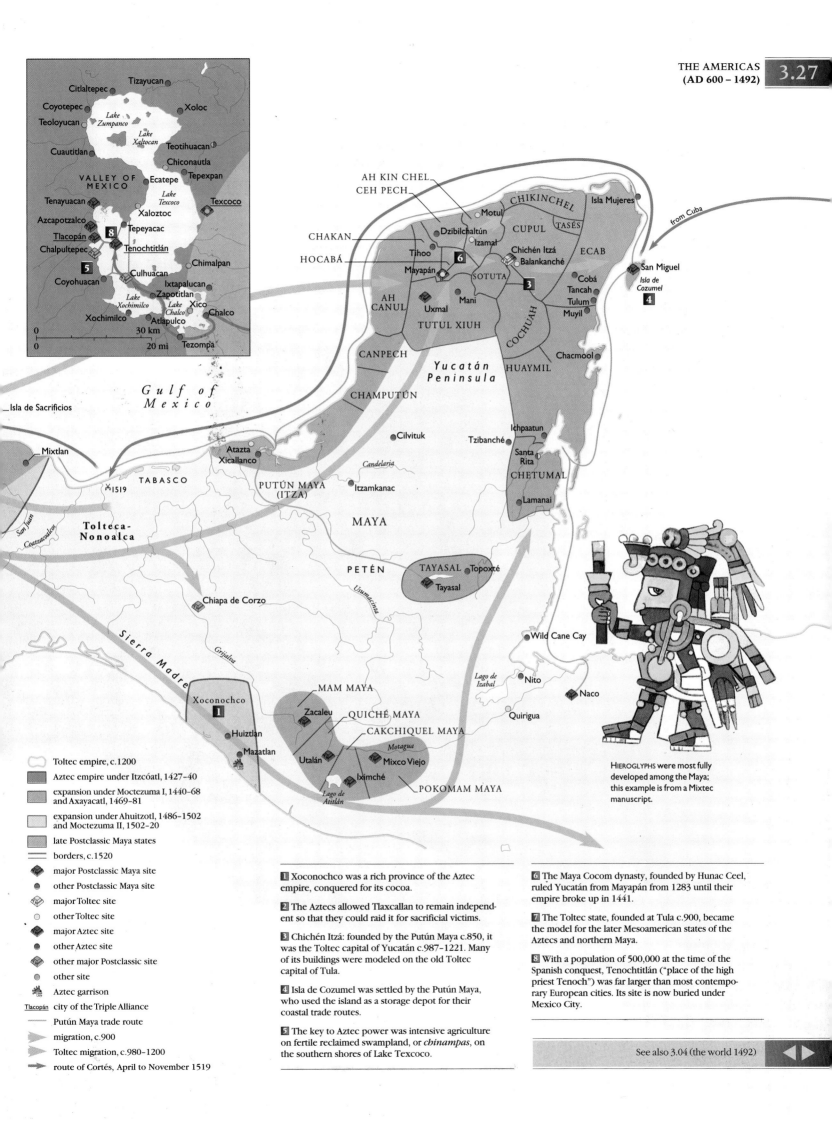

3.28 The Andean civilizations to the fall of the Incas • 700 – 1533 •

The collapse of the highland Tiahuanaco and Huari empires in about 1000 ushered in a long period of political fragmentation in the Andean civilizations. Both in the highlands and on the coast many local states emerged, most of which, like the Sicán state of Lambayeque, controlled no more than a single valley. Around 1200 the Chimú state, centered on Chan Chan in the Moche valley, began a period of gradual imperial expansion until in the 15th century it controlled over a thousand kilometers (620 miles) of the Peruvian coast. Around the same time that the Chimú began to expand, a semi-legendary figure, Manco Capac, founded the Inca state at Cuzco in the Killke cultural area of the highlands. For most of its history the Inca state controlled little more than the valley around Cuzco but in the 15th century it became the greatest of all the empires of the pre-Columbian Americas: it was also destined to be the last.

At its peak in around 1500 the Inca empire encompassed much of modern Peru and Bolivia, together with sizable portions of Chile, Argentina and Equador, and ruled over some 12 million people. The Incas' remarkable territorial expansion took place almost entirely during the reigns of Pachacutec (r.1438–71) and his equally able son Tupac Yupanqui (r.1471–93). The Incas overcame the Chimú, their only serious rivals as an imperial power, with little difficulty, capturing their capital Chan Chan in 1470. By the end of Tupac's reign the Inca empire was reaching the practicable limits of its expansion. The Amazonian rainforest to the east and the southern Andes had sparse, mobile populations that would have proved difficult to control and had environments that were unsuited to the settled intensive agriculture that might make their conquest and colonization worthwhile.

Some new territorial gains were made in the north under Huayna Capac (r. 1493–1525) but on his death a bloody civil war broke out between his sons Atahuallpa and Huáscar. Atahuallpa finally triumphed in 1532 but he had no opportunity to restore the weakened empire. In the same year the Spanish conquistador Francisco Pizarro invaded and captured Atahuallpa in a daring assault on Cajamarca. In 1533 the Spanish executed Atahuallpa and installed a puppet ruler at Cuzco: however, when he rebelled in 1536, they assumed direct rule. Inca resistance continued from inaccessible mountain strongholds but was finally crushed in 1572.

There are many reasons for the Incas' spectacular rise and equally rapid decline. They were fortunate in having able generals as rulers. Inca nobles were brought up in the arts of war and a standing army was maintained, so the empire was able to react quickly to any threat. Uniquely among Andean states, the Incas built a network of strategic roads estimated to have been more than 20,000 kilometers (12,500 miles) long – second only in size to the Roman empire's among pre-industrial civilizations – which allowed troops to move quickly to quell trouble on the borders or in the provinces. Conquests were consolidated by a policy of deporting rebellious populations to the heart of the empire where they could be supervised, while their lands were resettled by loyal Inca subjects.

Probably the main factor in Inca success, however, was their complex administrative system – maintained without any system of writing, and with record-keeping done using an elaborate system of knotted strings known as *quipu* – which allowed them to marshal the empire's human resources with great efficiency. Inca society was highly centralized and rigidly hierarchical. At its head was the semidivine emperor. Below the emperor, and directly answerable to him, were the prefects of the

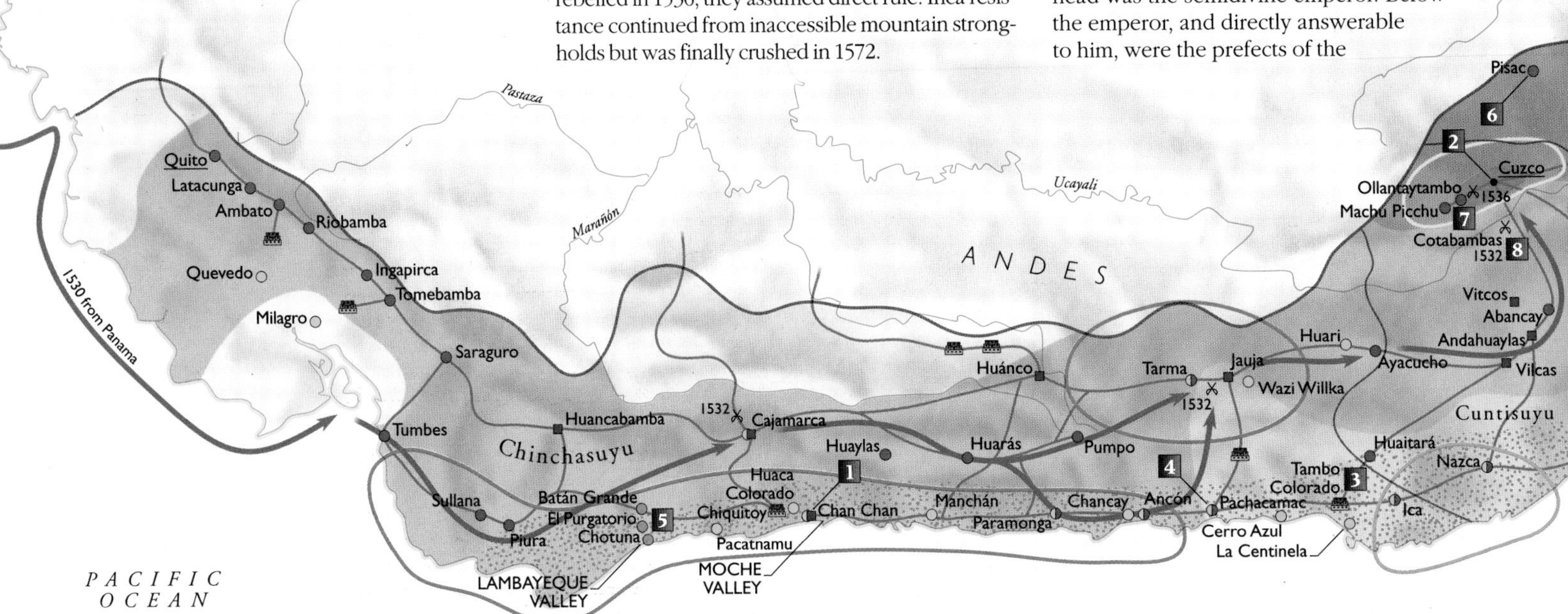

TIMELINE

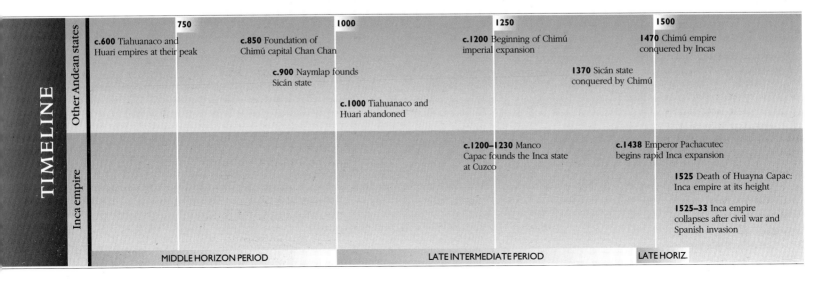

	750	1000	1250	1500
Other Andean states	**c.600** Tiahuanaco and Huari empires at their peak; **c.850** Foundation of Chimú capital Chan Chan; **c.900** Naymlap founds Sicán state	**c.1000** Tiahuanaco and Huari abandoned	**c.1200** Beginning of Chimú imperial expansion; **1370** Sicán state conquered by Chimú	**1470** Chimú empire conquered by Incas
Inca empire			**c.1200–1230** Manco Capac founds the Inca state at Cuzco; **c.1438** Emperor Pachacutec begins rapid Inca expansion	**1525** Death of Huayna Capac: Inca empire at its height; **1525–33** Inca empire collapses after civil war and Spanish invasion

MIDDLE HORIZON PERIOD | LATE INTERMEDIATE PERIOD | LATE HORIZ.

Four Quarters and below them provincial governors, followed by district officers, local chiefs and, at the bottom, foremen each responsible for supervising ten families. Farmland was divided into thirds, for the support of the state, the gods and the people respectively. All Inca men and women contributed taxation in the form of labor on those parts of the land allocated to the state and the gods. Able-bodied men also paid tax through a labor draft known as *mit'a*. This could last for months and range from military service to work on major construction projects, such as roads and fortresses, or agricultural improvements, such as terracing steep hillsides. This system enabled the empire to raise and supply large armies and keep them in the field for long campaigns.

Although Pizarro was fortunate in having his invasion coincide with the end of a long and destructive civil war, the centralized hierarchy of the Inca empire was also partly responsible for its swift demise. No major decision could be taken without the emperor, whch meant that the empire was paralyzed once Atahuallpa had been captured. Diseases also contributed to the Incas' defeat; as in Mesoamerica, the indigenous population had no resistance to epidemics brought by the Spanish. Indeed, the civil war that first weakened the Inca empire was indirectly caused by a disease introduced from Europe: Huayna Capac died of a smallpox epidemic that spread south from the Spanish base at Panama.

1 Chan Chan was the capital of the Chimú empire from c.850–1470: at the heart of the city were ten walled palace-mausoleum compounds.

2 The Inca capital Cuzco was regarded as the center of the universe, from which radiated the "Four Quarters" of the world. In the Quechua language of the Incas (still widely spoken in the Andes), *cuzco* means "navel".

3 *Tambos*, roadside hostels and storehouses, were sited at intervals of one day's journey on all the empire's roads; one of the largest and best preserved is Tambo Colorado.

4 The oracle of the god Pachacamac, dating to around AD 200, was a major pilgrimage center and rival to the Incas' state solar cult.

5 The Lambayeque valley was the center of the wealthy Sicán state from c.900 until its conquest by the Chimú in c.1370.

6 The Inca increased the area of farmland by terracing mountainsides: many, as at Pisac, are still farmed today.

7 Machu Picchu, the most famous Inca site, was a remote mountain-top religious center and frontier outpost.

8 The victory of Atahuallpa's forces over his rival Huáscar at Cotabambas ended the Inca civil war.

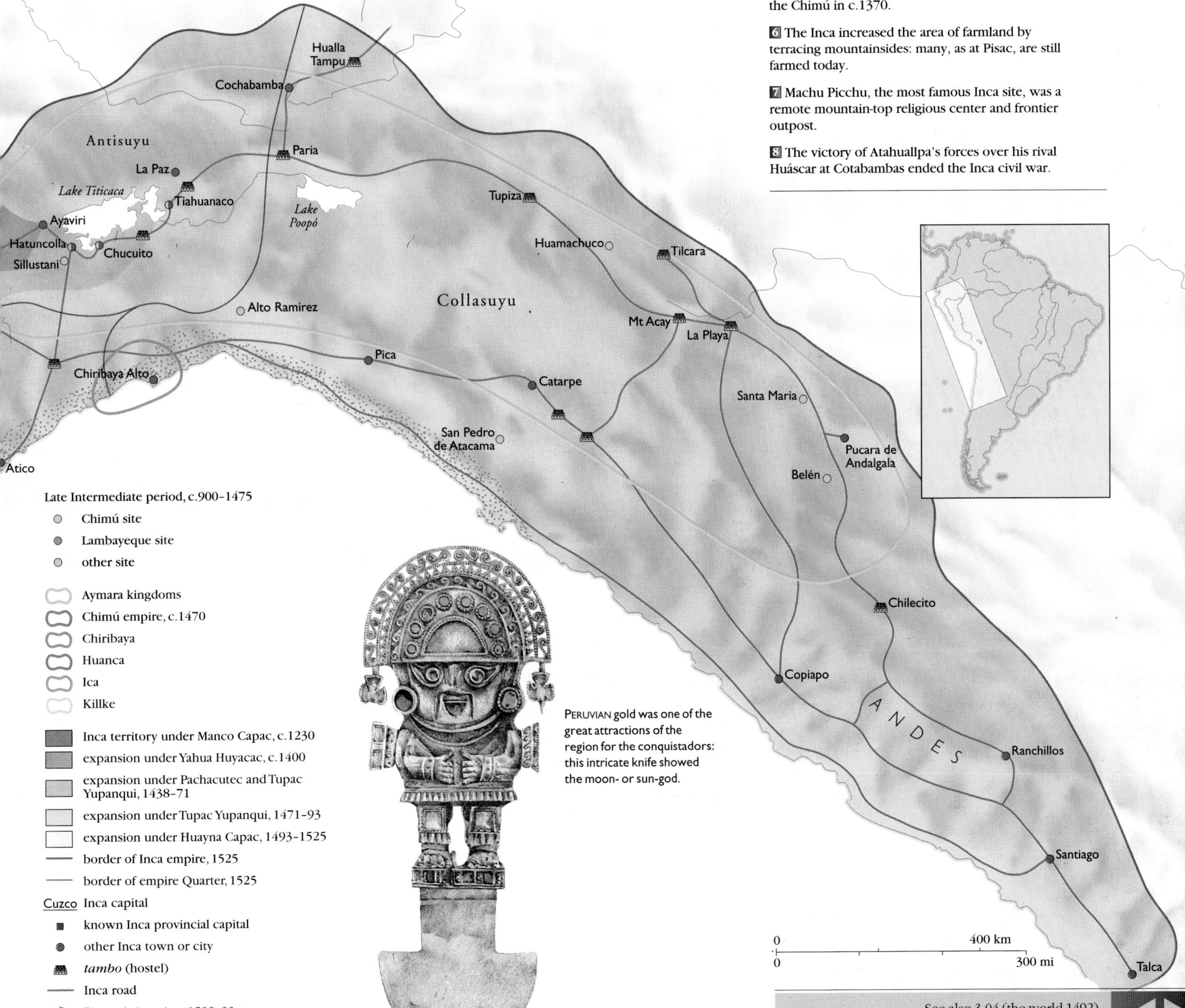

PERUVIAN gold was one of the great attractions of the region for the conquistadors: this intricate knife showed the moon- or sun-god.

See also 3.04 (the world 1492)

Cross-referencing
References to other dictionary entries are identified in small capitals (e.g. BATTLE OF AGINCOURT*); references to map spreads are denoted by the use of an arrow (e.g.* ▷ 3.17*).*

Chinese spellings
Since 1979 the standard international system for the transliteration of Chinese names into Roman characters has been Pinyin, and this is the system used throughout this dictionary.

AACHEN
The capital of the Frankish kingdom under the CAROLINGIANS, now in western Germany. In the 790s CHARLEMAGNE built a palace with adminstrative and religious functions, importing for the purpose marble from Italy. Aachen was a center of artistic and cultural patronage in the first half of the 9th century. ▷ 3.06

ABBASID CALIPHATE
ISLAMIC dynasty founded by ABU AL-ABBAS, ruling from 750 to 1258. Beginning as a revolutionary opposition, the Abbasids overthrew the UMAYYAD caliph at the Battle of the Zab. The Abbasids transferred the center of Islamic power from DAMASCUS to the newly founded city of BAGHDAD. Two phases can be identified in Abbasid history; the first (750–945) saw the gradual erosion of the political authority of the CALIPHS as power was delegated to military commanders; in the second (945–1258), the caliphate maintained only a nominal and moral authority while real power rested with secular dynasties. ▷ 3.01, 3.02, 3.03, 3.05, 3.07, 3.14, 3.16, 3.20

ABD AL-RAHMAN I
Restorer of the UMAYYAD dynasty in Spain. Fleeing the ABBASID conquest, he gathered support from Berber tribes in the Maghreb and invaded Iberia in 755. After defeating the governor Yusuf al-Fihri and successive revolts in the 760s, he established Umayyad rule at CÓRDOBA and maintained it until his death in 788. ▷ 3.14

ABD AL-RAHMAN III
The first CALIPH of Moslem Spain, ruling from 912 to 961. After establishing political unity in CÓRDOBA, he launched offensives against the Christian rulers of Spain and competed for influence in north Africa against the FATIMIDS. At his death Muslim Spain was a prosperous and peaceful state, and Córdoba was by far the most sophisticated city west of CONSTANTINOPLE. ▷ 3.14

ABU AL-ABBAS
The first ABBASID to be CALIPH. After the defeat of the UMAYYADS in 750 there remained only scattered resistance to the new dynasty. Those who did resist were eliminated by al-Abbas with fearsome violence. His victims included those of his own chiefs whom he suspected of having gained too great an authority. Having overseen the transformation of the Abbasids from a revolutionary movement to a governing dynasty, al-Abbas died in 754. ▷ 3.14

ABU BAKR
First CALIPH, a contemporary of MUHAMMAD and one of his earliest converts. A constant companion and supporter of the Prophet, Abu Bakr accompanied him to MEDINA and was instrumental in the conquest of MECCA in 630. Although never a military commander of note, he was appointed by the Prophet as his successor. From 632 until his death in 634 he was largely occupied as caliph in dealing with the *ridda* (apostasy) arising in the new state. His simplicity of life became legendary. ▷ 3.13

ACHAEA
Region of southern Greece and province of BYZANTIUM until 1204, when it became a LATIN principality after the Fourth CRUSADE sacked CONSTANTINTOPLE. Achaea extended over the Peloponnese and included the tributary duchies of Athens and Thebes. The Villehardouin family established a glittering court at Andravida. In 1275 Achaea passed to the ANGEVIN rulers of Naples. It was overrun by the OTTOMANS in 1460. ▷ 3.10, 3.17

ACRE
Town on the Palestinian seaboard, known in the Hebrew Scriptures as Akko and in Greek as Ptolemais. A naval base for the FATIMID CALIPHATE, it was captured by the Frankish CRUSADERS in 1104. Lost to SALADIN in 1187 and regained three years later by the Third Crusade, it was effectively the capital of the KINGDOM OF JERUSALEM until its final fall to the MAMLUKES in 1291. ▷ 3.07, 3.17

ADAL
ISLAMIC state of east Africa in the 14th to the 16th centuries. Its capital was at Harer in modern Ethiopia. Under Ahmed Gran (d.1543), Adal invaded Ethiopia, conquering much of the country by 1533. The Ethiopians were only saved by Portuguese intervention. Adal collapsed in the late 16th century following invasions by the nomadic Oromo. ▷ 3.18

AETHELBALD
King of the MERCIANS (r.716–57). Aethelbald campaigned vigorously against the Welsh, the Northumbrians and the West Saxons. He is credited with reforming the English Church, but he also violated ecclesiastical property. He was murdered by his bodyguard, and buried in a mausoleum built in the Roman style. ▷ 3.06

AGHLABID EMIRATE
North Africa during the 9th century, when the Aghlabids held the region for the ABBASID caliphate. The Aghlabid dynasty was founded by Ibrahim al-Aghlab in 800, who overcame initial opposition with the help of Berber tribes. The last Aghlabid, Ibrahim II, abdicated in 902, and the dynasty was ended by the SHIITE revolution instigated by Abu Abd Allah, which brought the FATIMIDS to power. ▷ 3.10, 3.07, 3.14

AGINCOURT, BATTLE OF
A major battle of the HUNDRED YEARS WAR, fought in northeastern FRANCE (25 October 1415) between an English army of about 6,000 men under HENRY V and a much larger French force. English tactics were superior, centered on dismounted men-at-arms and large numbers of bowmen. They secured a crushing defeat of the French, and this victory paved the way for Henry's conquest of NORMANDY. ▷ 3.12

'AIN JALUT, BATTLE OF
The defeat of the MONGOLS by the MAMLUKE army of Baibars at 'Ain Jalut in Palestine in 1260. It was decisive for the future of the Near East. The westward expansion of the Mongol ILKHANATE was checked and the Mamlukes assured as heirs of the AYYUBID empire in Syria and Palestine. The battle was a setback to the CRUSADER STATES, which had hoped to ally with the Mongols against the Mamlukes. ▷ 3.03, 3.16, 3.17, ▷ 3.22

ALAMUT
Fortress in the Alburz mountains of Khorasan (northeastern Iran). Here from 1090 to 1257, when Alamut was lost to the MONGOLS, a SHIITE sect known as the ASSASSINS ruled an enclave loyal to the FATIMIDS of Egypt. Public murder was used systematically as a means of spreading terror among the neighboring SUNNI populations, and a chronic state of war existed between the Assassins and the surrounding areas. ▷ 3.16

ALA-UD-DIN KHALJI
KHALJI Sultan of Delhi (r.1296–1316). He came to power by assassinating his uncle, Sultan Jalal-ud-Din Firuz Khalji. Ala-ud-Din gave the sultanate a stable economic basis through a heavy land tax to maintain a full-time army. Under him, the MONGOLS were repulsed from India several times and the DELHI SULTANATE's control was extended south of the Narmada river for the first time. ▷ 3.19

ALBERT II
(c.1397–1439) Duke Albert V of Austria, who became HOLY ROMAN EMPEROR Albert II (r.1438–39), initiating continuous Habsburg possession (except for 1740–45) of the imperial crown, until the empire's abolition in 1806. ▷ 3.12

ALBIGENSIAN CRUSADE
Launched by Pope INNOCENT III in 1208 after the murder of a papal legate, the Crusade was intended to extirpate the Cathar heresy from southwestern France. In a series of campaigns lasting 20 years, northern French barons invaded the Languedoc and confiscated territory under the banner of holy war. The

wars ended the independence from the French crown of the county of Toulouse, but they had less effect on heresy than did the INQUISITION and the preaching of the friars. ▷ 3.09

ALEUT
Native inhabitants of the Aleutian Islands of Alaska. The Aleut first appeared in about 2500 BC and are ethnically and linguistically related to the Inuit (Eskimo). They lived by hunting marine mammals and fishing. About 1000 Aleut survive today. ▷ 3.26

ALEXIUS I COMNENUS
BYZANTINE emperor (r.1081–1118) who succeeded a weak administration to save the Byzantine empire from the NORMANS of southern Italy and the Pechenegs by using the aid of first VENICE and then the CUMANS. He profited from the defeat of the SELJUK Kilij Arslan by using the First CRUSADE to recapture territory in Anatolia. ▷ 3.15, 3.17

ALFRED THE GREAT
King of WESSEX (r.871–99). Alfred's main achievement was the successful defense of the kingdom against the VIKINGS, culminating in his defeat of Guthrum at Edington in 878. This laid the foundation for his successors to create a unified English kingdom. Alfred's success was underpinned by reform of Anglo-Saxon military resources and the building of defensive fortifications. In his last decade he devoted himself to a revival of learning by importing scholars to his court. ▷ 3.07

AL-FUSTAT
The first city founded in Egypt by the Muslims (643). Sited on the east bank of the Nile by the small Greek town of Babylon, al-Fustat was later divided into a lower district on the river bank and a higher on the desert plain. The founding of neighboring al-Kahira (Cairo) in 969 did not at first harm the propserity of al-Fustat, which developed as a commercial center. In contrast, a military aristocracy dominated Cairo. SALADIN incorporated al-Fustat with Cairo in the 12th century. ▷ 3.13

ALI
Fourth CALIPH. Cousin and son-in-law of MUHAMMAD, he took part in most of the early military campaigns that established ISLAM in Arabia, and acted as secretary to Muhammad. After the Prophet's death he initially opposed the succession of ABU BAKR, but retired from public life until invited by the UMAYYADS to be caliph after the death of UTHMAN. Following the rebellion of MUAWIYA, Ali was forced to submit to an arbitration that resulted in his deposition. Murdered in 660, he became the figurehead of the SHIITES. ▷ 3.05, 3.13

ALJUBARROTA, BATTLE OF
Defeat of Juan I, king of CASTILE, during his invasion of PORTUGAL in 1385. The defending Portugese had been reinforced by English archers. Portugal thereafter remained safe from Castilian threat. ▷ 3.10

ALMANZOR (AL-MANSUR)
Vizier and effectively the ruler of Muslim Spain from 978 to 1002. Beginning his career in the administration of CÓRDOBA, he rose to become vizier under the young caliph Hisham II in 976. He fought 52 campaigns against the Christians, achieving suzerainty over Navarre in 982 and defeating LEÓN in 984. Almanzor is credited with having fostered Christian unity in Spain by his systematic aggression against the northern kingdoms. ▷ 3.14

ALMOHAD CALIPHATE
A Berber dynasty from Morocco. The Almohads invaded Spain in 1145 but were forced to withdraw after a defeat at LAS NAVAS DE TOLOSA (1212), which opened almost the whole of Spain to the Christians. The dynasty had begun as a movement of reform, founded by Muhammad ibn Tumart (d.1130), calling north African Muslims to spiritual renewal through purity of faith and living. At its peak (1130–63) the Almohad caliphate controlled the Maghreb as far east as Tripoli, in addition to Muslim Spain. ▷ 3.08, 3.09, 3.17

ALMORAVID EMIRATE
A Berber dynasty (1071–1147) from Morocco that succeeded in imposing ISLAM on west Africa as far south as Senegal before taking over Muslim Spain from the UMAYYADS in 1086. The name derives from *al-Murabitun*, a reference to the organization of warriors into groups known as *ribats*. ▷ 3.18

ALP ARSLAN
Second sultan of the SELJUK dynasty, (r.1063–73). He succeeded in bringing all Seljuk territory under his rule and was recognized as sultan by the ABBASID caliph. He campaigned against the BYZANTINES, the Armenians and the GEORGIANS on the Anatolian frontier, subduing Georgia in 1064, and in 1071 he crushed the Byzantine army at MANZIKERT. This victory laid Anatolia open to the Seljuks, but in 1072 Alp Arslan was fatally wounded while invading the Karakhanid territories on his eastern frontier. ▷ 3.16

AL-QADISIYA, BATTLE OF
This victory of the Muslims over the Sasanian king of Persia, Yazdadjird III, at some time in the period from 635 to 637 opened up the way to the ARAB conquest of Persia. The Muslims, though more numerous, were less well equipped than the Sasanians, who used elephants. One tradition says that many of the Sasanian soldiers were chained to one another to prevent their flight, but that they were drowned in a river when the Muslims used them as a human bridge. ▷ 3.13

ALWA
A Christian Nubian kingdom situated below the confluence of the White Nile and Atbara rivers, and extending beyond the confluence of the Blue and White Niles, with its capital at Soba, near modern Khartoum. It was overrun by ARAB tribes in the 16th century, when its independence and its Christianity ended. ▷ 3.01, 3.02, 3.03, 3.04, 3.05, 3.13, 3.14, 3.18

AN LUSHAN
(703–57) Chinese general of Turkish origin who led a rebellion against the TANG DYNASTY in 755. In 756 his forces captured the Tang capital CHANG'AN and he declared himself the first emperor of the Great Yen dynasty. He was murdered by a slave in 757, but the rebellion continued and was suppressed only in 763. The authority of the Tang dynasty never fully recovered. ▷ 3.20

ANASAZI CULTURE
An early maize-farming culture flourishing in the southwestern deserts of North America (AD 700–1500). At its peak the Anasazi attained considerable social and cultural complexity, but droughts caused its decline after 1300. The culture is noted for its multi-roomed apartment dwellings called pueblos and its superb painted pottery. One of the culture's most important sites is CHACO CANYON. ▷ 3.26

ANGEVIN DYNASTY
A royal dynasty descended from the counts of ANJOU that provided the kings of ENGLAND 1154–1485 (also known as the PLANTAGENETS) of which only the first three – HENRY II, RICHARD I and JOHN – are called Angevin monarchs. It was in this period that the dynasty dominated western Europe by means of its vast Angevin empire. Their lands stretched from SCOTLAND to the Pyrenees. In 1204 John lost the empire and the dynastic heartland of Anjou, after which the Plantagenet appellation is applied. ▷ 3.08

ANGKOR
Sacred temple city and capital of the KHMER EMPIRE from the time of its foundation by king Yasovarman I (r.889–910) until its sack by the Thais in 1431. Angkor was abandoned soon after and only rediscovered in the 1860s by French missionaries. The largest monument is the temple of Angkor Wat, dedicated to Vishnu, the patron god of SURYAVARMAN II, its builder. After Angkor was sacked by the CHAMS in 1177, Angkor Wat was replaced by the almost equally impressive temple precinct of Angkor Thom. ▷ 3.25

ANJOU
County of northwest FRANCE and seat of the ANGEVIN DYNASTY. When Count Henry of Anjou, son of Geoffrey PLANTAGENET, became king of ENGLAND in 1154, Anjou continued to be held by the English kings as a fief from the French crown until JOHN lost the county in 1204. Anjou became a duchy in 1297 and was fully annexed to the French crown by LOUIS XI in 1480. ▷ 3.08

Ankara, Battle of
In 1402 Timur the Lame defeated and captured in battle at Ankara the Ottoman sultan Bayezid I. The victory marked the western limit of Timur's expansion; at the same time it led to a temporary crisis in the Ottoman regime and an interregnum of ten years before Mehmed I was able to reunite the empire. ▷ 3.12, 3.16, 3.23

Anse aux Meadows, l'
Archeological site of a small Norse settlement in northern Newfoundland, which was occupied for about 20 years in about 1000. The site is the only certain evidence of Precolumbian European contact with the Americas. ▷ 3.26

Antioch, principality of
A largely Greek enclave in what is now Syria. The capture of Antioch by the Crusaders in 1098 marked the beginning of a Frankish state in north Syria. Byzantium claimed suzerainty, but only periodically could emperors assert their authority. Despite military setbacks in 1119 and 1164 the principality survived Muslim attack until 1268, when it fell to the Mamluke sultan Baibars. ▷ 3.17

Antipope
A rival pope to the one elected by canon law, as occurred during the Great Schism of 1378 to 1417.

Aquitaine
Duchy in southwest France ranging from the Pyrenees to the Loire, including Gascony. It passed to the Angevins in 1152 when Henry of Anjou married Eleanor of Aquitaine, and so to England when he became Henry II in 1154. From 1204 the French crown took possession of Aquitaine, but Gascony was not finally lost to France until 1453 at the end of the Hundred Years War. ▷ 3.06. 3.08, 3.10

Arabic
The language of the Arabs. It is a Semitic language, whose oldest written examples date from about 300, but whose oral history is much older. Most pre-Islamic Arabic takes the form of poetry. The language and script became an important vehicle for disseminating Islam through the Koran, the model for literary usage. The language took on new influences with the spread of Islam, and the classical period saw an extension of the corpus of Arabic writing through the translation of Greek works. ▷ 3.13

Arabs
Semitic people of the Arabian peninsula, the first to be converted to Islam. By the time of the emergence of Islam they were polarized between the nomadic tribes of the interior and the trading cities of the coast. The Arabs were polytheistic, but communities of Jews and Christians were important in the cities. Between 622 and 632 the Arabs adopted Islam, which became the vehicle of their expansion beyond the peninsula. ▷ 3.02, 3.08, 3.13, 3.14, 3.15, 3.16, 3.17, 3.18

Aragon
Region of northeastern Spain. The kingdom of Aragon was born from the union between Aragon and the county of Catalonia, formerly a fief of the West Frankish kingdom. The kingdom began to flourish after 1085, when the pace of the Reconquista quickened. The Balearic Islands were conquered by Aragon in the early 13th century, and later in the century Aragon developed an international role through King Peter I's involvement in Sicily. The marriage of King Ferdinand of Aragon to Queen Isabella of Castile in 1479 effectively united the kingdoms. ▷ 3.03, 3.04, 3.07, 3.08, 3.09, 3.10, 3.11, 3.12

Arcadiopolis, Battle of
Battle fought in 970 in Thrace, Greece, when the Greek general Bardas Sclerus defeated the invading army of Svjateslav, grand prince of Kiev. ▷ 3.15

Armagnac dynasty
Ruling family of Armagnac, originating in the 10th century, that held power from 1319 to 1525. It formed an opposing faction (also known as the Orléanists) to the Burgundian party, vying for control of King Charles VI of France. The conflict ended with the Treaty of Arras (1435) which reconciled the Burgundian court with France. ▷ 3.12

Arsuf, Battle of
Victory of Richard I's crusading army over Saladin on the coastal plain of Palestine near Arsuf as it marched south from Acre to Jaffa in 1191. Saladin's harrying tactics succeeded in disrupting the Crusader column, but Richard's generalship ensured that the battle was won by a decisive cavalry charge. The victory restored Frankish morale after the disastrous defeat of Hattin. ▷ 3.17

Ascalon, Battle of
Christian victory in the First Crusade. A month after the capture of Jerusalem in July 1099, Crusaders led by Godfrey of Bouillon won a decisive victory over the Fatimids near Ascalon. The victory secured the Crusaders in possession of Jerusalem. ▷ 3.17

Ashikaga shogunate
Japanese rulers (1336–1573). A branch of the Minamoto family, the Ashikaga shoguns controlled the emperor and government of Japan from Kyoto. The family came to power after the overthrow of the Kamakura shogunate and the attempt by emperor Go-Daigo to restore direct imperial rule. After the Onin War the dynasty's authority faded as power passed to the *daimyo* (provincial feudal warlords). By 1500 Japan had broken up into over 400 effectively independent states. ▷ 3.24

Assassins (Ismaili Nizari)
A Shiite sect ruling from Alamut between 1090 and 1257, and also active in Lebanon in the 12th century. In the late 12th and early 13th century they proselytized in India, maintaining a nominal connection to the movement in Iran until the 16th century. The name is derived from their supposed ritual use of hashish. The modern word "assassin" takes its meaning from the sect's murderous tactics against Sunni Muslims. ▷ 3.05, 3.16, 3.17

Asturias
Region of northwest Spain. The foundations of its kingdom were laid by the Visigothic nobleman Pelayo (Pelagius) whose victory over the Muslims at Covadonga in 718 is traditionally regarded as the beginning the Spanish Reconquista. In 866 Asturias became part of León. It was made a principality in 1338. ▷ 3.06, 3.07, 3.14

Atahuallpa
Last ruler of the Inca empire, Atahuallpa (r.1525–33) spent most of his reign fighting a civil war with his brother Huáscar. Shortly after defeating Huáscar in 1532, Atahuallpa was captured by the Spanish conquistador Francisco Pizarro and executed the following year. ▷ 3.28

Athos, Mount
Also known as the Holy Mountain, this was the center of Greek Orthodox monastic spirituality and theological study in the Byzantine period. Situated on the easternmost of the three peninsulas of Chalkidike, in northeast Greece, it comprised 20 separate monasteries, most but not all Orthodox and representing between them both communal and hermit traditions within monasticism. The Holy Mountain first flourished under Emperor Nikephoros Phokas (963–69) and by about 1100 was a self-governing monastic republic with immunity from the state. ▷ 3.09, 3.15

Austrasia
Eastern division of the Frankish kingdom following the death of Clovis I (511). It included Belgium and Lorraine. Ruled by Merovingian kings until the 8th century, it ceased to exist under Charlemagne's rule. ▷ 3.06

Avignon papacy
Period when the papal court resided at Avignon in southeast France (1309–77). The papacy, already under French influence, moved to Avignon to avoid the civil unrest raging in Italy. A magnficent, luxurious palace was built there to accommodate the court, leading contemporaries to denounce the "Babylonian captivity of the Church". All six popes of the Avignon papacy were French, creating unease among France's enemies, especially England. However, the papacy was generally sincere in its motivations and the period is marked by great advances in

bureaucratic efficiency and fiscal development. The court went back to Rome in 1377, but in 1378 the GREAT SCHISM returned it to Avignon until 1408. ▷ 3.04, 3.05, 3.10, 3.12

AYUTTHAYA
Thai kingdom named for its capital Ayutthaya, north of Bangkok, Thailand. It was the direct precursor of the kingdom of Siam (modern Thailand). The city, founded in 1351 by Ramathabodi I, was the Thai capital until it was sacked by the BURMESE in 1767. There are extensive ruins of Buddhist temples, royal tombs and palaces. ▷ 3.25

AYYUBID DYNASTY
ISLAMIC dynasty of Egypt, founded by SALADIN in 1177. The Ayyubids also controlled Syria and reduced the CRUSADER STATES of the HOLY LAND to a coastal strip. The dynasty was overthrown in 1250 by the MAMLUKES, Turkish slave soldiers recruited by the Ayyubids. ▷ 3.16

AZTECS
The dominant people of Mesoamerica from the 15th to the early 16th centuries. They were a farming people who migrated into the valley of Mexico in about 1200, settling at TENOCHTITLÁN in 1325. The Aztec monarchy and state was founded by ITZCÓATL in 1428. In alliance with the neighboring city-states of Texcoco and Tlacopan, the Aztecs had conquered most of central Mexico by 1500, their empire reaching its greatest extent under MOCTEZUMA II (r.1502–20). The empire was destroyed by the Spanish CONQUISTADOR Hernán Cortés in 1519–21. A driving force behind the Aztec conquests was the need to capture prisoners to sacrifice in religious rituals. Aztec society was hierarchical and class-based. The aristocracy were relatives of the king while the commoners were divided into 20 hereditary clans. Aztec civilization was derived largely from earlier Mexican civilizations, including the TOLTEC. ▷ 3.27

BAGHDAD
The capital of the ABBASID dynasty. Founded on the banks of the Tigris in 763, the city was built around a network of canals, and divided into quarters reflecting various ethnic and professional groupings. During the second half of the 9th century, when the capital moved temporarily to SAMARRA, Baghdad remained the commercial and cultural center. Building in the 10th century extended one side of the city to a length of 8 kilometers (5 miles). The population grew to 1.5 million, but under the BUWAYHIDS Baghdad was neglected and fell into decline from the mid-11th century. After the end of the ABBASID CALIPHATE in 1258 it was a provincial center. ▷ 3.01, 3.02, 3.03, 3.05, 3.14, 3.16

BAHMANI SULTANATE
Muslim sultanate of the Deccan region of India, founded in 1347 by Hasan Gungu, governor of the Deccan, following his rebellion against MUHAMMAD IBN TUGHLUK, sultan of DELHI. The Bahmani capital was at the fortress of Daulatabad. Bahmani expansion to the south was blocked by the powerful Hindu kingdom of Vijayanagara, and by the end of the 15th century it had broken up into five independent sultanates. ▷ 3.19

BALLIOL, JOHN
King of SCOTLAND (r.1292–96). Balliol was made monarch by EDWARD I of ENGLAND. His rebellion against Edward led to an English invasion of Scotland and his capture.

BANNOCKBURN, BATTLE OF
Battle fought in central SCOTLAND (24 June 1314) between the armies of Robert I (the Bruce) of Scotland and King Edward II of ENGLAND. The tactical superiority of the Scots ensured victory over the poorly led English. Its outcome resulted in English recognition of Scottish independence in 1328. ▷ 3.10

BASIL II (THE BULGAR-SLAYER)
BYZANTINE emperor (r.976–1025) who supported the peasantry against powerful landowners. His great success and ruthlessness against the BULGARS earned him his soubriquet; Bulgaria was annexed to the empire in 1018. Under his rule the empire dominated Europe and the Middle East. ▷ 3.15

BATU KHAN
A grandson of CHINGIS KHAN. Between 1236 and 1241 he conquered most of southern Russia, secured the vassalage of the local princes and founded the MONGOL state known as the GOLDEN HORDE. Although he penetrated as far west as the Danube in 1241, defeating the Poles and Hungarians, he failed to establish a permanent base in Europe before his death in about 1255. ▷ 3.23

BAYEUX TAPESTRY
A linen strip 48 centimeters (19 inches) wide and 70 meters (231 feet) long depicting the BATTLE OF HASTINGS (1066). It was completed soon after the battle, probably commissioned for Odo, bishop of Bayeux. ▷ 3.08

BAYEZID I
OTTOMAN sultan (r.1389–1403). After mastering Turkish rivals in western Anatolia, Bayezid turned to the Balkans, defeating the Bulgars in 1393 and blockading CONSTANTINOPLE (1394–1403). In 1396 he crushed a western crusading army at NICOPOLIS, but was himself defeated by TIMUR THE LAME in 1402 and died as his captive. ▷ 3.23

BECKET, THOMAS À
(c.1120–70) Archbishop of Canterbury and saint. He was appointed chancellor in 1155, and in 1162 HENRY II promoted him to the archbishopric of Canterbury, expecting his help and cooperation in issues opposing the church and the state, but Becket took the part of the church, especially in matters concerning benefits of the clergy. On his return from exile in FRANCE (1164–70) he was murdered in Canterbury Cathedral (29 December 1170) by four knights believing their action would help the king. He was canonized remarkably swiftly (February 1173) making Canterbury a popular destination for pilgrims. ▷ 3.08

BELGRADE, BATTLE OF
Battle fought on 10 September 1456. The OTTOMAN Turks, following up their great victory at CONSTANTINOPLE (1453) had their advances eastwards checked at Belgrade, where their siege of the city was lifted by Hunyady, HUNGARY's national hero. His rout of the Turks blocked their advance towards Hungary. ▷ 3.16

BENEDICTINE ORDER
Monastic followers of the Rule of St Benedict of Nursia (c.480–c.547). Followers sought to achieve personal sanctification through adherence to the Rule through study, labor, communal worship and obedience to superiors. By the 8th century it was the dominant monastic order, gaining further influence through the 10th-century CLUNIAC reform movement. Benedictines were known as "Black Monks" on account of their black habits. ▷ 3.09

BENIN
West African rainforest kingdom founded in about 1250, now part of modern Nigeria. The kingdom was at its peak from the 16th to 18th centuries as a result of its involvement in the slave trade. The kingdom was annexed by Britain in 1897. Benin was noted for the high technical and artistic standards of its cast bronze sculptures. The former French west African colony of Dahomey adopted the name in 1975. ▷ 3.18

BERNARD OF CLAIRVAUX, ST
(c.1090–1153) Charismatic and ascetic abbot of his foundation at Clairvaux, France. His influence as a philosopher, orator, theolgian and reformer was felt throughout the 12th-century church among laymen and popes. He preached the Second CRUSADE and reformed the CISTERCIAN ORDER. ▷ 3.09

BIBLE
The sacred book of the Jewish and Christian traditions, comprising the Old Testament (the Jewish Bible) and the New Testament (the gospels of the life of Christ, and writings of the early church). The definitive form of the Bible as known in western Christianity was established by St Jerome, who translated it into Latin (the Vulgate Bible) in the 5th century AD. The later Middle Ages saw increasing movements to translate the Bible into vernacular languages: one of the first was produced in English by John Wycliffe in the late 14th century.

Black Death
A devastating epidemic that swept Europe in the 14th century – the defining episode of the 1300s. A combination of Bubonic and pneumonic plague that was imported from eastern Europe in 1346, it was spread throughout the continent by rats infested with carrier parasitic fleas. Entering through ports and following trade routes it spread rapidly, with mortality rates averaging 47 percent in England (where almost half the population died within 18 months). In Europe over a third of the population succumbed to the plague from 1346 to 1351. Its impact may have been heightened when famine and malnutrition reduced resistance to the disease during crop failures from 1315 to 1317 and in the 1320s. Cattle and sheep plagues also reduced the food supply. Social repercussions included religious hysteria, civil unrest and persecution of the Jews; economic effects included asset deflation and wage inflation. ▷ 3.04, 3.10, 3.16, 3.23

Bogomils
A heretical movement that took its name from a 10th-century Bulgarian village priest. Active in the Balkans, the Bogomils preached against the Orthodox church and the Byzantine rulers, and for dualism (the material world is evil; the unseen spiritual world is good). They spread into Europe as Cathars. ▷ 3.09

Bohemond I
(c.1056–1111) Norman adventurer and soldier from Sicily. A leader of the First Crusade, he took Antioch, becoming its prince while the other Crusaders went on to take Jerusalem. ▷ 3.09, 3.17

Borobudur
A vast Buddhist monument in Java, built between 778 and 850 by the Sailendra dynasty. The site comprises over 70 stupas on a terraced platform 31 meters (103 feet) high. The monument was conceived as a model of the Buddhist path to enlightenment. The site was abandoned in about 1000 and restored by Dutch archeologists (1907–11). ▷ 3.25

Bosworth Field, Battle of
Final battle of the Wars of the Roses, fought on 22 August 1485 in the English Midlands between the armies of Henry Tudor and Richard III. Richard's death on the battlefield signaled the loss of the Yorkist cause and the ascendancy of the Tudor dynasty under Henry VII. ▷ 3.12

Bouvines, Battle of
French victory over imperial forces in northeastern France (27 July 1214), in which a coalition of anti-Capetian forces under Emperor Otto IV was routed by Philip II. The victory confirmed Philip's earlier conquests of Angevin territory in France, destroyed Otto's power and left France the strongest power in Europe. ▷ 3.08

Brétigny, Treaty of
Treaty signed between England and France in May 1360. It marked a nine-year peace in the Hundred Years War. By its terms the French ceded Aquitaine and Gascony to Edward III. Its most tangible outcome was the ransom and release of King John II of France, captured by the English at the Battle of Poitiers (1356). ▷ 3.10

Brittany
The northwestern peninsula of France. A duchy by the end of the 10th century, it remained a semi-independent state until absorbed into France by 1491 through royal marriages, and fully incorporated by 1532. ▷ 3.07, 3.08, 3.10, 3.12, 3.13, 3.14

Bruges
An important trading and maunfacturing city in northwest Belgium. Bruges was a central office of the Hanseatic League in the 13th century, by which time it had become the main port of exchange for goods from the Baltic and the Mediterranean. It was also the center for English wool exports and the Flemish cloth industry. Bruges's wealth was reflected in generous patronage of the arts, and it became a leading cultural city. Silting of its access to the sea hastened its decline in the 15th century. ▷ 3.11

Bubonic plague
Disease transmitted by fleas of the black rat, causing swelling of the lymph nodes (called buboes), usually leading to death. It broke out repeatedly in Europe, most devastatingly in the Black Death. ▷ 3.06, 3.10

Bulgar khanate
Khanate on the Danube, founded in about 679 by a group of Bulgars, a Turkic people originally from central Asia. By the late 9th century their language had been replaced by a new Slavic language and culture that took shape from their conversion to Orthodox Christianity in 864. The khanate was conquered by the Byzantine emperor Basil II in 1018. ▷ 3.02, 3.03, 3.06, 3.07, 3.14, 3.15

Burgundy, duchy of
Region in northeast France. An important but frequently hostile fief of France, it passed out of the royal demesne to Philip the Bold in 1364, thereby beginning its ascendancy and expansion until 1477 under a succession of notable dukes: John the Fearless, Philip the Good and Charles the Bold, all opponents of the Armagnac faction. Under Philip the Good it was probably the richest state of Europe. Following Charles the Bold's death at the Battle of Nancy (1477), King Louis XI annexed the duchy to the French crown. ▷ 3.10, 3.12, 3.17

Burmese
Alternative name for the Burman people, who originated on the southeast Tibetan plateau, migrated into the Irrawaddy valley in the early 9th century and set up the kingdom of Pagan (c.850). They overcame the Mons to dominate the region later known as Burma. ▷ 3.25

Buwayhids
A Persian Shiite tribal federation from Daylam by the Caspian Sea, whose conquest of Persia and capture of Baghdad in 945 ended the Abbasid caliphate's political power. Although the Abbasids retained the office of caliph, real power henceforth lay with chief emirs, the first of whom was Ahmad ibn Buya. One feature of their government was the use of *iqta'*, the financing of armed forces by the allotment of landed estates. ▷ 3.02, 3.14. 3.16

Byzantine empire
Empire of western Asia and southeastern and southern Europe, named for Byzantium, the Greek name of its capital Constantinople. Formed from the eastern Roman empire and lasting until the 15th century, it carried forward the fundamental ideas and ideals of the Roman empire for a thousand years after its fall. Heraclius (r.610–45) implemented long-lasting military and administrative reforms which are generally regarded as marking the end of the eastern Roman empire and the beginning of the Byzantine empire. Despite losing territory to the Arabs, Bulgars and Lombards the empire recovered and reached its peak in about 1000 under Basil II. A crushing defeat by the Seljuk Turks at Manzikert (1071) led to rapid decline. Calls to the Latin west for armed help began the Crusades but poor relations with the west resulted in the sack of Constantinople by the Fourth Crusade in 1204. The Byzantines recaptured Constantinople in 1261 and the empire lingered on until conquered by the Ottoman Turks in 1453. It was a state of outstanding Christian culture, alienated from Latin Christendom by the schism between the Roman Catholic and Orthodox churches. ▷ 3.02, 3.03, 3.04, 3.05, 3.06, 3.07, 3.08, 3.09, 3.10, 3.11, 3.12, 3.14, 3.15. 3.22, 3.23

Calais
Seaport of northeartern France. Taken from France by Edward III in 1347, it remained the only English possession in France after the Hundred Years War, finally falling to France in 1558. ▷ 3.12

Caliph
The office of successor to Muhammad. The caliph was the political and spiritual leader of the Islamic people, originally legitimized by the consensus of the community. This unity was shattered by the mid-7th century and the office disputed by rival dynasties – the Umayyads and Abbasids, and from the 10th century the Fatimids in Egypt. By the end of the 10th century the Abbasid caliphs had ceased to have political authority, and although the office survived until 1258 it became largely a titular position. ▷ 3.13

Calmar, Union of
Union in 1397 of Denmark, Sweden and Norway (which ruled Iceland). Sweden broke away in 1523, but Denmark and Norway remained united until 1814. ▷ 3.10, 3.12

Camel, Battle of the
A decisive engagement fought in 656 near al-Basra between Caliph Ali and 'A'isha, the widow of Muhammad, and her supporters, who rebelled against Ali after the murder of Uthman, the previous caliph. Ali was victorious when the camel ridden by 'A'isha was hamstrung and she was captured. ▷ 3.13

Canossa
Town in northern Italy and scene in 1077 (during the early stages of the Investiture contest) of a humiliating submission and public penance by the excommunicated Henry IV, king of Germany and Italy, before Pope Gregory VII.

Capet, Hugh
(c.938–996) King of France (r.986–96). He was elected monarch following the death of Louis V, the last Carolingian king. He founded the Capetian dynasty which ruled France until 1328. ▷ 3.07

Capetian dynasty
French royal family, founded by Hugh Capet in 987 and ruling France until 1328. Under such kings as Philip II and Louis IX, the existence of France was secured and it grew to become Europe's strongest state.

Carolingian dynasty
Frankish dynasty founded by the palace mayor Pepin of Herstal (d.714), named for his successor Charles Martel. Pepin III overthrew the Merovingian dynasty and became king of the Franks in 751. The Carolingians reached the peak of their power under Charlemagne (r.768–814) whose empire included most of western Europe. Carolingian rule continued in what is now Germany until 911, in what is now France until 987.

Carolingian empire
Frankish empire instituted by Charlemagne following his coronation as Roman emperor on Christmas Day 800. The imperial title was a confirmation of the territorial power he had amassed over former Roman territory, extending across France, the Low Countries, most of Germany west of the Elbe and Italy as far south as Rome. The empire, governed in accordance with written laws, sought consciously to revive Roman imperial forms. The empire was partitioned between Charlemagne's grandsons by the Treaty of Verdun in 843 and finally broke up in 888. ▷ 3.01, 3.02, 3.06, 3.07, 3.08

Casimir IV
(1427–92) Duke of Lithuania who became king of Poland-Lithuania (r.1447–92) by marriage, thus reuniting the kingdom of Poland-Lithuania. He campaigned successfully against the Teutonic Knights, recovering western Prussia from them in 1466 by the Treaty of Thorn. Under his rule Poland-Lithuania was the largest state in Europe. ▷ 3.12

Castile
Spanish kingdom. Originally a county of León, it became independent in the 11th century. Castile expanded southwards against the Muslims, finally defeating them with the fall of Granada in 1492. It was united with its great peninsular rival Aragon in 1479, following the marriage of Isabella of Castile and Ferdinand of Aragon. ▷ 3.03, 3.04, 3.08, 3.09, 3.10, 3.11, 3.12

Cathars
Heretics active from the 12th to the 14th centuries in southern France and Lombardy. Their power base was the city of Albi, hence the Albigensian Crusade (1209–29) launched against them, after which the Inquisition was established to deal with persistent Cathars. Adherents followed the dualist teaching, derived from the Bogomils, that all matter is evil. ▷ 3.05, 3.09, 3.17

Catholic church
See Roman Catholic church

Caxton, William
(c.1422–91) English printer responsible for producing the first printed English book (*Recuyell of the Historyes of Troyes*) and for England's first printing press (1476). ▷ 3.12

Chaco Canyon
Complex of sites of the Anasazi culture which flourished from 950 to 1300. The central site is Pueblo Bonito, a vast semi-circular apartment building of 800 rooms, probably once inhabited by 1,200 people. Chaco Canyon was linked to 125 subsidiary villages by a 400-kilometer (250-mile) road network. The relationship between the canyon sites and the outlying villages is uncertain but it may have been a central ritual and trade center. ▷ 3.26

Chagatai khanate
A Mongol state of central Asia. The western half was dominated by the silk-route cities of Samarkand and Tashkent, while the eastern half was inhabited largely by pagan nomads. Becoming emir of Samarkand in 1361, Timur the Lame attempted between 1370 and 1405 to use Chagatai as the foundation for a renewed Great Khanate, but his wars ultimately reduced the khanate to the area around Kashgar. ▷ 3.03, 3.04, 3.05, 3.23

Chalukyas
Hindu dynasty that dominated central India in the 7th century. Founded by Jayasimha in about 500, the Chalukya kingdom reached its greatest extent under Pulakeshin II (r.610–43). He defeated Harsha in 633, halting Harsha's plans to conquer the Deccan. The Chalukyas were overthrown by the Rashtrakuta dynasty in 756. ▷ 3.19

Champa
The kingdom of the Chams, an Austronesian people of Vietnam. Founded in 192, Champa was a considerable power up to the 11th century when it began to lose ground to the neighboring Vietnamese and Khmer peoples. The Chams were strongly influenced by Indian civilization. Champa was conquered by the Vietnamese kingdom of Cochin China in 1611. The Chams survive as a small ethnic minority in modern Vietnam. ▷ 3.25

Chams
See Champa

Chan Buddhism
See Zen Buddhism

Chandella
Rajput dynasty and kingdom on the central Gangetic plain. Its capital was the temple city of Khajuraho. The kingdom survived from around 836 until 1202 when it was destroyed by Qutb-ud-Din. ▷ 3.19

Chang'an
Ancient name of modern Xian, Shensi province, China. Chang'an was founded in 202 BC as the capital of the former Han dynasty (206 BC–AD 9). It was later also the capital of the Sui (581–618) and Tang (618–907) dynasties. With over 1 million inhabitants it was the world's largest city by the year 750. Chang'an was divided into three parts, the palace city, the imperial city (for the officials) and the outer city for craftsmen and for merchants. Many ancient buildings survive, including temples, pagodas and fortifications. ▷ 3.20

Charlemagne
Carolingian king of the Franks (r.768–814) and "Roman" emperor (r.800–814). He brought most of western Europe under his control, campaigning successfully against Saxons, Lombards, Bohemians and Avars to expand his empire northwards and eastwards. A devout Christian, he promoted church reform and the revival of learning – the Carolingian Renaissance. The exact significance of his imperial coronation in Rome in 800 is not clear; Charlemagne probably believed he was refounding the western Roman empire ▷ 3.01, 3.02, 3.06, 3.07

Charles II (the Fat)
King of France (r.884–87). As Charles III, emperor of the west (r.881–87), he reunited the Carolingian empire. Deposed following a humiliating treaty with the Vikings (887), when the final break-up of the Carolingian empire began, he died in 888. ▷ 3.07

CHARLES IV
(1316–78) HOLY ROMAN EMPEROR (r.1346–78). He defeated LOUIS IV to gain the imperial crown for the LUXEMBOURG DYNASTY. A shrewd and capable leader, he avoided traditional imperial entanglements in Italy. His reign saw stability and prosperity. In 1356 he issued the GOLDEN BULL to govern imperial elections. ▷ 3.10

CHARLES III (THE SIMPLE)
King of FRANCE (r.893–923). In 911 Charles granted Rouen to the VIKING leader Rollo, so establishing the duchy of NORMANDY. His attempts to strengthen royal power led to his deposition, imprisonment and, in 929, his murder. ▷ 3.07

CHARLES VII
(1403–61) King of FRANCE (r.1422–61). When Charles succeded to the throne, the northern half of France, including Paris, was under English rule. French recovery began when JOAN OF ARC relieved ORLÉANS in 1429. Charles was in Paris by 1436. Ultimate victory in the HUNDRED YEARS WAR was achieved by France in 1453, owing much to Charles's stabilization of royal finances, reconciliation with BURGUNDY in 1435 and reorganization of the French army.

CHARLES THE BOLD
Last reigning duke of BURGUNDY (r.1467–77) and one of the richest and most powerful princes of his time. An implacable foe of his feudal overlord, LOUIS XI, he attempted to unite his lands in the Low Countries and Burgundy by conquering the intervening territory. He was killed at the Battle of Nancy (1477) and his lands divided between FRANCE and the Habsburgs. ▷ 3.12

CHARLES MARTEL (THE HAMMER)
(c.688–741) CAROLINGIAN who was MAYOR OF THE PALACE from 719 to 741. He earned his soubriquet crushing the Muslims at the BATTLE OF POITIERS (732), a victory that checked Muslim expansion in Europe. ▷ 3.06

CHEN-LA
Early KHMER kingdom of Cambodia and southern Vietnam, flourishing from about 400 to about 800 on the lower Mekong river. The kingdom developed under Buddhist and Hindu influences. According to Chinese sources, Chen-la was divided into two, sometimes independent, parts: Land Chen-la and Water Chen-la, corresponding to inland and coastal regions. ▷ 3.25

CHERSON
An ancient trading post in the Crimean peninsula, long disputed by the BYZANTINES and Russians. In 989 VLADIMIR, prince of KIEV, took it to enforce his claim of marriage to a Byzantine princess. Destroyed by LITHUANIA, Cherson became a Turkish possession in 1475. ▷ 3.15

CHICHÉN ITZÁ
A leading Mayan city-state of the Yucatán peninsula in the Post Classic period (800–1500). Named for the Itzá (or Putun) Maya who settled there in about 850, it was captured by Kukulcán, a TOLTEC adventurer, around 1000 and remained under Toltec rule until it was conquered by HUNAC CEEL in 1221, after which it was abandoned. The surviving monuments show the influence of the Toltec architecture of TULA, though they are built on a far grander scale. ▷ 3.27

CHICHIMECA
See TOLTECS

CHIMÚ EMPIRE
Empire founded in about 1200, controlling about 1,000 kilometers (600 miles) of Peru's northern coastline by the 15th century. Its capital was at Chan Chan in the Moche valley. The Chimú were conquered by the INCAS in 1470. ▷ 3.28

CHINGIS KHAN (TEMUJIN)
MONGOL ruler and conqueror (r.1206–27), born Temujin. The title of Chingis Khan ("Universal Khan") was awarded in recognition of his unification of the Mongol tribes. In about 1211 he embarked on the conquest of northern China, but this was completed only in 1234. Meanwhile in 1218 he defeated the KARA KHITAI for mastery of central Asia, and by 1220 had captured SAMARKAND and Bukhara. In 1221 Balkh and Khorasan fell to him and the Mongol advance into and beyond the Caucasus began. Chingis himself returned to Mongolia between 1222 and 1225. He died in 1227. His military success, marked by astonishing mobility and savagery, was based on a strategy perfectly suited to the pasturelands of central Asia. By the mid-13th century most of Asia was under Mongol control. ▷ 3.03, 3.04, 3.16, 3.21, 3.22, 3.23

CHOE DYNASTY
Korean dynasty that came to power in 1196, following a military coup against the KORYO dynasty. The Choe gave ineffective leadership to determined popular resistance to the MONGOL invasions from 1231. War-weariness led the Koreans to overthrow the dynasty in 1258 and accept Mongol overlordship. ▷ 3.24

CHOLAS
TAMIL dynasty of south India from the early centuries AD to 1279. It emerged as a major maritime and imperial power between the 8th and 12th centuries, its power peaking under Rajaraja (985–1014) and his son Rajendra (1014–44), who conquered Ceylon and led naval raids as far as Bengal and Sumatra. Its power declined in the 12th century due to attacks by the PANDYAS and Hoysalas. ▷ 3.19

CISTERCIAN ORDER
A religious movement founded in 1098 at Cîteaux in FRANCE. The Cistercians were a reforming branch of the BENEDICTINES, reacting especially to the perceived laxity of CLUNY. Advocating literal adherence to the Rule of St Benedict and strict poverty, they met with great success under the leadership of Stephen Harding and BERNARD OF CLAIRVAUX, establishing some 700 houses (customarily in isolated places) across western Europe by 1300. Agricultural pioneers, they were called "White Monks" from the color of their habits. ▷ 3.09

CLERMONT, COUNCIL OF
Council held in November 1095 at Clermont in southern France, called by Pope URBAN II to preach the First CRUSADE in reponse to the BYZANTINE EMPIRE's call for help against the SELJUK TURKS. ▷ 3.08, 3.17

CLUNIAC MOVEMENT
BENEDICTINE reform movement founded at the French monastery of Cluny in 910. Under Abbot Odo (927–41) Cluny became the center of monastic revival and the first international monastic organization; by the abbacy of Peter the Venerable (1132–56) there were more than 1,000 Cluniac monasteries, famous for their elaborate liturgy. Eventually, Cluny's growing wealth prompted accusations of worldliness, and the CISTERCIANS became the leading reformers. ▷ 3.07, 3.09

CNUT (THE GREAT)
King of ENGLAND (r.1016–35), Denmark (r.1018–35) and Norway (r.1030–1035). Cnut inherited a claim to England from his father SVEIN FORKBEARD in 1014 but was only recognized as king by the English in 1016 after fierce resistance. Cnut was subsequently recognized as king in Denmark and Norway and as overlord in Sweden. Cnut's legal and military reforms brought justice and peace to England. His death resulted in the swift disintegration of his Anglo-Scandinavian empire. ▷ 3.07

COCOM DYNASTY
Mayan dynasty of the Late Classic period, founded by HUNAC CEEL in 1221. The Cocom dynasty dominated Yucatán from their capital Mayapán through marriage alliances and mercenary armies until 1441, when the dynasty was overthrown by Ah Xupan Xiu, a rebel nobleman of Mayapán. ▷ 3.27

CONGO
African kingdom south of the mouth of the Congo river, comprising parts of modern Congo and northern Angola. Congo probably dates from the 14th century. Contacts were made with the Portuguese in the 1480s, and in 1490 King Nzinga Nkuwu converted to Christianity. However, relations with the Portuguese soon broke down because of their slave raiding, and Christianization proper did not occur until the 17th century. The kingdom began to break up in the late 17th century. ▷ 3.18

Conquistadors
Spanish conquerors of the New World, such as Hernán Cortés and Francisco Pizarro, who overcame indigenous peoples of the Americas from the early 16th century. ▷ 3.27, 3.28

Constance, Council of
Church council held in southern Germany (1414–18), called by Pope John XXII to end the Great Schism. It deposed the antipopes, condemned the teachings of Wycliffe and burned the heretic Jan Hus. ▷ 3.12

Constantine VII
Byzantine emperor (r.913–57). A man of scholarly disposition, he wrote a number of invaluable works about the government of the empire, notably the *Book of Ceremonies*. But he was ineffective in political leadership, and conflicts in southern Italy and with the Arabs continued unresolved, although lively diplomatic relations were established with Russia and the Abbasid caliph. ▷ 3.15

Constantinople
Capital of the Byzantine empire and great trading port on the Bosphorus, founded by the emperor Constantine in 324. Attacked on many occasions, it was taken only twice, by the Fourth Crusade in 1204 (whose leaders held it until 1261) and finally by the Ottoman Turks in 1453. It became the Ottomans' seat of government until the early 20th century when it was renamed Istanbul. ▷ 3.05, 3.06, 3.07, 3.08, 3.09, 3.10, 3.11, 3.12, 3.13, 3.14, 3.15, 3.16, 3.17, 4.15, 4.16

Córdoba
Córdoba became the capital of Abd al-Rahman I's Umayyad state in Muslim Spain in 756. Its great age of prosperity lasted until 1031, when the Umayyad line in Spain was extinguished, but during this period Córdoba rivalled Baghdad in size and splendor and far outshone any western city. It passed into Almoravid control in 1091 and to the Almohads in 1148, but in 1236 was captured by Ferdinand III of Castile. Córdoba's great tradition of scholarship is represented by Ibn Hazm, Averroes and Maimonides. ▷ 3.06, 3.14

Cortes
The national assembly of Spain. Like the English Parliament it emerged from the king's court to become a bi-cameral, tax-raising representative institution. The first documented cortes was held in León in 1188.

Corvinus, Matthew
(c.1443–90) King of Hungary (r.1458–90). Under his rule Hungary dominated central Europe. He took Vienna in 1485, making it his capital, reformed Hungary's fiscal system and created a standing army. ▷ 3.12

Covadonga, Battle of
Defeat of an Arab army numbering 187,000 by the Visigothic chief Pelayo and a small band of followers supposedly in 718 or 719. Recent scholarship has questioned the traditional version of events, suggesting that the battle took place in 722, that the numbers have been exaggerated and that the story was embellished in order to provide justification for the Reconquista. ▷ 3.06, 3.14

Crécy, Battle of
First major land battle of the Hundred Years War, fought on 26 August 1346. A small English force under Edward III defeated the French army of Philip VI by means of superior infantry tactics and the use of archery. John of Luxembourg, king of Bohemia, was killed in the battle. Edward went on to take Calais. ▷ 3.10

Crusader States
Four new political entities established as a result of the First Crusade (1096–99): the kingdom of Jerusalem, the principality of Antioch and the counties of Tripoli and Edessa. Here Frankish dynasties ruled over largely Arab populations with varying degrees of assimilation. Of these, Jerusalem was the

THE CRUSADES

CRUSADES TO THE HOLY LAND

Crusade	Date	Leaders	Result
First	**1096–99**	Godfrey de Bouillon Raymond of Toulouse Robert of Normandy Bohemund of Taranto Baldwin of Flanders	Capture of Jerusalem (1099) Establishment of Crusader States
Second	**1147–49**	Louis VII of France Emperor Conrad III	Unsuccessful siege of Damascus
Third	**1188–92**	Emperor Frederick Barbarossa Richard I of England Philip Augustus of France	Recapture of the Palestine coast and Cyprus
Fourth	**1202–04**	William of Montferrata Baldwin of Hainault	Constantinople sacked (1204)
Fifth	**1217–21**	Andrew of Hungary Cardinal Pelagius John of Jerusalem Hugh of Cyprus	Capture of Damietta (1219)
Sixth	**1228–29**	Emperor Frederick II	Gain of Jerusalem (1229)
Seventh	**1248–54**	Louis IX of France	Capture of Damietta (1249)
Eighth	**1270–72**	Louis IX of France	Unsuccessful attack on Tunis (1270)

OTHER CRUSADES

Crusade	Date	Leaders	Result
Bogomil	**1168**	Stephen Nemanya	Suppression of heresy in the Balkans
Baltic	**1147**	Emperor Conrad III	Conversion of pagan Wends
Albigensian	**1209–29**	Simon de Montfort	Suppression of Cathar heresy
Children's	**1212**	Nicholas	Child crusaders dispersed in Italy
Prussian	**1227**	Teutonic Knights	Conversion of pagan Prussians
Nicopolis	**1396**	John the Fearless of Burgundy	Defeat by the Turks
Bohemian	**1420–32**	Emperor Sigismund	Suppression of Hussite heresy

largest and most important, for long periods in the 12th century controlling the others. Edessa fell to ZANGI in 1144 but the other states revived after SALADIN'S conquests (1187–89) to maintain a precarious existence until 1291. From the 1190s CYPRUS, taken from the BYZANTINES, became another Crusader kingdom, surviving until the 15th century. ▷ 3.16–17, 3.22

CRUSADES
The name given retrospectively to a series of campaigns preached by the PAPACY initially for the recovery of the HOLY LAND from the Muslims, but from the mid-12th century extending into other areas. Campaigns were mounted against the Baltic pagans, against heretics and political opponents of the PAPACY within Europe, and against the OTTOMAN Turks. Crusaders were given spiritual privileges in return for participation. The First Crusade (1096–99) established the CRUSADER STATES, but successive operations throughout the 12th and 13th centuries failed to achieve as much success. ▷ 3.03, 3.05, 3.08, 3.09, 3.10, 3.13, 3.15, 3.17

CUMANS
A nomadic people who formed the westernmost wing of a tribal confederation extending from the Danube to Kazakhstan. A series of migrations in the early 11th century saw Cumans ranging from the south Russian steppes to the Danube. In the 12th century Cumans were an important element in regional warfare, but they were overrun by the MONGOLS in the mid-13th century. ▷ 3.08, 3.09, 3.17, 3.22

CUZCO
Traditionally founded by MANCO CAPAC in the early 13th century, Cuzco was the capital of the INCA EMPIRE until the Spanish conquest in 1533. Cuzco is situated at the heart of a broad and fertile valley in the Peruvian Andes, over 3,300 meters (11,000 feet) above sea level. In the Quechua language of the Incas, *cuzco* means "navel" and the city was considered by them to be the center of the world. Although Cuzco was largely rebuilt by the Spanish, substantial Inca ruins survive. ▷ 3.28

CYPRUS, KINGDOM OF
Mediterranean kingdom established by RICHARD I during the Third CRUSADE when he captured the island. He sold it to Guy of Lusignan, king of JERUSALEM, in 1192; his dynasty ruled until 1474. It fell to the OTTOMANS in 1571. ▷ 3.16, 3.17

CYRILLIC ALPHABET
Slavic alphabet derived from the Greek. The emergence of a written language for the south Slavs in the Balkans came with their conversion to Christianity in the 9th century by the BYZANTINES. The conversion of the Russians in 988 spread a version of Cyrillic to the north and east. The use of a single language and script for sacred and vernacular purposes helped to promote a sense of Russian identity based on ORTHODOX Christianity.

CZARS
The title, deriving from the Latin "Caesar", adopted by IVAN III, prince of MOSCOW, when he married a BYZANTINE princess in 1472. The title reflected the emergence of a powerful unified Russian kingdom based on Moscow following Ivan's victories over the kingdom of Lithuania-Poland. ▷ 3.12

DAGOBERT I
MEROVINGIAN ruler (r.621–38) of the three Frankish kingdoms of AUSTRASIA, NEUSTRIA and BURGUNDY that between them covered most of northern and eastern France, the Low Countries and Germany west of the Rhine. He was the last effective Merovingian, and after his death in 638 the dynasty failed to control the MAYORS OF THE PALACE who eventually overthrew them. ▷ 3.06

DAI VIET
Vietnamese kingdom, also known by its Chinese name, Annam, founded in 939 after a long independence struggle against China. The Chinese reoccupied the kingdom in 1410 but were again driven out in 1427. Dai Viet conquered CHAMPA in the late 15th century but at the expense of internal cohesion. Royal authority weakened and after 1610 the southern province of Cochin China was effectively independent. Dai Viet was conquered by France (1858–83) and incorporated into French Indo-China as the provinces of Tonkin (north) and Annam (south). ▷ 3.25

DAMASCUS
Largely Greek city of Syria adopted by the UMAYYADS as their capital, preserving much of the heritage of the Greek population. The city's political importance waned when the ABBASIDS shifted the seat of power east in 750. ▷ 3.13, 3.14

DAMIETTA
Situated at the mouth of the Nile, Damietta was a frequent target for 13th-century CRUSADES launched against the AYYUBIDS who controlled Jerusalem from Egypt. The Fifth Crusade captured Damietta (1219–21) but was forced to withdraw by the flooding of the Nile. In 1249 the French king LOUIS IX also captured the city but fell prey to the same fate as the Fifth Crusade and left Egypt in 1250. ▷ 3.17

DANEGELD
Tax (*geld*) imposed in ENGLAND from 991 to pay tribute to the VIKINGS. It remained a general military tax until 1162. ▷ 3.07

DANELAW
Eleventh-century name given to area of northern and eastern ENGLAND settled by the Danes (VIKINGS) in the 9th and 10th centuries. Danish laws, language and customs prevailed over Anglo-Saxon ones. ▷ 3.07

DANIEL
Prince of MOSCOW (r.1263–1304) and founder of the principality of Moscow in the late 13th century. He fortified the town and expanded its territory through his military conquests. ▷ 3.10

DANISHMEND EMIRATE
A Turkish dynasty ruling in northern Anatolia and Cappadocia from the 1080s until 1178. The founder, the emir Danishmend, occupied Melitene and other strongholds, profiting from the distraction posed to the SELJUKS in Anatolia by the First CRUSADE. In 1101 he devastated a crusading army near Heraclea, and in the 1130s his successors held the BYZANTINES at bay. After 1142 succession disputes weakened the dynasty, and in 1178 Melitene fell to the Seljuks. ▷ 3.16

DAOISM
Religion of ancient China, based on the teachings of Lao Zi, contained in the Dao De Jing. Daoism emphasized the Dao (the way of nature) and taught that human actions should be in accordance with this. It promoted the principle of non-action. In the early medieval period it became a popular religion, with a strong monastic tradition, and its influence suffused much east Asian philosophy. Daoists seeking immutable substances as a reflection of immortality developed alchemical techniques and ideas that had were passed to ISLAM and later to Europe. ▷ 3.05

DELHI SULTANATE
The principal Muslim state of northern India from 1206 to 1526. Delhi was chosen as a regional capital by MUHAMMAD OF GHUR following his conquest of northern India. On his death, the general QUTB-UD-DIN (r.1206–11) broke away from GHURID control and Delhi became the capital of an independent sultanate. The sultanate became an imperial power under ILTUTMISH (r.1211–36), who consolidated Muslim control of northern India. The sultanate reached its greatest extent under MUHAMMAD IBN TUGHLUK (r.1325–51) who brought nearly all the subcontinent under his control. The sultanate declined rapidly after Muhammad's death and in 1398 Delhi was sacked by TIMUR THE LAME. Under the SAYYID DYNASTY (1414–51) the sultanate controlled only Delhi and its hinterland. The sultanate regained control of most of northern India under the LODI DYNASTY (1451–1526), but in 1526 it was destroyed by Babur, founder of the Mughal empire. ▷ 3.19

DIAS, BARTHOLOMEW
(c.1450–1500) Portuguese navigator. He became the first European to sail around the Cape of Good Hope, thereby opening the way to the Indian Ocean. ▷ 3.04

Dominican order
The Black Friars, founded by St Dominic in 1215 as a missionary order. Being rigidly orthodox they were entrusted to fill the offices of the Inquisition during the Counter-Reformation.

Dorset Inuit
Inuit (Eskimo) culture that flourished in Greenland, Newfoundland and the Canadian Arctic from 550 BC to AD 1100. Using very simple stone and bone technology – they lacked even bows and arrows – the Dorset hunted a wide range of land mammals, seals and walrus. The Dorset were replaced or assimilated by the more sophisticated Thule Inuit culture in about 1000–1200. ▷ 3.26

Dorylaeum, Battle of
Christian victory during the First Crusade. In June 1097 the Seljuk Kilij Arslan was routed by the army of the First Crusade as it marched across Anatolia. This was the first major engagement with the Turks in the field, following the successful siege of Nicea, and it demonstrated the superiority of the Frankish cavalry charge. ▷ 3.17

Dushan, Stephen
King (r.1331–46) and emperor (r.1346–55) of Serbia. He took advantage of the decline of the Byzantine empire to extend Serbian power into Macedonia, Bulgaria and Albania. His empire collapsed after his death. ▷ 3.10

Dvaravati
Mon kingdom of southern Thailand c.550–1050). Though never a great power, Dvaravati played an important role in the transmission of Indian cultural influence to the Khmers, Thais and Burmese. ▷ 3.25

Edessa, county of
The first of the Crusader States. The county owed its existence to the opportunism of Baldwin I while on a diversionary maneuver on the First Crusade. On Baldwin's succession to the throne of Jerusalem in 1100 the county passed to his cousin Baldwin of Le Bourg and in 1118 to the Courtenay family. Edessa, always the most vulnerable of the Crusader States, fell to Zangi in 1144 and was never recovered. The population comprised large numbers of Armenians and Syrian Christians in addition to Muslims. ▷ 3.17

Edinburgh, Treaty of
Treaty signed on 17 March 1328 by which the English, following their defeat by the Scots at Bannockburn, recognized Scottish independence under Robert the Bruce. ▷ 3.10

Edward I
King of England (r.1272–1307). Edward's active role as a prince taught him valuable political and military skills. He fought in Wales (which he completely conquered), in the baronial civil wars in England against Simon de Montfort and on the Eighth Crusade (1270). He defeated John Balliol and William Wallace in Scotland in the 1290s, earning the soubriquet "Hammer of the Scots". His need to fund simultaneous wars with Scotland and France elevated the importance of Parliament.

Edward III
King of England (r.1327–77). He was skillful in politics and war, winning victories against Scotland at Halidon Hill (1333) and Neville's Cross (1346). His claim to the French crown initiated the Hundred Years War in which his reputation was made by spectacular successes at Sluys, Crécy, Calais and Poitiers. His later years were marked by financial difficulties and decline. Edward's reign also witnessed the outbreak of the Black Death. ▷ 3.10

Edward IV
(1442–83) King of England (r.1461–70 and 1471–83). Edward became Yorkist king against the background of the Wars of the Roses. His energy and ability outmatched the feeble Henry VI whom he deposed and murdered. However, later policies, cruelty and hedonistic indulgences blackened his reputation and lost him popularity. His governmental reforms were built on by the Tudors.

Edward the Confessor
King of England (r.1042–66) and saint. His reign saw political tensions arising between Edward's pro-Norman faction and the party of Earl Godwin, but was otherwise relatively peaceful and stable. However, Edward's lack of an heir caused the crisis of 1066. He founded Westminster Abbey where he was buried. ▷ 3.07

England
Northern European kingdom. Anglo-Saxon invaders of post-Roman Britain founded several small kingdoms. Of these only Wessex survived the Viking invasions of the 9th century. Under the leadership of Wessex, the Vikings were defeated and a united English kingdom was created. By 1016 renewed Viking invasions had forced England into Cnut's Scandanavian empire. In 1066 a successful invasion of England brought the Norman dynasty to power (1066–1154), under which the country was feudalized. Henry II's accession founded the Angevin-Plantagenet dynasty (1154–1485). Baronial unrest in the 13th century led to Magna Carta and curbs on royal power. Conflicts with France were frequent throughout the Middle Ages, culminating in the Hundred Years War (1337–1453). Ultimate French victory was followed by the civil Wars of the Roses (1455–85) which were concluded by the accession of the new Tudor dynasty. In 1536 Wales was legally incorporated into England; in 1707 Scotland united with the two (now Protestant) to form Great Britain.
▷ 3.01, 3.02, 3.03, 3.04, 3.05, 3.06, 3.07, 3.08, 3.09, 3.10, 3.11, 3.12

Epirus, despotate of
Byzantine state founded after the fall of Constantinople to the Fourth Crusade in 1204. It was conquered by the Ottomans in the 1430s. ▷ 3.17

Erik the Red
Norse colonizer. Born in Norway, Erik settled in Iceland as a child. In about 980 while exiled for manslaughter, Erik explored the southwest coast of Greenland, establishing a colony in 982. His favorable description of Greenland had attracted about 1,000 Scandinavians by 1000. ▷ 3.07

Fatimid caliphate
Shiite dynasty. The Fatimids conquered Egypt in 969, proclaimed a rival caliphate to the Abbasids, and from the new capital of Cairo they became the leading Mediterranean power until the 12th century. At their height in the mid-11th century the Fatimids controlled Palestine and Syria, but these were lost to the Seljuks. The Fatimid caliphate, weakened by Crusader invasion in the 1160s, was ended by Saladin in 1171. Shiite groups throughout the Islamic world regarded the Fatimid caliphate alone as legitimate. ▷ 3.02, 3.03, 3.14, 3.16, 3.17

Ferdinand of Aragon (the Catholic)
King of Aragon (r.1479–1516); king of Naples (r.1504–16). His marriage to Isabella of Castile in 1469 led to the unification of Spain. He conquered Granada (1492), completing the Christian Reconquista, and established the Spanish Inquisition. ▷ 3.12, 4.07

feudalism
A contractual system in which a lord (usually a king or great magnate) granted protection and a fief (usually an estate) to a vassal (usually a knight or nobleman) in return for military service. The name derives from the Latin *foedum* (agreement). The contract was symbolically, and publically, sealed by the vassal swearing an oath of homage to his lord. Feudalism was losing its military significance in Europe by the 12th century as military service was commuted for a cash payment and fiefs came to regarded as heritable property. ▷ 3.08

Five Dynasties and Ten Kingdoms
A period of disunion (907–60) during which China was divided into 11 independent states following the collapse of the Tang empire. In order to maintain the fiction of continuous imperial rule, later Chinese historians treated the five short-lived dynasties that ruled the Yellow river valley in this period as legitimate imperial dynasties, while the rulers of the other ten kingdoms were usurpers. The last of

the Five Dynasties was overthrown in 960 by SONG TAIZU (r.960–76) who began the reunification of China. ▷ 3.21

FLANDERS
Duchy in the Low Countries made prosperous in the Middle Ages by the textile industry, trade and the privileges of its principal towns, GHENT and BRUGES. Traditionally it allied with ENGLAND, its chief supplier of wool, and opposed FRANCE, against whom it inflicted a crushing defeat at Coutrai (1302). In 1384 Flanders became a BURGUNDIAN fief when PHILIP THE BOLD inherited it and moved his court to Bruges. Divided variously between France, Holland and Belgium, its commercial and strategic importance made it a theater of conflict up to 1945. ▷ 3.10, 3.11

FLORENCE
Capital of Tuscany, Italy. It grew rich on the profits of local industry and trade between northern and southern Europe, introducing an international gold coinage with GENOA in 1253. Increasingly autonomous from the 11th century, it became a fully fledged republic by the 1260s, expanding its territory and its influence. It was a cradle of the RENAISSANCE, at the time probably the leading cultural center of western Europe, a position owing much to the patronage of its MEDICI rulers. GIOTTO, Dante, Donatello, Boccaccio, da Vinci, Machiavelli, Masaccio, Brunelleschi and Michaelangelo were among its citizens. ▷ 3.12

FRANCE, KINGDOM OF
Western European country that emerged from the break-up of the CAROLINGIAN EMPIRE in 888. It was ruled by a CAROLINGIAN DYNASTY until 987 when HUGH CAPET founded the CAPETIAN DYNASTY. The king's central authority remained weak until the 12th century. In 1204 PHILIP II conquered ANGEVIN possessions in France, and power was consolidated under LOUIS IX. The Valois dynasty, founded in 1328, eventually defeated the English in the HUNDRED YEARS WAR and drove them out of the country. LOUIS XI absorbed BURGUNDY and other great fiefs into the kingdom, uniting most of modern France by 1483. France's expansionist foreign polices and borders remained causes of European wars throughout its history. It became a republic during the French Revolution of the 1790s. ▷ 3.01, 3.02, 3.03, 3.04, 3.05, 3.06, 3.07, 3.08, 3.09, 3.10, 3.11, 3.12, 3.17

FRANCHE-COMTÉ
Region of eastern France. A county of the HOLY ROMAN EMPIRE from the 11th century, it passed to BURGUNDIAN rule in 1384. It reverted to imperial control in the late 15th century until final incorporation into FRANCE in 1678. ▷ 3.10, 3.12

FRANCIS OF ASSISI, ST
(1181–1226) Saint and the founder of the FRANCISCAN ORDER. He renounced his wealthy background and lifestyle to embrace poverty and preaching. ▷ 3.09

FRANCISCAN ORDER
Friars who followed the Rule of St Francis. Founded in 1209, approved by Pope INNOCENT III and confirmed by Pope Honorius III in 1223, the order adhered to the ascetic evangelism of the New Testament. Their numbers and influence expanded rapidly. Success and temporal pressures divided the order between Spirituals and Conventuals, the former espousing the absolute poverty of St Francis, for which they were charged with heresy. Franciscans were known as "Grey Friars" by virtue of their simple habits. ▷ 3.09

FRANCONIA
One of the five tribal duchies of medieval Germany. Franconia became the nucleus of the new East Frankish Kingdom after 843. Duke Conrad I became the first German king (r.911–18), but the crown soon passed to the SAXON DYNASTY. After this, Franconia produced no ducal dynasty and remained a royal demesne until its fragmentation in the late 13th century. ▷ 3.07, 3.08

FREDERICK I (BARBAROSSA)
HOLY ROMAN EMPEROR (r.1152–90) of the HOHENSTAUFEN DYNASTY, called "Barbarossa" for his red beard. His reign was troubled by domestic unrest and wars in Italy. His attempts to impose imperial authority in Italy earned the hostility of the PAPACY, and he was excommunicated. The Lombard cities revolted, driving him from Italy after his defeat at Legnano (1176). Peace with the papacy allowed him to complete his pacification of Germany, quelling the rebellious HENRY THE LION, and to stamp his control over its neighbors. He drowned on his way to the HOLY LAND to lead the Third CRUSADE. Considered one of Germany's most able monarchs, he achieved far more through conciliatory politics than military confrontation. ▷ 3.08

FREDERICK II
HOHENSTAUFEN king of SICILY (r.1198–1250) and HOLY ROMAN EMPEROR (r.1212–50). Frederick defeated the WELF Otto IV for the imperial crown. Frederick's reign was dogged by conflicts with the popes who, with some cause, feared his ambition. A successful CRUSADER (1228–29), he won back Bethlehem, Nazareth and JERUSALEM for the Christians by treaty negotiations rather than military action; he crowned himself king of JERUSALEM. An excommunicate at that time (one of three such occasions), he returned to regain quickly his Neapolitan territories seized in his absence by Pope Gregory IX. He made peace with the PAPACY in 1230 and directed his energies to reducing Lombardy to submission; but renewed conflict with Rome prompted open rebellion in Germany and defeat in Italy. An accomplished linguist, poet, humanist and scholar of the arts and sciences, he was a politically and intellectually enlightened leader and one of the most cultured men of his day. The breadth of his accomplishments earned him the appellation "Stupor Mundi" (Wonder of the World). ▷ 3.08

FUGGER BANK
Bank founded in Augsburg in 1380 by Hans Fugger, becoming Europe's greatest financial house by the 16th century, funding princes and imperial policy, for which the family was ennobled. ▷ 3.11

FUJIWARA DYNASTY
Aristocratic Japanese family that dominated the imperial government in the HEIAN PERIOD (794–1185) through a permanent regency founded by Fujiwara Yorifusa in 858. The Fujiwara maintained their position by marrying their daughters to members of the imperial family. In this way Fujiwara no Michinga (966–1028), one of the most powerful members of the family, was father of four empresses and grandfather to three successive emperors. The Fujiwara used their power to amass huge tax-exempt landholdings. The rise of SAMURAI clans in the 12th century led to the decline of Fujiwara influence. ▷ 3.24

GAJA MADA
Prime minister of the Javanese MAJAPAHIT empire from 1331 until his death in 1364. His expansionist policies made Majapahit the dominant power in Indonesia. He is regarded as a hero by modern Indonesian nationalists for his role as an early unifier of the archipelago. ▷ 3.25

GAOZU
See LI YUAN

GASCONY
Coastal region of southwestern FRANCE from Bordeaux in the north to the Pyrenees in the south. It was the only part of AQUITAINE not conquered by France in the thirteenth century. It maintained a flourishing wine trade with England. At the end of the HUNDRED YEARS WAR the French victory at Castillon (1453) brought it under French control. It was fully incorporated into France in 1607. ▷ 3.08, 3.10, 3.11, 3.12

GEMPEI WAR
Decisive civil war in medieval Japan between the TAIRA and Minamoto SAMURAI clans (1180–85). The war began with the rebellion of the Minamoto, led by MINAMOTO YORITOMO, against the dominance of Taira Kiyomori at the imperial court. It ended with the destruction of the Taira clan at the naval battle of Dannoura (1185). Following the war, Yoritomo founded the KAMAKURA SHOGUNATE beginning a period of military government in Japan that would last until 1868. ▷ 3.24

GENGHIS KHAN
See CHINGIS KHAN

GENOA
Seaport of northwest Italy. It recovered from stagnation under the Lombards to achieve independence in the 10th century and had acquired a coastal Mediterranean empire by the 13th. The western Mediterranean's main commercial center, it clashed with its rivals, defeating Pisa by 1284 but was defeated by VENICE at Chioggia (1380). Thereafter it declined, riven by political divisions and dominated by foreign powers. Genoa issued the first marine insurance premium (c.1350). ▷ 3.08, 3.10, 3.11, 3.12, 3.15

GEORGIA
Autonomous Christian kingdom of the Caucasus from 788, when the KHAZARS helped Leon II to end BYZANTINE suzerainty. Its period of glory came under King Davit' Aghmashenebeli (1089–1125), when the use of CUMAN merceneries made the kingdom the most powerful in the region. The MONGOL invasion of the Caucasus in the 1220s ended Georgian independence. ▷ 3.02, 3.03, 3.04, 3.05, 3.08, 3.09, 3.10, 3.11, 3.12, 3.14, 3.15, 3.16, 3.22, 3.23

GHANA
The earliest known kingdom of west Africa. Ghana emerged in about 700 as a response to increased trans-Saharan trade and local population growth. The name of the kingdom was derived from the title of its king, the *ghana*. Ghana was centered in modern Mali and shared no territory with the modern state which bears its name: its population was mainly SONINKE. Through the influence of traders from north Africa, ISLAM had become established in Ghana by 1000. Ghana declined in the 11th century as a result of attacks by the ALMORAVIDS, who briefly captured the capital Koumbi Saleh in 1076. However, the kingdom survived until 1240 when it was conquered by Sundiata, the emperor of MALI. ▷ 3.18

GHAZNAVID EMIRATE
A Turkish dynasty taking its name from Ghazna, the base from which the Ghaznavids ruled eastern Persia and Afghanistan in the 11th and 12th centuries. The founder, Mahmud (998–1030), brought the Punjab and part of Sind under his control. In the early 11th century the dynasty fought the QARAKHANIDS, but was crushed by the SELJUKS in 1040 and withdrew from Persia to its wealthy Indian territories. Internal discord weakened the Ghaznavids in the 12th century, and in 1187 the dynasty was overthrown by the GHURIDS. ▷ 3.02, 3.03, 3.14, 3.16, 3.19

GHENT
City port of FLANDERS, rich in Gothic art and architecture and involved in wars against BURGUNDY. Ghent became part of Belgium on that country's foundation in 1830. ▷ 3.11

GHURID SULTANATE
Sultanate centered at Ghur (now Ghowr) in western Afghanistan, founded by Ala-ud-Din Husayn in 1151, following his rebellion against the GHAZNAVID EMIRATE. Ghurid power reached its peak under Ghiyas-ud-Din (r.1173–1202) and his brother and co-ruler Mu'izz-ud-Din, better known as MUHAMMAD OF GHUR (r.1173–1206), who brought all of Afghanistan and much of northern India under their control. The sultanate broke up on the death of Muhammad of Ghur. The general QUTB-UD-DIN broke away, founding the independent DELHI SULTANATE, while the remaining Ghurid lands were conquered by the KHWARIZM SHAHDOM in 1215. Though shortlived, the Ghurid sultanate laid the foundations for Muslim rule in India. ▷ 3.19

GHUZZ TURKS
Generic term for the nomadic Turkic people of the region between the Caspian and Aral Seas. Among the loose confederation of these tribes the SELJUKS became dominant in the 11th century and expanded south into central Asia, where they crushed the GHAZNAVIDS, before expanding west into Iraq, Syria and Anatolia. ▷ 3.02, 3.03, 3.14

GIOTTO DI BONDONE
(c.1226–1337) Italian painter and architect whose revolutionary painting technique introduced realism to art, preparing the way for RENAISSANCE innovations. ▷ 3.10, 3.12

GO-DAIGO
Emperor of Japan (r.1318–39) who attempted to overthrow the shogunate and restore direct imperial rule. With the support of Ashikaga Takauji, Go-Daigo overthrew the KAMAKURA SHOGUNATE in 1333. However, his failure to reward Takauji led Takauji to proclaim himself shogun in 1335. In 1336 Takauji captured the imperial capital at Kyoto and appointed a puppet emperor, so founding the ASHIKAGA SHOGUNATE. Go-Daigo fled to the Yoshino mountains and held out until his death. ▷ 3.24

GOLDEN BULL
Any important medieval European document with a gold seal attached. The most famous is Emperor CHARLES IV's imperial edict of 1356 regulating the law of imperial elections. It strengthened electors at the expense of cities, the PAPACY and minor rulers. ▷ 3.10

GOLDEN HORDE
A translation of *Altan Ordu*, the MONGOL name for the state established by BATU KHAN. It dominated southern Russia from 1236 to 1502. Nominally dependent on the GREAT KHANATE, it retained its autonomy until weakened by defeats at the hands of the Russians in 1380 and TIMUR THE LAME at the end of the 14th century. From about 1419, independent provinces emerged within the state. ▷ 3.03, 3.04, 3.05, 3.10, 3.11, 3.12, 3.23

GRANADA
Region of southern Spain conquered by Muslims from north Africa in 711, and the last Spanish Muslim state to fall to the RECONQUISTA under FERDINAND OF ARAGON and Isabella of Castile in 1492. ▷ 3.08, 3.10, 3.11, 3.12

GREAT KHANATE
The overlordship over all MONGOL tribes accomplished by CHINGIS KHAN in 1206 led to the creation of a Great Khanate based in KARAKORUM. During the 13th century subordinate khanates were established to rule the western conquests, but after the death of MÖNGKE KHAN in 1259 these were effectively independent. The last phase of expansion was the conquest of the SONG empire by KHUBILAI KHAN. By 1355 the Great Khanate had fragmented. ▷ 3.03, 3.22, 3.23

GREAT PLAINS INDIANS
Bison-hunting (buffalo-hunting) peoples of the Great Plains of North America. This way of life was established as early as 9000 BC. Bison were hunted on foot, a favorite strategy being to stampede herds over cliffs (buffalo jumps). By the 16th century bison hunting was gradually dying out as maize farming spread west along river valleys. However, the introduction of the horse to the plains in the 18th century made bison hunting far more efficient and led many settled plains peoples to abandon farming for nomadism. In historical times the Plains Indians have included the Plains Cree, Assiniboin, Cheyenne, Sioux and Kiowa. ▷ 3.26

GREAT SCHISM (1054)
The final breach between the ROMAN CATHOLIC CHURCH and the Greek ORTHODOX CHURCH following the excommunication of the Patriarch of CONSTANTINOPLE for refusing to recognize the authority of Rome.

GREAT SCHISM (1378–1417)
Division of the ROMAN CATHOLIC CHURCH in which rival popes sat in Rome and Avignon. The election of the volatile Italian Pope Urban VI (a reaction to the French-dominated AVIGNON PAPACY) led to the election of a rival pope, the French Clement VII. The two sat respectively at Rome and Avignon, causing the schism. Christian Europe divided into two politically determined camps: FRANCE, SCOTLAND, CASTILE and PORTUGAL for Clement; ENGLAND, FLANDERS, HUNGARY and the HOLY ROMAN EMPIRE for Urban. In 1409 the Council of Pisa attempted to resolve the split but only served to exacerbate matters, producing a third rival pope. A further council was called at CONSTANCE (1414) which healed the schism with the election of one, sole pope, Matin V. The schism weakened the papal office and strengthened conciliarism

(the view that popes should be guided by church councils). ▷ 3.04, 3.05, 3.10, 3.12, 3.16

GREAT SELJUK SULTANATE
Empire established by the conquests of the SELJUKS in the mid-11th century. At its greatest extent under MALIK SHAH, the sultanate stretched from the Bosphorus to the Hindu Kush, but after 1192 a succession of crises caused it to fragment. ▷ 3.16, 3.17, 3.23

GREAT WALL OF CHINA
System of masonry and brick defensive walls, around 9 meters (30 feet) high and 6,400 kilometers (4,000 miles) in length, built by the Ming dynasty in the 15th and 16th centuries to protect northern China from invasions of steppe nomads. The Great Wall was the final development of a tradition of frontier walls going back to the Warring States period (480–221 BC). The first continuous frontier wall, built by the emperor Shi Huangdi (221–210 BC), was a rampart of compressed earth situated more than 80 kilometers (50 miles) to the north of the later line of the Great Wall.

GREENLAND
The world's largest island. Two-thirds of it lies above the Arctic Circle, and about 85 percent of its surface area is covered by ice sheets. Its first inhabitants were people of the Arctic Small Tool Tradition, an early Inuit culture, who arrived in about 4000 BC. Successive waves of Inuit colonizers followed, the most recent being the DORSET (c.500 BC) and the THULE INUIT (c.AD 1200). Southwest Greenland was also settled by the Norse from 987 to about 1500. The island was recolonized by the Danes in 1721 and is at present a Danish dependency. ▷ 3.36

GREGORY VII
Pope (r.1073–85) and saint. As cardinal Hildebrand, Gregory was an active reformer, and when pope his reforms against simony (the sale of church offices) and for clerical celibacy caused great controversy. His prohibition of lay investiture of bishops led to the bitter conflict with the German monarchy known as the INVESTITURE CONTEST. ▷ 3.09

GUILDS
Associations, usually economic by trade (artisans, merchants, etc.) formed to protect the interests of members. Many became extremely wealthy, controlling local government. ▷ 3.11

GURJARA-PRATIHARAS
Major Hindu dynasty of northern India (8th to 12th centuries). Founded by Nagabhata I in the 8th century, the Gurjara-Pratihara kingdom reached its peak under Bhoja (836–90) and Mahenjapala (890–910) when it stretched across northern India from Gujarat to Bengal. From 816 the capital was at KANAUJ on the Ganges. The dynasty was weakened by attacks by the RASHTRATKUTAS in the 10th century and its power was finally broken when MAHMUD OF GHAZNI sacked Kanauj in 1018. ▷ 3.19

GUTENBERG, JOHANNES
(1400–68) German printer, generally attributed with the invention of modern printing and the development of movable type, which led to the first printed books. He published the Gutenberg Bible in about 1455. ▷ 3.04

HAFSID CALIPHATE
One of three Muslim states to emerge in the Maghreb in the 13th century. Until the 1270s it expanded its territory, based on Tunis, but the interference of the ANGEVINS in Italy weakened the state. In the mid-14th century Tunis was occupied by the MARINIDS, but the Hafsids returned in 1370 and a further period of prosperity lasted until absorbtion into the OTTOMAN empire in 1574. ▷ 3.03, 3.04

HAJJ
The obligation imposed by MUHAMMAD on all Muslims to make the pilgrimage to the Kaaba at MECCA at least once in a lifetime. Although the Kaaba had been a cult site in pre-Islamic Arabia, its retention by Muhammad after the spread of ISLAM enabled the new religion to maintain a focal point for communal devotion. ▷ 3.18

HANSEATIC LEAGUE
Confederation of trading cities in northern Europe originating with the commercial, protectionist alliance of Lübeck and Hamburg in the early 13th century. It reached its peak in the later 14th century. The league used its great influence to acquire trading privileges and monopolies (almost total in the case of Scandanavia). It also engaged in military activity to further its own economic ends (as in its 1369 victory over Valdemar of Denmark). The league's main stations, *kontors*, were in London, Bergen, NOVGOROD and BRUGES, with overall control remaining in Lübeck. New trade routes to Asia and the New World, as well as increasing competition, eroded Hanseatic power in the 16th century. The league held its last general assembly in 1669. ▷ 3.11

HARALD BLUETOOTH
King of Denmark (r.c.950–c.985) who in 965 was baptized the first Christian king in Scandinavia, an event marked in the RUNIC inscription on the Jellinge Stone in Jutland. In 975 Harald was forced to submit to OTTO I after the defeat of his incursion into eastern Germany. In 983 he was deposed by his son SVEIN FORKBEARD, having succeeded in establishing a coherent state out of a collection of rival chieftainships. ▷ 3.05, 3.06, 3.07

HAROLD II
ENGLAND's last Anglo-Saxon king (r.1066). He was an able and active nobleman and monarch but his claim to the throne was challenged by Harald Hardrada of Norway and WILLIAM THE CONQUEROR, duke of NORMANDY. He defeated Harald at the Battle of Stamford Bridge but shortly afterwards was defeated and killed at the BATTLE OF HASTINGS by William. ▷ 3.08

HARSHA
The most powerful king of early medieval India (r.606–47). Harsha became king of Thaneswar, a minor kingdom in the Punjab, at the age of 16. In 618 he captured KANAUJ, which he made his capital. An energetic campaigner, he controlled most of northern India by 630 but his attempt to conquer the Deccan was defeated by the CHALUKYA king Pulakeshin II in 633. In 641 Harsha established the first diplomatic relations between India and China. A convert to Buddhism, he founded institutions for the poor and sick. Harsha's empire was not a centralized state; ruled mainly through vassal kings, it broke up quickly after his death. ▷ 3.01, 3.13, 3.19

HARUN AL-RASHID
ABBASID caliph (r.786–809). He strengthened the religious character of the office of CALIPH, and established BAGHDAD as a center of artistic patronage. Al-Rashid led armies against the BYZANTINES, penetrating as far as Heraclea in 806, and restored Muslim naval power in the Mediterranean. Nevertheless, under his rule there were upheavals almost everywhere from IFRIQIYA to Khorasan, and the division of territory between his sons fragmented the empire. The historical personality of the caliph has been distorted by misleading portraits in *The Arabian Nights*. ▷ 3.14

HASTINGS, BATTLE OF
One of the most important battles of English history, fought between HAROLD II of ENGLAND and WILLIAM THE CONQUEROR, duke of NORMANDY, on 14 October 1066 on the southeastern coast of England. Harold's army, depleted and tired after its victory over Norwegian invaders at Stamford Bridge three weeks earlier, fought a strong defensive action, but the Normans had more archers and their cavalry broke the English line late in the day. The consequent Norman victory was complete: the death of Harold and many English nobles enabled William to take the crown of England. ▷ 3.08

HATTIN, HORNS OF, BATTLE OF THE
BATTLE IN SALADIN's invasion of the KINGDOM OF JERUSALEM in 1187. He was met by a huge CRUSADER army led by King Guy. Trapped and encircled by Saladin's army, the Crusaders were crushed and Guy himself was taken prisoner. Saladin took Jerusalem shortly after. ▷ 3.08, 3.17

HEIAN PERIOD
Period of Japanese history (794–1185) that began with the removal of the imperial court from NARA to Heian (modern Kyoto). It ended

with the rise of the SAMURAI class and the establishment of the military government of the KAMAKURA SHOGUNATE. The move to Heian was ordered by the emperor KAMMU as a means of escaping the excessive influence of the Buddhist clergy of Nara. However, at Heian the emperors came under the influence of the FUJIWARA family and imperial authority was gradually eroded. The court was famous for its exquisitely refined cultural life. ▷ 3.24

HENRY III
HOLY ROMAN EMPEROR (r.1039–56). Under his rule the empire reached great heights, asserting and extending imperial authority over HUNGARY, Bohemia, Poland and southern Italy. He successfully intervened in ecclesiastical and papal matters, encouraged CLUNIAC and papal reform and patronized arts and learning. ▷ 3.08

HENRY IV
(1050–1106) King of Germany and Italy (r.1056–1105). Henry's reign was marked by the INVESTITURE CONTEST with the PAPACY and a power struggle with the German aristocracy. His quarrel with Pope GREGORY VII involved excommunication and his humiliation at CANOSSA. It permanently weakened the German monarchy. ▷ 3.08

HENRY VI
HOHENSTAUFEN HOLY ROMAN EMPEROR (r.1190–97). Henry became king of SICILY following its conquest in 1194. He held RICHARD I of England to ransom, exerted his power over the PAPACY and strengthened imperial authority. His early death threw the empire into disorder. ▷ 3.08

HENRY I
NORMAN king of ENGLAND (r.1100–35). Henry made his mark through his introduction of legal and bureaucratic reforms which earned him the appellation "Beauclerc". The death of his heir in a Channel shipwreck led to a disputed succession and the anarchy of King Stephen's reign.

HENRY II
King of ENGLAND (r.1154–89). The first ANGEVIN monarch, he controlled extensive territories in FRANCE, and his empire became the foremost political power of western Europe. Henry ruled his vast dominions by itinerant government, displaying great military and administrative skills. He began the conquest of Ireland and consolidated royal power in England after the anarchy of Stephen's reign. The extensive program of legal and administrative reforms that he initiated included clarification of common law, establishing the Exchequer and developing an efficient civil service. He clashed with THOMAS À BECKET in his unsuccessful attempt to impose the authority of royal courts over ecclesiastical ones (as he had done with feudal courts). ▷ 3.08

HENRY III
King of ENGLAND (r.1217–72). He was a poor politician and soldier. His unpopularity led to clashes with the baronage, culminating in the rebellion of 1264–66 led by SIMON DE MONTFORT, which EDWARD I, Henry's son, did most to quell. Lack of military success in FRANCE resulted in the TREATY OF PARIS (1259).

HENRY IV
King of ENGLAND (r.1399–1413). England's first LANCASTRIAN monarch. As Henry Bolingbroke he usurped the throne after leading a revolt against RICHARD II. In his troubled reign, he suffered conflicts with the church, with PARLIAMENT and in WALES. ▷ 3.12

HENRY V
King of ENGLAND (r.1413–22). An outstanding monarch and soldier, Henry earned renown for his exploits in the HUNDRED YEARS WAR, including a great victory at AGINCOURT and the conquest and colonization of northern FRANCE. Educated and pious, Henry was a generous patron of learning and a persecutor of the LOLLARDS.

HENRY VI
(1421–71) Last LANCASTRIAN king of ENGLAND (r.1422–61 and 1470–71). Cultured and religious, Henry was also nervous, indecisive and lacking in courage. His disastrous reign, exacerbated by his weak character and bouts of madness, witnessed defeat in the HUNDRED YEARS WAR and the outbreak of civil conflict, the WARS OF THE ROSES, for which his inability to govern was largely responsible. In 1471 he was murdered and replaced by his Yorkist opponent, EDWARD IV.

HENRY THE FOWLER
King Henry I of Germany (r.919–36) and founder of the SAXON DYNASTY. He secured Germany's borders and waged war successfully against the WENDS. ▷ 3.01

HENRY THE LION
(1125–95) WELF Duke of Saxony and Bavaria. His economic and military strength made him the most powerful German prince of his time, causing widespread resentment and his eventual defeat by Emperor FREDERICK I in 1180, when he was temporarily exiled from the empire. ▷ 3.08

HENRY THE NAVIGATOR
(1394–1460) Portuguese prince and navigator. He combined military campaigning with his love for exploration, sponsoring voyages that mapped the west coast of Africa.

HERACLIUS
BYZANTINE emperor (r.610–41). He came to the throne in a period of crisis precipitated by Avar and Persian invasions. Reorganization of the military administration enabled Heraclius to drive the Avars out of the Balkans and the Persians out of Syria, but only after enduring a siege of CONSTANTINOPLE itself in 626. His reign was a cultural watershed, for by the time of his death in 641, Greek had replaced Latin as the empire's official language, and the Byzantine period may be said to have begun. ▷ 3.01, 3.15

HIJRA
The flight of the Muslims to MEDINA after losing support from the QURAYSH in MECCA. The Prophet MUHAMMAD was permitted to propagate the new faith in Medina and it was from there that he launched the conquest and conversion of Arabia. Muslim dating begins from the first day of the lunar year in which the Hijra took place (16 July 622). ▷ 3.01, 3.05, 3.13

HILDEBRAND
See GREGORY VII

HOHENSTAUFEN DYNASTY
Family of German princes that provided several HOLY ROMAN EMPERORS (1138–1208 and 1214–54), who aggrandized the imperial office. The most famous were FREDERICK I and FREDERICK II. A bitter struggle with the PAPACY ended in 1268 with the execution of Conrad, last of the Hohenstaufens. ▷ 3.08

HOHOKAM
Early maize farming culture of the southwestern deserts of North America from 400 to 1450. Ballcourts at Snaketown and Casa Grande show that the culture was in contact with the Mesoamerican civilizations. ▷ 3.26

HOLY LAND
Name given by Christians to the homeland of Jesus Christ, roughly equivalent to Palestine. Christian reverence for the Holy Land began in the 4th century with the building of shrines on sites associated with the life of Jesus. Christian pilgrimage to the Holy Land reached a peak under the CRUSADER STATES, but continued long after the Muslim reconquest. The major shrines were the churches of the Holy Sepulchre in Jerusalem and of the Nativity in Bethlehem. ▷ 3.03, 3.16

HOLY ROMAN EMPIRE
European empire claiming to be the successor to the Roman and CAROLINGIAN empires, it was formalized as a political entity when OTTO I, king of Germany and Italy, adopted the imperial title in 962. In effect a German empire (the First Reich), the empire covered most of Germany, the Low Countries, Austria, Switzerland, Italy and Bohemia. Believing themselves to be successors of the Roman emperors, the Holy Roman emperors frequently had pretensions above their means. Frequent conflicts with the PAPACY undermined imperial power, and by the 13th century the empire had become a decentralized confederation of princely states under a weak emperor. From 1438 it was continuously

in Habsburg hands (excluding 1742–45) until its abolition by Napoleon in 1806. As an institution it was split by the Reformation and fatally weakened by the Thirty Years War. ▷ 3.01, 3.02, 3.03, 3.04, 3.05, 3.06, 3.07, 3.08, 3.09, 3.10, 3.11, 3.12, 3.22, 3.23

Hospital of St John, Order of the
Founded as a hospice for sick pilgrims in the late 11th century, the Hospital took its name from the parish of St John in Jerusalem which was its headquarters until 1187. The Hospital was recognized as an independent Order by the Papacy in 1113, and from the 1130s expanded its role to include garrisoning castles and providing a standing army for the Kingdom of Jerusalem. With resources from its western endowments, the Hospital increased in wealth and influence until the Muslim conquest of the Holy Land in 1291 forced it to withdraw in 1310 to Rhodes and in 1522 to Malta. ▷ 3.10, 3.11, 3.12, 3.17

Hülegü
Grandson of Chingis Khan, and the first ilkhan (r.1256–65). Hülegü's conquest of Samarkand (1255) and Persia and Iraq (1256–58) founded the Ilkhanate. His sack of Baghdad in 1258 ended the Abbasid caliphate. In 1260 Hülegü took Damascus and Aleppo, but defeat at 'Ain Jalut at the hands of the Mamlukes meant he could never dominate the Middle East. ▷ 3.23

Hunac Ceel
Founder of the Mayan Cocom dynasty of Yucatán. Hel conquered Chichén Itzá in 1221, ending the Toltec dynasty there. Shortly after his victory, Hunac Ceel founded Mayapán which remained the dominant Mayan city until 1441. ▷ 3.27

Hundred Years War
Series of wars (1337–1453) – including famous encounters at Sluys, Crécy, Poitiers, Agincourt, Orléans, Formigny, and Castillon. – between England and France. Instigated by Edward III's claim to the French crown, the struggle ended when France took control of Bordeaux, leaving Calais as the only English possession in France. The war continued the Angevin–Capetian struggle and was largely prompted by French economic interests and English concerns over French intervention in Scotland ("The Auld Alliance"). ▷ 3.10, 3.12

Hungary
Central European state founded by the Magyars. Its first, and greatest, king was St Stephen Istvan (r.1000–38) who introduced Christianity and centralized government to create a powerful, repressive state. Between 1301–1490 Matthias Corvinus was its only native ruler. In 1526 Louis II died facing the Ottomans at Mohacs. Thereafter Hungary was a battleground of shifting borders until Habsburg possession in 1699 led to the Austro-Hungarian empire and the dual monarchy of 1867. It lost vast tracts of territory after defeat in World War I. Defeated again in 1945 it came under Communist rule (which an uprising in 1956 could not shake off) until democratization in 1989. ▷ 3.04, 3.05, 3.06, 3.07, 3.08, 3.09, 3.10, 3.11, 3.12, 3.16, 3.17, 3.22, 3.23

Hus, Jan
(c.1369–1415) Bohemian religious reformer and national hero influenced by the doctrines of John Wycliffe's Lollardy. He was condemned as a heretic and burned at the Council of Constance, prompting the Hussite wars (1419–36). ▷ 3.12

Husain
A grandson of Muhammad, Husain was recognized in 661 as the rightful caliph by the supporters of the murdered Caliph Ali. He took no action against Caliph Muawiya, but after his death he rebelled against his son Yazid. He was defeated and killed at Karbala in 680. His supporters saw him as a martyr and their schism from the caliphate was to lead to the establishment of the Shiite branch of Islam. ▷ 3.05, 3.13

Hussites
Followers of Jan Hus who wished to remove imperial and papal influence in Bohemia and continue Hus's religious reforms through the Four Articles of Prague (1420), which insisted upon clerical morals, free preaching and universal communion. In the Hussite wars (1419–36), the established powers prevented them from creating a theocratic peasant state. ▷ 3.12

Ibn Battuta
(1304–68/9 or 1377) Arab traveler and writer. Ibn Battuta began traveling across north Africa in 1325. For the next 30 years he traveled constantly, traversing the entire Islamic world as far as India and penetrating China. His account of his journeys is a description of the known world, much valued for the quality of his observations. ▷ 3.16

Ica
Culture centered in the Ica Valley on the coast of southern Peru. It flourished in the Late Intermediate period (c.900–c.1475) until the region was conquered by the Incas. The culture is distinguished by its high-quality textiles and painted pottery. ▷ 3.28

Iceland
North Atlantic island settled by Vikings in about 870. In 930 the settlers created the Althing, an aristocratic assembly, to rule the island. Christianity was adopted in about 1000. Increasingly troubled by aristocratic feuding, Iceland joined Norway in 1262, becoming a Danish possession by the Union of Calmar (1380). Icelandic independence was achieved in 1918. ▷ 3.02, 3.03, 3.04. 3.07

Iconoclast controversy
Conflict in the Byzantine empire over the use of icons of saints in worship. It threatened the stability of the empire between 726 and 843. Leo III's edict (726) banning icons provoked opposition, particularly from monasteries, and in 787 the 7th Ecumenical Council declared veneration of icons orthodox. Fresh conflict arose in 815 when Leo V renewed the ban on icons, but in 843 Empress Theodora reversed this policy. ▷ 3.05, 3.15

Idrisid caliphate
A Moroccan dynasty founded in 789 and reaching its peak in the mid-9th century, when the Idrisids extended their authority over the Berber tribes. By 929, however, a Fatimid invasion had wrested control of Ifriqiya from the dynasty, and by 985 the Idrisids had been extinguished. ▷ 3.01, 3.07, 3.14

Ife
Kingdom and city of the Yoruba people of what is today southwestern Nigeria. Probably in existence by the 12th century, Ife came under the political domination of Oyo in the 16th century, but its autonomy was protected by its status as a religious center: it is regarded by the Yoruba as the legendary birthplace of humanity. Ife was finally conquered by Ibadan in 1882 but it remains an important religious center. ▷ 3.18

Ifriqiya
Province of the eastern Maghreb, centered on Tunis. Muslim geographers seldom agreed about its precise limits. In early writings it extends from Tripoli to Tangier, but in the 10th century it was more loosely the whole of north Africa, including the Sahara. The province is most often identified with the Aghlabid dynasty. ▷ 3.13, 3.14, 3.15

Igbo (Ibo)
A numerous people of southeastern Nigeria, in pre-colonial times living in several tribal confederations. The Igbo were incorporated into the British colony of Nigeria in 1886. In a civil war fought between 1967 and 1970, the southeast attempted unsuccessfully to secede from Nigeria as the independent state of Biafra.

Ilkhanate
The Mongol state created by Hülegü's conquests in Persia, Iraq and Syria in the 1250s, and including as satellites Armenia and Anatolia. Until 1295, when they adopted Islam, its rulers (ilkhans) enjoyed close relations with Christian Europe. Although the Ilkhanate lasted only until 1355, it created in Persia for the first time in centuries a single territorial unit. ▷ 3.03, 3.04, 3.11, 3.23

Iltutmish
Sultan of Delhi (r.1211–36). The son-in-law of Qutb-ud-Din, the founder of the Delhi

SULTANATE, he consolidated Muslim rule in northern India. A sensitive statesman and fine administrator, Iltutmish transformed Delhi from a minor fortress town into an imperial capital. Iltutmish's sons were incompetent, and he wished to be succeeded by his daughter Raziyya. However, she could not establish her authority and was deposed in 1240, after which the dynasty went into decline. ▷ 3.19

INCA EMPIRE
The last and greatest of the states of the pre-Columbian Americas. At its peak in about 1500, the Inca empire was one of the largest states on earth, comprising much of modern Peru, Equador, Bolivia, Chile and Argentina. It ruled around 12 million people. The Incas were a Quechua-speaking people of the Peruvian Andes. According to Inca traditions, MANCO CAPAC founded the Inca state at CUZCO (c.1200–30). Spectacular imperial expansion began under PACHACUTEC (r.1438–71) and continued under his son TUPAC YUPANQUI (r.1471–93). A war of succession broke out on Huayna Capac's death (1525) between his sons Huáscar and ATAHUALLPA. Atahuallpa's victory came only months before the CONQUISTADOR Francisco Pizarro invaded the fatally weakened empire in 1532. Though Inca resistance to the Spanish continued for many years after Atahuallpa was executed by Pizarro in 1533, the empire died with him. The Inca state was highly organized, had an extensive road system and a rigidly hierarchical social structure. The emperor, held to be an incarnation of the sun god Inti, had autocratic powers. The Incas consolidated their conquests by imposing their language and culture on conquered peoples. Inca civilization was not original but drew freely on the traditions of 2,000 years of Andean history. ▷ 3.28

INNOCENT III
Pope (r.1198–1216) – one of the greatest incumbents of the Holy See, and the leading exponent of the PAPACY's temporal and spiritual supremacy. ENGLAND, SICILY and ARAGON became papal fiefs during his pontificate. His reign is a series of major events: he elevated Otto IV to the position of emperor, and then deposed him. He placed England under interdict. He preached the Fourth, Fifth and ALBIGENSIAN CRUSADES, promoted the FRANCISCAN ORDER, and in 1215 held the Fourth, and most important, LATERAN COUNCIL. ▷ 3.08, 3.09, 3.17

INQUISITION
Tribunal of the church to suppress heresy by investigation and punishment. It was established in the wake of the ALBIGENSIAN CRUSADE to eliminate CATHARISM and it spread throughout Europe. In 1252 Pope Innocent IV permitted it to use torture. Punishments included fines, imprisonment and, for unyielding heretics, burning. ▷ 3.05, 3.09

INVESTITURE CONTEST
Conflict between the PAPACY and lay rulers, principally the HOLY ROMAN EMPERORS, over the right to appoint bishops to vacant sees. Its most famous protagonists were HENRY IV of Germany and pope GREGORY VII. It was concluded by the Diet of Worms in 1122, largely in the papacy's favor. ▷ 3.08

IRISH PALE
Also known as the English Pale, the area of Ireland under direct English governance. By the 15th century it had shrunk to a small area around Dublin, when English preoccupations with the HUNDRED YEARS WAR were exploited by the Irish. ▷ 3.12

ISABELLA OF CASTILE
Queen of CASTILE (r.1479–1504). Her marriage to FERDINAND OF ARAGON made possible the unification of Spain. With him she established the SPANISH INQUISITION and expelled the Jews from Spain in 1492. Isabella funded Columbus's voyages of exploration westward across the Atlantic Ocean. ▷ 3.03, 3.12

ISLAM
The religion established by the Prophet MUHAMMAD following divine revelations beginning in 610. After a series of military campaigns to convert the ARAB people, from 632 Islam spread, largely by conquest, extending eventually from the Atlantic to southeast Asia. Islam is monotheistic and claims to be the last of a series of divine revelations to humans. Its success was aided by its capacity to assimilate the cultural heritage of conquered territories without compromising the core of the religion itself. ▷ 3.01, 3.02, 3.03, 3.04, 3.05, 3.06, 3.07, 3.08, 3.09, 3.10, 3.11, 3.12, 3.13, 3.14, 3.15, 3.16, 3.17, 3.18, 3.19

ISMAILI NIZARI
See ASSASSINS

ITZCÓATL
King of the AZTECS (1428–40), Itzcóatl strengthened the authority of the monarchy and was responsible for forging the TRIPLE ALLIANCE with the neighboring cities of Texcoco and Tlacopan, which made the Aztecs the dominant power of the valley of Mexico and laid the foundations for their later imperial expansion. ▷ 3.27

IVAN III (THE GREAT)
Prince of MOSCOW and first czar of Russia (r.1462–1505). He extended the territory of Moscow, subjugated its rival, NOVGOROD, in 1478 and in 1480 ceased tribute payments to the Mongol GOLDEN HORDE. CONSTANTINOPLE having fallen to the Turks in 1453, Ivan promoted Moscow as a third Rome, adopting the title czar (Caesar) in 1470. ▷ 3.12

JACQUERIE
French peasant revolt of 1358 in the wake of deprivations inflicted by the HUNDRED YEARS WAR. The peasants targeted the nobility and were in turn bloodily suppressed. ▷ 3.10

JAYAVARMAN II
Founder of the KHMER EMPIRE of Cambodia (r.802–50). He was a vassal ruler in the ANGKOR district in about 800, under an unknown Javanese or Sumatran dynasty. In 802 he declared independence, proclaiming himself *devaraja* (god-king), so establishing the Khmer monarchy on a theocratic basis. In the remainder of his career he united the Khmer people and built an empire approximating to modern Cambodia. ▷ 3.25

JERUSALEM, KINGDOM OF
CRUSADER STATE founded in 1099. The kingdom extended at its height in the mid-12th century from the Red Sea to Beirut and included territory east of the Jordan. The conquests of SALADIN (1187–89) reduced the kingdom to a rump around Tyre, but during the 1190s the coastline, which included the most important commercial centers, was restored to Frankish hands and the kingdom enjoyed a revival based on a new capital at ACRE. The kingdom was weakened in the 1180s by baronial factionalism and in the 13th century by dwindling military resources and a failure of the royal succession. ▷ 3.09, 3.17

JEWS
Descendants of and converts to the religion of a people expelled from Palestine by the Romans in the 1st century. Their religion contributed the Old Testament of the BIBLE. Important Jewish settlements could be found from central Asia to Britain in the medieval period. In the west they were subject from the 12th century onward to persecution. Jews were periodically massacred, for example in 1096 in the Rhineland. Excluded from England and France by 1300, they took refuge in Spain until 1492 and in north Africa. In Islamic lands Judaism was a protected religion, though Jews were second-class citizens. ▷ 3.05, 3.05, 3.09, 3.10, 3.12

JIHAD
The obligation on Muslims to wage war to establish ISLAM. It was used to justify the initial military conquests of the 7th century. The revival of the concept in 12th-century Syria helped to unify the Islamic Near East against the SHIITES and the CRUSADER STATES. ▷ 3.16

JOAN OF ARC, ST
(c.1412–31) French heroine and military leader of the HUNDRED YEARS WAR. She led a successful counterattack against the English, breaking their siege of ORLÉANS in 1429. Captured by the BURGUNDIANS, she was burned by the English as a witch. ▷ 3.12

JOHN
ANGEVIN king of ENGLAND (r.1199–1216). John lost all Angevin territory in FRANCE except GASCONY in war with PHILIP II (1202–04), so

earning the appelation "Lackland". He was excommunicated and England laid under interdict for his quarrel with Pope Innocent III over the archbishopric of Canterbury; John was forced to submit, with England becoming a papal fief. An able and innovative administrator but a poor soldier, John's arbitrary rule led to baronial rebellion and Magna Carta to restrict royal authority. He died during a French invasion of England. ▷ 3.08

John the Fearless
Duke of Burgundy (r.1404–19). Despite its failure, John won fame for his role in the Nicopolis Crusade against the Turks in 1396. His assassination of Louis, duke of Orléans, in 1407 precipitated a civil war and in 1418 he took advantage of French defeats in the Hundred Years War to sieze Paris. John was murdered while negotiating with the future Charles VII of France. ▷ 3.10, 3.12

Jürchen
A Siberian pastoralist people related to the Manchus. In 1124 they conquered the Khitan state of Liao in northern China and founded the Jin dynasty. ▷ 3.21

Kalmar
See Calmar, Union of

Kamakura shogunate
First military government of Japan. Following his victory in 1185 over the Taira clan in the Gempei War, Minamoto Yoritomo founded a *bakufu* (military government) at Kamakura, south of Edo (modern Tokyo) to rule alongside the imperial court. In 1192 the emperor recognized Yoritomo's dominant position and granted him the title *shogun* (generalissimo). The major achievement of the Kamakura shogunate was the repulse of the Mongol invasions of 1274 and 1281, but the high costs of this weakened the authority of the shogunate and it was overthrown in 1333 by the emperor Go-Daigo. ▷ 3.24

kamikaze
Japanese for "divine wind".The term was first applied to the typhoons that scattered the Mongol invasion fleets at Hakataka Bay, Kyushu, in 1274 and 1281. It was later used to describe the Japanese navy suicide pilots who attempted to crash explosive-packed aircraft onto Allied warships in the closing years of World War II. ▷ 3.23

Kammu
Emperor of Japan (r.781–806). To escape the excessive influence of the Buddhist clergy, in 794 he removed the imperial court from Nara to Heian (modern Kyoto), initiating the Heian period (794–1185). Heian remained the imperial capital until 1868. ▷ 3.24

Kanauj
Ancient city, now in Uttar Pradesh, India. Kanauj rose to prominence as the capital of the short-lived empire of Harsha in the 7th century and was later the capital of the Gurjara-Pratiharas. The city was sacked by Mahmud of Ghazni in 1018 and again by Muhammad of Ghur in 1193. ▷ 3.19

Kara-Khitai
Central Asian khanate, with its capital at Balasaghun, now in Kyrgizstan. The khanate was founded by the Khitan ruler Yeh-lü Ta-shih when he conquered the Kharakhanid Turks in 1137. In 1141 Yeh-lü consolidated his conquest by defeating the Great Seljuk sultan Sanjar near Samarkand. The khanate was weakened in about 1200 by attacks from the Khwarizm shahdom and in 1218 it collapsed precipitately when the Mongols invaded. The governmental institutions of Kara-Khitai were taken over by the Mongols to form the foundations of their own imperial administration. ▷ 3.22

Karakorum
Capital of the Mongol empire, in the Mongolian steppes. Built by Chingis Khan in 1220 and walled in 1235. After the great khans settled in China in the later 13th century, Karakorum lost its importance. ▷ 3.22, 3.23

Karbala, Battle of
The revolt in October 680 of Husain against the Umayyad caliphate. It ended when he was defeated at Karbala by the caliph Yezid, whose authority he had refused to recognize. Husain's death was regarded as martyrdom by his Shiite followers. ▷ 3.05, 3.13

Kediri
The dominant kingdom of eastern Java from the 11th century until its absorption by the Singhasari empire in the mid-13th century. It was an important naval and trading power. ▷ 3.03

Khajuraho
Capital of the northern Indian Chandella dynasty (9th–12th century) and an important religious center, now in Madhya Pradesh state. It was abandoned in the 14th century and lost in thick forest until its rediscovery in 1838 by a British army officer. Of the city's original 85 Hindu and Jain temples about 20 remain largely complete: they are famous for their richly decorative carvings. ▷ 3.19

Khalji dynasty
The second ruling dynasty of the Delhi sultanate (1290–1320), founded by Firuz Khalji (r.1290–96) following the collapse of the Slave dynasty of Qutb-ud-Din, founded in 1206. The greatest Khalji ruler, Ala-ud-Din (r.1290–1316), extended the sultanate's control into the Deccan. Mubarak, the third and last Khalji ruler, was murdered in 1320 by his chief minister Khusrav Khan who ruled briefly before being overthrown by Tughluk I, founder of the Tughluk dynasty. ▷ 3.19

Khazars
A central Asian people who had settled by the 7th century in the south Russian steppes. The Khazars already numbered Christians and Muslims when, in about 800, the khaghan (tribal chieftain) converted to Judaism. During the 10th century the Khazars lost territory to the Rus, and by the early 11th century had disappeared as a political force. ▷ 3.01, 3.02, 3.05, 3.07, 3.13, 3.14, 3.16

Khitans
Nomadic tribe from the Manchurian plain, of Turko-Mongolian origins, who threatened northern China from 500. In the 10th century they invaded China and helped to bring down the Tang dynasty. They were ruled by the Liao dynasty to 1125 when they were destroyed by their Jürchen vassals. ▷ 3.21

Khmer empire
Empire of the Khmer people founded by Jayavarman II in 802. The empire's capital was established at the spectacular temple-city of Angkor by Yasovarman I (r.889–910). At its peak under Suryavarman I (r.1010–50) and Suryavarman II (r.1113–50) the empire controlled all of modern Cambodia and most of Thailand and Laos. Attacked by the expanding Thai peoples, the empire declined in the 15th century. In 1431 the capital was moved from Angkor to the safer location of Caturmukha (near Phnom Penh) and by 1500 the Khmer were a minor regional power. ▷ 3.25

Khmers
Austroasiatic-speaking people of modern Cambodia, also known as Kampucheans. Small numbers of Khmer also live in Thailand and southern Vietnam. Linguistically, they are related to the Mons of Thailand and Myanmar. The earliest Khmer state was Funan, which emerged in about 100. It was succeeded in about 400 by Chen-la and in about 800 by the Khmer empire.

Khubilai Khan
(1215–94) Grandson of Chingis Khan and great khan of the Mongols (r.1260–94). Khubilai completed the conquest of Song China (begun 1252) in 1279, transferring the capital of the Great Khanate from Karakorum to Dadu (Beijing) in 1266. His later campaigns against Japan (1274, 1281) and Java (1292) were costly failures. Khubilai was the first Mongol ruler to become the founder of a Chinese dynasty, that of the Yueh. ▷ 3.03, 3.23

Khwarizm shahdom
The traditional title given to a north Persian province. Its ruling Ma'murid dynasty was in 1017 incorporated by the Ghaznavids, and in the 1030s by the Seljuks. After the fragmentation of the Great Seljuk sultanate in the 12th century, the dynasty flourished until

destroyed by the MONGOLS in the 1250s. ▷ 3.14, 3.16, 3.22

KIEV
Capital of KIEVAN RUS (c.882–1240). Kiev was already a flourishing town when captured by the Varangian (VIKING) Askold in about 860. Askold was expelled by Oleg of the RYURIK dynasty in 882, who transferred his capital there from NOVGOROD. After the conversion of the Russians to Christianity in the 10th century, Kiev became a major cultural center and was impressively fortified by Yaroslav the Wise (r.1019–54). Destroyed by the MONGOLS in 1240 it passed to LITHUANIA (1362) and the Poles (1569) before returning to Russian control in 1654. It is now capital of the Ukraine. ▷ 3.07–09

KIEVAN RUS
RUS state, founded by Oleg of the RYURIK dynasty when he moved his capital from NOVGOROD to KIEV in about 882. Under Igor (913–45) and Svyatoslav I (r.945–72) Kievan control extended from the Gulf of Finland to the Black Sea. The Kievan state adopted ORTHODOX Christianity in 987, forging close cultural and political links with the BYZANTINE EMPIRE which had a formative effect on early Russian culture. Kievan Rus broke up into several principalities in 1132, though all were nominally subject to the prince of Kiev. The principality was overrun in 1240 by the MONGOLS. ▷ 3.07, 3.08, 3.09

KILLKE
A culture of the Peruvian Andes whose architectural and artistic traditions were ancestral to those of the INCAS. It flourished in the LATE INTERMEDIATE PERIOD (c.1000–1475). ▷ 3.28

KILWA KISIWANI
City-state off the coast of modern Tanzania. Founded in about 800 as a trading center, Kilwa was ISLAMIZED in about 1000 through the influence of visiting ARAB traders. Around 1200 Kilwa became the first state in sub-equatorial Africa to issue coinage. It was occupied briefly by the Portuguese (1505–12) and declined thereafter. Substantial ruins remain, including those of a 14th-century mosque and palace. ▷ 3.18

KOGURYO
One of the THREE KINGDOMS of early Korea. Koguryo developed in the T'ung-chia river valley around Kungnaesong, its first capital, (c.37 BC). At its peak in the 5th century the influence of Koguryo extended from central Korea far into Manchuria. Koguryo was eventually destroyed in 660–68 by the Chinese TANG DYNASTY empire in alliance with SILLA. ▷ 3.24

KONARAK
In ORISSA, India, Konarak is famous for the Surya Deula, the 13th-century temple of the Hindu sun god Surya, one of the masterpieces of Hindu architecture. Carved in the form of a gigantic 12-wheeled chariot, the temple is richly ornamented with erotic sculptures. When complete the temple exceeded 60 meters (200 feet) in height, its remains stand to half that height. ▷ 3.19

KONGO
See CONGO

KORAN
The revelation received by MUHAMMAD from 610 onward, held by Muslims to be the word of God and providing the basis of ISLAM. The Koran in its present form was compiled by the third caliph UTHMAN (644–56), who arranged the texts into 114 *suras*. The order is not chronological and the revelation itself is difficult to understand without knowledge of the historical context. ▷ 3.01, 3.05, 3.13

KORYO
Kingdom, founded between 918–36 by WANG KON (r.918–45) of the Koryo dynasty, from which Korea gets its name. Koryo was a successor state to SILLA which collapsed in about 900. By 960 Koryo had established control of most of the Korean peninsula south of the Yalu river. The dynasty was overthrown by a military coup in 1170 and the country was ruled by generalissimos until the CHOE DYNASTY won power in 1196. ▷ 3.24

KOSOVO, BATTLE OF
Battle fought on 28 June 1389 in southern Serbia, in which the OTTOMANS defeated the Serbs, ending the Serbian kingdom. The battle has had a lasting impact on the Serbian national consciousness, with murderous consequences for Bosnian Muslims and Kosovans during the break-up of Yugoslavia in the 1990s. ▷ 3.10

KOTTE
SINHALESE kingdom in Ceylon in the 13th to 15th centuries. King Parakrambahu VI (1412–67) brought all of Ceylon under his control but thereafter the kingdom declined rapidly. In 1505 Kotte became a tributary to the Portuguese who imposed direct colonial rule in 1597. ▷ 3.19

KUFIC
A stylized ARABIC script developed at al-Kufa, Iraq, and used primarily in transcribing the KORAN, in official documents, on coins and in monumental inscriptions.

KURDS
Indigenous people of northern Iraq, Syria, Iran and southeast Turkey. The conversion of the Kurds to ISLAM began in the 640s. They were later brought under the control of the ABBASID CALIPHATE. The AYYUBID DYNASTY, established in the 1170s by SALADIN, himself of Kurdish origin, temporarily brought Kurds into positions of political influence. ▷ 3.16

KÜYÜK KHAN
Khan of the MONGOLS (r.1246–48). The son and successor of OGEDAI, and a patron of NESTORIAN CHRISTIANITY. During Küyük's reign, disputes over the succession between the descendants of CHINGIS became increasingly bitter. Küyük died while preparing to campaign against his cousin BATU KHAN. ▷ 3.22

LAMAISM
The TIBETAN form of Buddhism. Lamaism developed in the 7th to 9th centuries when the traditional Tibetan shamanistic Bon religion was assimilated to Mahayana Buddhism, which was introduced from India. Lamaism was persecuted in the 9th century by King gLang Dar Mar but made a strong recovery in the 11th century when the monasteries became powerful landowning institutions. Lamaism was reformed by Tsong-kha-pa (1357–1419) who founded the dGe-lugs-pa sect (or Yellow Hats). From this sect descends the line of Dalai Lamas who, from the 17th century, have been recognized as the temporal as well as spiritual leaders of Tibet. ▷ 3.05

LAMBAYEQUE
See SICÁN STATE

LANCASTRIAN DYNASTY
A branch of the PLANTAGENET DYNASTY, which ruled ENGLAND from 1399 to 1461 under HENRY IV, HENRY V and HENRY VI. Its great struggle with the rival House of York erupted into the WARS OF THE ROSES. ▷ 3.12

LAS NAVAS DE TOLOSA, BATTLE OF
The decisive battle (fought on 16 July 1212) of the Spanish RECONQUISTA. An Iberian crusading army won a great victory over the Muslims, permanently breaking their power. ▷ 3.08

LATE HORIZON PERIOD
The period (c.1475–1532) in the history of the Pre-Columbian Andean civilizations of South America which saw the dominance of the INCA empire. ▷ 3.28

LATE INTERMEDIATE PERIOD
The period in the history of the Pre-Columbian Andean civilizations of South America between the fall of the Tiahuanaco empire in about 1000 and the INCA conquest of the ICA in about 1475. The dominant state of the period was the CHIMÚ EMPIRE. ▷ 3.28

LATERAN COUNCIL
General council of the church held in Rome. Those of 1123, 1139, 1179 and 1215 are numbered I-IV; although strictly not the first they are the most signficant. Of these, IV is the most important: called by Pope INNOCENT III, it defined transubstantiation, reaffirmed reforms and laid down many central tenets of the Catholic faith. ▷ 3.09

LATIN EMPIRE
Eastern Mediterranean empire founded by the Fourth CRUSADE. The Crusaders who captured CONSTANTINOPLE in 1204 displaced the ruling BYZANTINE dynasty and partitioned former Byzantine territory between the house of Flanders, the Courtenay family, other baronial families – notably the Villehardouins in ACHAEA – and the Venetians, who controlled Crete and most of the Aegean, Cycladic and Ionian islands. The empire dwindled in influence until its fall in 1261 to Michael VIII Palaeologus, who re-established Byzantine rule. ▷ 3.11, 3.16, 3.17

LECHFELD, BATTLE OF
Victory of the German king OTTO I over the MAGYARS in 955. Otto's victory over the still pagan Magyars gained him prestige as protector of Christendom as well as defining the eastern borders of the German empire. ▷ 3.07

LEO III
Pope (r.795–816). The factional conflicts in Rome to which Leo fell victim in 799 led to his appeal to CHARLEMAGNE, and to his restoration to power with Frankish help. Perhaps in return for this Leo crowned Charlemagne emperor in 800, an event of great significance for relations between spritual and secular authority throughout the medieval period. ▷ 3.06

LEO VI (THE WISE)
BYZANTINE emperor (r.886–912). A prolific writer, Leo was the most important legislator since Justinian. The omnipotence of the emperor was given legal standing in his *Basilica.* He reformed the military administration to face a revival of BULGAR power in the Balkans. ▷ 3.15

LEÓN
Region and medieval Christian kingdom of northwest Spain, evolving from ASTURIAS in the 10th century. It was united with CASTILE (1037–1157), broke away and rejoined (1230). PORTUGAL gained its independence from León in 1128. ▷ 3.02, 3.07, 3.08, 3.09

LI YUAN
First emperor of the TANG DYNASTY of China, known also as Gaozu (r.618–26). Li Yuan was military governor of Taiyuan in northern China. With the empire facing collapse as a result of the disastrous rule of the Sui emperor Yang (r.604–17), Li Yuan mounted a military coup. In 617 he captured the Sui capital Luoyang and executed Yang. The following year at CHANG'AN he proclaimed the Tang dynasty. In 626 Li Yuan abdicated in favor of his son Li Shih-min who became emperor under the title TAIZONG: he died in 635. ▷ 3.20

LIAO
State founded by the KHITAN chief A-pao-chi in Manchuria, Mongolia and northeastern China (916–1125). Its rulers adopted the Chinese dynastic name Liao. Liao had a dual government. The Chinese population of the south were ruled by a government based on the TANG DYNASTY administration while a tribal assembly ruled the nomads of the north. Liao fought the SONG DYNASTY for control of northern China, settling in 1004 for regular payments of tribute by the Chinese. Liao was destroyed in 1125 by the Manchurian JÜRCHEN who took over their institutions and established the Jin empire. ▷ 3.21

LITHUANIA
Baltic state emerging from a 13th-century duchy to expand rapidly in the 14th century. It was the last pagan state in Europe, adopting Christianity only in 1386 when it formed a dynastic union with Poland. Thereafter it was intermittently ruled by Poland, Russia and Germany until independence in 1991. ▷ 3.08, 3.09, 3.10, 3.11, 3.12

LODI DYNASTY
The last ruling dynasty of the DELHI SULTANATE (1451–1526). Of Afghan origin, the Lodis came to power in Delhi when Bahlul Lodi (r.1451–89) deposed the last sultan of the weak SAYYID DYNASTY (1414–51). Under Bahlul and his son SIKANDER LODI, the sultanate recovered control of much of northern India. The attempt by Ibrahim (1517–26) to strengthen royal authority caused opposition and induced the governor of the Punjab to invite Babur, the Mughal ruler of Kabul, to invade India. When Ibrahim was killed by Babur at the Battle of Panipat in 1526, the sultanate collapsed. ▷ 3.19

LOLLARDS
English followers of the religious reformer John Wycliffe, espousing evangelical heresy, individual faith and scriptural supremacy. They sparked political revolt in 1414 and influenced the HUSSITES. ▷ 3.10

LOMBARD DUCHIES
Two independent Lombard-ruled duchies of southern Italy – Spoleto and Benevento. Founded in the 7th century they were conquered by the NORMANS and the BYZANTINE EMPIRE in the 11th, eventually becoming part of the kingdom of SICILY. ▷ 3.13, 3.14, 3.15

LOMBARD KINGDOM
Kingdom of northern Italy under Lombard rule from 569 until crushed by CHARLEMAGNE in 774 after a request for military help against them by Pope Hadrian. ▷ 3.13, 3.14, 3.15

LOMBARD LEAGUE
An alliance of northern Italian city-states formed in 1164 to protect their independence against imperial encroachment. It won a geat victory over FREDERICK I at Legnano (1176) and supported the WELF cause until the League's final dissolution in 1250. ▷ 3.08

LORDSHIP OF THE ISLES
Lordship covering the Hebrides and northwest SCOTLAND and, for a while, the Isle of Man. Theoretically subject to Scotland, it was ruled by the MacDonalds in virtual independence from the 14th century until its absorption by Scotland in 1493. ▷ 3.12

LOUIS IV (THE BAVARIAN)
HOLY ROMAN EMPEROR (r.1314–47). As Wittelsbach duke of Bavaria he beat his Habsburg rival to the imperial crown. He warred with the PAPACY, taking Rome (1328–30), but his dynastic ambitions were thwarted by the LUXEMBOURG DYNASTY. ▷ 3.10

LOUIS VI (THE FAT)
CAPETIAN King of FRANCE (r.1108–37). A colorful and, despite his corpulence (by middle age he was unable to mount his horse), an energetic monarch whose vigorous military campaigning did much to increase the power and prestige of the monarchy.

LOUIS VII
CAPETIAN King of FRANCE (r.1137–80). He took part in the disastrous Second CRUSADE (1147–49) and inadvertently created the ANGEVIN empire by divorcing his wife, the heiress Eleanor of AQUITAINE in 1152. She married Henry of ANJOU, the future HENRY II of ENGLAND. Henry thus added her enormous landholdings in southwestern France to the Angevin lands he took with him to the English throne. Louis countered the huge threat to France posed by the Angevin empire through shrewd politics, including eliciting papal support, and through efficient management of the royal desmesne.

LOUIS IX (ST LOUIS)
CAPETIAN king of FRANCE (r.1226–70) and saint. A renowned CRUSADER, he led the Seventh Crusade (1248–54) to Egypt where he was captured and ransomed. In France he consolidated the important territorial gains made by his father (Louis VIII) and grandfather (PHILIP II). His reign was long and peaceful, ending conflict with ENGLAND by the TREATY OF PARIS (1259). He died besieging Tunis. ▷ 3.17

LOUIS XI
King of FRANCE (r.1461–83). An unpopular king, he was renowned for his Machiavellian attitude. He defeated a BURGUNDIAN-led coalition in 1465, and his greatest success followed the death of CHARLES THE BOLD in 1477, when he added extensive Burgundian territories to France. ▷ 3.11

LOUIS THE PIOUS
CAROLINGIAN emperor (r.814–40). During Louis' reign the CAROLINGIAN EMPIRE was weakened by disputes between him and his sons. Civil war followed his death, resolved by the three-way division of the TREATY OF VERDUN in 843. ▷ 3.06, 3.07

Luxembourg dynasty
An imperial dynasty founded in 1308 when Henry VII of Luxembourg became Holy Roman emperor. It built a power base in Bohemia, making Prague a cultural center, with territories to rival the Habsburgs'. It held the imperial crown for 80 years between 1346 and 1437, its greatest emperor being Charles IV. ▷ 3.10, 3.12

Macchu Picchu
Inca city, situated high above the Urabamba valley, Peru, Macchu Picchu was probably a border outpost or religious center. The city was unknown to the Spanish conquerors and lay undiscovered until 1911. Macchu Picchu, built in the typical Inca style with massive dry-stone masonry, remains in a remarkable state of preservation. ▷ 3.28

Macedonian dynasty
Byzantine dynasty (867–1056) founded by Basil I in 867, so called because of the family's place of origin, though in fact the family was Armenian. The achievements of the Macedonian emperors in the 9th to 10th centuries were the reform of the army and civil administration that enabled the empire to overcome the Bulgar threat. After 1028 the failure of direct succession led to a series of weaker emperors coming to the throne through marriage to Empress Zoe. ▷ 3.15

Magna Carta
The "Great Charter", signed at Runnymede in England on 15 June 1215 by King John and baronial representatives, setting out personal and political liberties and responsibilities in the relationship between king and subjects. The charter aimed to curb excessive and arbitrary royal power and is regarded as an early human-rights document. ▷ 3.08

Magyars
A Turkic people who migrated to central Europe from the forest-steppe zone of Asia in the 9th century under the leadership of Arpád. During the 10th century the Magyars penetrated as far as eastern France, but were decisively defeated in 955 by Otto I. Under István (Stephen) they were converted to Catholic Christianity (c.1000–20) and formed a kingdom that flourished until falling to the Ottomans in the 16th century. ▷ 3.01, 3.02, 3.06, 3.07, 3.09, 3.15

Mahmud of Ghazni
(b.c.971) The son of Sebuktigin, a Samanid Turk slave who made himself the independent ruler of Ghazni in Afghanistan (r.977–97). Mahmud became ruler of Ghazni (r.999–1030) after defeating his brother in battle in 998. Mahmud conquered most of Iran and, a militant Muslim, he launched 17 separate invasions of Hindu India. Although the Punjab was brought under Mahmud's rule, his main objective in invading India was plunder and the destruction of Hindu temples. Under his rule Ghazni became a major Muslim cultural center. The Ghaznavid empire declined rapidly after Mahmud's death. ▷ 3.14

Majapahit
Javanese state and dynasty (1293–1527). Named for its capital city, Majapahit was the greatest pre-Islamic state of Indonesia. At its peak under the able leadership of its prime minister, Gaja Mada, who held office from 1330 to 1364, Majapahit exercised a loose dominance over most of the Indonesian islands and the coast of Malaya. Majapahit was a major trading and naval power. The empire collapsed in the 15th century after the introduction of Islam undermined the authority of its Hindu-Buddhist monarchy. ▷ 3.25

Mali empire
Medieval kingdom of the Malinke people. Mali's heartland was on the upper Niger river. The empire was founded when the Malinke rebelled against their Susu overlords under Sundiata in 1230. It reached its height under Mansa Musa (r.1307–32), when it controlled most of the west African Sahel. Trans-Saharan trade, particularly in gold, made an important contribution to Mali's prosperity and power. Beginning in 1400 Mali faced rebellions by its subject peoples and it had ceased to exist by 1550. ▷ 3.18

Malik Shah
Seljuk sultan (r.1072–92). The heir to Alp Arslan, Malik overcame rivals for the Great Seljuk sultanate, including his own brother, by 1084. Under his rule the sultanate reached its greatest extent, though on his death it soon fragmented. ▷ 3.16

Mamluke sultanate
The dominant force in the Near East from late 13th to the early 16th century. Originally formed from an army of Circassian slaves, the Mamlukes overthrew their masters, the Ayyubid dynasty, to become rulers of Egypt, in 1249. They halted the Mongol invasion in 1260 at 'Ain Jalut and had extinguished the Crusader States by 1291. ▷ 3.03, 3.04, 3.10, 3.11, 3.16, 3.17, 3.22, 3.23

Man, kingdom of
Kingdom comprising the Isle of Man and the Hebrides founded in about 1079. It owed allegiance to Norway but in practice was independent before breaking up in the late 13th century. ▷ 3.08

Manco Capac
Semi-legendary founder of the Inca state, possibly lived in about 1200–30. According to legend, the ancestors of the Inca people emerged from openings in a hill called Paccari Tampu ("Dawn Hostel"). Led by Manco Capac they made their way to the nearby Cuzco valley, drove out its inhabitants and settled there. ▷ 3.28

Manorial system
The domiant agricultural system of medieval Europe. It was a system of landholding centered on the lord's manor (demesne) in which land was divided among free and unfree tenants (serfs), under the jurisdiction of the manorial court. Tenants paid a proportion of their crops as rent and serfs also had to peform labor dues. Many manors were geographically fragmented, comprising several villages. ▷ 3.11

Manzikert, Battle of
Victory, in 1071, of the Seljuks under Alp Arslan over the Byzantine empire. The emperor Romanos IV was captured and the Seljuks occupied Byzantine Anatolia. Byzantine power never recovered from the defeat. ▷ 3.03, 3.09, 3.15, 3.16

Marinid caliphate
Muslim dynasty ruling Fez in Morocco from 1248 to 1465. During the mid-14th century the Marinids also controlled neighboring Tlemcen. ▷ 3.03

Maritime Edict
Edict issued in 1371 by the Chinese Ming dynasty forbidding all Chinese to engage in overseas trade. The measure, part of a xenophobic reaction following liberation from Mongol rule, was meant to protect China from foreign influences but it also destroyed Chinese maritime commerce and led to widespread smuggling. ▷ 3.23

Mayors of the palace
Palace officials under earlier Merovingian kings, effective rulers of the Franks by the mid-7th century. The most prominent, such as Charles Martel, commanded the kingdom's armies. In 752 the mayor Pepin III deposed the last Merovingian, establishing his own Carolingian family on the throne. ▷ 3.06

Mecca
The holiest city in the Islamic world. Before the arrival of Islam this oasis on the trading route from the Red Sea coast of Arabia to Syria was already a commercial and (polytheistic) religious center. After Muhammad's victory over Mecca in 630, the Kaaba shrine in Mecca became the foremost place of worship of the new religion. ▷ 3.01, 3.03, 3.05, 3.13

Medici
Family of bankers who ruled Florence (1434–1737). Under their patronage the city became the leading cultural center of Renaissance Europe. Notable members include Catherine de' Medici, queen of France, and Popes Leo X and Clement VII. ▷ 3.12

Medina
The traditional burial-place of Muhammad. A cosmopolitan trading city in pre-Islamic times, Medina was suffering political disruption when Muhammad emigrated there in 622. His

ability to unify the Medinans and to use the city as the springboard of his conquest of Arabia between 622 and 630 assured the success of ISLAM. ▷ 3.01, 3.05, 3.13

MEHMET II
OTTOMAN sultan who began preparations for the conquest of CONSTANTINOPLE on his accession in 1451, finally capturing it on 29 May 1453. The transformation of the declining city into the new capital of the Ottoman empire occupied him until his death in 1481. Greeks remained prominent at Mehmet's court, and he was praised by contemporaries for his personal virtues and cultural patronage. ▷ 3.16

MERCIA
An Anglo-Saxon kingdom extending from the Thames valley to the Humber and Dee, and enjoying its greatest period of influence under AETHELBALD (r.716–57) and OFFA (r.757–96). Offa attained loose overlordship over other English kingdoms and corresponded with CHARLEMAGNE. Mercia was conquered by the Danes in the 9th century and fell under the sway of WESSEX in the 10th century. ▷ 3.06

MEROVINGIAN DYNASTY
Frankish dynasty established by Childeric in about 460, but claiming descent from the semi-mythical Merovech, Frankish ally of the Romans. At its peak under Clovis (r.482–511), the Merovingian custom of dividing lands between male heirs led to the weakening of the regime, and by the mid-7th century effective control had passed to the MAYORS OF THE PALACE. The last Merovingian king, Childeric III, was deposed in 751. ▷ 3.06

MICHOACAN
AZTEC name for the kingdom of the Tarascans in western Mexico. The state was founded in about 1325 by the semi-legendary chief Taríakuri. Michoacan became a powerful kingdom, well able to keep the expansionist Aztecs at bay in the 15th century. ▷ 3.27

MINAMOTO YORITOMO
Founder of the KAMAKURA SHOGUNATE, the first of the military governments that would rule Japan until 1868. Yoritomo (1147–99) was a leading member of the Minamoto SAMURAI clan. In 1180 he joined a rebellion (the GEMPEI WAR) against the dominant samurai clan, the TAIRA. By 1185 he had defeated both the Taira and his rivals within the Minamoto clan and he established a *bakufu* (military government) at his headquarters at Kamakura. Unable to challenge Yoritomo's power, the emperor granted him the title of *shogun* (generalissimo) in 1192. ▷ 3.24

MISSISSIPPIAN TEMPLE MOUND CULTURES
A group of cultures of the Mississippi basin of North America, including Middle Mississippian, South Appalachian Mississippian, Plaquemine Mississippian (on the lower Mississippi), and the related Caddoan, Fort Ancient and Oneota cultures. The cultures developed in about 800 after the introduction of maize and beans led to the beginning of full-time agriculture in the region. By the 12th century the Mississippian cultures had developed complex hierarchical societies and towns had begun to grow up around the massive earth temple mounds for which the culture is named. The cultures declined in the 15th century for unknown reasons. Epidemic diseases introduced accidently by Europeans completed the destruction of the cultures in the early 16th century. ▷ 3.26

MIXTECS
Native people of Mixteca, western Oaxaca, Mexico. A Mixtec kingdom emerged in the 10th century. In the 14th century the Mixtecs began to encroach on the neighboring Zapotec kingdom and had virtually eliminated it by the time of European contact in 1520. ▷ 3.27

MOCTEZUMA II
Last king of the AZTEC empire of Mexico (r.1502–20). A fine warrior and administrator, Moctezuma acted indecisively when faced by the invasion of the Spanish CONQUISTADOR Hernán Cortés in 1519, possibly believing him to be the god Quetzalcóatl, whose return to Mexico from the east was foretold by Aztec legend. On his arrival at TENOCHTITLÁN, the Aztec capital, Cortés captured Moctezuma and held him hostage. Moctezuma later died from injuries received during an uprising which temporarily drove the Spaniards from the city. ▷ 3.27

MOGOLLON CULTURE
Maize-farming culture of the southwestern deserts of North America (300–1450). The culture is noted for its geometrically decorated pottery, especially that from the Mimbres valley in New Mexico. The early Mogollon lived in pit houses, but after 1000 they adopted the multi-roomed pueblos of the ANASAZI CULTURE. The modern Zuni Pueblo Indians are thought to be, in part, descended from the Mogollon people. ▷ 3.26

MOLDAVIA
Principality formed by the Vlachs, who had emigrated from the Carpathian mountains. Moldavia emerged as an independent state under Bogdan I in 1349. Stephen IV (r.1457–1504) defended the kingdom against the OTTOMANS, but under Bogdan the One-Eyed (r.1504–17) it became a vassal of the Ottoman empire. ▷ 3.10, 3.12, 3.16

MÖNGKE KHAN
Khan of the MONGOLS (r.1251–59). In 1252 Möngke initiated the conquest of SONG China (completed by KHUBILAI KHAN) and of the ABBASID CALIPHATE (completed by HÜLEGÜ). ▷ 3.22, 3.23

MONGOLS
General name for a group of Mongolian-speaking central Asian nomad peoples, including the Mongols, TATARS, Buryats, Naimans, Kereyits and Tayyichi'ut (and, later, the Oirats and Khalkas). United by CHINGIS KHAN in 1206, over the next 70 years they conquered the largest contiguous land empire in world history in campaigns that were notorious for their savagery. At its peak in the late 13th century, the Mongol empire included China, Korea, Tibet, central Asia, Russia, Iran and Iraq, but by this time it had already been divided into four effectively independent khanates. By the mid-14th century Mongol power was in decline in Iran, and China won back its independence in 1368. On the western steppes, the Mongols were absorbed by their Turkic subjects but in their heartland on the eastern steppes of Asia they remained a potent force until the 17th century, when they were conquered by the Manchus. On the fall of the Manchu dynasty in China in 1911, the Mongols of Outer Mongolia became independent, forming the Republic of Mongolia. There are today 5 million Mongols, about 3 million of whom still live under Chinese rule in the Autonomous Region of Inner Mongolia. ▷ 3.22, 3.23

MONOPHYSITE CHRISTIANS
Term covering all churches – specifically the Armenian, Coptic and Syrian Orthodox churches – that did not accept the formula of the Council of Chalcedon (451) for determining the relationship between human and divine elements in the person of Christ. The Monophysites maintain that Christ's nature was wholly divine. Divisions between Monophysites and ORTHODOX reflected regional divisions within the eastern Roman empire. ▷ 3.13

MONS
An Austroasiatic-speaking people of the Irrawaddy delta of modern Myanmar and also eastern Thailand. The Mons probably originated in western China from where they migrated to their present homelands by the 6th century. They adopted Buddhism in the 9th century. In 1057 the Mons of the delta were conquered by the BURMESE of PAGAN. The destruction of Pagan by the MONGOLS allowed the Mons to regain their independence in 1317 as the kingdom of Pegu, but they were reconquered by the Burmese Toungou dynasty in 1535. The Mon kingdom of DVARAVATI (c.550–1050) played a significant role in the development of Thailand. ▷ 3.25

MONTEZUMA II
See MOCTEZUMA II

MONTFORT, SIMON DE
Soldier, CRUSADER and leader of the baronial reform movement rebelling against HENRY III of ENGLAND in the Barons' wars (1264–67), during which he was killed. He sought to

curb royal power by the Provisions of Oxford (1258) and called England's first representative PARLIAMENT in 1265.

MOSCOW, PRINCIPALITY OF (MUSCOVY)
Russian principality founded by DANIEL in the late 13th century. Centered on the fortified Kremlin, it extended its territory, uniting with the principality of Vladimir in the 14th century. Under IVAN III (r.1462–1505) and Ivan IV (1533–84) Moscow became the capital of the emerging Russian empire. ▷ 3.10. 3.12

MUAWIYA
CALIPH (r.661–80), founder of the UMAYYAD dynasty. Governor of DAMASCUS, Muawiya rose to prominence as the avenger of the murder of UTHMAN and overcame Caliph ALI in 657. He became caliph in 661 on the murder of Ali, ruling from Damascus until his death in 680. ▷ 3.01, 3.05, 3.13

MUHAMMAD
(570–632) Prophet of ISLAM. A member of the dominant QURAYSH tribe of MECCA, he lived in obscurity as a merchant until he began in 610 to receive the divine revelations that comprise the KORAN. After unsuccessful attempts to convert the Meccans to the new religion of Islam, Muhammad was invited to proselytize in MEDINA, and it was from here that the conquest and conversion of Arabia began, secured in 630 by the defeat of Mecca. Muhammad is venerated in Islam as the last of the series of prophets bringing divine revelation to humans. ▷ 3.01, 3.05, 3.13

MUHAMMAD OF GHUR
Sultan of Ghur (Afghanistan) (r.1173–1206). Full name Mu'izz-ud-Din Muhammad ibn Sam, he was the brother of Sultan Ghiyas-ud-Din, who appointed him subordinate ruler of Ghazni in 1173. In 1175 Muhammad began the conquest of northern India but after his decisive victory over the RAJPUTS at the second Battle of Tarain (near Delhi) he left campaigning to his lieutenant QUTB-UD-DIN. After Ghiyas's death in 1202, Muhammad ruled Ghur until his assassination in 1206, which was followed by the break-up of the sultanate. ▷ 3.19

MURAD I
An OTTOMAN sultan (r.1362–89) under whose guidance the Anatolian sultanate evolved into an empire stretching as far as the Balkans. From 1369 BYZANTIUM was effectively a tributary principality whose policies were directed by Murad. No attempt was made to conquer the city. In 1389 Murad was killed by insurgents in the BATTLE OF KOSOVO. ▷ 3.16

MYRIOCEPHALUM, BATTLE OF
Defeat in 1176 of the BYZANTINE emperor Manual Comnenos by the SELJUK SULTANATE OF RUM. The defeat ended Byzantine hopes of recovering control of Anatolia, lost since the BATTLE OF MANZIKERT. ▷ 3.15, 3.16

NAN CHAO
A Thai kingdom, now part of Yunnan province, China. Nan Chao emerged in about 600 and by 800 had became a major power. Its capital was at Dali. The kingdom was conquered by the MONGOLS in 1253 and came under the rule of the Ming dynasty in 1368. ▷ 3.25

NANAK, GURU
(1469–1538) Founder of SIKHISM, a monotheistic religion combining Hindu and (to a much lesser extent) Muslim influences. Born near Lahore, Nanak became a mendicant in the Indian tradition and visited both Hindu and Muslim holy sites. He settled at Kartarpur in the Punjab in 1520, where he was recognized as a guru (an inspired teacher). The Punjab remains the main center of Sikhism. ▷ 3.05

NARA
The imperial capital of Japan from 710 until 784. Founded in 706, the city was modeled on the Chinese TANG DYNASTY capital at CHANG'AN and was an integral part of the imperial government's attempt to build a centralized state on Chinese lines. The increasing power of the Buddhist clergy forced the court to abandon Nara, eventually settling at HEIAN in 794. Several Buddhist monuments survive, including the Horyuji monastery (built 670) and the Todaiji temple (built 745–52). ▷ 3.24

NESTORIAN CHRISTIANS
Followers of Nestorius, the patriarch of CONSTANTINOPLE, who was deposed by the Council of Ephesus in 431 for his doctrine that Christ's nature comprised in equal measure but separately the human and divine. His followers were banished from the Roman empire and from the 6th century they spread eastward from Iraq, establishing churches as far away as China. ▷ 3.02, 3.05, 3.20

NEUSTRIA
The western division of the Frankish kingdom after the 6th-century conquests of King Clovis, roughly equivalent to northeastern France. ▷ 3.06

NEVSKY, ALEXANDER
Prince of NOVGOROD (r.1236–63). He saved Novgorod from attack by the MONGOLS in 1240 by becoming their vassal. He was rewarded by appointment as prince of KIEV and grand prince of VLADIMIR-SUZDAL. His submission freed him to concentrate on defeating the Swedes (1240) and TEUTONIC KNIGHTS (1242) who threatened Novgorod from the west. ▷ 3.08

NICAEA, EMPIRE OF
BYZANTINE state, founded following the Fourth CRUSADE's seizure of CONSTANTINOPLE in 1204. Nicaea recaptured Constantinople in 1261, reestablishing the Byzantine empire until its final conquest by the OTTOMANS in 1453. ▷ 3.16–17

NICOPOLIS CRUSADE
Disastrous CRUSADE of 1396 under Franco-Hungarian leadership. It attempted to stop OTTOMAN expansion in Europe but ended with a humiliating defeat by an Ottoman army under BAYEZID I at the Battle of Nicopolis. Desertions and poor discipline contributed to the severity of the defeat. ▷ 3.10, 3.16, 3.17

NOBATIA
The most northerly of the medieval kingdoms of Nubia, with its capital at Faras. In the 7th century Nobatia became united with Makuria, and the seat of political power moved to Dongola. Faras became an ecclesiastical center. ▷ 3.13

NONOALCA
See TOLTECS

NORMAN CONQUEST
Conquest of ENGLAND by the NORMANS, which began with WILLIAM THE CONQUEROR's victory at the BATTLE OF HASTINGS in 1066. The last English resistance had been crushed by 1071. The conquest was achieved by warfare and colonization. It forced a new, foreign governing class upon England with its own language and culture and it severely repressed English resistance with harsh measures, such as the brutal "Harrying of the North". The Normans introduced feudal institutions but they also preserved many Anglo-Saxon institutions. ▷ 3.08

NORMANDY
Duchy of northern FRANCE named after Norse settlers under Rollo, to whom King CHARLES III ceded it in 911. A troublesome fief of France, in 1066 it was united with ENGLAND by WILLIAM THE CONQUEROR. Annexed by PHILIP II in 1204, Normandy was recovered by HENRY V of England in the early 15th century. It was finally incorporated into France after 1450. ▷ 3.07, 3.08, 3.12

NORMANS
Descendants of Duke Rollo and the VIKINGS who settled in NORMANDY. An energetic and belligerent race, they conquered ENGLAND (1066) and parts of WALES and Ireland. In the 11th to 12th centuries they dominated much of the Mediterranean through conquests of SICILY, southern Italy and Malta. They were notable CRUSADE leaders. They owed their success to military skill and pragmatic government, adapting local practices to their rule. ▷ 3.08, 3.09

NORSEMEN
See VIKINGS

NORTHUMBRIA
Powerful Anglo-Saxon kingdom of northern ENGLAND and southeastern SCOTLAND founded

in the 7th century and destroyed by VIKING invasions in the 9th century. ▷ 3.06, 3.07

NOVGOROD
Leading city of Russia and flourishing commercial center throughout the Middle Ages, it became a principal office of the Hanseatic league. At the peak of its power under ALEXANDER NEVSKY (r.1236–63) it was a bulwark against eastward German and Swedish expansion. It was absorbed by MOSCOW in 1478. ▷ 3.02, 3.03, 3.07, 3.08, 3.09, 3.10, 3.11, 3.12

NUR AL-DIN
Ruler of Aleppo (r.1146–74). The son of ZANGI, he united Syria under his rule in 1154 and conquered the FATIMID CALIPHATE of Egypt in 1171 by mobilizing SUNNI orthodox sentiment against both the SHIITES and the Franks. Although he lost control of Egypt to his general SALADIN, the ISLAMIC unity established in the Near East in the late 12th century was Nur's achievement. ▷ 3.16

OFFA
King of MERCIA (r.757–96). His conquests made him the foremost ruler in Britain. He used the title of king of the English and considered himself equal to his great contemporary, CHARLEMAGNE. He built OFFA'S DYKE, a practical symbol of his power. ▷ 3.06

OFFA'S DYKE
An earth and timber rampart, originally up to 240 kilometers (150 miles) long (including river boundaries and the earlier Wat's Dyke), built along MERCIA'S Welsh frontier by OFFA. Its main function was probably to stop cross-border raiding. ▷ 3.06

OGEDAI KHAN
MONGOL khan (r.1229–41). The third son and successor of CHINGIS KHAN. Ogedai continued the Mongols' expansion – eastward into China and Korea, westward into Iran and, through BATU KHAN, into Russia. ▷ 3.22, 3.23

ONIN WAR
Japanese civil war (1467–77), fought in the Kyoto region between supporters of rival heirs to the ASHIKAGA SHOGUNATE. The weakness of the shogunate was clearly exposed and Kyoto heavily damaged in this prelude to a century of civil strife. ▷ 3.24

ORISSA
Medieval kingdom of northeastern India, properly known as Odra Desa. At its peak under the Ganga (1078–1435) and Surya (1435–1568) dynasties, Orissa was a stronghold of Hinduism against ISLAM. Conquered by Muslim Bengal in 1568, Orissa later formed part of the Mughal empire. ▷ 3.19

ORLÉANS
City and duchy in northern FRANCE. It was the center of a royal duchy (1344–1498). Besieged by the English in the HUNDRED YEARS WAR it was famously relieved by JOAN OF ARC in 1429, a turning point in the war. It was the base of the ARMAGNAC party in the 15th century. ▷ 3.08, 3.12

ORTHODOX CHURCH
Also known as the Eastern Orthodox church and (incorrectly) the Greek Orthodox church it was the chief form of Christianity in the BYZANTINE EMPIRE, for which it was the official religion, and in the Slavic lands it converted. After centuries of disputes and growing mistrust, it finally broke from Rome in 1054. Like the ROMAN CATHOLIC CHURCH, it was heavily involved in politics and experienced heretical and reform movements, such as the ICONOCLAST CONTROVERSY (762–843) and the BOGOMILS. ▷ 2.17, 3.05, 3.06, 3.07, 3.09, 3.15

OSMAN I
Eponymous founder of the OTTOMAN DYNASTY. Osman's date of birth is unknown, but he was active from about 1300 to about 1325 and died in about 1326. By 1308 Osman controlled western Anatolia, having pushed the BYZANTINES back to the vicinity of NICAEA. ▷ 3.04, 3.16

OTTO I (THE GREAT)
SAXON king of Germany (r.936–73) and Italy (r.951–73) and HOLY ROMAN EMPEROR (r.962–73). His assumption of the imperial title in 962 was seen, like CHARLEMAGNE'S in 800, as restoring the western Roman empire. He was successful in Italy, operated the royal government through ecclesiastical structures and overshadowed the PAPACY. He further strengthened the imperial office by asserting control over the German nobles and ending Magyar invasions by his famous victory at LECHFELD (955). ▷ 3.02, 3.07

OTTOMAN DYNASTY
Turkish dynasty (c.1300–1924) founded by OSMAN I. After its capture by MEHMET II in 1453, CONSTANTINOPLE remained the capital of the dynasty until its overthrow after World War I. ▷ 3.04

ÖZBEG
Khan of the GOLDEN HORDE (r.1312–40). He survived an attempt by MONGOLS unhappy with his pro-ISLAMIC policy to assassinate him on his accession, contracted a dynastic alliance with the Mamlukes in 1320 and converted to Islam himself. Yet he was liberal in his treatment of Christians and permitted Italian trading colonies to be built on the Black Sea. ▷ 3.23

PACHACUTEC
Ninth emperor of the INCAS (r.1438–71). He was a great general who initiated the Incas' period of rapid imperial expansion by conquering a vast area from Lake Titicaca to Quito. In his later years Pachacutec left campaigning to his equally able son TUPAC YUPANQUI and supervised a program of monumental building at CUZCO. Pachacutec abdicated in favor of Tupac in 1471, dying a few years later. ▷ 3.28

PAEKCHE
One of the THREE KINGDOMS of early Korea, Paekche developed in the southeast of the Korean peninsula around 18 BC. Paekche was conquered by an alliance of its neighbor SILLA and the Chinese TANG empire in 668 and was occupied first by the Tang and then, in 671, by Silla. Paekche played a key role in the transmission of Buddhism and Chinese culture to Japan. ▷ 3.24

PAGAN
BURMESE kingdom which at its height in the 11th to 13th centuries dominated an area roughly equivalent to modern Myanmar. The kingdom is named after Pagan on the middle Irawaddy, its capital from the reign of king Anawrahta (1044–77). The city of Pagan was founded in 849 but its spectacular growth began only after the Burmese adopted Buddhism in 1056. Pagan was sacked by the MONGOLS in 1287 after which the kingdom collapsed and the city was largely abandoned. Of the thousands of Buddhist shrines, stupas and temples built at Pagan, several hundred still survive. ▷ 3.25

PALLAVAS
TAMIL dynasty of east-central India that ruled from the 4th century to the 9th century, when their lands were conquered by the CHOLAS. The dynasty was at its peak under Mahendra-Varman I (r.c.600–30). ▷ 3.19

PANDYAS
TAMIL dynasty of southernmost India whose origins may go back to the 4th century BC but which was at its peak between the 8th and 12th centuries, when its power sometimes extended to Ceylon. The dynasty's capital was at Madurai from the 7th century onwards. The power of the dynasty was broken by Muslim invasions in 1311 but became extinct only in the 16th century. ▷ 3.19

PAPACY
The office of the pope (the bishop of Rome), the leader of the ROMAN CATHOLIC CHURCH. Traditionally founded by St Peter, the first pontiff, the office has been continuous from the 3rd century to the present day. According to Catholic teaching the authority of the papacy was conferred on St Peter by Christ (Matthew 4.18–20) and is inherited by each successive pope. The institution has survived repeated sackings of Rome, the AVIGNON PAPACY, the GREAT SCHISM, heresy and the Protestant Reformation, achieving its greatest influence in the 11th to the 13th centuries, especially under Popes GREGORY VII and INNOCENT III. In 1978 John Paul II became the first non-Italian pope since 1542. ▷ 3.04, 3.05, 3.06, 3.08, 3.09, 3.10, 3.12

THE POPES 600–1492

Gregory I	**590–604**
Sabinian	**604–06**
Boniface III	**607**
Boniface IV	**608–15**
Deusdedit (Adeodatus I)	**615–18**
Boniface V	**619–25**
Honorius I	**625–38**
Severinus	**640**
John IV	**640–42**
Theodore I	**642–49**
Martin I	**649–54**
Eugenius I	**654–57**
Vitalian	**657–72**
Adeodatus II	**672–76**
Donus	**676–78**
Agatho	**678–81**
Leo II	**682–83**
Benedict II	**684–85**
John V	**685–86**
Conon	**686–87**
Sergius I	**687–701**
John VI	**701–05**
John VII	**705–07**
Sisinnius	**708**
Constantine	**708–15**
Gregory II	**715–31**
Gregory III	**731–41**
Zacharias (Zachary)	**741–52**
Stephen	**752**
Stephen II	**752–57**
Paul I	**757–67**
Stephen III	**768–72**
Adrian I	**772–95**
Leo III	**795–816**
Stephen IV	**816–17**
Paschal I	**817–24**
Eugenius II	**824–27**
Valentine	**827**
Gregory IV	**827–44**
Sergius II	**844–47**
Leo IV	**847–55**
Benedict III	**855–58**
Nicholas I	**858–67**
Adrian II	**867–72**
John VIII	**872–82**
Marinus I	**882–84**
Adrian III	**884–85**
Stephen V	**885–91**
Formosus	**891–96**
Boniface VI	**896**
Stephen VI	**896**
Romanus	**897**
Theodore II	**897**
John IX	**898–900**
Benedict IV	**900**
Leo V	**903**
Sergius III	**904–11**
Anastasius III	**911–13**
Lando	**913–14**
John X	**914–28**
Leo VI	**928**
Stephen VII	**929–31**
John XI	**931–35**
Leo VII	**936–39**
Stephen VIII	**939–42**
Marinus II	**942–46**
Agapetus II	**946–55**
John XII	**955–64**
Leo VIII	**963–65**
Benedict V	**964**
John XIII	**965–72**
Benedict VI	**973–74**
Benedict VII	**974–83**
John XIV	**983–84**
John XV	**985–96**
Gregory V	**996–99**
Sylvester II	**999–1003**
John XVII	**1003**
John XVIII	**1004–09**
Sergius IV	**1009–12**
Benedict VIII	**1012–24**
John XIX	**1024–32**
Benedict IX	**1032–44**
Sylvester III	**1045**
Benedict IX	**1045**
Gregory VI	**1045–46**
Clement II	**1046–47**
Benedict IX	**1047–48**
Damasus II	**1048**
Leo IX	**1049–54**
Victor II	**1055–57**
Stephen IX	**1057–58**
Nicholas II	**1059–61**
Alexander II	**1061–73**
Gregory VII	**1073–85**
Victor III	**1086–87**
Urban II	**1088–99**
Paschal II	**1099–1118**
Gelasius II	**1118–19**
Calixtus II (Callistus)	**1119–24**
Honorius II	**1124–30**
Innocent II	**1130–43**
Celestine II	**1143–44**
Lucius II	**1144–45**
Eugenius III	**1145–53**
Anastasius IV	**1153–54**
Adrian IV	**1154–59**
Alexander III	**1159–81**
Lucius III	**1181–85**
Urban III	**1185–87**
Gregory VIII	**1187**
Clement III	**1187–91**
Celestine III	**1191–98**
Innocent III	**1198–1216**
Honorius III	**1216–27**
Gregory IX	**1227–41**
Celestine IV	**1241**
Innocent IV	**1243–54**
Alexander IV	**1254–61**
Urban IV	**1261–64**
Clement IV	**1265–68**
Gregory X	**1271–76**
Innocent V	**1276**
Adrian V	**1276**
John XXI	**1276–77**
Nicholas III	**1277–80**
Martin IV	**1281–85**
Honorius IV	**1285–87**
Nicholas IV	**1288–92**
Celestine V	**1294**
Boniface VIII	**1294–1303**
Benedict XI	**1303–04**
Clement V (at Avignon from 1309)	**1305–14**
John XXII (at Avignon)	**1316–34**
Benedict XII (at Avignon)	**1334–42**
Clement VI (at Avignon)	**1342–52**
Innocent VI (at Avignon)	**1352–62**
Urban V (at Avignon)	**1362–70**
Gregory XI (at Avignon, then Rome from 1377)	**1370–78**
Urban VI	**1378–89**
Boniface IX	**1389–1404**
Innocent VII	**1404–06**
Gregory XII	**1406–15**
Martin V	**1417–31**
Eugenius IV	**1431–47**
Nicholas V	**1447–55**
Calixtus III (Callistus)	**1455–58**
Pius II	**1458–64**
Paul II	**1464–71**
Sixtus IV	**1471–84**
Innocent VIII	**1484–92**

Papal States
Territory of central Italy under the temporal control of the PAPACY from 768 to 1870, when the states merged with the newly formed Italian state. ▷ 3.03, 3.04. 3.08, 3.10, 3.11 3.12

Parhae
Kingdom of northern Korea and Manchuria. It developed in about 694 as a successor state to KOGURYO after its destruction by SILLA and the TANG in 668. Parhae was a centralized state on Chinese lines. The kingdom was destroyed in 926 by the KHITANS. ▷ 3.24

Paris, Treaty of
Treaty concluded in May 1259 between ENGLAND and FRANCE by which England relinquished all claims to NORMANDY, ANJOU, Touraine, Maine and Poitou, thereby formally ending the ANGEVIN empire. In partial reciprocation, the English king was acknowledged as duke of AQUITAINE, held as a French fief.

Parliament
The legislative assembly of ENGLAND comprising the House of Lords and the House of Commons. It arose from the 1230s, called by the king to settle issues of particular importance. It soon covered taxation, a measure that required consent and hence representation. In 1265 SIMON DE MONTFORT included commoners for the first time. Regular parliamentary sessions were not held until after the Glorious Revolution (1688); the Lords dominated Parliament until the Reform Acts of the 19th century.

Parsees
Followers of the prophet Zoroaster who fled Persia to escape Muslim persecution in the 8th century and settled in Gujarat, India. A further wave of emigration followed in the 10th century. The Parsees retained their ethnic, religious and cultural individuality in India but lost contact with remaining Zoroastrians in Persia. ▷ 3.05

Pasai
See SAMUDRA

Patrimony of St Peter
Territory of central Italy originally granted to the PAPACY by CHARLEMAGNE and developing into the PAPAL STATES. ▷ 3.06, 3.07

Peasants' Revolt
Peasant and artisan uprising of 1381 in ENGLAND. Led by Wat Tyler, it demanded the repeal of the Statute of Labourers (a wage restriction policy introduced in the wake of the BLACK DEATH) and the abolition of SERFDOM and the poll tax. King RICHARD II quelled this most serious of revolts and executed its leaders. ▷ 3.10

Pegu
See MONS

Pepin II of Herstal
MAYOR OF THE PALACE and effective ruler of the MEROVINGIAN kingdom of the Franks between 679 and 714. Pepin is regarded as the founder of the CAROLINGIAN DYNASTY. ▷ 3.06

Pepin III
First CAROLINGIAN king of the Franks (r.751–68). He succeeded his father CHARLES MARTEL as MAYOR OF THE PALACE. Pepin allied with the PAPACY against the LOMBARDS in Italy in 751. In return Pope Zacharias authorized him to depose the last MEROVINGIAN king and become king of the Franks himself. ▷ 3.06

Philip II Augustus
King of FRANCE (r.1180–1223). During his reign the CAPETIAN DYNASTY and the French

kingdom were both secured. He consolidated and expanded the royal domain and was joint leader of the Third CRUSADE (1190–91) with RICHARD I. In 1204 he conquered most of the ANGEVIN possessions in France, increasing French territory fourfold. His crushing victory over the emperor Otto IV at BOUVINES (1214) confirmed his gains and simultaneously removed the imperial threat to his crown. He supported the ALBIGENSIAN CRUSADE which brought Languedoc under French control by 1229. He added important financial and legal innovations to his great achievements. ▷ 3.08

PHILIP THE BOLD
Duke of BURGUNDY (r.1363–1404). Philip was granted the duchy by his father, John II of FRANCE in 1363. He inherited FLANDERS and FRANCHE-COMTÉ by marriage in 1384. He ruled as regent in France during the bouts of madness of his nephew, Charles VI, giving rise to the Burgundian–ARMAGNAC conflict with his brother and court rival, Duke Louis of ORLÉANS. He was a heroic leader, and his government is regarded as one of the best in medieval Europe. ▷ 3.10, 3.12

PHILIP THE GOOD
Duke of BURGUNDY (r.1419–67). He became duke on the assassination of his father, JOHN THE FEARLESS by the future Charles VII of FRANCE. In his quest for vengeance, Philip allied with ENGLAND (1420). His reconciliation with France in 1435 was a decisive blow to English ambitions. Inheritance more than doubled his dominions, leaving his realm the most prosperous in Europe, reflected by its magnificent RENAISSANCE court at BRUGES boasting Jan van Eyck as its official artist. ▷ 3.12

PLAGUE
See BLACK DEATH, BUBONIC PLAGUE

PLANTAGENET DYNASTY
Royal dynastic family of ENGLAND founded by HENRY II in 1154, lasting until RICHARD III's death in 1485, with a dynastic split between the cadet houses of Lancaster and York occuring after RICHARD II's deposition in 1399. The first three kings of the dynasty are also known as the ANGEVIN DYNASTY. ▷ 3.08, 3.10, 3.12

PLISKA
The fortified palace and capital city of the BULGAR KHANS, flourishing in the late 8th century. Pliska was destroyed by the BYZANTINE emperor Nikephoros Phokas in 811. ▷ 3.15

POITIERS, BATTLE OF (732)
Battle fought in 732 in central FRANCE in which CHARLES MARTEL, palace mayor of the Franks, repulsed an ARAB move north from Spain, checking their European ambitions north of the Pyrenees. ▷ 3.06

POITIERS, BATTLE OF (1356)
Battle of the HUNDRED YEARS WAR fought on 19 September 1356 in central FRANCE, won by Edward the Black Prince for the English. The capture of the French king, John II, enabled the English to negotiate a huge ransom payment and favorable terms in the TREATY OF BRÉTIGNY. ▷ 3.10

POLAND-LITHUANIA
State formed in 1386 when the Polish crown fell to Duke Wladyslaw II of LITHUANIA, founder of the Jagiellon dynasty (1386–1572). Victory over the TEUTONIC KNIGHTS at TANNENBERG enabled CASIMIR IV to make it the largest state in Europe, recovering Prussia from the knights by the Treaty of Thorn (1466). Lithuania was formally united to Poland in 1569 by the Union of Lublin. ▷ 3.12

POLO, MARCO
(c.1254–1324) Venetian merchant and traveler whose account of his travels in China was the most important influence on European perceptions of the Far East until the 19th century. Marco's father and uncle had visited China as merchants (1260–69). When they began a return journey in 1271 Marco, then aged 17, accompanied them. Crossing central Asia, the Polos arrived at SHANGDU, KHUBILAI KHAN's summer capital, in 1275. Marco entered the khan's service and spent 17 years traveling in China before returning to VENICE in 1295 by way of southeast Asia. Marco dictated the account of his travels to the writer Rustichello while imprisoned by the Genoese. ▷ 3.23

POLONNARUVA
Ancient city in eastern Ceylon, founded in the 4th century. Polonnaruva was occupied by the CHOLAS in the 11th century but in the 12th century it became the capital of a powerful Buddhist kingdom. From its peak under Parakramabahu I (r.1153–86) and Nissanka Malli (r.1187–96) the kingdom declined rapidly because of attacks from southern India. Extensive ruins, including palaces, temples and colossal images of the Buddha survive. ▷ 3.19

POPE
See PAPACY

PORTUGAL
Iberian country, originally a county of CASTILE. It won its independence between 1128 and 1143. In 1147 the Second CRUSADE won Lisbon from the Muslims and it became Portugal's capital; by the mid-13th century Portugal had established its present boundaries. Beginning in the 15th century maritime expansion led to the creation of a far-flung colonial empire in Africa, Asia and Brazil. Portuguese power never fully recovered from a period of union with Spain (1580–1640). In 1974 Portugal embraced democracy after 50 years of dictatorship. ▷ 3.08, 3.09, 3.10, 3.11, 3.12

PURE LAND BUDDHISM
One of the most popular forms of Mahayana Buddhism in East Asia, the Pure Land school promises its followers rebirth in the Western Paradise, free of pain and want until they are ready for full Enlightenment. Although it originated in northern India, Pure Land achieved its greatest influence in China, where it was introduced in the 4th century, and Japan, where it was introduced in the 12th century and known as Amida. ▷ 3.05

PUTÚN MAYA
Also known as the Itzá Maya, the Putún homeland was on the Bay of Campeche in Mexico. Prominent as merchants in the early Post Classic period (900–1200), the Putún dominated trade routes along the Caribbean coast of Mesoamerica. In about 850 they founded CHICHÉN ITZÁ which became the dominant Mayan city of the Yucatán. ▷ 3.27

QADISIYA, BATTLE OF
Decisive ARAB victory on the banks of the river Euphrates over Sasanian Persia in 637: it opened the way for the Arab conquest and ISLAMIZATION of Persia. ▷ 3.13

QARAKHANID TURKS
A dynasty ruling in central Asia between the 10th and 13th centuries. Though rivals to the SAMANIDS, they never formed a unitary state but remained a loose tribal grouping, and in the mid-11th century split into two khanates. Overshadowed by the mid-12th century, the dynasty collapsed in 1210. ▷ 3.14, 3.16

QARMATIANS
Ismaili followers of Hamdan Qarmat, a 9th-century Muslim apocalyptic revolutionary who attracted support in Iraq, Bahrayn, north Africa and Khorasan for his vision of the coming of the Mahdi, who would ensure social justice. The Qarmatians provoked hostility with their violent methods. ▷ 3.14

PLANTAGENET KINGS OF ENGLAND 1154–1485

1154–89	Henry II	1327–77	Edward III	1470–1	Henry VI
1189–99	Richard I	1377–99	Richard II	1471–83	Edward IV
1199–1216	John	1399–1413	Henry IV	1483	Edward V
1216–72	Henry III	1413–22	Henry V	1483–85	Richard III
1272–1307	Edward I	1422–61	Henry VI		
1307–27	Edward II	1461–70	Edward IV		

Quraysh
Bedouin tribe of Arabia that had settled and become dominant in Mecca by the late 6th century. The tribe opposed the revalation of Muhammad, which threatened its leadership. The early caliphs were of the Quraysh, but succession disputes within the tribe had by 680 split the unity of Islam. ▷ 3.13

Qutb-ud-Din
A Turkish slave-general who, beginning in 1192, conquered northern India in the service of Muhammad of Ghur. On Muhammad of Ghur's death (1206), Qutb-ud-Din established an independent sultanate at Delhi under the Slave dynasty. At his death in 1210 Muslim control of northern India was still far from secure and his son-in-law and successor Iltutmish faced serious Hindu revolts. ▷ 3.19

Ragusa
Croatian seaport (present-day Dubrovnik) founded in the 7th century. Ragusa was a medieval cultural center and trading rival to Venice. It was an independent republic until Napoleon's conquest in 1808. ▷ 3.10, 3.12

Rajputs
People of northern India who between the 8th and 16th centuries established several dynasties, the most important of which was the Gurjara-Pratihara. The origins of the Rajputs lie in an assimilation which took place between the indigenous peoples of northwest India and the White Huns (or Ephthalites) who invaded in the 6th century. The Rajputs are divided into a number of clans. Four of these, the Pratiharas, Chauhans, Solankis (or Chaulukyas) and Parmaras, claim descent from the sacrificial fire pit of Ajmar while the others belong to Solar and Lunar races. About 12 million Rajputs live in India today. ▷ 3.19

Rashtrakuta dynasty
Hindu dynasty of the central Indian Deccan founded in 756 by Dantidurga after his overthrow of the Chalukya dynasty. Dantidurga established his capital at Malkhed. At their peak under Indra III (r.915–27) and Krishna III (939–65) the Rashtrakutas dominated an area extending from Kanauj on the Ganges to the Tamil plains of the far south. Most of this territory was only loosely held and the empire collapsed in 973. ▷ 3.19

Ravenna, exarchate of
Province of the Byzantine empire in northeast Italy centered on Ravenna. It was ruled by a governor called the exarch. Established in 553, it was conquered by the Lombards in 752. In 756 the Franks drove the Lombards out and Charlemagne formally granted the exarchate to the papacy as part of the Patrimony of St Peter. ▷ 3.06, 3.15

Reconquista
The Spanish Christian reconquest of the Iberian peninsula from Muslim control, traditionally regarded as beginning in 718 with the victory at Covadonga in Asturias. Political divisions among the Christians prevented its completion until 1492, when unification of Castile and Aragon facilitated the expulsion of the Muslims from Granada. The Reconquista earned the status of a Crusade. ▷ 3.06, 3.07, 3.08, 3.09, 3.10, 3.11, 3.12

Renaissance
Cultural rebirth of Europe between about 1350 and about 1550. It originated in northern Italian city-states such as Florence, spreading across Europe to other centers (for example, to Bruges). The Renaissance revived the learning of ancient Greece and Rome and the spirit of universal inquiry and experimentation in all art forms, stressing individualism and scientific observation of the natural environment. Many of the great names in culture and learning spring from this period: Masaccio, Raphael, da Vinci and Michaelangelo in art; Petrarch and Boccaccio in literature; Donatello in sculpture; Erasmus and Machiavelli in thought and politics. ▷ 3.12

Richard I (the Lionheart)
Angevin king of England (r.1189–99). He was an oustanding military commander who spent most of his life at war. With Philip II of France he co-led the Third Crusade with appreciable success: he conquered Cyprus, marched to within sight of Jerusalem and secured the existence of the Crusader States. Shipwrecked on his return and imprisoned by the Duke of Austria and Emperor Henry VI, he was heavily ransomed. On his return, he regained the lands lost to Philip II in his absence, but died from a crossbow wound received at a siege. Frequently criticized for spending less than six months in England and instead fighting abroad, Richard, in doing so, gained prestige and security for his kingdom. ▷ 3.08, 3.12

Richard II
Plantagenet king of England (r.1377–99). He began his reign with promise, quelling the Peasants' Revolt. However, he grew arbitrary and ruthless in his exercise of power, clashing with Parliament and the lords appellant and exiling his cousin Henry Bolingbroke (the future Henry IV). Bolingbroke invaded England and deposed, imprisoned and murdered Richard. ▷ 3.10

Richard III
Last Plantagenet king of England (r.1483–85). Protector to his young nephew Edward V, Richard usurped the throne and governed well. However, he was dogged by persistent rumors, almost certainly true, that he had murdered Edward and his younger brother (the Princes in the Tower). Abandoned by many of his supporters, Richard died at the Battle of Bosworth Field fighting Henry Tudor who, as Henry VII, founded the Tudor dynasty. ▷ 3.12

Roman Catholic church
Christian church based in Rome under the leadership of the papacy, traditionally founded by St Peter in the 1st century AD. The early church survived Roman persecution to become the official religion of western and central Europe by the end of the Middle Ages. Its organizational structure, based on that of the Roman empire, and its monastic learning carried the church through the barbarian invasions and made it an important agent of cultural continuity between the ancient and medieval worlds. As the main repository of literacy and learning, the church was heavily involved in politics and governmental administration during the Middle Ages. Although Rome claimed universal authority over all Christians, its claims were never accepted by the eastern Orthodox church. In the west Rome successfully contained challenges to its spiritual authority until, in the 16th century, the Reformation saw the rise of a rival Protestant church. Thereafter Portuguese, Spanish and French colonialism spread Catholicism around the world, helping to guarantee its continuing position as the largest Christian church. ▷ 3.09

Rum, sultanate of
The Seljuk state established in Anatolia in the 11th century and lasting until the Ottoman advance of the 14th century. Its capital was at Iconium. "Rum", denoting Anatolia, derives from the Arabic word for the Byzantine empire (in turn from the Greek *Rhomaioi*). ▷ 3.16, 3.17

runic script
The system of writing developed in pre-Christian Scandinavia, surviving largely on monumental inscriptions such as tombs or to record ownership of objects. An example is the inscription made in 965 on the Jellynge Stone of Harald Bluetooth. The figures were designed for incision or carving and are thus typically angular. Runes are also associated with pagan cultic practices.

Rus
Name originally applied to Scandinavian settlers in the northwest of Russia who in about 860 took control of Novgorod under the leadership of Ryurik and later founded a powerful state based on Kiev. These Scandinavian Rus were quickly assimilated into the subject Slavic population which also became known as Rus or Russians. In 987 the Rus converted to Orthodox Christianity as a result of a political alliance with Byzantium. ▷ 3.02, 3.07, 3.08, 3.15

Russian Orthodox church
Russian church established after the conversion of the Rus by Greek Orthodox missionaries in 987. Although the Russian church was effectively independent from its parent, it was in theory subordinate to the Greek Orthodox Patriarchate in Constantinople. ▷ 3.09

Ryurik
A possibly legendary Viking who ruled Novgorod from about 862 to about 879. He gave his name to the Ryurik dynasty, founded by his successor Oleg (r.c.879–913), which ruled Novgorod and Kiev from about 879 to 1271. ▷ 3.02

Saffarid dynasty
Persian dynasty ruling from Seistan, on the frontier of Iran and Afghanistan (861–1003). The name, meaning coppersmith, derives from the founder's profession. By the 890s the Saffarids had expanded to India in the east and threatened Baghdad in the west, but the defeat of 'Amr in 900 and the rise of the Ghaznavids in the 10th century ended their influence. ▷ 3.14

Saladin
Sultan of Egypt (r.1174–93). A Kurd by descent, in 1169 Saladin was appointed vizier of Egypt by Nur al-Din. In 1171 he deposed the Fatimid caliph, a Shiite, and restored Sunni orthodoxy. On the death of Nur al-Din in 1174 he seized Syria. In 1187 he conquered the kingdom of Jerusalem, but in 1191–92 he was pushed back from the Palestinian coast by Richard I. His Ayyubid dynasty remained in power in Syria and Egypt until the mid-13th century when it was overthrown by the Mamlukes. ▷ 3.03, 3.08, 3.16, 3.17

Samanid dynasty
Persian dynasty ruling Transoxiana and Khorasan (819–1005). Victory over the Saffarids in 900 and the reign of Nasr (914–43) marked the apogee of their power, reflected in the sophisticated court at Bokhara. The Kharakhanid invasions of the later 10th century put an end to the dynasty. ▷ 3.14

Samarkand
An ancient city of Transoxiana, which owed its eminence to being located at the intersection of trade routes from China and India to the west. A cosmopolitan population included Jews and Nestorian Christians. At its peak under the Samanids in the 10th century, Samarkand was destroyed by the Mongols in 1220, but after 1367 regained its former influence under Timur the Lame. ▷ 3.01, 3.04, 3.22, 3.23

Samarra
A city on the Tigris about 160 kilometers (100 miles) north of Baghdad. Between 836 and 892 it was the Abbasid capital, but suffered depopulation after the caliphate moved to the new foundation of Baghdad. ▷ 3.14

Samudra
City in northern Sumatra, also known as Pasai. With nearby Perlak, it was the earliest Muslim state in Indonesia. The earliest evidence of major Islamic influence is a set of royal inscriptions in Arabic from 1295. The city was easily accessible to merchant shipping from the Indian Ocean and had a hinterland rich in gold and spices. In the 15th century it was gradually overshadowed by Malacca. ▷ 3.25

Samurai
Member of the warrior class that dominated Japan in the period of the shogunates (1185–1868). The samurai developed an austere culture in contrast to the refinement of the imperial court in the Heian period (794–1185). By the 16th century the samurai code of behavior had become formalized as *bushido*, which held stoicism, bravery, honor and loyalty above life and made ritual suicide the respectable response to defeat or dishonor. The samurai lost their privileged status when feudalism was abolished in 1871. ▷ 3.24

Santiago de Compostela
Shrine in northwestern Spain. Bones discovered in Santiago in 812 were believed to be those of St James the Apostle, making it the third holiest pilgrimage center in Christendom, after only Jerusalem and (in Europe) Rome. ▷ 3.05, 3.09

Saxon dynasty
Saxon line of German kings founded by Henry the Fowler in 919 and lasting until Henry II in 1024. After 962 they also held the title Holy Roman emperor. ▷ 3.07

Saxons
Natives of northern Germany who remained pagan until conversion to Christianity was forced on them after defeat by Charlemagne in protracted campaigning from 772 to 797. The duchy of Saxony was one of the constituent territories of the kingdom of Germany from the 10th century, providing the Saxon dynasty that ruled from 919 to 1024. Saxons migrated in large numbers to Britain in the 5th century. ▷ 3.06

Saylac
Also called Zeila, a port in the far north of Somalia. It was an important Arab trading settlement from the 9th century to the 19th century, exporting ivory, slaves and other products of the Ethiopian interior. Saylac declined after the building of the Djibouti–Addis Ababa railway at the beginning of the 20th century. ▷ 3.18

Sayyid dynasty
Ruling dynasty of the Delhi sultanate from 1414 to 1451. The dynasty saw the sultanate reduced to little more than its capital. ▷ 3.19

Scotland, kingdom of
Kingdom formed when Kenneth I (r.842–58) united the Scots (originally from Ireland) and Picts under his rule. It was nominally subject to England in the 12th and 13th centuries, but Edward I's attempts to incorporate Scotland more fully into his kingdom caused a rebellion. Scottish independence was won at the Battle of Bannockburn (1314) and confirmed by the Treaty of Edinburgh (1328).The country achieved its modern borders in the 15th century. In 1603 King James VI of Scotland became James I of England; in 1707 the two countries joined by the Act of Union to form Great Britain. ▷ 3.08, 3.09, 3.10, 3.11, 3.12

Seljuk Turks
A branch of the Ghuzz Turks who between 1028 and 1038 swept into Persia, defeating the ruling Ghaznavids and establishing control over Qarakhanid lands to the east and over Iraq, Syria and Anatolia to the west. Seljuk power in Transoxiana ended in 1141, but continued in Syria and Anatolia until the mid-13th century. ▷ 3.08, 3.03, 3.14, 3.15, 3.16, 3.17, 3.22

Serf
In medieval Europe an unfree tenant farmer, legally tied to the land of his lord's estate. His status was inherited by his children. Certain rights elevated serfs above slaves: they had rights of inheritance and could not be bought and sold separately from the land they worked on. ▷ 3.10, 3.11

Shan
A Thai people who live mainly in eastern and northern Myanmar. Between the 14th and 16th centuries about 30 small Shan states developed, which later paid tribute to the Burmese kings of the Toungou dynasty. Several Shan separatist groups are currently engaged in warfare against the government of Myanmar. ▷ 3.25

Shangdu
The summer capital of the Mongol rulers of China, founded by Khubilai Khan in 1260. The city was made famous as Xanadu in the poem by Samuel Taylor Coleridge. ▷ 3.23

Shiite Muslims
The party of religious and political opposition to the Umayyad dynasty, originating as the followers of Ali and his son Husain in the 7th century. The Shiites awaited the coming of a just imam to exercise leadership over all Muslims. Historically the Shiites, a minority within Islam, have been opposed and sometimes persecuted by the majority Sunni. Shiites have their own distinct schools of Koranic and legal interpretation. ▷ 3.05, 3.13, 3.14, 3.16

Shintoism
Indigenous polytheistic religion of Japan, based on ancestor worship and on reverence of the spirits (*kami*) of nature and of places. Shinto can be traced back to the 6th century but is probably much older. The emperor was accorded a divinity based on descent from the goddess Amaterasu. Shinto acquired many

Buddhist and Confucian traits. As a state religion it was proscribed in 1945, when the emperor Hirohito renounced his divinity, but it remains a powerful influence.

Shoa
Muslim state of northeast Ethiopia and Djibouti, founded sometime before the 12th century by the Muksumite family of Mecca. Internal disputes caused the state's collapse at the end of the 13th century. ▷ 3.03

Sicán state
State of the arid Lambayeque valley of north coastal Peru, founded in about 900 by Naymlap, a semi-legendary but almost certainly real figure. Vast irrigation systems supported intensive agriculture, allowing the Lambayeque valley to become the most densely populated region of the Andes under the Naymlap dynasty. Following a period of disastrous flooding and famine, the Sicán state was conquered by the Chimú empire in 1370. ▷ 3.28

Sicily, Norman kingdom of
Kingdom comprising southern Italy and the Mediterranean island of Sicily (the "kingdom of the Two Sicilies"), created by the Normans following their conquest of Byzantine Italy (1042–71) and Arab Sicily (1072). In 1130 Roger II, an enlightened ruler who cultivated a sophisticated court and government that adopted Arab bureaucracy and learning, was recognized as its first king. In 1194 the kingdom passed to imperial Hohenstaufen control by marriage. ▷ 3.15, 3.16, 3.17

Sikander Lodi
The second and most successful ruler of the Lodi dynasty of the Delhi sultanate (r.1489–1517). Sikander rebuilt the power of the sultanate, making it once again the dominant power of northern India. ▷ 3.19

Sikhism
A monotheistic Indian religion combining Hindu with limited Muslim influences, founded by Guru Nanak (1469–1539). Sikhism teaches the unity of God, the brotherhood of man, rejection of caste and the futility of idol worship. The holiest site for Sikhs is the Golden Temple of Amritsar founded by the 4th guru Ram Das (guru from 1574 to 1581). Sikhism drew most of its converts from Hinduism. Sikh men vow not to cut their hair and are readily identified by their turbans. About 14 million Sikhs live in India today, mostly in the Punjab, with smaller communities overseas.

Silla
The most successful of the Three Kingdoms of early Korea. Silla developed in about 57 BC in the southeast of the Korean peninsula. In 660–68 Silla allied with the Chinese Tang dynasty against its neighbors Paekche and Koguryo. Silla gained nothing from the alliance, and when it was treated as a tributary state it rapidly drove the Chinese out of the Korean peninsula. Despite this Silla's administration and education systems were modeled on those of the Tang and were adopted by all subsequent Korean dynasties. In 780 a long conflict between the monarchy and aristocracy broke out and by 900 the kingdom had broken up. ▷ 3.24

Singhasari empire
Empire of the Javanese Singhasari dynasty (c.1225–92). The empire brought about the final collapse of the declining Sumatran Srivijaya empire in 1280 and briefly dominated much of Indonesia. The dynasty was overthrown following a Mongol attack on Java in 1292 and its empire dissolved. ▷ 3.25

Sinhalese
The majority ethnic group of modern Sri Lanka (Ceylon). Their ancestors are believed to have originated in northern India and to have migrated to Ceylon in about 500 BC, overwhelming the aboriginal Veddas. The Sinhalese speak an Indo-European language and are mainly Buddhists.

Solomonid dynasty
Christian ruling dynasty of Ethiopia (1270–1777, 1868–1975). The dynasty claimed descent from Menelik I, the supposed son of King Solomon and the queen of Sheba. However, the first historical ruler of the dynasty was Yekuno Amlak (r.1270–85). During the 14th century the Solomonids won control of most of the Ethiopian highlands but from the 15th century onwards they were on the defensive against attacks by Muslims. The emperors of modern Ethiopia also claimed descent from the Solomonids. ▷ 3.18

Song dynasty
Chinese imperial dynasty (960–1279) founded by Song Taizu (r.960–76) who, with his brother Song Taizong (r.976–97), reunified China at the end of the Five Dynasties and Ten Kingdoms period (907–60). The Song dynasty is divided into two periods: Northern Song (960–1127), when the capital was at Kaifeng, and Southern Song (1127–79), when the Jin conquest of northern China had forced the dynasty to move to Hangzhou. In 1234 the Song empire was attacked by the Mongols, who took Hangzhou in 1276. The last Song emperor died in battle against the Mongols at Yaishan in 1279. ▷ 3.21

Soninke
A mainly Muslim Mande-speaking farming people of Senegal and neighboring countries of west Africa. They were the founders of the kingdom of Ghana, the first historically attested state of west Africa. ▷ 3.18

Spanish Inquisition
Inquisition established in Spain in 1478 by Ferdinand of Aragon and Isabella of Castile against a background of popular anti-Semitic and anti-Muslim feeling. Its original aim was to restore lapsed *conversos*, Jews and Muslims who had been baptized Christians, but it was also largely responsible for the expulsion of Jews from Spain in 1492. ▷ 3.12

Srivijaya empire
An early Indonesian state of the 7th to 13th centuries. Srivijaya was probably located at modern Palembang in southern Sumatra. At its peak in the 9th and 10th centuries, it controlled the Strait of Malacca and the maritime trade route between China and India, which passed through it. Srivijaya was sacked by the Cholas of southern India in 1025, went into decline and lost control of the strait to nearby Malayu. Srivijaya was conquered by the Javanese Singhasari empire in 1280. ▷ 3.25

Sron-btsan-sgampo
The first Buddhist king of Tibet (r.605–49), responsible for the emergence of Tibet as a centralized state. He introduced writing based on Indian scripts and expanded his control over the Tibetan plateau and Nepal. His attacks on the Chinese Tang empire forced the emperor Taizong to give him a princess in marriage to buy peace. ▷ 3.20

Strathclyde
Welsh kingdom centered on the river Clyde, with its capital at Dumbarton. It was absorbed by Scotland in about 1020. ▷ 3.06, 3.07

Sufism
Ascetic movement within Islam, so called because of the coarse wool *suf* worn by adherents. Islam encouraged solitary contemplation as a means of achieving closeness to God. The movement reached its peak in the late 10th century. ▷ 3.05, 3.19

Sui Wendi
See Wen

Sukhothai
The capital of an early Thai kingdom in the mid-13th century, now a ruined city in northern Thailand. Under Ramkhamhaeng (r.c.1279–98), Sukhothai won control of much of modern Thailand and Laos. Sukhothai began to decline after a rival Thai dynasty established itself at Ayutthaya in 1351. In 1438 it was conquered by Ayutthaya and was abandoned in about 1500. ▷ 3.25

Sunni Ali
King of Songhai (r.1464–92). He created an empire based on Timbuktu, which he conquered in 1468. Sunni's brutality toward Timbuktu's scholars gave rise to the tradition that he was an unbeliever. ▷ 3.18

Sunni Muslims
Those Muslims who accepted the succession to the caliphate of Muawiya and the Umayyad

family against the claims of ALI and his secessionist followers in the later 7th century. The political split widened into one of theology and legal practice. Sunna referred to the practices of the Prophet that became, along with the Hadith, the cornerstone of the ISLAMIC legal tradition. The term as applied to the majority of Muslims, in contrast to the SHIITES, has the connotation of following orthodoxy as opposed to a deviant tradition. ▷ 3.05, 3.13, 3.14, 3.16

SURYAVARMAN II
King of the KHMER EMPIRE (r.1113–50). He was responsible for the building of the magnificent temple of ANGKOR Thom. From 1126 to 1134 he campaigned against DAI VIET and from 1145 to 1150 fought to annexe CHAMPA. His campaigns brought no lasting territorial gains and they left his realm exhausted and impoverished. ▷ 3.25

SUTRI, SYNOD OF
The church council convened by Emperor HENRY III in December 1046 for the purpose of reforming the PAPACY. Pope Benedict IX, who had already been persuaded to abdicate, was deposed along with his godfather and successor, Gregory VI, as well as Silvester III, the candidate of a rival family. ▷ 3.09

SVEIN FORKBEARD
King of Denmark (r.987–1014). Svein began to raid ENGLAND from 994 and by 1013 he had conquered the country and forced Aethelred II to flee. Svein himself died in 1014 before he could be crowned king. He was succeeded in England by his son CNUT and in Denmark by his son Harald II (1014–18). ▷ 3.07

SWABIA
From the 10th century a duchy in southern Germany which held a strategically important position between the Danube and the Rhine. It was ruled by the HOHENSTAUFENS from about 1077 to 1268 when the duchy ceased. ▷ 3.07–08

TAIRA CLAN
Japanese SAMURAI clan, also known as the Heike. The origins of the Taira family have been traced to the 9th century. Between 1156 and 1180 the Taira dominated the imperial court but were overthrown by the MINAMOTO in the GEMPEI WAR (1180–85). Their final defeat at the sea Battle of Dannoura in 1185 is the subject of the *Tale of Heike*, one of the most important literary works of medieval Japan. ▷ 3.24

TAIZONG
The second emperor of the TANG DYNASTY of China (r.626–49). He came to power after forcing his father LI YUAN (r.618–26) to abdicate. He was a ruler of exceptional ability who extensively restructured the central and local goverment of China and reformed the judiciary. Land was redistributed to the peasantry and their taxes were reduced, so promoting a rapid increase in agricultural production and general economic prosperity. Export of silks and ceramics was encouraged. Between 628 and 647 the vast Tarim basin in central Asia was conquered and the first diplomatic relations with TIBET were established. ▷ 3.20

TAIZU, SONG
First emperor of the Chinese SONG DYNASTY, Song Taizu (r.960–76) was a general under the Later Zhou dynasty of Kaifeng during the period of disunity known as FIVE DYNASTIES AND FIVE KINGDOMS. In 960 he overthrew the Zhou in a military coup and began a series of campaigns to reunify China, a task which was completed by his brother and successor Song Taizong (r.976–97). Taizu was a most able ruler and statesman who rebuilt the civil government of China and ruled humanely according Confucian ethics. ▷ 3.21

TALAS RIVER, BATTLE OF
ARAB victory in 751, near present-day Aulie-Ata, which ended Chinese domination over central Asia. Henceforth, central Asia was to become part of the ISLAMIC rather than the Chinese world. The loss of central Asia at one stroke hastened the collapse of the TANG dynasty. ▷ 3.01, 3.14, 3.20

TAMILS
A Dravidian-speaking Hindu people of southern India. The Tamils, many of whom migrated to Ceylon between 300 BC and AD 1200, form the majority population (54 million) in Tamil Nadu state in India and about 12 percent (3 million) of the population of modern Sri Lanka. Historically important Tamil states include the medieval kingdoms of Jaffna, the PANDYAS, PALLAVAS and CHOLAS. ▷ 3.19

TANG DYNASTY
One of the most successful imperial dynasties of China (618–907), founded by LI YUAN who overthrew the Sui dynasty and ruled under the name Gaozu (r.618–26). Li Yuan was deposed by his son Taozong (r.626–49), an exceptional ruler who built a strong central government, introduced land and tax reforms and conquered the Tarim basin in central Asia. Further conquests were made in central Asia and Korea under Gaozong (r.649–83) but these overextended the empire and were lost before the end of his reign. The central Asian provinces were completely lost in the 8th century after defeats by the ARABS and TIBETANS. The authority of the Tang was also undermined by the rebellion of AN LUSHAN (755–63). In the 9th century, peasant rebellions became common and power was seized by semi-independent regional warlords. The dynasty finally collapsed in 907 and China fragmented, beginning a period of disunity known as the FIVE DYNASTIES AND TEN KINGDOMS. ▷ 3.20

TANNENBERG, BATTLE OF
Battle fought in northern Poland (15 July 1410), in which POLAND-LITHUANIA won a great victory over the TEUTONIC KNIGHTS. It precipitated the decline of the knights and their withdrawal from Poland. ▷ 3.12

TARASCANS
See MICHOACAN

TARTARS
See TATARS

TATARS
A nomadic Turkic people of north-central Asia. Conquered by CHINGIS KHAN in the early 13th century, they became assimilated to the MONGOLS. After this the Mongols were frequently known as Tatars (or Tartars). ▷ 3.02, 3.04, 3.12, 3.22, 3.23

TEMUJIN
See CHINGIS KHAN

TEN KINGDOMS
See FIVE DYNASTIES AND TEN KINGDOMS

TENOCHTITLÁN
Capital city of the AZTEC empire, now buried under Mexico City. Tenochtitlán was founded in 1325 on two islands in Lake Texcoco. The city grew rapidly and by 1519, when the CONQUISTADOR Hernán Cortés arrived, the population was about 400,000. Tenochtitlán was connected to the mainland by causeways and supplied with food grown on *chinampas* (floating gardens) on the surrounding lake. At the city's heart was the royal palace and the Great Temple complex, the scene of regular human sacrifices. ▷ 3.27

TEUTONIC KNIGHTS
A German CRUSADING order founded in 1190 during the Third Crusade. In the 13th and 14th centuries they crusaded against pagans, winning extensive territories in LITHUANIA and the Baltic region. The order never recovered from its defeat at TANNENBERG in Poland in 1410. It was secularized in the 16th century. ▷ 3.03, 3.04, 3.08, 3.10, 3.11, 3.12, 3.17, 3.23

THESSALONICA, KINGDOM OF
Frankish state established in Greece as a result of the Fourth CRUSADE. The kingdom, which included Thrace and western Greece as far as the Attic peninsula, lasted only until 1224, when it was conquered by the DESPOTATE OF EPIRUS, one of the successor states to the BYZANTINE EMPIRE. ▷ 3.15

THREE KINGDOMS
The three earliest kingdoms of Korea, from the 1st century BC to the 9th century AD: SILLA, PAEKCHE and KOGURYO. ▷ 3.24

THULE INUIT
Inuit (Eskimo) who originated on St Lawrence and other islands in the Bering Strait before

800 and began to expand along the Arctic coasts of Alaska and Canada in about 1000, displacing or assimilating the earlier DORSET INUIT. By the 13th century they had reached GREENLAND, where they made contact with Norse settlers, with whom they traded and fought. The Thule specialized in hunting marine mammals, including seals and whales, and developed a sophisticated technology which enabled them to flourish in the high Arctic until modern times. ▷ 3.26

TIBET

Himalayan region whose recorded history begins in the 6th century AD. A unified kingdom emerged under SRON-BTSAN-SGAMPO (r.605–49). Buddhism, introduced from India, was the dominant cultural influence on the developing kingdom. During the 8th century Tibet embarked on a remarkable expansion, conquering much of Chinese TANG DYNASTY'S central Asian empire and sacking their capital at CHANG'AN in 763. By 800 Tibetan control extended south of the Himalayas to the Bay of Bengal. Growing internal problems caused the empire to collapse in about 850. Tibet was conquered by the MONGOLS in 1251 but after KHUBILAI KHAN'S death in 1294 Mongol control weakened and Tibet regained independence in 1368. Chinese influence in Tibet increased in the 18th century after the Tibetans called on the Manchu to help repel Mongol and Nepalese invasions. Tibet was garrisoned by China after 1720 and the Manchu controlled the succession of the Dalai Lama from 1751. Tibet regained its independence from China in 1912 following the fall of the Manchu dynasty but was reconquered in 1950 and since 1965 has been a nominally autonomous region of the People's Republic of China. ▷ 3.20

TIMUR THE LAME

Central Asian conqueror (r.1369–1405). The vizier of the great khan of CHAGATAI, he usurped the khan's authority and from 1380 to 1387 overran eastern Persia, Afghanistan, Azerbaijan and Kurdistan, establishing a capital in SAMARKAND. In 1391 he defeated the GOLDEN HORDE, in 1393 took BAGHDAD and in 1397 invaded India. In 1402 he defeated the OTTOMANS on his western frontier at ANKARA. The Timurid empire soon broke up and by 1500 was restricted to Transoxiana. ▷ 3.04, 3.16, 3.19, 3.23

TIMURID EMIRATES

Lands divided between the heirs of TIMUR THE LAME. After his death in 1405 his empire was divided between his older grandsons and his fourth son, Shah Rukh (r.1407–47). Nominal suzerainty was given to the oldest grandson, but succession disputes effectively split the empire into rival emirates, of which Shah Rukh's, based in Transoxiana and eastern Persia, was the most lasting, powerful and civilized. By the early 16th century UTHMAN had driven out the last Timurids. ▷ 3.04

TOLTECS

The dominant people of central Mexico from the 9th to the 12th centuries AD. The Toltecs arose from the amalgamation of farming tribes, including the Chichimeca and Nonoalca, who migrated into central Mexico in about 800. The Toltec state emerged in about 900 with the foundation of TULA, the capital, 80 kilometers (50 miles) north of Mexico City. In about 1000, Toltec migrants, possibly led by TOPILTZIN-QUETZALCÓATL, conquered the Mayan city of CHICHÉN ITZÁ in Yucatán. The Toltec state collapsed in about 1168 but its civilization exercised a lasting influence in Mexico, especially on the AZTECS. ▷ 3.27

TOPILTZIN-QUETZALCÓATL

TOLTEC king born in 935 or 947 who came to be identified with the god Quetzalcóatl ("Feathered Serpent"). According to legend, now almost certainly disproven by archeological evidence, his opposition to human sacrifice offended the god Texcatlipoca and he was overthrown. Topiltzin-Quetzalcóatl fled east overseas vowing that one day he would return and reclaim his kingdom. He may be the same person as Kukulcán (also "Feathered Serpent", but in Mayan) who conquered the Mayan city of CHICHÉN ITZÁ in Yucatán in 987. The story of Topiltzin-Quetzalcóatl may have influenced the reaction of MOCTEZUMA II to Hernán Cortés when he invaded the AZTEC empire in 1519. ▷ 3.27

TREBIZOND, EMPIRE OF

One of the three successor states to the BYZANTINE EMPIRE, Trebizond was the creation of the Comnenos dynasty after their removal from CONSTANTINOPLE in 1185. The empire consisted only of a narrow strip of coast around the trading city of Trebizond, and survived through dynastic alliance with Caucasian powers until falling to the OTTOMANS in 1461. ▷ 3.03, 3.12, 3.17

TRIPLE ALLIANCE (MESOAMERICA)

Alliance between the AZTECS of TENOCHTITLÁN and the nearby cities of Texcoco and Tlacopan, forged by the Aztec king ITZCÓATL in 1434. The alliance was the basis of Aztec power, and Texcoco and Tlacopan soon became junior partners. ▷ 3.27

TRIPOLI, COUNTY OF

CRUSADER STATE founded between 1102 and 1104 by Raymond, count of Toulouse, one of the leaders of the First CRUSADE. Largely dependent in the 12th century on JERUSALEM and in the 13th on the military orders, the county fell to the MAMLUKES between 1263 and 1290. Tripoli itself was destroyed in 1289. ▷ 3.17

TUGHLUK, MUHAMMAD IBN

Sultan of Delhi (r.1325–51). Muhammad was an energetic administrator and fine soldier whose campaigns in the Deccan brought the DELHI SULTANATE to its greatest territorial extent. To consolidate his conquests in the south Muhammad moved his capital to Daulatabad but was forced to return to Delhi after rebellions broke out in the north. As a result, Muhammad lost control of Daulatabad in 1347 when its governor rebelled and founded the independent BAHMANI SULTANATE. Though in many ways a harsh ruler, Muhammad was tolerant in religious matters and genuinely concerned for the welfare of the poor, personally supervising famine relief.

TULA

The capital of the TOLTEC empire, now a ruined city 80 kilometers (50 miles) north of Mexico City. Founded in about 900, Tula was sacked by unknown attackers in 1168 and subsequently abandoned. The AZTECS later removed many monuments and sculptures for their capital TENOCHTITLÁN, but impressive ruins of temple-pyramids and ball courts remain.

TULUNID EMIRATE

Egyptian dynasty (868–905) founded by Ahmad ibn Tulun. Tulun, a sub-governor of Egypt, built up a slave army and exploited the weakness of the ABBASID government to seize control of the province. The Abbasids recovered Egypt in 905. ▷ 3.02, 3.14

TUPAC YUPANQUI

Emperor of the INCAS (r.1471–93). He showed great ability as a general during the reign of his father PACHACUTEC, leading the conquest of the CHIMÚ EMPIRE in 1470. Tupac campaigned tirelessly during his own reign, more than doubling the size of the Inca empire. ▷ 3.28

TURKS

Generic term for peoples of central Asia, comprising various tribes, languages and cultures. Originally nomadic steppe-dwellers, many Turkic peoples adopted the sedentary life of the urban Middle East or eastern Europe after successive waves of invasion and conquest from the 7th century onward. ▷ 3.01, 3.02, 3.03, 3.04, 3.05, 3.09, 3.10, 3.11, 3.14, 3.16, 3.20, 3.21, 3.22

TVER

Branch of the RYURIK dynasty founded by Yaroslav (1246–71), the younger brother of ALEXANDER NEVSKY. Although grand prince of Vladimir, Yaroslav chose to rule from the city of Tver. Throughout the 14th and 15th centuries Tver and MOSCOW competed for dominance of northern Russia, but in 1485 Tver was annexed to Moscow. ▷ 3.10

UIGHUR TURKS

Dominant Turkic people of the eastern steppes, frequently allied with the Chinese from 744 until 840, when they were defeated by the Kirghiz, another Turkic people. The Uighurs withdrew to the northern Tarim and western Kansu, where they ruled until 1028. The Uighurs had from the 760s embraced Manicheism and advanced the religion in China. ▷ 3.01, 3.02, 3.05, 3.20, 3.21, 3.22

UMAR
Father-in-law of MUHAMMAD, and the second CALIPH (r.634–44). Umar presided over the first ISLAMIC conquests in Syria, Egypt and Persia. He was murdered by one of his slaves. ▷ 3.01, 3.13

UMAYYAD CALIPHATE
Dynasty ruling the Islamic world from 661 to 750, founded by MUAWIYA. The Umayyads shifted the center of Muslim power from Arabia to DAMASCUS, as ISLAM absorbed the culture of the ancient Middle East. They established a compromise between the ideal of Islamic society and the needs of secular government, and in so doing allowed Islam to spread from central Asia to the Atlantic. ▷ 3.01, 3.02, 3.05, 3.06, 3.07, 3.13, 3.14

URBAN II
Pope (r.1088–99). An ally of GREGORY VII, Urban continued his reformist policies and the struggle against HENRY IV of Germany. In 1095 at the COUNCIL OF CLERMONT he preached the First CRUSADE demonstrating the prestige and influence achieved by the reformed papacy. ▷ 3.08, 3.09, 3.17

UTHMAN
The third CALIPH (r.644–56). He was responsible for collecting in a single text the KORAN, providing the basis for a unified system of law and belief within ISLAMIC lands. ▷ 3.13

UZBEGS
Turkic nomad people of central Asia. Under Abu'l Khair (r.1428–68), they founded a kingdom in southern Siberia. His grandson, Muhammad Shaybani (r.1468–1510), established Uzbeg mastery over the TIMURID EMIRATES in Transoxiana, Ferghana and Khorasan until 1599. ▷ 3.04

VALDEZ, PETER
Religious reformer from Lyons who in about 1173 abandoned a mercantile career to preach against wealth. His preaching without episcopal licence provoked the hostility of the church, and he became increasingly radical in his attacks on religious authority and the sacraments. He and his followers, called WALDENSIANS, were declared heretical and subjected to persecution. ▷ 3.09

VENICE
Italian seaport and city-state. Established by the 7th century, Venice was under nominal BYZANTINE rule until about 1000. Venice dominated the Dalmatian coast and Adriatic Sea, gaining possession of Crete in 1216 and colonies further afield. In the 15th century Venice became the most powerful Italian city-state, and Europe's major commercial power, after defeating GENOA, its main trading rival, at Chioggia (1380). Its wealth made Venice a major cultural center of the RENAISSANCE. Decline soon followed because of OTTOMAN expansion and French and Habsburg intervention in Italy. The republican government of Venice was dissolved by Napoleon in 1797 and Venice was added to Italy in 1866. ▷ 3.08, 3.09, 3.10, 3.11, 3.12, 3.15, 3.17, 3.23

VERDUN, TREATY OF
Treaty of August 843. By its terms the CAROLINGIAN EMPIRE was divided between LOUIS THE PIOUS's three sons into East Francia, WEST FRANCIA and the Middle Kingdom. ▷ 3.07

VIKINGS
Generic term for the pagan raiders from Norway and Denmark who began to attack coastal settlements in the British Isles in the 790s and during the 9th century penetrated into the Frankish kingdom. Their ferocity and mobility took defenders by surprise. The Danes conquered much of England after 865, while the Norse (Norwegians) established settlements in the Scottish Isles, Ireland, ICELAND and NORMANDY. The impetus for Norse expansion came from the emergence of a centralized and competitive Scandinavian society, from land shortages and the potential for trade. ▷ 3.01, 3.02, 3.06, 3.07, 3.26

VLADIMIR OF KIEV
Russian prince (r.980–1015) of the RYURIK dynasty, Vladimir introduced ORTHODOX Christianity to the RUS in 987 by his marriage to a BYZANTINE princess. His division of territory according to a strict hierarchy established the dynasty throughout Russia. ▷ 3.09

VLADIMIR-SUZDAL
Neighboring cities of northeastern Russia, important regional centers that developed in the 12th and 13th centuries a notable school of religious painting. The essentially BYZANTINE style was heightened by a distinctive expressionism. The province was overrun by the TATARS in the 13th century. ▷ 3.10

WALDENSIANS
Heretical sect – the followers of Peter Valdes, a wealthy merchant turned reformer from southern FRANCE. He founded the movement in about 1173 to promote the apostolic life through evangelism and poverty. He broke with the church over the right to preach without ecclesiastical authority. The movement survives today. ▷ 3.09

WALES
Principality of western Britain. Its Celtic princes repulsed Anglo-Saxon invasions and briefly united in the 11th century under Gruffydd ap Llywelyn. NORMAN incursions into south Wales marked the beginning of two centuries of warfare until EDWARD I conquered Wales, making it a principality by the Statute of Wales (1284). A rising in 1400 by Owen Glyndwr failed to regain independence. In 1536 the Act of Union incorporated Wales into ENGLAND. ▷ 3.09, 3.12

WALLACHIA
Vlac province north of the Danube between Transylvania and the Black Sea. Founded in 1290, it was dominated by HUNGARY until 1330. By 1391 Prince Mircea was paying tribute to the OTTOMANS, and in 1417 became their vassal. ▷ 3.10, 3.12, 3.16

WANG ANSHI
(1021-86) Senior minister of the SONG DYNASTY who in 1068 introduced the most far-reaching program of reforms to improve conditions for the Chinese peasantry before modern times. Opposition by the rich land-owning class prevented the reforms being enforced and they were abolished in 1086. ▷ 3.21

WANG KON
Founder of the KORYO dynasty from which Korea gets its name. Also known as T'aejo ("Great Progenitor"), Wang Kon (r.918–45) was a castle lord from the northern border of SILLA. When Silla began to break up in about 900, Korea descended into chaos, with the emergence of many competing dynasties. Wang Kon declared himself king in 918 and had defeated all his rivals by 936, so reunifying Korea. ▷ 3.24

WARS OF THE ROSES
English civil wars (1455–85) between the Houses of Lancaster and York, named for their respective emblems of a red and white rose. Conflicts and power struggles on a local and national scale broke out against a background of defeat in the HUNDRED YEARS WAR and the weakness of HENRY VI's monarchy. The fortunes of each side ebbed and flowed throughout this period of sporadic warfare until the BATTLE OF BOSWORTH FIELD (1485) secured the throne for the Tudor dynasty under Henry VII. Henry defeated the last Yorkist uprising at Stoke in 1487. ▷ 3.12

WATTASID CALIPHATE
Moroccan dynasty. Regents for the MARINIDS from 1428, they usurped the sultanate from 1472 to 1549. ▷ 3.04

WELF DYNASTY
A Saxon and Bavarian aristocratic family whose most celebrated members are HENRY THE LION and his son, the HOLY ROMAN EMPEROR Otto IV. In Italy it lent its name to the pro-papal Guelph faction in the struggle against the imperialist Ghibellines. ▷ 3.08

WEN
Ruling name of Yang Jian, first emperor of the Sui dynasty (r.589–604) of China. Yang Jian

came to power in the Northern Zhou state in 581, following a military coup, and in a series of skillful campaigns reunited China after more than 350 years of disunity. ▷ 3.20

Wends
Slavonic people of the Baltic coast of Germany and Poland. They were forcibly converted to Christianity by the bloody Wendish Crusades in the 12th century. Their lands were then colonized by Germany, especially under the lead of Henry the Lion. ▷ 3.08, 3.17

Wessex
Southern English kingdom of the West Saxons, founded in about 500. It emerged from Mercian domination in 825 and, under the leadership of Alfred the Great (r.871–99), was the only Anglo-Saxon kingdom to survive the 9th-century Viking invasions intact. Alfred's successors united the Anglo-Saxons under their leadership and conquered the Danelaw to create by 954 the kingdom of England. ▷ 3.06, 3.07

West Francia
Western division of the Carolingian empire following the Treaty of Verdun (843), approximating to present-day France. ▷ 3.07

Whitby, Synod of
General council of the English church, held in Northumbria in 664, in which the Roman church took precedence over the Celtic church, especially concerning the dating of Easter, marking the final conversion of England and its convergence with European church structures. ▷ 3.06

White Huns (Ephthalites)
A Turkic nomad people established in central Asia at the end of the 5th century. During the 6th century the Ephthalites invaded Persia, Chinese Turkestan and India, where they are considered by some to be ancestral to the Rajputs.

William I (the Conqueror)
Duke of Normandy (r.1035–87) and king of England (r.1066–87). An illegitimate child, William used his great military and political skills to secure his precarious position in Normandy, quelling rebellion and repulsing French invasions. With papal blessing, he claimed the English throne from his cousin Edward the Confessor, defeating and killing his rival Harold II at the Battle of Hastings in 1066. He reformed the church, introduced feudal institutions and replaced the Anglo-Saxon aristocracy with his own supporters from Normandy and France. The Domesday Book, a survey of the resources of England, was compiled on his orders in 1086. ▷ 3.08

witan
The council of Anglo-Saxon kings. It encompassed the realm's great men (nobles and prelates), called by the king to assist in formulating government policy, thereby acting as a check on royal power and securing collective agreement for it.

Wittelsbach dynasty
Bavarian ducal family, continuing into the 20th century, that provided three Holy Roman emperors, including Louis IV. ▷ 3.10

Xixia
Tibetan state founded in the late 10th century and comprising Tanguts, Tibetans and Chinese. It was mostly Buddhist and by the 13th century had adopted some elements of Chinese culture, including literacy. Xixia was conquered between 1205 and 1226 by Chingis Khan as a prerequisite to the Mongol conquest of northern China. ▷ 3.02, 3.21, 3.22

Yarmuk river, Battle of
The Arab victory over the Byzantines at the Yarmuk, a tributary of the Jordan, on 20 August 636. It was followed by the conquest of Palestine and Syria. ▷ 3.13, 3.15

Yi dynasty
Ruling dynasty of Korea from 1392 to 1910. The dynasty was founded, with Chinese support, by Yi Songgye (r.1392–98), who ended a period of political instability that followed the end of Mongol rule in 1356. The Yi gave Korea a long period of stable government that lasted until the Japanese invasions of the late 19th century. The last ruler of the dynasty was forced to abdicate when Japan annexed Korea in 1910. ▷ 3.24

York
City of northern England, a Viking trading center and capital of the Viking kingdom of York (c.870–954). ▷ 3.07, 3.08

Yuan dynasty
The dynastic name of the Mongol rulers of China, adopted by Khubilai Khan (r.1260–94) following his defeat of the Song dynasty in 1279. With the exception of Khubilai Khan, the Yuan were rapacious but mediocre rulers who were never able to build a stable administration or win the acceptance of their Chinese subjects. The Yuan were afflicted with frequent succession struggles after 1328, and the dynasty was finally overthrown in 1368 by a Chinese uprising under Zhu Yuanzhang. ▷ 3.23

Zangid emirate
A vassal dynasty of the Seljuks founded by Zangi, atabeg of Mosul, who in the 1130s extended his power throughout northern Syria and in 1144 seized the county of Edessa from the Franks. Zangi's son Nur al-Din brought Egypt and Syria under a single ruler. The Zangid dynasty was overthrown by Saladin between 1174 and 1177. ▷ 3.03, 3.16, 3.17

Zaydite emirate
Shiite dynasty of northern Yemen from 893 to 1962, founded by Yahya, a Zaydi, who was invited by the local Arab tribes to arbitrate between them. ▷ 3.14

Zayyanid caliphate
A regional north African regime ruling the area between Tlemcen and the Sahara after the fall of the Almohads. The Zayyanid caliphate was seldom able to control much territory and remained vulnerable to tribal insurgence. By the early 16th century the Zayyanids had given way to the Ottomans. ▷ 3.03, 3.14

Zen Buddhism
Form of Pure Land Buddhism practiced in China (where it is known as Chan) and Japan. It places emphasis on sudden enlightenment (*satori*) through intuition. Chan practitioners emphasize meditation on paradoxical questions designed to challenge intellectual or common-sense assumptions. It was introduced to China by Bodhidharma in the 5th century AD, and flourished from the 8th century. It spread to Japan during the 14th century.

Zheng He
(1371–1435) Chinese court eunuch, admiral and statesman. He led a series of seven maritime expeditions around southeast Asia and the Indian Ocean as far as the east African coast between 1405 and 1433. The expeditions were intended to promote trade and increase the prestige of the Ming dynasty but were discontinued because of their cost, and the Chinese gave up their aspirations to become a major maritime power.

Zimbabwe, Great
Ruined city in Zimbabwe, southern Africa. First occupied by iron-using pastoral farmers in about 300, it was an important religious, trading and political center between 1000 and 1450, when impressive stone structures were built there. The largest of these is the Great Enclosure, a ritual structure, built in about 1200. With an outer wall 244 meters (805 feet) long and 10 meters (33 feet) high, it was the largest stone building in sub-Saharan Africa. Great Zimbabwe had a population of 5000–18,000 people at its peak in about 1400 but was superseded by Mwenemutapa in about 1450 and abandoned. ▷ 3.18

Zoe
Byzantine empress, last of the Macedonian dynasty. In 1028, aged almost 50, she was married to Romanos III Argyrus. In 1034 she had Romanos murdered and married her lover Michael. After Michael's death in 1041 she was banished to a convent, but popular feeling ensured her restoration and marriage to Constantine IX Monomachos (1042–55). Zoe died in 1050. ▷ 3.15

Acknowledgments & Index

Text, timelines and maps

The authors and publishers readily acknowledge the work of a large number of scholars and published works, on which they have drawn in the preparation of this atlas. Many of these works remain in print, and can be used as reliable secondary reading on the many topics covered in this atlas. Among them are the following:

Ajayi, JFA and Crowder, Michael (eds) *Historical Atlas of Africa* (Cambridge and New York 1985)
al Faruqi, Ismail Ragi (ed) *Historical Atlas of the Religions of the World* (New York and London 1974)
Almond, M, Black, J, McKitterick, R, and Scarre, C *The Times Atlas of European History* (London and New York 1994)
Ardagh, John with Jones, Colin *Cultural Atlas of France* (London and New York, 1991)
Bagot Glubb, J *The Great Arab Conquests* (London 1963)
Barraclough, G (ed) *The Times Atlas of World History* (4th ed , London 1993 and New York 1994)
Bartlett, R *The Making of Europe, Conquest, Colonisation and Cultural Change 950–1300* (London 1993)
Black, C and others *Cultural Atlas of the Renaissance* (London and New York, 1993)
Blunden, Caroline and Elvin, Mark *Cultural Atlas of China* (London and New York, 1986)
Braudel, Fernand *Civilization and Capitalism* (3 vols., Princeton, rev. ed. 1992)
Chadwick, Henry and Evans, Gillian R (eds) *Atlas of the Christian Church* (London and New York, 1987)
Coe, Michael, Snow, Dean and Benson, Elizabeth *Atlas of Ancient America* (London and New York, 1986)
Coe, Michael *Mexico: from the Olmecs to the Aztecs* (London and New York 4th ed 1994)
Cohn-Sherbok, D *Atlas of Jewish History* (London and New York 1994)
Collcutt, Martin, Jansen, Marius and Kumakura, Isao *Cultural Atlas of Japan* (London and New York, 1988)
Connah, G *African Civilizations: Precolonial cities and states in tropical Africa* (Cambridge and New York 1987)
Cotterell, A *East Asia* (London 1993, New York 1995)
Darby, HC and Fullard, Harold *The New Cambridge Modern History Atlas* (Cambrdge 1970)
Davies, RHC *A History of Medieval Europe* (London and New York 2nd ed 1988)
Davis, Norman *Europe: a History* (Oxford and New York 1996)
de Lange, Nicholas *Atlas of the Jewish World* (London and New York, 1984)
Elliott, JH (ed) *The Hispanic World* (London and New York 1991)
Fage, JD and Oliver, R (eds) *The Cambridge History of Africa* (Cambridge and New York 1975–)
Falkus, M and Gillingham J *Historical Atlas of Britain* (London and New York revised ed 1987)
Fernández-Armesto, Felipe (ed) *The Times Atlas of World Exploration* (London and New York, 1991)
Freeman-Grenville, GSP *Historical Atlas of the Middle East* (New York 1993)
Gilbert, Martin *The Atlas of Jewish History* (London and New York 5th ed 1996)
Gottfried, RS *The Black Death* (London 1983)
Graham Campbell, James (ed) *Cultural Atlas of the Viking World* (London and New York, 1994)
Grosser Historischer Weltatlas (3 volumes (Munich 1981)
Hall, DGE *A History of South-east Asia* (London 4th ed 1981)
Haywood, John *Historical Atlas of the Vikings* (London and New York 1995)
Haywood, John *Dark Age Naval Power* (London and New York 1991)
Holt, PM, Lambeth, AKS and Lewis, B (eds) *The Cambridge History of Islam* (Cambridge 1970–)
Hooper, Nicholas and Bennett, Matthew *The Cambridge Illustrated Atlas of Warfare: The Middle Ages 768–1487* (Cambridge and New York 1996)
Johnson, Gordon, Bayly, C and Richards JF *The New Cambridge History of India* (Cambridge 1987–)
Johnson, Gordon *Cultural Atlas of India* (London 1995, New York, 1996)
Kinder, H and Hilgemann, W *Atlas of World History* (2 vols, Munich, London and New York 1974)
King, PD *Charlemagne* (London 1986)
Kulke, H and Rothermund, D *A History of India* (London 1990)
Langer, William L *An Encyclopedia of World History* (5th ed, London and New York 1973)
Lee, K *A New History of Korea* (Cambridge, Mass 1988)
Ling, T *A History of Religion East and West* (London 1968)
Lynch, JH *The Medieval Church* (Harlow 1992)
Matthew, Donald *Atlas of Medieval Europe* (London and New York, 1989)
Milner-Gulland, Robin with Dejevsky, Nikolai *Cultural Atlas of Russia and the Soviet Union* (London and New York, 1989)
Moore, RI (ed) *The Hamlyn Historical Atlas* (London 1981)
Morgan, D *The Mongols* (Oxford 1986, Cambridge, Mass 1990)
Moseley, ME *The Incas and their Ancestors* (London and New York 1993)
Ostrogorsky, G *History of the Byzantine State* (New Brunswick revised ed 1986)
Parker, WH *An Historical Geography of Russia* (London 1968)
Phillipson, DW *African Archaeology* (Cambridge, 2nd ed 1993)
Pitcher, DE *An Historical Geography of the Ottoman Empire* (Leiden 1972)
Pounds, Norman JG *An Historical Geography of Europe* (Cambridge 1990)
Reid, Anthony (ed) *Southeast Asia in the Early Modern Era: Trade, Power and Belief* (New York 1993)
Riasanovsky, NV *A History of Russia* (Oxford and New York 5th ed 1993)
Riley-Smith, Jonathon *The Atlas of the Crusades* (London and New York 1991)
Roberts, JM *The Hutchinson History of the World* (London 1976)
Robinson, Francis *Atlas of the Islamic World since 1500* (London and New York, 1982)
Roolvink, R *Historical Atlas of the Muslim People* (Amsterdam 1974)
Scammell, GV *The World Encompassed: the First European Maritime Empires c.800–1650* (London 1981)
Schmidt, KJ *An Atlas and Survey of South Asian History* (New York and London 1995)
Schwartzberg, Joseph E (ed) *A Historical Atlas of South Asia* (Chicago and London, 2nd ed 1992)
Sharer, RJ *The Ancient Maya* (Stanford Ca 5th ed 1994)
Shepherd, William R *Shepherd's Historical Atlas* (New York and London, 9th ed 1974)
Sinclair, Keith (ed) *The Oxford Illustrated History of New Zealand* (Oxford and Auckland 1990)
The Times Atlas of the World (London and New York, 8th ed 1990)
Thornton, John K *Africa and Africans in the Formation of the Atlantic World 1400–1680* (Cambridge and New York, 1992)
Tindall, G and Shi, DE *America, a Narrative History* (New York, 1996)
Todd, M *The Early Germans* (Oxford and Cambridge, Mass 1992)
Twitchett, D and Fairbank, J (eds) *The Cambridge History of China* (15 vols, Cambridge and New York 1978–91)
Vincent Mary and Stradling, RA *Cultural Atlas of Spain and Portugal* (London 1994, New York 1995)
Wallace-Hadrill, JM *The Barbarian West 400–1000* (5th ed Oxford and Cambridge, Mass. 1996)
Watson, F *India, a Concise History* (London and New York 1993)
Webster's New Geographical Dictionary (Springfield, Massachusetts, 1984)

Artwork

Artwork references have been assembled from a wide variety of sources. Any individual or institution who can demonstrate that copyright may have been infringed is invited to contact Andromeda Oxford Ltd.

Figures refer to map numbers; **bold** type indicates major references.